MW01517799

Contemporary Urbanism in Brazil

UNIVERSITY PRESS OF FLORIDA

Florida A&M University, Tallahassee
Florida Atlantic University, Boca Raton
Florida Gulf Coast University, Ft. Myers
Florida International University, Miami
Florida State University, Tallahassee
New College of Florida, Sarasota
University of Central Florida, Orlando
University of Florida, Gainesville
University of North Florida, Jacksonville
University of South Florida, Tampa
University of West Florida, Pensacola

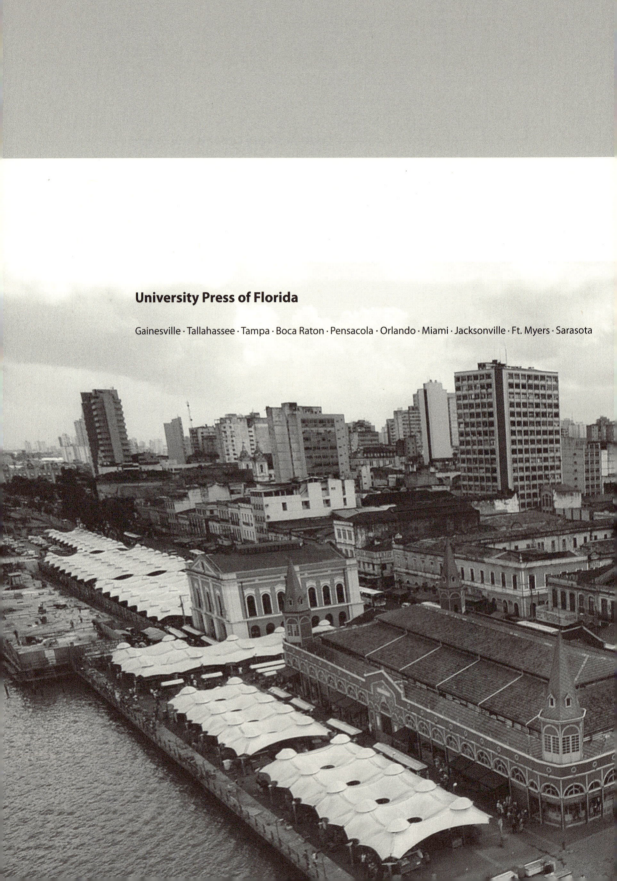

University Press of Florida

Gainesville · Tallahassee · Tampa · Boca Raton · Pensacola · Orlando · Miami · Jacksonville · Ft. Myers · Sarasota

Contemporary Urbanism in Brazil

Beyond Brasília

Edited by Vicente del Rio and William Siembieda Foreword by Jon Lang

Copyright 2009 by Vicente del Rio and William Siembieda
Printed in the United States of America. This book is printed
on Glatfelter Natures Book, a paper certified under the
standards of the Forestry Stewardship Council (FSC). It is a
recycled stock that contains 30 percent post-consumer waste
and is acid-free.
All rights reserved

13 12 11 10 09   6 5 4 3 2 1

Library of Congress Cataloging-in-Publication Data
Contemporary urbanism in Brazil: beyond Brasília/edited by
Vicente del Rio and William Siembieda; foreword by Jon Lang.
p. cm.
Includes bibliographical references and index.
ISBN 978-0-8130-3281-8 (alk. paper)
1. City planning—Brazil. I. Rio, Vicente del, 1955–
II. Siembieda, William J.
HT169.B7C675 2008
307.1'21609819–dc22   2008025850

The University Press of Florida is the scholarly publishing
agency for the State University System of Florida, comprising
Florida A&M University, Florida Atlantic University, Florida
Gulf Coast University, Florida International University, Florida
State University, New College of Florida, University of Central
Florida, University of Florida, University of North Florida,
University of South Florida, and University of West Florida.

University Press of Florida
15 Northwest 15th Street
Gainesville, FL 32611–2079
http://www.upf.com

Contents

Illustrations

List of Tables

Foreword

Almost all, if not all, design professionals know of the design of Brasília and can sketch a conceptual diagram of the city's layout. Many laypeople know of it too. Many people know of the planning and design of Curitiba during the 1980s and 1990s, for it has been widely described in the popular media. The experience there has already influenced planning and design decisions in cities outside Brazil, such as Bogotá and Los Angeles. Few, however, know of the issues confronting planners in Curitiba today. Some scholars may know of recent innovative planning activities and of some internationally acclaimed urban open spaces in Rio de Janeiro's Corredor Cultural or in Porto Alegre's Largo Glênio Peres market square revitalization. Not much is known about what else is happening in those cities or, for that matter, anywhere else in Brazil, however. That is a pity because as Brazil flexes its growing economic muscles and its cities burgeon, the rest of the world can learn much from the success and limitations of recent planning and urban design work in that country.

It is often thought that the major urban design paradigms and design ideas all originated in Western Europe and the eastern United States and then were transmitted across the world through the globalization of investment markets, education, and professional practice. Indeed, many did. Many planners and architects from other countries have been educated, particularly at the graduate level, in the United States and Western Europe, and consultants from those countries have taken their design knowledge and attitudes from home and have planted them in alien territory. Often those design models have been applied in sociopolitical and geographical contexts very different from those in which they were developed. Some design concepts have flourished everywhere but many have not. There is much truth in all these assertions, but the picture is really more complex.

Design ideas have flowed back and forth across the continents and oceans of the world. The development of modernist architecture and urban design is one example. Many ideas now considered to be those of the Bauhaus or of Le Corbusier had their roots in the Soviet schools of architecture. The City Beautiful had antecedents in Mughal gardens as much as in the baroque. The influence of Japan on the picturesque tradition in Europe is well known. In addition, the work of European architects abroad shaped their ideas and thus what they did at home. French architects explored design possibilities in France's colonies in North Africa and Indo-China before applying them in France (to the extent they could in less authoritarian contexts than existed in the colonies). There is nothing new in these observations, even if they are yet to be fully documented. The contribution to the world scene of design in Latin America has, however, been largely neglected.

The layout and architecture of precincts of cities as diverse as Buenos Aires, Santiago de Chile, and Brasília show their debt to European models, particularly those of French architects, their design ideas, and their philosophical attitudes embedded in the Napoleonic code. Sometimes subtly but often boldly, the transformation of European architectural paradigms in Latin America has had a largely unrecognized impact on urban design everywhere. This observation is particularly true of modern architecture and urban design in Brazil.

In the 1950s and 1960s the sculptural qualities of Brazilian modern architecture and the enthusiasm with which it was created and built were inspirations for architects throughout the world, particularly those in the economically developing world. Consider the reflections of the first of India's modern architects, Habib Rahman: "We returned from our training abroad full of the ideas of Brazil and the manner in which architects there had embraced modernism" (interview by Lang, 1984). Since then Brazilian architects have had to confront the contradictions in modernist thought, particularly in the urban design precepts promulgated in documents such as CIAM's Athens Charter.

Much has been built in Brazil since the audacious concept of Brasília, the boldness of its design, and the rapidity of its implementation—largely in the hands of two people, Lucio Costa as planner and Oscar Niemeyer as architect—captured the world's attention. For all its strengths and weaknesses and the opportunity costs it incurred, the city has a firm place in international architects' minds. Misguidedly, many of them believe that is all Brazilian planning, urban design, and architecture have to offer the world. Much has indeed been learned from the development of Brasília. The city has been visited by innumerable architects, praised by such urban design luminaries as Edmund Bacon in his classic *Design of Cities,* and been subjected to much sociological analysis. We can continue to learn from the initial experience of the building of Brasília, but the world has evolved. Matters may not have changed as rapidly in the countries of the economically developed world as we want to believe, but the opportunities now facing city planners and urban designers in the rapidly developing world are substantially different than in the past.

The field of urban design has evolved from its roots in civic design—grand architectural gestures—to a concern with enhancing the quality of life of a city's citizens. It has changed its focus from eliminating problems (and often throwing out the baby with the bathwater) to developing what is worthwhile in urban and suburban life. The concern is not only with the development of cleared greenfield and brownfield sites but even more so with revitalizing existing business districts and a range of city precincts: neighborhoods, including squatter settlements, campuses of various types; and other schemes too numerous to mention. The range of projects and the range of mechanisms used to implement them have been prodigious.

The work of urban designers has to be seen within the processes of urbanization and urban transformation as shaped by market economies and legal rights. The reason is simple. Planners and urban designers in the public sector, or working on behalf of the public sector, intervene on behalf of some perceived public good in the actions of the invisible hand of economic forces and the invisible web of laws that govern market transactions and property development practice. When working for the private sector, planners and urban designers may well be intervening on behalf of developers attempting to maximize their profits. At an abstract level, property development processes are similar everywhere, but much can be learned from the particularities of unique situations.

The experience of Brazil is particularly instructive because the country is modernizing rapidly. The economy is growing at a remarkable speed. Cities such as São Paulo are expanding on their peripheries at a great pace, and their infrastructures and precincts are being regenerated in response to international capital flows. Their skylines are increasingly impressive, matching those of Manhattan and Hong Kong when seen from afar. Yet Brazilian cities are known internationally primarily for negative reasons: they are congested, crime ridden, and bathed in smog. Rio de Janeiro may be known for its backdrop of hills and its beaches, but it is also known for its favelas, or shantytowns. Yet one reads little in either the professional or lay press about the procedures used to incrementally upgrade the quality of squatter settlements. One hears of the deforestation of the Amazon basin, but not of efforts to deal with the problems incurred. Rio's Carnaval, with its arrays of scantily clad samba dancers, appears on television screens around the world every year, but one hears little about the efforts to preserve those aspects of the country's Afro-Brazilian heritage worth retaining. Many of these planning and design efforts, while unique to Brazil, have generic features that have to be addressed by planners and urban designers everywhere, particularly in those parts of the world where there are major differences in income level between the rich and poor or where development is occurring at a rapid pace.

Brazil is a large country in which a great variety of planning and urban design necessities and opportunities have been confronted during the past two decades. The country is blessed with an extraordinarily competent and creative set of professionals. A wide variety of planning and design issues have been confronted. A state capital for the recently formed state of Tocantins has been developed to add to those planned in the past. Efforts have been made to revitalize a range of precincts in cities large and small. Waterfronts have been exploited to enhance the amenities of cities. Squatter settlements have been improved. New large-scale building types such as shopping centers have had catalytic effects (as well as negative side effects) on the areas around them. Much has happened in Curitiba since the initial planning and design of its infrastructure systems drew worldwide attention to the magnificent (not in a bombastic sense but in a quiet piece-by-piece manner) design interventions that changed the city's character. One needs to understand the issues now facing planners there when they are having to deal with a second generation of design concerns. Much can be learned from the mechanisms used to achieve the variety of positive outcomes in Brazilian cities, provided one sees them within the sociopolitical and economic context of Brazil.

It is time to understand how the globalization of the economy and of information flows affects the designing of cities. It is time for city planners, urban designers, and architects to look at Brazil and to learn from the goals that politicians and design professionals have set for themselves in improving the ways of life of people in cities, the creative mechanisms they have used to achieve those goals, and the successes and limitations of the patterns and procedures they have used to meet the desired objectives. Understanding the evolution of Brasília is as important as understanding the political and design ideology behind its original creation, but few architects and urban designers have the slightest idea of what Brasília is like now. No such grand design gesture as Brasília has been made since in Brazil, but equally important interventions have been made in the country's many cities. They are important because they have directly addressed the situation at hand. That is the greatest lesson that one can learn from Brazil. That is the important lesson we need to learn. The publication of this book is indeed timely.

Jon Lang

Professor, Faculty of the Built Environment,
University of New South Wales, Australia

Preface   What Can We Learn from Brazilian Urbanism?

Large cities around the world are in the process of reinventing themselves and learn-ing how to deal with the contradictions of urbanism. Cities are more heterogeneous, more politicized, more plural, and more pragmatic than ever. The links between the global and the local reflect a process of adaptation more than schemes of grandeur. We now work more often with fragmented territories of the city than with one uni-fied territory. This new logic defines a new urbanism as expressed in space, place, and locality, and this is nowhere more evident than in the struggle large cities of the developing world face as they attempt to overcome their political, social, and eco-nomic difficulties.

This book views urbanism as the social production of cities in their material and symbolic dimensions, as best expressed recently by Alexander Cuthbert (2006). We posit that Brazilian cities may be looked upon as examples of contemporary urbanism not only because they present all the contradictions of capitalism in the developing world, but also because of the failures, successes, and promises of their planning and urban design efforts. The lessons learned from Brazilian contemporary urbanism will help us understand and deal with cities throughout the world, in an effort to con-tribute to the advancement of state-of-the-art urbanism as well as to "postcolonial-izing urban studies . . . decentering the reference points for international scholarship" (Robinson 2006: 168).

Contemporary Urbanism in Brazil: Beyond Brasília is an assessment of how cities in Brazil have overcome the hegemony of the modernist paradigm and how they are being shaped at the dawn of the twenty-first century. Twelve case studies in eight dif-ferent cities show exciting developments and advances in planning and urban design practice, as well as discussing the different state, civil society, and political forces that act upon them. The case study discussions demonstrate that the most significant chal-lenge for contemporary urbanism in Brazil—and not unlikely for the vast majority of developing countries—is to help build a more equitable city, one that bridges the spatial and economic gaps between different social groups and between the public and the private realms. Through the Brazilian experience, we begin to see the ways in which modernism, high modernism, and postmodernism coexist and interact to form new logics for the utilization of urban space.

With the disruption of the modernist paradigm, the dismantling of the military regime, and the return to full democracy in Brazil in the mid-1980s, Brazilian urbanism started to pursue a new paradigm and new models with which to respond to pressing political, economic, and social challenges at the global, national, and local levels. Despite the social gaps caused by historically uneven development and more recently by globalization and liberalism, Brazilian urbanism has evolved beyond Brasília and modernism, and has become more effective in meeting societal needs.

Innovative perspectives and solutions in the Brazilian experience provide many lessons to be learned, particularly concerning the role of the state and planning agencies in reducing social inequalities, responding to community needs, and guaranteeing the quality of the public realm. It is important to note that Brazil is the only country in Latin America—and perhaps one of the few in the world—where re-democratization was followed by decision making on what type of urban space would be compatible with a more inclusive notion of citizenship (Jones 2004). For instance, the Brazilian Constitution of 1988 includes a vision of the social function of property and of the city, as well as articles on urban and environmental policies. The 2001 national Statute of the City (Federal Law 10.257) responds to the constitutional goals and regulates their provisions, setting a very progressive legal framework for urban land use and development control. Both the constitution and the law resulted from lengthy national popular debates regarding "urban reform," and provided municipalities with fundamental tools for making better and more just cities. These are fundamental changes: as Lefebvre (1968) states, the right to the city is a superior form of human rights.

Needless to say, this book does not aspire to be a complete account of current urbanism in Brazil. Not only is this a complex theme with many different facets and prisms through which it can be studied, but the scale of such a task would be literally continental: Brazil is larger than the continental United States; its population in 2006 is estimated at more than 180 million, of which 80 percent live in urban areas; and fifteen capital cities have more than 200,000 inhabitants.[1] Brazil has 5,560 municipalities and at least an equal number of cities (if we use the country's official definition of city, which is that the municipality's main urban settlement is considered a city).

In this book we have identified the major trends of Brazilian contemporary urbanism and have selected representative cities and experiences that contribute to our goals. We sincerely hope that readers benefit from the discussions herein, and that these discussions provoke further curiosity about Brazilian urbanism and contribute to a larger conversation about urbanism and the quality of cities.

Dualities in Brazilian Cities

Brazil's harsh social and economic contrasts are deeply engraved in its cities and its spaces. Over the last two decades, most depictions of the country and of Rio de Janeiro in the international media have been negative. Both tourism agencies and the U.S. consulate rank large Brazilian cities—particularly Rio—as areas of high risk due to the high rates of street crime and burglary. Newspapers constantly expose police inefficiency, brutality, and corruption, as well as widespread poverty. Recent films such as *City of God* and *City of Men* (both filmed in Rio) and *Carandiru* (filmed in São Paulo) worsen Brazil's image abroad and increase the fears of the international audience. Albeit somewhat exaggerated and distorted, these images and pieces of news do expose some of the real problems that Brazil faces today.

We can best exemplify the contradictory nature of urban development in Brazil by looking at Rio de Janeiro, which represents well the social, political, and economic processes that dictate form in Brazilian cities. Maybe more than any other city in Brazil, Rio, like Brazil as a whole, is perceived internationally in conflicting images.

Without doubt Rio is one of the most problematic cities in Brazil. To start with, the city's housing deficit is enormous. In 2005, an estimated total of 1.4 million people in the metropolitan area lived in substandard housing (including favelas,[2] overcrowded tenements, illegal subdivisions, and others). Of these individuals, 88 percent were families earning less than three times the minimum wage per month.[3] Census data from the Brazilian Institute of Geographical Statistics (IBGE) indicate that the total number of favelas in the city grew from 384 in 1991 to 513 in 2000, and that in 2001 more than one million people—almost 20 percent of Rio's total population—were *favelados* (favela residents). And the reality is probably worse: most researchers agree that these totals are underestimates because of methodological problems in the collection of census data from favelas. Rio's cityscape and city-building processes constantly produce first world opulence and amenities side by side with third world misery and lack of basic services.

The increasing strength and boldness of criminals and drug traffickers in Rio is alarming. In 2004, there were 43.8 homicides and 1,251 recorded thefts per 100,000 inhabitants—the highest rate among Brazil's big cities.[4] A curious example of crime occurred in Rio in 2006: in a little more than twenty-four hours, all the electric cables in one of the city's most important and busiest tunnels were stolen by thieves, who resold them to scrap yards. The escalation in crime has generated a cityscape of fear characterized by gated communities and fenced residential buildings, and has reduced public nightlife, all of which obviously has negatively affected the tourism industry.

Continued Inequality

Thomas Skidmore, a longtime international researcher of Brazilian development history, notes that the ultimate contradiction in Brazilian society is between the country's "justifiable reputation for personal generosity" and the fact that it remains one of the world's most unequal societies, representing "all the problems of capitalism in the developing world" (Skidmore 1999: xiii). Researchers agree that throughout history the development models chosen by the ruling classes in Brazil have never favored a more equal distribution of wealth, and the country's asymmetrical participation in globalization is only making the situation worse (Skidmore 1999; Sachs 2001; MacLachlan 2003).

Even after democratization, the economic profile of the Brazilian population did not change much. Although the total number of poor has decreased and their buying power has increased in the two decades since the inflation spiral was halted, social inequalities and the concentration of income have worsened. Census data indicate that 52 percent of the employed workforce earns less than two times the minimum wage per month, and whereas in 1960 the richest 10 percent of the population possessed 54 percent of the national income, by 1995 they held 63 percent of it.[5] Sachs (2001) noted that Brazil is a poorly developed country because it adopted a growth model that is socially perverse and leads to increasing concentration of wealth. We hope that the democratic process will eventually change this situation.

Within this context, the scale and complexity of the urbanization issue in Brazil are immense. The total population grew from 52 million in 1950 to more than 180 million people in 2001, and in the same period the percentage of urban dwellers grew from 36.1 percent to more than 80 percent. In 2001 there were twelve cities with a population of more than one million; the fact that their demographic growth has been slowing significantly in the recent census periods indicates that although the larger cities are not experiencing as much migration as they did in the past, the medium-sized cities are growing at a much faster pace, and as expected, they are developing the same problems as the large metropolises. For instance, greater São Paulo—the city itself plus a conglomeration of thirty-eight municipalities—covers almost forty-eight square miles, and its current population of almost eighteen million is projected to reach twenty-one million by 2015 (Wilheim 2001: 476). In 1991–2000, greater São Paulo grew at a rate of 1.63 percent while nine of its municipalities grew by more than 5 percent and even by as much as 8.36 percent (Meyer, Grostein, and Biderman 2004: 57).[6] In the case of Rio de Janeiro, census data indicate that in 2001 the city had almost six million inhabitants while the greater Rio area had more than nine million.

Brazilian cities also experience strong conflicts at another level. Globalization, transnational and market forces, and the entrepreneurial paradigm are generating fragmented cities of increasingly privatized spaces, shopping centers, gated communities, and social enclaves. In Brazil over the last two decades, economic globalization met liberalism in city building, and many see the city as a commodity to be branded and sold in national and international markets, as an enterprise that should be run as any other business, and as a place for the "creative economy" (Arantes, Vainer, and Maricato 2000). In big cities comprehensive planning is losing out to strategic planning based on an "urbanism of results": long-term planning is giving way to projects that are visible and have short-term effects.

Let us now look at the positive side of the coin, beginning with Rio de Janeiro. First, like Brazil, Rio has definitely retained long-lasting positive images since Carmen Miranda's naïve films of the 1960s and 1970s and the international reputation of Brazilian music and soccer. Certainly, several aspects of Brazil's second largest and showcase city—such as the urban environment, the beautiful landscape, the ocean and beaches, the music, and a complex network of cultural attractions and thriving public spaces—make Rio diverse, interesting, and an "internationally celebrated city" (Kotler et al. 2006: 151). Rio is known as the capital of samba and Carnaval parades, bossa nova and *garotas de Ipanema,* beach culture, and a distinct Carioca lifestyle (*Carioca* refers to a person or product native to Rio), and it is the country's cradle for many other cultural movements, styles, and symbols. Also, despite the increasing street crime, nightlife is still alive and well: traditional bohemian areas and revitalized spaces downtown are packed with people. The Carnaval parades, the now-traditional New Year Eve's fireworks along the beaches, and the year-round free events and concerts attract hundreds of thousands. In February 2006, for instance, a record-breaking audience of more than one million people packed Copacabana beach for a free Rolling Stones concert paid for by the city of Rio.

Despite the negative images of Rio, a six-year-long survey of twenty-three countries conducted in 2003 by a team of social psychologists from California State University at Fresno concluded that Rio de Janeiro was the "friendliest city in the world," followed by San José in Costa Rica and Madrid in Spain. The study suggests that the friendliness, spontaneity, and openness of the Carioca, who are always ready to help and to make new friends, are fundamental virtues in the overcrowded metropolis of nine million. More recently, a survey of members of the Urban Land Institute cited Rio as one of their favorite non–North American cities because of its distinctive qualities (Miara 2007).[7]

From a macroeconomic point of view, things are going well in Brazil, which has long been South America's economic leader and is regarded as one of the most important economies in the world. With the return to a stable democracy in the mid-1980s and the establishment of a stable economy in the 1990s, Brazil has earned a new position in the community of nations (Kotler et al. 2006). Confidence in Brazil has grown immensely in the last decade among international bankers and external investors, and the "Brazil cost" has decreased significantly.[8] For instance, although in 2001 Brazil occupied a modest fortieth position on the IMD Global Business School world competitiveness ranking, from 2001 to 2003 foreign investments totaled $22.5 billion and placed the country second only to Mexico in Latin America (Kotler et al. 2006). According to World Bank data, between 2000 and 2004, the Brazilian gross internal product (GIP) grew at a rate of 2.66—very close to the world average of 2.84.

In May 2006, President Luis "Lula" da Silva celebrated Brazil's independence from oil imports which, together with the successful shift to sugarcane-based ethanol for powering automobiles that started in the 1970s, was an important step in economic development. Interestingly, with the growing international awareness of the negative effects of burning fossil fuels, Brazil has been praised internationally for its pioneering use of ethanol and natural gas as alternative fuel sources. In a 2006 political advertisement in California, former U.S. President Bill Clinton supported a proposition to provide state financial support for projects that use alternative energy and hailed Brazil's accomplishments. "If Brazil can do it, California can," he said.

Institutional and judicial reforms have paved the path toward better and more just cities and opened more channels for public participation. Since the fall of the military regime in the mid-1980s, national social movements and growing citizen participation in public life have elevated expectations for a new social order and increased pressures to develop cities that are more just and appropriate for Brazil's social needs and cultural heritage. We have already mentioned the 1988 National Constitution and the 2001 Statute of the City, but other progressive steps should also be mentioned, such as the participatory planning processes adopted in several municipalities, the more than one thousand municipal master plans finalized between 2006 and 2007, the important work of the Ministry of the City formed in 2002, and other advances in planning and design. As Skidmore (1999: xiii) notes, Brazil is "one of the more stunning accomplishments of nation-building in the modern world."

Theoretical Underpinnings of This Book

Contemporary Urbanism in Brazil is an exploration of how Brazilian urbanism is responding to old and new dualities and adapting to the complexities of the contemporary city. While it is transforming itself into a modern state, Brazil still faces many serious, longstanding problems; yet its leaders have also realized that the city is a major arena for fostering well-balanced development, social justice, and full citizenship.[9] We will see that this realization is generating many different, effective urban responses and new models of urbanism.

If we understand modernism as an expression of a specific process of modernization (Harvey 1990; Jameson 1991), then we see that in many respects the modern condition has never been fully achieved in Brazil, and thus modernity is incomplete. But in contrast to Jameson (1991), who sees postmodernism as occurring only after the logic of modernism has triumphed, in our analysis of Brazilian urbanism we note that modernism and postmodernism exist concurrently.

On one level, the implementation of a modernization agenda still drives Brazilian city building, as the vision contained in the country's political and legal frameworks clearly suggests. Despite the significant growth of democratic participation and public-private partnerships in recent years, the culture of Brazilian urbanism is based primarily on a national political project and on a centralized and paternalistic government-oriented system that pursues public welfare. Political projects and thus actions at national, state, and municipal levels influence city form and structure as partial reflections of the logic of property capital. We also see in terms of morphology, function, and expression that postmodern urbanism is occurring in Brazilian cities and that multiple logics of urban space production are emerging. This may lead to a rich set of local projects led not by an overarching ideology of collective advancement, but by a localized expression of what works for people in their city or neighborhood.

As Erminia Maricato (1997) noted, planning in Brazil has a strong positivistic (and thus modernist) heritage, which historically has led the state to take on a central role in promoting economic and social equilibrium and the existence of a consumer market. Even in times of deregulation and liberalization of the economy, the state has still been responsible for preventing market dysfunction, as well as for guaranteeing the reproduction of the labor force. In this vision, urbanism is as fundamental for social equity and development strategies as it is for capital and social investments, reproduction of the labor force, and increased value for real property.

On another level, Brazil's postmodern condition came about in the sense that the nation's project of modernization moved away from a process of "creative destruction" (Harvey 1990: 22) and came to accept different concurrent realities. Maybe the concurrency of both paradigms is a reminder that the modernist project was left unfinished (Jameson 1991; del Rio and Gallo 2000). The conceptual framework of postmodernism is perhaps the best tool for understanding the Brazilian urban experience and, by extension, that of other countries with a history of colonialism and dictatorship. Postmodernism's attention to the role of space and the construction of everyday life provides a means of understanding social action (Dear 2000). For example, São Paulo, like Los Angeles, is multi-centered and fragmented and has substantial expansion (mostly urban working class and poor neighborhoods) at its edges. The mechanisms for social and symbolic production of space, while driven by historical bases, do reflect strong postmodern tendencies.

With democratization in the late 1980s and the new political and economic forces being expressed in the cities, Brazilian urbanism faces a postmodern dilemma similar to what the United States and most European countries have faced for decades: the contradiction between playing a synoptic and reactive role (more in pace with universal truths and ideals) versus an opportunistic and proactive role (more in pace with responses to market demands and political opportunism) (Loukaitou-Sideris and Banerjee 1998). This dilemma haunts contemporary planners and designers and reflects the oppositions between modernist and postmodernist value systems (Ellin 1999): should our fight be for lasting structural changes, or should we act to promote limited and localized differences? Brazilian cities express this dilemma, and both sides of it seem to complement each other and feed off each other's consequences as cityscapes around the country reveal the tensions between global versus local, private versus public, and individual versus collective realms. Like the culture of Brazil, this tension results in positive attempts to make the city a valued part of Brazilian life.

In recognizing these needs, the various problems of development, and the necessity for a broad spectrum of solutions, Brazilian urbanism has overcome the dominance of modernism and now regards it as one among possible models. Paraphrasing Lang (2005), Brazilian urban design moved away from "total design" into piecemeal or incremental solutions. The universality of the modernist solution, its functionalism, one-size-fits-all mentality, and perception of design as beginning with a tabula rasa, for instance, are no longer part of the design and cultural discourses. Complex problems cannot be reduced to simple formulas anymore, and neither can the solution be based solely on rationalism. In this sense, Brazilian urbanism has become postmodern, but not in a reactionary sense as a reproduction of the status quo under new forms nor as a new aesthetic discourse—which is totally irrelevant here—but rather because it recognizes fragmentation, heterogeneity, differences, pluralism, and pragmatism (Harvey 1990; Jameson 1991; Dear 2000). It changes the conception of the city and its culture, recognizes historical precedents and different typologies, values place-based solutions and public-private partnerships, and leans on community participation and democracy as a leading force (Watson and Gibson 1995; Ellin 1999). Thus, recognizing different kinds of city-building processes can allow for diversity and allow responses to different publics, while accepting different forms of cultural expression.

The essays and case studies in this book reveal postmodern urbanism as a social process of production and consumption of urban space (Dear 2000), where there is a constant polarity on one level between markets versus places and detachment versus belonging, and on the other level, between public versus private realms as expressed through the use and significance of urban space (Zukin 1988). Deregulation, for instance, is an interesting facet, as it seems to be one of the modus operandi of postmodern urbanism. Undoubtedly, deregulation is setting new economic and power relationships at the level of national and regional superstructures; however, its effects on cities are not so evident. In contrast, democratic participation and the new national legislation introduced cities into a new era of land-use and urban-development regulation. These are likely to result in more heterogeneity, pluralism, and pragmatism throughout the country. These effects are in evidence in cities such as Porto Alegre, which has been experimenting with reinventing itself and its social purpose through programs such as the participatory city budget. And yet, Brazilian society firmly believes in a nationalist, forward-looking development model and that cities and a conscious urbanism can change society and achieve higher states of human and social development.

Readers will certainly notice that an optimistic tone about the development of contemporary urbanism in Brazil underlies this book. We hope to demonstrate that Brazil is forging a creative urbanism that is postmodern in the sense that it welcomes different logics and models in embracing the nation's quest for better and more just cities.

The Structure of the Book

No matter what prism we look through, we find several positive changes in Brazilian urbanism since re-democratization in the mid-1980s. Many cities are investing in reshaping the public realm through different approaches that prove modernism and postmodernism do coexist. A positive aspect of Brazil's contemporary urbanism is the use of complementary strengths of both modernism and postmodernism to achieve more useable and equitable cities.

We start this book by discussing the evolution of urbanism in Brazil in order to provide readers not familiar with this facet of Brazilian development with a historical foundation for understanding present conditions. This introduction will introduce the main reasons why modernism continues to be a strong influence in city building for better (by incorporating the functionality much needed in rapidly developing areas, for instance) and for worse (by facilitating spatial and social segregation, for instance). We also comment on some of the negative effects of the free market and global economy on Brazilian cities, and also on recent positive changes in the political and legal contexts leading toward more democratic processes and a socially responsive urbanism.

The book is divided into three parts reflecting the major trends in contemporary Brazilian urbanism. The decision to concentrate on these trends was based on our initial research on how urbanism was developing in Brazil. We chose those city-building experiences that could contribute to a better understanding of a developing nation and could teach helpful lessons to the developed world. Unfortunately, as we stated before, due to the enormity of our task, we had to be very selective in our choice of case studies.

Eighteen researchers contribute twelve case studies in eight different cities, representing different regions and different realities in Brazil.[10] The map in figure P.1 shows the localities, and their populations are given in table P.1. The selected cities range from the country's largest urban areas to small regional capitals. These case studies illustrate different ways that Brazilian urbanism tries to meet the overarching goal of helping to advance society—and thereby responds to the original paradigm of modernity. Unlike when modernity dominated Brazilian urban development, there is at present no universally accepted model or tenets dictating solutions in all cities.

In the introduction to each part of the book, we introduce the relevant major trend and the case studies representing it. That we have identified the first trend as Late Modernism should come as no surprise given the enormous political and cultural importance of modernism from the formative years of Brazil as a modern state in the 1930s to the end of the military dictatorship in the early 1980s. The modernist paradigm was the perfect fit for the positivistic ideals of the industrializing, modernizing, and development-thirsty young nation well into the 1950s and guided the construction of Brasília. The military regime centralized power in the government and relied on modernism in its totalitarian, technocratic, and rationalist pursuit of an ideal social order (Holston 1989; Harvey 1990). Modernism served well the large development projects and state-supported capitalist development of the 1960s and 1970s.

After half a century of dominating the Brazilian cultural and political scene, modernism, as one would expect, remains a strong influence today. The case studies will show how modernist precepts are still present in much of Brazilian urbanism, par-

Figure P.1. Map of Brazil and its states, indicating the state capitals and case study cities.
(Map by Vicente del Rio)

Table P.1. Populations of Brazil and case study cities, 2000 and 2006.

	2000	2006
Belém	1,280,614	1,428,368
Brasília	2,051,146	2,383,784
Curitiba	1,587,315	1,788,559
Porto Alegre	1,360,590	1,440,939
Rio de Janeiro	5,857,904	6,136,652
Salvador	2,443,107	2,714,018
São Paulo	10,435,546	11,016,703
Brazil	169,872,856	186,770,562

Source: Instituto Brasileiro de Geografia Estatística (IBGE)website: www.ibge.gov.br.

Data for 2000 are from the national census; data for 2006 are IBGE estimates.

ticularly in existing zoning regulations and in the positivistic perspective of urban policies and political leaders. Forced to recognize the existence of different sets of values, however, modernist urbanism in Brazil came to coexist with other urbanisms, mutated into what we call Late Modernism. The case studies will take the reader from Brasília (where a "classic modernism" survives among other urban morphologies that are not always recognized) to the new capital of Palmas (a great example of a rationalist city built in the 1990s), to the dominating vertical cityscape of São Paulo and its shopping centers as nodes for growth. Late Modernism is thus about the struggle to exercise control over the development of city form and function.

The second part addresses Revitalization, the second trend in Brazilian contemporary urbanism. Because the resurgence of democracy in Brazil in the mid-1980s coincided with the peak of a grave economic crisis and stagnation, making the best out of the existing city and respecting social and physical contexts made a lot of political and economic sense. By that time, public participation and a renewed interest in history, architectural preservation, and place-based city marketing started reorienting urbanism away from the previous modernist paradigm of "creative destruction" (Harvey 1990: 16). Politically and economically, Le Corbusier's model of bulldozed clear-site urbanism became almost impossible.

From the successful efforts of the Cultural Corridor project in Rio de Janeiro to the controversial renovation of the Pelourinho district in Salvador, the riverfront revitalization in Belém, and the privately led revitalization of brownfields in Porto Alegre, the case studies of Revitalization demonstrate Brazil's struggle to improve the existing city, using history and context as social, economic, and cultural resources. In this respect, Brazilian contemporary urbanism is closer to postmodernist ideals: as the case studies demonstrate, it recognizes the value of historical precedents, multiple uses, sustainable development, and the growing role of the private sector as a partner in public projects.

The third part of this book addresses what we term Social Inclusion, the struggle to make a better city for the entire community of residents. In the introduction to this book, we briefly discuss how democratization and the changes in the political and economic frameworks redirected urbanism, given that both the 1988 National Constitution and the 2001 Statute of the City regard the city as a place for social justice and as a public domain. Efforts resulting from this legal framework have been generating projects that are responsive to community needs, rebuild the urban public realm, and recognize that all social groups have a right to a quality urban environment. Due to the enormous and longstanding social inequality in the country, Brazil certainly has a long way to go in creating cities that are socially equitable and livable for all, but the case studies demonstrate that many efforts have been made in that direction.

The "Social Inclusion" section opens by discussing urbanism in Curitiba, a city that international analysts have repeatedly called a model of sustainable planning practices and that recently placed first in the Smart Cities list compiled by the Urban Land Institute (see *Urban Land,* April 2007). The discussion will focus not only on Curitiba's achievements but also on the challenges it presently faces in managing its own success. Next, a citywide urban design project designed to reconstruct the image of Rio de Janeiro and make the streets more livable is presented, followed by a study of three different ways that the city of São Paulo is reshaping its fragmented territory and making it more accessible to the public. The last case study in this book discusses the award-winning Favela-Bairro program in Rio de Janeiro, a cutting-edge project to upgrade squatter settlements and integrate them physically and socially into the city.

We hope that the discussions and case studies in this book will lead the reader to share our optimism about contemporary Brazilian urbanism and its fundamental role in expanding democracy, making cities more socially just, and increasing the quality of the public realm. We also hope that the various projects and programs, particularly the successful examples, will inspire others and contribute to the advancement of planning and urban design in both developing and developed nations.

Brazil has repeatedly been called "the country of the future" and "the sleeping giant" due to its enormous latent potential for development, in both natural and human resources. Yet the growth in the 1960s and the economic boom of the 1970s were followed by the international financial crisis of the 1980s, high inflation rates, and a political crisis that finally ousted the military government, all of which proved the shallowness of that growth and exposed the ugly reality that while some groups enjoy a first world quality of life, the majority of Brazilians barely make a living. On entering the new millennium, Brazil still faces the same old historical social injustices and repeated patterns of uneven development, all deeply engraved in cities. For the past decade, however, the political avenues opened by re-democratization, the success of economic plans that stopped inflation, the opening of the market to international investments, and the increase in political accountability have improved the quality of life of a significant portion of the population. We firmly believe that Brazilian contemporary urbanism has rightfully assumed a fundamental role in this process of reinventing the city and responding to concurrent territorial logics.

Notes

1. Data from the Instituto Brasileiro de Geografia Estatística (IBGE; Brazilian Institute of Geographical Statistics) website at www.ibge.gov.br (retrieved 10/18/2006).
2. *Favela* is the Brazilian term most commonly used for a squatter settlement. Initiated by land invasions, these informal settlements generally lack basic public infrastructure and services. The buildings are precariously built, and occupants lack property titles. See, for instance, the essay by Duarte and Magalhães (chapter 12) in this book.
3. The national minimum wage (SM) was created by populist dictator Getúlio Vargas during the Estado Novo in 1936. Although its value against the U.S. dollar has been increasing since the country's re-democratization in the mid-1980s, it is still much below a livable wage for workers. Historic average values are Cz$804, or US$58 (March 1986); R$70, or US$79 (September 1994), and R$380, or US$186 (April 2007). The first two wages coincide with Brazil's last two economic plans, which affected the exchange rate (see Brazil's Central Bank website: www.bcb.gov.br).
4. Based on studies presented at the "Revitalização do Rio: Os Principais Desafios da Região Metropolitana" (Revitalization of Rio: The Main Challenges to the Metropolitan Region) seminar, organized by the *O Globo* newspaper and published as a series of articles in 2005.
5. Census data are from the IBGE website at www.ibge.gov.br (retrieved 10/18/2006).
6. The annual population growth rate in the São Paulo metropolitan area (thirty-nine municipalities) actually dropped from 6.17 percent in 1950–60 to 1.63 percent in 1991–2000. (Meyer, Grostein, and Biderman 2004).
7. In Jim Miara, "What Makes Great Cities?" *Urban Land,* April 2007: 60–67.
8. Economists understand the "Brazil cost" as "a combination of actual negative realities and perceptual myths" that indicates the international perception of the risk in investing in Brazil and that determines its degree of political and economic vulnerability (MacLachlan 2003: 214).
9. "Full citizenship" is a term popularly used in Brazilian planning to refer to the concept that all citizens have a right to all modern amenities, employment, and property ownership; it is only through having these things that a person can acquire full citizenship.
10. Most contributors to this volume are Brazilian and originally wrote their chapters in Portuguese. These texts, including any quotations from Brazilian sources within them, were rendered into English by paid translators then reviewed by the editors. We hope that we have provided a readable and accessible resource on a topic not often written about in English.

Acknowledgments

Editing and writing a book is no easy task, and each book presents new challenges. The many challenges represented by the preparation of *Contemporary Brazilian Urbanism: Beyond Brasília* were not overcome by the editors alone, but required the help of many individuals and institutions that we wish to acknowledge. First, our contributing colleagues from Brazilian universities deserve strong recognition since their multitask jobs and chronic lack of resources made participating in this book so much more difficult for them. Thankfully, they were highly motivated to publicize Brazilian contemporary urbanism to an international readership, and agreed to endure the editors' picky demands: we are particularly grateful to them for their dedication.

We are very grateful to the Graham Foundation for Advanced Studies in the Fine Arts, the LEF Foundation, and Cal Poly San Luis Obispo's Research and Graduate Programs Office, which provided grants for various phases of the research, manuscript preparation, and editing.

Professors Jon Lang (University of New South Wales, Australia) and Larry Herzog (San Diego State University) reviewed the manuscript and provided us with valuable comments and insights. We are indebted to Professor Jon Lang for writing the book's foreword. We thank our guiding hands at the University Press of Florida, particularly Amy Gorelick for believing in the book, and Jacqueline Kinghorn Brown, project editor.

Thank you to Jon Tolman, who took the translation job so promptly, and to Kirsteen Anderson, who was an incredibly diligent copy editor and magically put the manuscript in much better shape.

We would also like to thank the following individuals for their comments on parts of this book: Iára Castello (Federal University of Rio Grande do Sul, Porto Alegre); Michael Dear (University of Southern California, Los Angeles); Edésio Fernandes (University College, London); Jorge Guilherme Francisconi (Brasília); David Gertner (Pace University, New York); Octavio Costa Gomes (IBAM, Porto Alegre); Zeljka

Howard (Cal Poly, San Luis Obispo); Silvio Macedo (University of São Paulo); and Geoffrey K. Payne (GKP Consultants, London). We want to thank Adauto Cardoso, Luciana Lago, and Luiz Cesar Ribeiro, Federal University of Rio de Janeiro, for participating in a lengthy interview on urban reform in Brazil. Needless to say, our colleagues added a great deal to this book and helped us come closer to a perfection that, unfortunately, can never be reached. Many thanks to the friends, photographers, and institutions that contributed the images that enhance the book.

Cal Poly State University, San Luis Obispo, supported our endeavor in many ways. We particularly thank Dr. Susan Opava, Dean of Research and Graduate Programs, and R. Thomas Jones, Dean of the College of Architecture and Environmental Design. Our colleagues in the City and Regional Planning Department were supportive, patient, and even learned to refrain from asking "How's the book going?" for the sake of our own sanity. Thank you also to Ryan Brough, Maria Cristina Gosling (for the initial translation efforts), Kathy Lehmkuhl, Joy Miller, Lilly Schinsing, and Melany Reese Senn.

Vicente del Rio would like to thank his wife, Miriam, and daughter, Deborah, for putting up with his grumpy researcher persona while the book was in development. He thanks his mother, Beatriz, and his late father, Edgard, for providing him with so much love and inspiration, and for bringing him to life in that incredible place called Rio de Janeiro. He is also much indebted to his former and present students, constant sources of inspiration who keep scholarship alive.

William John Siembieda thanks his wife, Leslie, for sharing her nights and weekends with this book. Over the years, various members of ANPUR (the Brazilian Urban and Regional Research Association) have shared their thoughts, writings, and sometimes their homes with him. They certainly have influenced his approach to this topic. Finally he thanks Gilda and Paulo Bruna for first bringing him to Brazil in 1985 and for beginning a conversation on how to understand and do something about the form and function of Brazilian cities.

Contemporary Urbanism in Brazil

Introduction Historical Background

Vicente del Rio

This introduction discusses the evolution of urbanism in Brazil, beginning with the birth of modernism, then covering the military regime, the democratic movements of the 1980s, the expansion of the notion of urban intervention, and, finally, the multiplicity of approaches to tackle the city at the dawn of the twenty-first century. Our goal is to help readers become familiar with Brazilian urbanism as a foundation for a clear understanding of the contents and implications of the book's case studies. As such, this introduction is not meant to be a complete, systematic account, which for a country as large as Brazil with such a complex history and more than 80 percent of its population living in urban areas, would require a book of encyclopedic proportions.

There is no English-language literature assessing the same time span in the evolution of Brazilian urbanism, although a number of publications—particularly those dealing with modernism and architecture—discuss specific issues over shorter periods. We make use of many of these works and provide as many bibliographical references as possible to assist readers in pursuing further studies. Moreover, since the history of the city and urbanism cannot be dissociated from an understanding of the political, economic, and social framework of development, our discussion also covers the most important correlations between these topics and urban development.

From a quest to create a progressive, developed nation and the corresponding paradigm of commitment to modernism, Brazil has moved toward a quest for democracy and social equity through city building. Brazilian contemporary urbanism accepts modernism as one of the possible models by which to understand and act upon the city, but it also accepts other, equally valid models. From the positivistic, reductionist, and rigid universal discourse of modern urbanism to the fragmented, pluralistic, and multifaceted shift in sensibilities that characterizes postmodernism (Ellin 1999; Dear 2000) and the transnational processes of globalization (King 2004),

1

Brazilian contemporary urbanism is re-creating itself and allowing for the coexistence of multiple territorial logics in its search for multiple ways to respond to societal needs and urban problems. This brief historical account helps to frame the case studies within a larger picture and, we hope, helps to explain why contemporary Brazilian urbanism is able to absorb multiple perspectives and possibilities, which is the reason we perceive it to be postmodern.

The Birth of Modern Brazilian Urbanism

Brazil's love affair with modernism has been long and intense, and is still deeply embedded in all cultural spheres. As in other Latin American countries, in Brazil after independence cultural production and city building became increasingly dependent on first French and then British models until after World War II, when the United States became the dominant cultural power.[1] Interventions on the city were increasingly seen as "part of a more ambitious package of reforms intended to modernize the social structures" (Almandoz 2002: 17). In fact, modernism in Brazil would never have developed so quickly and strongly without the patronage of the ruling classes. It has long been a tool for promoting the state's vision of progress.

Starting with the dictatorship of Getúlio Vargas (1930–1945) and his populist Estado Novo (New State; 1937–1945), modernism would provide the perfect official vocabulary for government projects and buildings. This regime's dedication to modernizing the state apparatus, developing the country, and creating a new industrial economic base had to be accompanied by a new symbolism, one representing a nationalist, industrializing, and forward-looking new nation.[2] The rise of Vargas and the Estado Novo would be fundamental for a group of Brazilian intellectuals, architects, and artists who had been discussing modernism in the arts and literature and its relationship to industrial production since the Semana de Arte Moderna (Modern Art Week) in São Paulo in 1922.[3] These early modernists discussed the idea of Brazilianism—that there was a legitimate Brazilian culture—and adopted a "metaphor of cannibalism . . . to define their relationship to European culture as that of . . . deliberate, selective ingestion, by which a foreign product was transformed into something entirely Brazilian" (Fraser 2000: 9).

The quest for a new national identity and structure included incursions into architecture, planning, urban design, and low-income housing (Borges 1995; Sisson and Jackson 1995). An important example of urbanism supported by Vargas was the construction of Goiânia, the new capital of the state of Goiás, designed by modernist architect Attílio Corrêa Lima in the early 1930s for a population of fifty thousand (fig. I.1). The modernity of his design—although still heavily influenced by the garden city movement—would serve Vargas as a symbolic gesture of rupture with the old rural oligarchies and the establishment of a new industrial center in the undeveloped interior of Brazil (Borges 1995). Similarly important was São Paulo's 1930 Plano de Avenidas, the first city-wide comprehensive master plan based on modern circulation needs, highly influenced by U.S. circulation planning of the time (Leme 1999; Pereira 2002). Other similar projects were being carried out throughout the country as the positivist discourse in urbanism defended the idea of promoting development, social discipline, and order through urban design. During the Estado Novo, planning departments were created in major Brazilian cities, the first zoning laws were approved, and many urbanists were appointed mayors by Vargas (Leme 1999; Outtes 2002).

Figure I.1. Plan for Goiânia by Attílio Corrêa Lima, including the changes by Armando Godoy (top of drawing), 1934.

In both his regime and later in the political agenda of his Estado Novo, Vargas acknowledged the importance of extending education to the masses in order to garner support for the regime's goals for national progress and to expand middle-class values. The entire educational system received deep reforms, including the creation of the Ministry of Education and Health in 1933, which would become a strong ally in the institutionalization of modernism. Higher education was expanded through, for instance, the creation of the University of São Paulo in 1934 and the reorganization of the University of Brazil (now the Federal University of Rio de Janeiro) in 1938. A group of intellectuals headed by the famous writer Mario de Andrade, Rodrigo Mello Franco, and Lucio Costa, interested in the preservation of the Brazilian memory, received the support of the Vargas regime to create the first agency for historic preservation in 1936. The SPHAN (Serviço de Patrimonio Historico e Artistico Nacional, or National Historic and Artistic Patrimony Service) was created within the structure of the Ministry of Education and Health, which meant that historic preservation could also be made to serve the regime, if only as a means of stressing the importance of modernity.[4]

In keeping with the regime's ideals of modernism, in 1931 the minister of education appointed Lucio Costa—a young modernist architect who at that time worked for the ministry and who would eventually create Brasília—as the new director of the Escola Nacional de Belas Artes (National Fine Arts School) with the charge of fully reforming it. Costa instituted a "functional" course parallel to the old beaux arts curriculum, hired modernist architects and urban designers as new faculty members, and had instant success with the students. Evidently, he also aroused strong opposition among the old faculty, who forced his resignation one year later, but not before he had inspired a group of students who would become the influential first generation of modern architects, including Oscar Niemeyer and Roberto Burle Marx (Deckker 2001). Costa's curriculum changes in Rio would influence architectural education throughout Brazil, and eventually modernism would dominate the debates at the first Brazilian Congress of Urbanism in 1941. Urbanism would soon become institutionalized as a specific profession with the creation of a graduate program for architects and engineers in the School of Architecture of Rio de Janeiro's University of Brazil in 1945.

As many other authors have noted, modern architecture and urbanism in Brazil owe a great deal to Le Corbusier's visits and his influence on young Brazilian architects (Fraser 2000; Deckker 2001; Andreoli and Forty 2004). Their alignment with Estado Novo objectives was fundamental for the political recognition of modernism and for its eventual adoption as the official architectural vocabulary for government buildings, as well as the official style in architectural education. Deckker (2001), for instance, narrates the political intricacies of the famous 1935 design competition for the new Ministry of Education and Health building built in Rio. The minister rejected the winning entry—a beaux arts classicist project—and handed the design over to Lucio Costa, who decided to gather a small group of young collaborators, including Oscar Niemeyer. With Le Corbusier acting as a consultant, the team produced a groundbreaking new design for the building, which became one of the most internationally celebrated modernist buildings and an icon of "modern Brazil." The paradigmatic design for this building includes two elegant intersecting volumes in the middle of the site and on *pilotis* (columns), allowing the ground floor to integrate with the landscaping (by Roberto Burle Marx); extensive use of *brise-soleils* (external sun blocking panels); and other architectural novelties (Fraser 2000; Deckker 2001).

In their aggressive professional marketing, these "first modern thinkers" headed by Costa and Le Corbusier also ridiculed their competitors, and they were influential in the consolidation of the modernist discourse within the Estado Novo apparatus. Examples were their criticisms of the 1930s master plan for Rio by French urbanist Alfred Agache and of the project for the Cidade Universitária (university campus) by Italian Marcello Piacentini, who would later become Mussolini's architect. It is interesting to note that at that time, the Estado Novo shared some populist and philosophical roots with fascist regimes such as Mussolini's—and thus with Piacentini's monumental style.

Agache was a leading French urbanist with a beaux arts background who adopted a "sociological urbanism" approach and was hired after his seminars on planning and socioeconomic reforms in Rio de Janeiro (Underwood 1991; Pereira 2002). Agache's beaux arts plan for Rio included sociological innovations: satellite towns for the working classes, citywide plans for infrastructure, impressive city embellishments, and a total renewal of the downtown (fig. I.2). Later, he would move his practice to Brazil and develop master plans for other Brazilian cities such as Curitiba and Vitoria, and for land developments such as São Paulo's Interlagos district

Agache's plan for Rio was further battered at the end of the 1930s, when political maneuverings inside the city government forced its abandonment. At that time Vargas enthusiastically supported a project to build a monumental new downtown

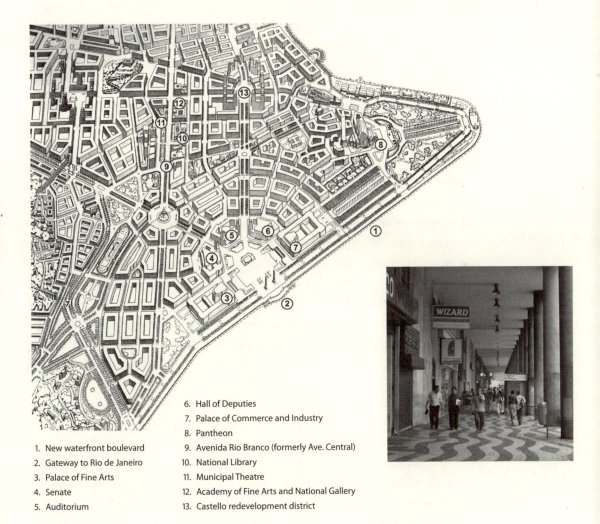

1. New waterfront boulevard
2. Gateway to Rio de Janeiro
3. Palace of Fine Arts
4. Senate
5. Auditorium
6. Hall of Deputies
7. Palace of Commerce and Industry
8. Pantheon
9. Avenida Rio Branco (formerly Ave. Central)
10. National Library
11. Municipal Theatre
12. Academy of Fine Arts and National Gallery
13. Castello redevelopment district

Figure I.2. Alfred Agache's master plan for Rio de Janeiro, 1933: (*left*) A bird's-eye rendering of the downtown area, showing all major buildings and urban elements. (Adapted by Vicente del Rio); (*right*) One of the proposals in the Agache plan, a pedestrian arcade in downtown Rio. (Photo by Vicente del Rio)

boulevard that ultimately destroyed a stretch of twenty blocks of old colonial morphology and 958 residential buildings, replacing them with the 150–foot-wide Avenida
Presidente Vargas and buildings towering twenty-two stories on both sides.

Le Corbusier made his first visit to Brazil on his own initiative in 1929, visiting four
cities, including São Paulo and Rio de Janeiro. He was attracted by the possibility of
obtaining new work, particularly because he had heard of Brazil's desire to build a
new capital and because of the presence in Brazil of Agache, his competitor. He de-
livered lectures based on his Cité Contemporaine and other projects; entertained his
followers, including Lucio Costa; and made numerous sketches of Rio's landscape and
women. Researchers agree that this visit marked a turning point in his career, when
his vocabulary started adopting more curvilinear forms. Fraser (2000: 10) notes that,
impressed by the city's "larger-than-life landscape," Le Corbusier adapted his rigid
geometry of city blocks and his superhighway to the curvilinear topography (fig. I.3).
Later, in 1936, he made his second trip to Rio as a consultant to Lucio Costa and his
team in the development of the design for the Ministry of Education and Health
building.

In the 1940s and 1950s, when modernism was at its peak internationally, the world
admired the "Brazilian style" of architecture and urban design. The previously mentioned Ministry of Education and Health building, Lucio Costa's and Oscar Niemeyer's
collaboration on the celebrated Brazilian Pavilion at the 1939 New York World's Fair,
Costa's Park Guinle residential project in Rio (1948), Niemeyer's Pampulha Lake complex in Belo Horizonte (1940), and several other modern buildings—these all became
international icons, examples of a perfect adaptation of the tenets of modern architecture to local conditions (Fraser 2000; Deckker 2001; Andreoli and Forty 2004). The
U.S. "Good Neighbor" policy of the 1940s; the 1943 New York Museum of Modern Art
exhibition and accompanying book, Brazil Builds; and countless international publications in the United States and Europe all helped to publicize Brazilian architecture
worldwide.

American political and industrial interests during World War II were allied to
Getúlio Vargas's policies; this along with the development of Brazil's steel industry
generated an interesting new town project next to Rio de Janeiro, commissioned
to Josep Luís Sert and Paul Wiener in 1943 (Fraser 2000). The Cidade dos Motores
(Motor City), designed to house twenty-five thousand people, was to be built around
an airplane engine factory and the new steel plant in nearby Volta Redonda. Soon
after the war ended, the factory began building engines for trucks. Although the town
was never built, according to Fraser (2000) its design represented a development of
Sert's theories as he moved away from the rigidity of the four CIAM precepts and
adopted the "civic core" as the fifth one.

Figure I.3. Le Corbusier's concept sketch for Rio de Janeiro, 1929. (© 2007 Artists Rights Society [ARS], New York/ADAGP, Paris/FLC)

The political platform of Vargas and the Estado Novo included the financing and construction of low-income "workers' housing"—in the jargon of those times—with moneys from new pension funds and institutes linked to social security and the Ministry of Labor (Bonduki 1998). Housing was an important political issue; providing housing was intended to increase the regime's legitimacy and encourage public support for other social reforms. The housing could not be built fast enough, however, as the Estado Novo's industrial policies and the rapid pace of industrialization encouraged more migration to major cities; in Rio de Janeiro, for instance, the 1940s saw the greatest growth of favelas, which totaled 105 in 1948 (Abreu 1987).

Beginning in the mid-1950s, modernism and the CIAM precepts, together with Perry's 1929 neighborhood unit principles, would guide the design of public housing throughout Brazil; although not numerous enough to meet demand, these public housing projects did have significant effects and allowed for experimentation with the new design principles (Bruand 1981; Segawa 1998; Bonduki 1998). As a measure of their prominence, two housing projects were included in the "Brazil Builds" exhibition and book: a partially built project with 4,038 housing units in São Paulo by Attílio Corrêa Lima (designer of the new city of Goiânia), and another one with 2,344 units in Rio de Janeiro (Segawa 1998). Probably the most internationally famous of the modernist "workers' housing" projects is the Pedregulho Residential Complex in Rio de Janeiro, built in 1947. This complete "neighborhood unit" included a school, day-care and health centers, a swimming pool, 478 housing units, and a serpentine apartment building on *pilotis* (fig. I.4).[5] Not unlike what was going on in other parts of the world, modernism had become the vocabulary for low-income projects by the time Brasília was being built.

The ambitious economic, industrial, and national development programs set forth in 1956 by President Juscelino Kubitschek—who as mayor of Belo Horizonte had built the Pampulha modernist complex—included the construction of a new national cap-

Figure I.4. The Pedregulho Residential Complex in Rio de Janeiro, designed by Affonso Reidy and built in 1947, a modernist icon of Brazilian public housing. (Photo by Vicente del Rio)

ital not only as a progressive national symbol but also as a means to bring development into the country's interior. The territorial logic was to develop and modernize Brazil's heartland and populate the middle of the country. Kubitschek's agenda was pivotal in consolidating Brazilian modernism. His economic strategy was successful in promoting overall optimism and encouraging industrialization, but it also sped up migration to urban areas and urbanization (Skidmore 1999; MacLachlan 2003).

Vargas's and later Kubitschek's drive for industrialization was pivotal in the population explosion of Brazil's major cities in the 1940s and 1950s. Abreu (1987) noted that Rio de Janeiro's metropolitan area grew by 103 percent between 1950 and 1960 and that in 1960, 53 percent of its population consisted of migrants—half of whom lived in areas just outside Rio, most in illegal land subdivisions—those without land titles, built without official approval, or without the infrastructure the developer was supposed to provide. The situation was similar in the São Paulo metropolitan area, where Meyer, Grostein, and Biderman (2004) registered a growth rate of 6.17 percent between 1950 and 1960, compared to a growth rate of 3.04 percent for Brazil as a whole in the same period.

At the end of the 1950s, belief in economic growth and the positivism of modernism drove two paradigmatic projects in Rio de Janeiro that helped set the pace of Brazilian modern urban design. Both were under the charge of Affonso Reidy at the city's Planning Department. The first was an urban renewal project that demolished a hill and part of the historic downtown to build office towers along two major avenues, and the other was the famous Parque do Flamengo (Flamengo Parkway). Built in the 1960s on a major landfill over Guanabara Bay, this project was conceived by Affonso Reidy—architect of the Pedregulho complex—and consisted of a high-speed vehicular corridor connecting downtown to Copacabana and higher-income districts along the beaches integrated with a major public park. Carefully landscaped by Roberto Burle Marx with sports grounds, bike and pedestrian paths, and numerous indigenous plant species, the Flamengo Parkway became an important recreational resource and an international icon of Brazilian urban design and landscape architecture (fig. I.5).

The new capital of Brasília, inaugurated in 1960, represented the apex of President Kubitschek's development policies and cultural optimism: in a little more than four years a whole city was built from scratch (Evenson 1973; Fraser 2000). The product of a national design competition with an international jury (interestingly, Kubitschek had turned down Le Corbusier's offer to design it free of charge), Brasília was a symbol of deep transformations, representing the culmination of the country's dreams of modernization, industrialization, and advancement from an agrarian past. It was Brazil's biggest attempt to achieve a more balanced urbanization of its national territory. Brasília's architecture and urban design helped consolidate modernism in the Brazilian cultural repertoire. The city is the most complete realization of modernist urbanism and of Le Corbusier's teachings (Holston 1989; Fraser 2000), and was declared a World Heritage Site by UNESCO in 1987.

Despite the construction of Brasília and the optimism generated by Kubitschek's development policies in the late 1950s, the early 1960s were troubled times for modernism, for Brazil, and for the international reputation of its architecture and urban design. Inflation and the foreign debt—driven up by Kubitschek's international borrowing and the construction of the new capital—were extremely high; political unrest

Figure I.5. Parque do Flamengo, built 1962–64 in Rio de Janeiro: urban design by Affonso Reidy (of the city's planning department) and landscape architecture by Roberto Burle Marx. (Courtesy of Silvio Macedo, Projeto Quapá)

increased due to the expansion of communism and the clash of ideologies between progressive values and the conservative middle class (Skidmore 1999; MacLachlan 2003). By the late 1950s and early 1960s, modernism was already deeply installed in architectural and planning circles and was accepted outside the intellectual elite and among the lower classes in Brazil. But soon after the construction of Brasília, there was little or no mention of Brazilian architecture in international magazines or in standard architectural history books, as contemporary researchers have noted (Fraser 2000; Andreoli and Forty 2004). Fraser (2000: 2) stated poignantly that "Brasilia . . . marked the end of the love affair . . . one ambition too far, and the architectural establishment in the USA and Europe turned against it."

Internationally, the 1960s mark the beginning of the end for modernist architecture and urbanism as Le Corbusier's authoritarian teachings and the cold rationalism of modernism were increasingly criticized from all sides—by academics, professionals, and users (Frampton 1992; Ellin 1999). As an interesting side note, in comparison to Le Corbusier's radicalism, Brazilian modernism was actually much more respectful of historical patterns, having incorporated some of these elements in its architectural solutions, as can easily be seen in the architecture of that time and in Lucio Costa's pivotal role in Brazil's movement for historic preservation (Deckker 2001; Cavalcanti 2003).

Nevertheless, in the geopolitical dimension, with the cold war and the shift of political and cultural interests toward the U.S.–European axis, Latin American and Brazilian architecture and urban design lost the interest of the intelligentsia and the media for several decades until the recent relative resurgence of interest in modernism among some key architectural publications (Deckker 2001; Cavalcanti 2003; Andreoli and Forty 2004; el-Dahdah 2005).

In addition to the progressive dismantling of modernism in the international intellectual arena, the Brazilian military coup of 1964 and the military government that remained in power until the mid-1980s worked against the international popularity of Brasília and Brazilian architecture. Fraser (2000) notes how easily Brasília's modernist urban settings and symbolism lent themselves to the new dictatorship. The monumental architecture, strict zoning, and large open spaces became the perfect representation of the power of a centralized military government. Moreover, the capital's strict adherence to a segregated urbanism led to the crystallization of a ring of poverty around the Pilot Plan area, expressing spatially the perverse social dichotomy of Brazilian society.

By and large, until the early 1980s, Brazilian urbanism—in both the professional and educational realms—reflected this paradigm and offered no novelties for international observers. Actually, it offered opportunities for tough criticism, such as

Holston's (1989) critique of Brasília, although this criticism sometimes came from observers who overemphasized negative perspectives or did not entirely understand the phenomenon.[6]

Modernism, which in Brazil had been embraced by the state since the early 1930s, would also serve the military regime and all its government agencies. The military would welcome the efficiency, functionalism, and technocracy of modernism; its urbanism of segregated land uses; its emphasis on private vehicles; its grandiose public works, and its role in promoting the growing gap between the rich and poor. Given its authoritarian and functionalist nature, modernist urbanism was well suited to the new power structure.

The Military and Technocratic Modernism

In a backlash against the economic and political unrest of the early 1960s and the popular socialist tendencies of the presidency succeeding Kubitschek's, the military took power in 1964, amply supported by the middle class and conservative parties.[7] The regime's political and economic agenda was to create a powerful, developed nation with a strong, independent internal market. Industrialization, urbanization, and the concentration of investments and population in the larger metropolises would be the means for developing and integrating the national territory.

As a result of the military's agenda for development, state-led capitalism, and a large influx of international capital, inflation was reduced significantly between 1968 and 1974, Brazil's foreign debt was renegotiated, and the average annual growth of the Brazilian economy reached the 10 percent mark (Segawa 1998). This period of economic expansion was nicknamed the "economic miracle." Economic growth was attained at the expense of social justice, however, and the gap between the rich and poor actually increased. The "economic miracle" did not last long; the oil price shocks of 1973 and 1980, increasing foreign and internal debts, and the return of inflation all pushed Brazil toward a huge economic crisis during the 1970s and 1980s. This crisis would eventually feed the growing political and popular opposition that would lead the country back to democracy in 1985.

From 1964 until the late 1970s, reflecting the centralized power structure of the military regime, national urban planning came into being (Schmidt 1983; Serra 1991). At the national level, the new order tried to balance development and reduce regional discrepancies in development. Federally controlled regional development agencies were created—such as SUDAM and SUDESUL (development agencies for the Amazon and the southern regions, respectively)—following the model of SUDENE, the development agency for the Northeast. (Modeled on the Tennessee

Valley Authority in the United States, SUDENE was created in 1959 by the Kubitschek government to help develop what was—and still is—Brazil's most backward region.) For virtually every development sector national funds and programs would be created, as well as national agencies responsible for overseeing policies and investments. The national program for road construction was part of the national agenda and produced the famous Transamazonia—a road meant to open up the Amazon region for development, connect it to the rest of the country, allow further exploration of natural resources, and colonize the interior.

Urbanization and city building at this time were seen from an economic and national development perspective. Urban problems became almost exclusively economic problems, and solving the exploding housing shortage in big cities became a question of increasing the supply of cheap residential units. The state would favor "rational" and administrative actions; it moved away from the quest for an "ideal city" toward the rational and efficient management of the existing city and the elimination of "internal dysfunctionalities" (L. Ribeiro and Cardoso 1994). A national planning system was implemented to try to limit the growth of the large metropolises such as São Paulo and Rio while strengthening midsized cities in order to generate a more balanced and integrated urban network.

In a sign of these new times, in 1965 the governor of Rio de Janeiro—one of the supporters of the military coup—hired the Athens-based firm of Constantinos Doxiadis Associates to develop a new city master plan. Rio had been deprived of its status as national capital with the inauguration of Brasília and needed planning to control its growth and to establish development policies. As noted by Evenson (1973), Doxiadis's study of the city was the most comprehensive to that date, and included sophisticated social, economical, and statistical projections based on his *ekistics* theory for human settlements. The plan aimed at directing the city toward an ideal grid model of hierarchically structured communities and highways, in sharp contrast to the city's historical radial growth pattern. Although the Doxiadis plan was never implemented, it represented the arrival of a somewhat scientific and rational planning model much aligned with the culture of master planning of the time. It also inspired local decisions in highway planning and defined the ideal modernist building typology adopted by Rio's zoning and building codes in 1976, which would, in turn, influence codes in all Brazilian cities (fig. I.6).[8]

Also influential during the mid-1960s was the Rio de Janeiro state government's conservative approach to low-income housing. Centered around the destruction of existing squatter settlements and the eviction of the families to low-quality modernist cookie-cutter public housing far from the city, this approach caused more problems than it solved; however, it was backed by an international paradigm and agencies

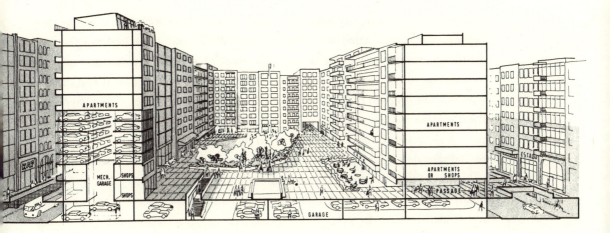

Figure I.6. Cross-section of the block concept for Copacabana, Rio de Janeiro, in the Doxiadis plan, 1965.
(Courtesy of Constantinos A. Doxiadis Archives)

such as the U.S. Alliance for Progress (Perlman 1976). Rio's urban and, particularly, its architectural model for public housing would be adopted by the National Housing Bank and all public housing agencies until the revision of paradigms with the re-democratization process in the mid-1980s. Using the same approach, in 1967 in Guarulhos—a municipality in the greater São Paulo area—the state agency started the construction of Conjunto CECAP, a 312–acre housing project designed by three of the most important modernist architects of São Paulo to house a total population of fifty-five thousand; this was designed to be a model of the state housing policy.

Reis (1996) points out that during the military period, the Brazilian network of cities demonstrated a centralizing political and economic framework with four fundamental aspects: rapid urbanization, increasing concentration of the population, exceptional scale of progress, and worsening of social and income inequalities. Census data indicate that whereas in 1960 only two cities—Rio and São Paulo—had more than one million inhabitants, by 1980, nine metropolitan regions and Brasília had all passed that mark; in addition, 70 percent of the country's population lived in urban areas (Reis 1996). By 1980, these nine metropolitan regions accounted for 29 percent of the country's total population and 42 percent of its urban population! Due to a lack of understanding of the social dimension of development, techno-rational national planning did not account for the pace of migration to large cities and the expansion of pirate subdivisions and favelas in major cities.

During the military era's "developmental techno-bureaucracy" (L. Ribeiro and Cardoso 1994), urbanism would embrace a "functional modernism"—not much different from what was being practiced in other parts of the world—and would focus on restructuring the existing city. The logic of the city and its prevailing structure became dependent on the functionality of vehicular circulation and transportation systems. Yet the national planning system was not without internal contradictions: from 1976 to 1982 large sums of federal funds were poured into urban public transportation systems like subways and trains, while the market and the city master plans encouraged the use of private vehicles. Villaça (1998) points out that the logic of the city and its prevailing structure became dependent on traffic circulation systems, on reproduction of capital through land development and speculation, and on an increasing spatial segregation of the upper classes from the rest of the city territory. Because of the highly volatile and historically inflationary economy, capital investments in land and real estate became extremely profitable and a fundamental factor fueling the urban economy and urban growth, generating increasingly denser and more vertical cities and more socially unjust urban territorialities.

Probably the federal government had its biggest direct effect on city building through the provision of investment funds for urban development, sanitation, housing, and transportation. Among these, house construction and ownership were seen by the powerful elite as strategic investments, not only in the face of the social unrest of the 1960s, but also because of the multiplying effects that the construction sector has over the economy. Months after the 1964 coup, the military government created the Sistema Federal de Habitação (SFH), a national housing financing system with two branches: a market-oriented sector (based on savings) and a socially oriented sector (based on a compulsory percentage taken from the worker's wage). This system financed public works dedicated to urban development, helped consolidate the real estate development market, generated an explosion in the construction of tower blocks and apartment buildings, and changed the land market and several aspects of the chain of production (Maricato 2001). This system had profound impacts on city building and on the Brazilian cityscape.

The same act that created the SFH also established the BNH (National Housing Bank) and SERFHAU (Federal Service for Housing and Urbanism), both under the umbrella of the Ministry of the Interior. For its first ten years, SERFHAU was a powerful agency responsible for defining national and regional urban policies. It supported planning research and graduate education, and promoted the making of numerous local "integrated master plans" by private planning firms following a uniform "multidisciplinary and rational" approach. Unfortunately, the implementation of these plans was very limited to say the least, and their efficiency was ideological rather than practical(Serra 1991; Maricato 1997). The split between policy-making and implementation agencies, as well as the growth in power of those commanding the financial resources, led to SERFHAU being abolished in 1974 and its role being taken over by the BNH, which became the strong arm implementing the governmental development agenda.

The BNH was initially created as a "second line" bank responsible for recapturing SFH money and lending it to other banks, regulating both market-oriented and socially oriented sectors of the national housing system, setting policies, operating funds, distributing investments, and supervising the entire system, including the implementation of public housing through state and local agencies (Valença 1999).[9] When SERFHAU was eliminated, the BNH became responsible for setting national policy for urban development, showing that the military techno-bureaucrats believed that the solution to the urban crisis lay mostly in solving housing and financial demands, not demands related to participatory democracy.

At the time of the BNH's creation in 1964, the estimated low-income housing demand in Brazil was eight million units; by the early 1980s the BNH had produced a little more than one million units for these groups (Valença 1999). By approaching the housing demand through financial means and simply increasing the construction of houses, the BNH produced very low-quality housing architecturally, in terms of bad typologies and very cheap construction materials (fig. I.7). In addition, the bank's

Figure I.7. Typical public housing following the National Housing Bank (BNH) precepts, in Pirituba, São Paulo. (Photo by Silvio Macedo, Projeto Quapá)

policies encouraged the eradication of favelas and the removal of residents to housing projects which, due to the high costs of land in the central city, were built far away from traditional employment opportunities—an extra burden on workers in addition to the mortgage imposed on them by the BNH.

Projeto Rio in Rio de Janeiro was the last BNH project and can be cited as a paradigmatic example of such projects. Its political goals and high costs were perhaps the last straw that would eventually drive the national housing system to bankruptcy. This ambitious regional project was meant to tackle the pollution of Guanabara Bay, in part through the urbanization of a complex of six favelas with almost 100,000 residents, hydraulic infilling of 5,600 acres of the water surface, and construction of a residential project with more than two thousand units for the displaced families. Fatal blows to the BNH were, on the one hand, the high costs of the infrastructure projects and the political commitment of the bank to charge families only 10 percent of the minimum wage for their thirty-year mortgages, and on the other, the low quality of the design. The minimal lots and houses—750 and 250 square feet respectively—and the cheap construction (buildings deteriorated completely in just a couple of years) generated high vacancy rates and delinquencies, which together with the good location of the project, resulted in a certain degree of gentrification.

The effects of the national housing system and the bank on consumers' lives and on cities were not positive and didn't solve the real problems. Moreover, during its last decade or so, the national housing financing system would concentrate on construction for middle- and high-income groups, siding with the dominant classes and securing a better return on investments. The SFH and the BNH were in many respects basic determinants of Brazilian urbanism and city building until the bankruptcy and closure of the housing bank in 1986 and the subsequent restructuring of the national housing system (Azevedo 1990; Valença 1999).

In 1973 SERFHAU managed to get the federal government to approve the creation of metropolitan regions around the nine largest cities, as well as special state agencies to oversee their planning and management. To establish an integrated planning system, these agencies provided three basic types of services for all municipalities within the metropolitan regions: basic support for municipal management (training of local staff, aerial and land surveys, mapping, and so on), development of master plans and staff support for plan implementation, and management of inter-municipal issues and services such as transportation, water supply, and garbage disposal. Although these were important services for the poorer municipalities around the main metropolises, the real power of the metropolitan agencies was political, since they were responsible for approving the local use of earmarked federal and state tax monies and investments. Although some critics argued that the metropolitan agencies represented an imposition of state and federal policies on local affairs disguised under a "rational and neutral" cover, these agencies left an important planning legacy.

Although SERFHAU was closed in 1974, its influence and that of its personnel on the national planning system continued through CNPU (National Commission of Metropolitan Urban Regions and Urban Policy) created in 1974 within the National Planning Secretariat, and the EBTU (National Agency of Urban Transportation), created in 1976. SERFHAU and the work of the CNPU was instrumental in defining a national vision of territorial development and the inclusion of urban policies in the II Plano Nacional de Desenvolvimento (PND, or national plan for development) approved in 1974.

The II PND was the first to fully reflect the importance of urban planning to the state as a coherent set of goals and policies aimed at integrating the national territory socially, economically, and spatially, and it dedicated special attention to the challenge of urban growth management (Schmidt 1983; M. Santos 1999). Chapter IX of the PND was the PNDU (Politica Nacional de Desenvolvimento Urbano, or national urban development policy) and one of its most important outcomes was a national program for development of state capitals and medium-sized cities. The goal was to encourage investments in medium-sized cities and draw them away from the large ones in order to strengthen Brazil's urban network, attain balanced social and regional development, and eliminate internal dysfunctions within cities and regions (Serra 1991; M. Souza 1999). Unfortunately, as Maria Adelia dos Santos (1999) observed, the economic and urban development directives within the II PND contained fundamental contradictions, and the economic directives translated into the worsening of regional disparities.

In 1979 the CNPU was restructured as the CNDU (National Council of Urban Development) and moved to the Ministry of the Interior, having helped gain approval of a national law to regulate and define minimum standards for urban land subdivisions (1979), and having proposed a project for a national development law which in 2001 would be the basis for the Statute of the City (discussed in the next section).

After the military left power in the mid-1980s, most of the metropolitan planning agencies were decommissioned by the state governments until practically all closed their doors. Important exceptions are EMPLASA, São Paulo's metropolitan planning agency—which now also plans for two other metropolitan regions in the state, serving a population of twenty-four million people—and METROPLAN of Porto Alegre, now a statewide agency in Rio Grande do Sul that concentrates on metropolitan transportation systems and on channeling resources for training local urban planning technicians to help municipalities prepare their own master plans.

The military era also influenced education in planning and urbanism through a series of educational reforms: new federal, state, and private institutions were created, and new curricula were promoted. In the late 1960s, undergraduate architecture programs started to include classes on urban and regional planning, and the title of their graduates was changed to "architect-urbanist," a move that was accompanied by the formation of professional boards and that strengthened the power of architects to direct urbanism and planning. In the 1970s matters got a bit more complicated epistemologically. "Urban and regional planning" became a fashionable discipline, following an international trend led by Great Britain and the United States. SERFHAU was a major influence on this shift, not only because all its work was based on interdisciplinary comprehensive planning, but also because the agency supported research and graduate education. A few two-year graduate programs in urbanism that followed the French tradition of *urbanisme* had been enrolling engineers and architects since the early 1950s, but the first master of science programs in urban and regional planning, which appeared in the early 1970s under the auspices of SERFHAU, followed the then-famous model of the University of Edinburgh Planning School. In the following decade, several other master's programs in planning were created, and soon economists, sociologists, transportation engineers, and other professionals would join architects as experts in urbanism.

Ambitious plans, large projects, and technocratic modernism were the trademarks of Brazilian urbanism and of its large supporting bureaucratic and financial apparatus created by the military. Particularly during the late 1960s and the 1970s, as Segawa (1998) notes, the euphoria of the Brazilian "economic miracle," together with the "planning syndrome" of the military regime, encouraged extensive public works and the relocation of investments and population to the interior of the country. Until the early 1980s, public works endeavors throughout Brazil typically reflected this approach to urbanism: urban renewal plans; construction of highways and viaducts; eviction of *favelados*; and construction of huge low-income residential projects, new city and state administrative centers, university campuses, airports, bus and train terminals, hydroelectric power stations, and new independent and company towns.

Two not-so-well-regarded examples of Brazilian urbanism from this period are the 1969 plan by Lucio Costa for Barra da Tijuca and Baixada de Jacarepaguá in Rio de Janeiro, and the new state administrative center in Salvador, Bahia, built in the early 1970s. Costa's plan, nicknamed Plano da Barra, is paradigmatic in representing the same search for an ideal city that Brasília did. Covering more than 11,800 acres, it intended to create a whole new district—including a metropolitan Central Business District—that would expand Rio de Janeiro toward the west along the coast, and it deeply altered the city's growth vector and land market. Costa's original plan was to provide panoramic views and the feeling of vast horizons, as well to protect the fragile beach and lagoon environments by concentrating density. The traditional city morphology was totally rejected in favor of a large grid defined by avenues and composed of triangular sections of eight- to ten-story residential buildings interconnected by clusters of shops with pedestrian arcades. At the junctions between sections, the plan located groups of lower buildings for specific private uses and public utilities. Over time, Costa's design mutated to reflect economic interests and became the city's largest real estate development for the middle and upper classes (G. Leitão 1999). Land uses are much more intense than planned, tower blocks are much taller and closer together, zoning codes mandate a rigid separation of functions, and gated communities and shopping centers prevail in an automobile-dominated environment (fig. I.8).

Figure I.8. Baixada de Jacarepaguá and Barra da Tijuca, Rio de Janeiro: (*above*) Lucio Costa's pilot plan, 1969 (Courtesy of Casa de Lucio Costa, Rio de Janeiro); (*left*) Costa's modernist vision morphed into an auto-dominated environment with segregated land uses, easily adapted to market speculation. (Photo by Silvio Macedo, Projeto Quapá)

The area covered by Costa's original plan is now the perfect representation of the fragmented territory of the postmodern city overlaid on a modernist spatial structure.

Also following modernist development models, the state of Bahia decided in the early 1970s to build a new government administrative center in Salvador. The urban design of the new center was typically modernist, with single-use buildings set apart from each other and a new highway leading to it that allowed the state to promote a large real estate development. The project created a new growth vector, restruc-

Figure I.9. Avenida Atlantica, along Copacabana beach, including the intricate mosaic by Roberto Burle Marx on the sidewalks. (Photo by Silvio Macedo, Projeto Quapá)

tured land values in the whole city, and seriously impacted the historic downtown.[10] Both Costa's Plano da Barra and the plan in Salvador were typical of the rationale of the regime at the time: to promote real estate development as one of the forces of economic development, and of the deep influence that modernism had in formulating the vision of the ideal city and determining the official architectural and urban vocabularies.

During Brazil's "economic miracle"—from the early 1970s until the big economic and political crisis of the early 1980s—many of the large modernist projects marking the urban landscape resulted from traffic circulation and public transportation plans backed up by federal monies. New urban highways and widening of arteries, and notably the construction of subway systems in São Paulo and Rio de Janeiro, generated extensive renovations and land-use and spatial transformations. Subway lines became new structural corridors not only because of their major transportation function, but also because they led to a new design on the surface which promoted the demolition of old buildings and higher densities, renovations and gentrification, and appreciation of real estate values. Some of these interventions would become models, as did the new waterfront boulevard in Copacabana built in the 1970s. In order to ameliorate vehicular traffic congestion between the downtown and high-income neighborhoods, the three-mile-long Copacabana beach was totally transformed by its widening through a costly land infill and construction of a new boulevard with wide sidewalks elegantly designed by the famous landscape architect Roberto Burle Marx (fig. I.9).

On the positive side, besides the creation of a national planning culture, particularly in major cities, some important and interesting urban plans and projects happened during the military era. Perhaps the best-known example internationally is the 1965 plan for Curitiba—a city now famous for its sustainability and public transit.[11] Resulting from a public competition and federally financed, the plan was innovative in its participatory methodology that brought in leading local institutions, its integrated land-use and transportation solutions, and the local planning system it proposed. Initial implementation of the plan was feasible due to support from both the state and the military, and to the growing influence of a team of local planners who even today continue to implement world-famous projects in Curitiba.

Planners in Curitiba came up with many innovative and influential projects starting as early as 1972 with the *calçadão* (big sidewalk), a downtown commercial street turned into a successful pedestrian corridor, and with their preoccupation over increasing the number of parks and green areas. Curitiba tied city growth, zoning, and higher densities to an integrated public transportation system and "structural axes" where highly efficient express buses run on dedicated lanes. This system succeeded in lessening traffic congestion in the center city and increasing ridership among middle-class as well as working-class users. Curitiba would also become an international model for sustainable development, and its urbanism has inspired other cities in Brazil and elsewhere, such as in Bogotá and Los Angeles.

Two other interesting urban projects built under the military regime deserve mention. One was the new town of Caraíba, planned in 1976 for employees of a mining company and designed for an estimated population of fifteen thousand.[12] The town's urban design and architectural solutions avoided the "company town" environment through using an open grid and reflecting vernacular traditions, avoiding strict zoning, providing six central squares with significant buildings around them, and designing in harmony with the local climate (M. Bastos 2003). Another example was the planning and design for the new town of Itá, built between 1977 and 1988 for a community displaced from their original settlement by the construction of a dam and hydroelectric power station in Santa Catarina, in southern Brazil. The state energy company's planning team conducted typological studies of the old settlement as well as participatory workshops with the two hundred resident families, resulting in urban design and architectural solutions that were responsive to the local cultural and social contexts (Rego 1996; M. Bastos 2003).

Probably the longest lasting effects of modernist urbanism on the Brazilian cityscapes resulted from a mix of the CIAM precepts, technocracy, and an economic model that led to land speculation and predatory real estate development practices. Echoing other analysts, Maria Bastos (2003: 99) states that "modern urbanism in Brazil allowed the domination of the signature building over the urban context." These effects are represented in the land-use legislation and building codes of virtually every Brazilian city, which by and large encourage a modernist typology of towers-in-the-green, vehicle-dominated environments, curtain-wall architectural solutions, separation of functions, and proliferation of shopping centers and commercial development.[13]

Analysts such as Segawa (1998) and Maria Bastos (2003) have observed that the military regime in Brazil served to isolate Brazilian architecture and urban design from the international scene. First, the military's cultural repression combined with an aggressive attempt by the architectural intelligentsia to develop an independent Brazilian architecture and urban design. Second, the military's technocratic development model and the "economic miracle" of the late 1960s and early 1970s positioned the state as a major client that hired Brazilian architects and planners for local and regional plans, urban renewal projects, government buildings, low-income housing projects, and so on (although there was also plenty of work in the private sector due to the construction boom). Not surprisingly, until the demise of the military regime and the rise of democracy again in the 1980s, urbanism and city building in Brazil—by both public and private developers—was dominated by a rationalist and functional modernism that permeated all cultural spheres, including architectural education.

Beyond Brasília: Democracy as a Prelude to Contemporary Urbanism

The 1980s represent an important turning point for Brazilians that set the stage for the rise of a new type of urbanism. The country was in the midst of a deep economic crisis brought on by the massive foreign debt, oil price hikes of the 1970s, skyrocketing inflation rates, and growing public opposition to the military government. Large national political movements for re-democratization, strengthening of the labor movement, social unrest, and the largest ever public protests in the country finally brought down the military dictatorship that had ruled the country since 1964 (Skidmore 1999; MacLachlan 2003). In April 1984, crowds of one million–plus people gathered in Rio de Janeiro and São Paulo demanding full democracy and direct elections at all levels of government. After reestablishing direct elections for state governors and mayors in all but the largest cities in the early 1980s, the military relinquished power in 1985 and Congress elected a new president. In 1988 a new National Constitution was passed, and in 1989 the country held its first universal direct elections for president since 1961.[14]

The 1980s introduced a deep crisis in the national planning system and the closure of various federal and metropolitan agencies. Of particular importance was the closure of the National Housing Bank and the total restructuring of the national housing financing system in 1986. This, as Valença (1999) noted, derailed the housing sector and dismantled the country's main policy think tank, decision makers, and promoters of social housing, leaving the housing demand to be met by either the private sector or by timid public financing. For better or worse, the BNH and the SFH had, after all, financed the construction of 2.4 million residential units from 1964 to 1986 (Maricato 2001: 44). The closing of federal and metropolitan planning agencies was also a serious blow to an already fragile system of planning and development control: much of the previous work by these agencies was lost and the well-trained staff was spread out among several other agencies.

During this difficult decade, there were few advances in Brazilian urbanism other than an incredible growth of academic and professional debates regarding the new roles of architecture and planning in society. Brazilian urbanism was facing many questions: How should it respond to the nation's new political and social agendas? How should it help fight social inequities? How should international trends be incorporated in design without sacrificing national and regional identities? Meanwhile, cities were continuing to suffer from a predatory real estate market and urban land speculation (natural consequences of the high inflation rates), a weak economy, and a planning system that became even weaker after the dismantling of the apparatus the military had overseen. Spatial fragmentation and social segregation in cities continued to worsen in the 1980s.

On the other hand, a series of important political changes were starting that would send planning and urbanism in new directions. The reestablishment of democracy strengthened public forums and community participation, and played a fundamental role in helping urbanism to overcome the modernist paradigm and the hegemonic image of Brasília. Different ways of understanding and coping with urban problems and community demands now emerged to compete with modernism. It was the start of a new *postmodern* era where local politics, public participation, and a pluralistic urban context became important ingredients in the urban equation. Community participation also brought a new awareness of the importance of architectural and cultural preservation.

The most significant project of the early 1980s, marking the beginning of Brazilian postmodern urbanism, was the Projeto Cultural Corredor (Cultural Corridor Project) in Rio de Janeiro.[15] Born from an alliance of city planners, community groups, and a coalition of shop owners fighting big private investors and land developers, the Cultural Corridor employed novel and imaginative policies and design guidelines designed to preserve, carefully renovate, and revitalize a large part of the historic downtown. The project's concepts, methods, and implementation tools became models for other Brazilian cities. Its success would help it survive several city administrators from different political parties, expand downtown, and ultimately affect wider cultural concerns.

By the mid-1980s, the national debates being held across Brazil on the writing of a new constitution spotlighted the need for an urban reform that would move away from the notion that city problems resulted exclusively from demographics and uncontrolled growth. The urban question was reframed as an expression of societal needs in the larger sense, and two issues became central to the quest for better cities: social inclusion and democracy. The Movimento Nacional da Reforma Urbana (National Movement for Urban Reform) sponsored debates in a variety of forums, including city, state, and federal elected officials; universities; and professional and nongovernmental organizations. The final document emerging from this process carried 140,000 signatures and was organized around four major goals: (a) democratic and participatory city governance; (b) social equity in the distribution of urban rent and urban land; (c) redirection of public investments to prioritize social investments; and (d) equitable accessibility to public services and facilities.

The proposals by the National Movement for Urban Reform were partially adopted in the 1988 National Constitution, which introduced extremely important political changes to the country, some of them with strong effects on city governance and urban development. First, it defined the municipality as an "entity" of the federation, granting it political, financial, and economic autonomy—a novelty in Latin America. This "municipalization" of the country's power structure pressured the states to change their constitutions and the municipalities to reorganize their *leis orgânicas municipais* (the body of laws that governs a municipality's functioning and organization). Second, it introduced the concept of the social role of urban property and of the city and recognized the need for more socially inclusive urban development. The National Constitution dedicates a chapter to urban policies and mandates that cities with populations of twenty thousand or more have master plans, besides introducing new mechanisms for controlling development, although these are general and depend on further elaboration at both national and local levels through further legislation.[16] States and municipalities would then replicate this demand for master planning in their own constitutions and *leis orgânicas*, and most would include the new constitutionally endorsed development control mechanisms. With regard to urban development, the 1988 National Constitution relied on the city as a locus for the redistribution of wealth and for the re-democratization of society (E. Fernandes 2001; L. Ribeiro and Cardoso 2003). Cardoso (1997) notes that this constitution brought new life to urban planning, redirecting it toward solving social inequities.

Moreover, although Brazil had had environmental protection laws in place since the 1970s, the new constitution advanced the environmental issue by dedicating a whole chapter to it and by requiring that impact studies be completed for projects that might affect the environment. Most important, by recognizing that environmental impacts affect the entire population, the constitution introduced the notion of diffuse rights—which in legal terms means that *anyone* can bring a lawsuit against a project because of its potential environmental impacts, not just those who are directly affected by those impacts. Because it extends the scope of environmental impacts, the concept of diffuse rights can be utilized in actions against urban and neighborhood projects, which makes it a powerful instrument for local groups and nongovernmental organizations. Based on the notion of diffuse rights, the law recognizes the environment as a collective entity and the city as a social reality. Additionally, the constitution also created an independent national Public Ministry which any citizen can access free of charge to bring a lawsuit against any of the three levels of government in matters of public interest, including environmental issues. These are early signs of the country's shift towards a participatory democracy.

Rio de Janeiro was the first city to follow the new constitutional mandates in the development of its 1991 master plan, which became a national model. It addressed and regulated the application of several of the progressive instruments for development control predicated in the constitution—such as the neighborhood impact statements and the transfer of development rights. In contrast to prior technocratic plans under the military regime, the Rio master plan represented a real political pact between the different stakeholders—political parties, nongovernmental organizations, professional and community groups, and so on—as its development involved a process of public participation and public referendums.

Predictably, the political and social climate of the 1980s was reflected in how urbanism was reinventing itself as well as how it was taught and practiced. Centered on the urban question and on the new role of urbanism, fierce academic debates were accompanied by significant developments in urban theory and applied research. The importance of the city to national development and the new social agenda was reflected in a strengthening of the urbanism curriculum in architecture programs and in the creation of several graduate programs in urban planning from the 1980s on.

Undergraduate education in schools of architecture and urbanism covers specific content outlined in a "minimum curriculum" supported by the ABEA (National Association for Education in Architecture and Urbanism)[17] and endorsed by the Ministry of Culture as a requirement for accreditation. Since 1994, a nationwide five-year minimum curriculum for undergraduate programs granting the degree of architect-urbanist includes courses in urban and regional planning, urban and landscape design, environmental studies, and sustainability. Learning how to solve urban problems and how to respond to community needs is part of the training required for this degree. According to the ABEA, in 2006 there were forty thousand students in eighty-five accredited architecture programs in private and public schools throughout Brazil.

At the graduate level, the importance of urbanism is safeguarded in the hands of the ANPUR (National Association for Research and Graduate Studies in Urban and Regional Planning). This association has grown from the five founding member programs throughout the country in 1983 to fifty affiliated programs in 2007, in schools of architecture and urbanism, geography, social sciences, economics, and public administration.[18] At the institutional level, the Ministry of Culture recognizes the importance of graduate education in planning and urbanism through CAPES (National Program for Faculty Training), which maintains a continuous evaluation system for the programs and provides some financial support, and CNPq (National Research Council), which has a national research network and provides research grants.

Finally, democratization opened up academia and professional organizations to an ongoing debate on urbanism through national and regional events, such as the biannual National Congress of Architects, biannual national conferences sponsored by ANPUR, seminars on urban design at the University of Brasília from 1986 to 1989, yearly seminars on the histories of various cities and of urbanism held in different universities since 1997, and many others. In recent years in Brazil, a large number of publications—proceedings, books, journals, online resources, and so on—dedicated to city planning and urban design have been helping to develop Brazilian contemporary urbanism, moving it toward a multitude of socially and place-conscious approaches.

Spatial Segregation and the City

Despite the increasingly democratic route taken by Brazil and Brazilian urbanism since the 1988 National Constitution was ratified, the majority of the country's population still suffers from social inequities and struggles to gain a more just distribution of resources and better quality of life. As we have noted, inequities and conflicts are highlighted and clearly expressed in the urban landscapes. Villaça (1998) notes that spatial segregation of the bourgeoisie is common in Brazilian cities and that it is always expressed in the patterns of investment of real estate capital and in zoning regulations. Rolnik (2001) agrees and observes that if one were to name a single element that most fully describes the Brazilian city in both time and space, it is the existence of deeply contrasting urban conditions affecting different social groups within the same city. In an eye-opening special issue of the journal *Geoforum* titled "Urban Brazil," the editors point out that Brazilian cities today reflect clearer and more definitive social and spatial divisions between legal and illegal, rich and poor, formal and informal (E. Fernandes and Valença 2001).

The recent positive changes generated by democratization have to overcome a long history of social fragmentation of the city environment that actually dates back to colonial times. The disparities between the formal and the informal city and the social and economic inequities between income classes actually worsened during the technocratic development agenda of the military government and with the economic crisis of the late 1970s and early 1980s. Unfortunately, global capitalism and neoliberalism contribute to a socially unjust urban environment through the notion that good urban governance must rely on concepts such as competitive entrepreneurship and creative economy.

As L. Ribeiro (2001: 153) notes, current analyses point out that "urban problems result from a dissociation between the city and the global economy, because of the incapacity of local governments to make them [cities] competitive in attracting international capital." Arantes, Vainer, and Maricato (2000) also point out that contemporary strategic planning and city governance models imported to Brazil from advanced capitalist countries advocate running cities as enterprises and mask the true intentions of transnational interests and neoliberalism. This so-called "barcelonization"[19] of planning and urban design led several Brazilian cities toward a search for results that were economically attractive in the short term. Rio de Janeiro, for instance, was the first city in Brazil to adopt this approach in the development of its strategic plan in the early 1990s and in most of the city actions and projects that followed.[20] This vision tends to divert public investments from comprehensive and socially just initiatives to projects benefiting only a small portion of the population—sometimes supporting the privatization of public spaces and the expansion of constructed, inauthentic places.

Longstanding social inequities exacerbated by globalization and a large increase in urban crime rates and street violence have resulted in an even more perverse spatial fragmentation in Brazilian cities as first the upper and later even the lower middle classes retreated to gated environments. Caldeira (2000), for instance, demonstrates the relationship between the increase in urban poverty and the escalation of street crimes in São Paulo, and how both contribute to the fear syndrome, the segregation of space, and the control of accessibility.

Reflecting these new realities and moving in the opposite direction from the re-democratization of the city mandated in the National Constitution, urbanism in Brazil is also being used for social exclusion, limiting social encounters, secluding and controlling the types of users of particular spaces, and preventing unexpected encounters between different social classes or the development of a real urbanity. In this sense, the large cities in Brazil begin to reflect the internal structure of world cities described by Friedmann and Wolff (2006: 64): a division between "citadel" and "ghetto" in a geography of inequality and class domination. Much of the urban landscape is being taken over by controlled environments and fenced parks, plazas, shopping centers, business parks, and even individual buildings. Along residential and commercial streets, city codes allow property owners to build fences along front setback limits, thus erecting another barrier separating public and private realms. This somewhat illusory perception of security negates the street environment and creates extremely negative visual impacts on the streetscape (fig. I.10).

The "city of walls" is now a common landscape, particularly in areas developed according to modernist zoning codes and spatial morphologies. The Corbusian model of towers-in-the-green, single-use zoning, and attention to traffic circulation generated disjointed districts, large distances between buildings, a landscape of highways, "no-man's-land" public areas that proved to be easily appropriated by the private sector, and segregated social realms (del Rio and Santos 1998). In contemporary Brazil, the majority of successful residential developments are gated and generally follow

Figure I.10. The increasing use of fences to segregate environments and create a perception of safety: (*top*) new residential area in São Paulo where all residential towers are gated communities detached from the street. (Photo by Silvio Macedo, Projeto Quapá); (*left*) all buildings in this residential street in Leblon, Rio de Janeiro, have fenced front yards. (Photo by Vicente del Rio)

architectural styles inspired by Miami-style imageries so dear to the middle class. New postmodern social and cultural metaphors have been adopted across all social classes, reflecting the strength of global consumerism based on North American models. This is ironic for a country where modern architecture was heroic and important enough to influence even the most humble residences from the 1950s to the early 1970s (Lara 2006).

Districts and suburbs in São Paulo, Rio de Janeiro, and other large cities are being transformed by new sites of social exclusion—gated communities and shopping malls—a phenomenon which Brazilian researchers now recognize as a major generator of new and complex urban and territorial dynamics. In the case of São Paulo, for instance, there are entire walled suburban neighborhoods at the outskirts of the city, such as Alphaville, which is so large that it has become more powerful than the municipality itself. The aforementioned Barra da Tijuca, a district in Rio originally planned by Lucio Costa in the 1960s, has become a collection of urban fragments, shopping centers, and walled communities linked by highways (see fig. I.8B). These are what King (2004) calls supraurbs or globurbs, referring to suburbs that become independent of their host city and develop direct connections to the global sphere. This phenomenon adds complexity to a pattern of urban growth largely dominated by low-income communities, land invasions, and pirate subdivisions on the fringes of metropolitan areas. As Sachs (2001) correctly notes, Brazil is a poorly developed country because it adopted a growth model that is socially perverse and promotes the increasing concentration of income in the hands of the elite: whereas in 1960 the richest 10 percent of the population held 54 percent of the national income, by 1995 they had 63 percent. In the global economy these inequalities will tend to worsen: in a recent study of São Paulo, Buechler (2006) points out that the changing nature of labor makes it more difficult for the poor to compete for jobs that are being globalized.

Recent Promising Developments

Despite the fact that spatial fragmentation and historically entrenched social injustices present a pessimistic side of Brazilian cities, recent developments in politics and in the growth of democracy suggest the beginnings of a "third way." In a recent analysis of the geopolitics of democracy and citizenship in Latin America, Jones (2004) notes that democratization is broadening the public sphere and has resulted in significant investments in the quality of public spaces and services. He adds that Brazil is the only Latin American country where democratization has been accompanied by a debate on what type of city is compatible with a more inclusive notion of citizenship.

Indeed, Brazil's return to full democracy allowed new political avenues to be paved toward more just cities and a better quality of urban life. As discussed earlier, the mandates of the 1988 National Constitution, the resurgence of leftist parties, and organized social and community movements have forced state and local governments to revise their planning systems in order to include more public participation and social programs. Important progress was made in this direction in cities such as Rio de Janeiro with the creation of the Controladoria Geral do Municipio (Municipal Comptroller of Expenditures) and an information system that is available to the public. Most large cities have made important advances toward more participatory governance by using various means to involve stakeholders and solicit community input in city building. This is particularly true in cities where the PT (Partido dos Trabalhadores, the Labor Party) is in power, such as Porto Alegre, a city of 1.2 million people which pioneered the innovative concept of participatory municipal budgeting.

The participatory budget program was started in 1989 by Olivio Dutra, then the mayor of Porto Alegre, then a member of the PT. A decision-making system was established whereby communities can decide via a complex series of popular assemblies which projects should be implemented in their territories (Abers 1998; A. Ribeiro and Grazia 2003). Whereas in 1990 only a little more than nine hundred people participated in the community assemblies, by 2003 there were almost fifty thousand participants. The scope and implications of the issues discussed also evolved from simple, localized problems—such as street paving and garbage collection—to cultural programs and citywide policies. The program led the United Nations to include the Porto Alegre program in its list of best practices in city management, and the World Bank to name it as a model of participatory democracy. Despite the program's inherent limitations and its frequent abuse by politicians, its potential for increasing civic participation prompted several other cities to adopt versions of it.[21] The potential of such a participatory and educational system to improve planning, control over development, and accountability is obvious.

In the 1990s, several cities started to develop citywide projects in response to either community pressures or market demands at national and global levels. Again, Rio de Janeiro is an interesting example in this respect: in the early 1990s the city developed a strategic plan that outlined ways to make the city more competitive in attracting investments and led to beautification, urban design, and favela upgrading projects.[22]

The 1992 Earth Summit (United Nations World Conference on Environment and Development) in Rio de Janeiro and Agenda 21 (a comprehensive plan of action to be followed by UN agencies and signatories of the document) also had significant repercussions for national and local development policies and regulations, particularly concerning the broadening notions of sustainability and environmental protection. Agenda 21 would also influence the regularization of the national constitution's vision of urban development and its chapters on urban and environmental policies, which took the form of the Estatuto da Cidade (Statute of the City; Federal Law 10.257).

Approved after years of national forums, debates, and political negotiations, the statute is a powerful tool towards implementing the constitution's conception of the social role of urban property and of the city, and provides the legal framework for the implementation of its urban and environmental policies (E. Fernandes 2001, 2007). Besides gathering legal instruments that were spread out in different pieces of legislation, the Statute of the City defines new and progressive mechanisms and instruments for urban land-use control, plan implementation, public participation, and development control. It injected new life into planning and urbanism and started to forge a path to a contemporary and more just city.

According to Edesio Fernandes (2001: 13), the Statute of the City was aimed at making cities more inclusive and it "confirmed and widened the fundamental legal-political role of municipalities in . . . directives for urban planning and in conducting the process for urban development and management." This new law will have a far-reaching impact on Brazil's legal and urban structure since it broke a longstanding tradition of civil law and set the basis for a new legal-political paradigm in establishing that the "right to urban property is ensured provided that a social function is accomplished, which is determined by municipal urban legislation" (E. Fernandes 2001: 13).

Some of the progressive planning tools defined and regulated by the Statute of the City and available for implementation by local governments include mandatory public participation and participatory budgeting, public-private partnerships, transfer of development rights (allowing land exchanges between the city and private developers), a five-year residence period after which squatters can claim adverse possession rights,[23] easier land tenure regularization and special zoning for favelas, flexibility in real estate taxation to discourage or encourage urban development, and the city's right to exercise the first option to buy any property, among others. Although the statute also introduced the important concept of neighborhood rights, municipalities were left to regulate these rights, which some believe will generate interesting political possibilities because each city will eventually have to define this notion in keeping with its particular social and political circumstances.[24] A progressive piece of legislation, the statute will no doubt have a strong influence on urbanism and on the political forces shaping Brazilian cities.

These effects are already starting to appear because the statute decreed that municipalities with more than twenty thousand inhabitants, those located in metropolitan regions, those declared of interest for tourism, and those to be affected by large projects should all have master plans prepared (or revised) and approved by their city councils—as required by the 1988 National Constitution—by October 2006. The mandate affected 1,684 municipalities (almost 30 percent of the total municipalities in Brazil!), of which 1,550 had finished preparing their plans by the set date, although some were still to be approved by their city councils.[25]

The first major cities to develop new master plans that incorporate the directives of the Statute of the City appear to have been Porto Alegre in 2001 (even before the statute was approved by Congress) and São Paulo in 2002. São Paulo's plan, developed by the city's second PT administration and fashionably titled Strategic Master Plan, resulted from a series of public meetings with different stakeholders and decentralizes city governance into districts and advisory councils with community and private-sector representatives. The São Paulo plan contains 308 articles (not surprising for a city of fourteen million people) and includes various innovations and progressive planning tools such as public-private partnerships and linked operations (developers can get a zoning change for one site in exchange for building low-income housing somewhere else), transfer of development rights, special zoning for favelas, and a progressive taxation mechanism that encourages urban infill by forcing landowners to develop underutilized land.

Another recent big institutional step forward in making cities better places to live and in setting the stage for contemporary urbanism was the formation of the Ministério das Cidades (Ministry of Cities) under the current Labor Party president elected in 2002 and reelected in 2006. The new ministry is divided into four secretariats—housing, urban programs, sanitation, and transportation and urban mobility—and its basic mission is to implement the PNDU (national policy for urban development) and the Politica Nacional de Cidades (national policy for cities). It has been accomplishing this mainly through investment programs in infrastructure, support for master planning at the local level, and capacity building and training of local public officials.[26] Interestingly, some of the ministry's policies are similar to those of SERFHAU—the federal planning agency during the initial years of the military regime. It has been instrumental in maintaining a national support network for the development of the master plans mandated by the constitution and the Statute of the City and in providing financial support to enable poorer municipalities to develop their plans. Above all, the formation and the work of the ministry reflect institutional recognition of the importance of urban issues for national development and for the pursuit of social equity called for in the constitution.

According to Edesio Fernandes, former director of the Department of Urban Land Tenure in the Ministry of Cities, the main urban issues that Brazil faces now are the provision of deeds and other forms of legal ownership as well as infrastructure and services to favelas and the irregular and substandard subdivisions on the peripheries of major cities (Fernandes, personal communication November 11, 2006). In 2006 the National Assembly, lobbied by the Ministry of Cities, was discussing upgrading the minimum standards and environmental requirements for urban subdivisions set by a 1979 national law, an important move toward higher-quality private urbanization, but one that could end up reflecting perversely on the market by pushing land prices up and dispossessing the poor.

Conclusion

As the new millennium progresses, Brazilian urbanism faces interesting and promising possibilities that will significantly affect the future of cities in Brazil. These possibilities result from forces coming from many directions, mediated by the historically entrenched spatial and social fragmentation in cities and the desire of the upper and middle classes to maintain the status quo. On one hand, re-democratization, increasing political and community participation in local governance, and the new laws contained in the National Constitution and the Statute of the City have opened important avenues toward more socially equitable urban development and a more inclusive and accessible public realm. On the other hand, the retreat from radical modernism, the sustainability debate, the need for more humanitarian values, and the economics and culture of globalization all press for a shift in theoretical paradigms and urban models. As Brazilian development moves unavoidably towards deeper globalism, the city risks losing its importance as the basic spatial-social unit of society.

Permeating the dynamics of these opportunities is the enormous role that the public realm and its manifestations in public spaces of cities have in Brazilian sociocultural life. While privatization expands over the public realm and produces entrenched spaces, many strong sociocultural expressions can only happen "outside the home" and "in the streets," and therefore depend on accessible and at least minimally developed public spaces. On one hand, Carnaval parades, religious celebrations, soccer matches and other sporting events, the beach culture, and big public events must happen in the public sphere of cities—in visible, large, and accessible areas. On the other, social encounters like dating, visiting extended family, social networking, showing off, family recreation, and even small retail businesses in poorer neighborhoods traditionally demand outdoor spaces within the public realm. Moreover, the space of the street and spaces outside the home are particularly important for low-income people who depend on social networking for survival, rely on the public realm to mediate class distinctions, and do not rigidly demarcate the social domains of street (public) and house (private) (da Matta 1991). The street, the square, the sidewalk, the park, and the beach will always be fundamental places for socialization and plurality, and thus for Brazilian urbanism.

In contrast to the modernist paradigm, which relies on centralized control and a rigid model of what a city should be, contemporary Brazilian urbanism is postmodern in the sense that it accepts and incorporates a multitude of social values and different visions of quality; it is more participatory and responsive to community needs, and it strives to produce more socially just environments. The late-modern city, the reutilized city, and the socially inclusive city are different contemporary urbanisms that coexist within the territory of all Brazilian cities and in the minds of all Brazilian academics and professionals. Urbanism in Brazil has overcome the limitations of a single paradigm and the limited possibilities of rigid models; it accepts and incorporates different shifts and influences. Brazilian urbanists are aware that the quality of the city environment and the social utility and cultural meaning of the public realm are fundamental pillars of society. To be truly effective as a societal tool, urbanism has to focus increasingly on the quest for a truly pluralistic and culture-specific city and for equitable and nonexploitative social and economic development.

Notes

1. For the transmission of early European urbanism to Brazil and other Latin American countries, see Almandoz (2002).
2. On this complex period of Brazilian political and social development, see, for instance, Skidmore (1999) and MacLachlan (2003).
3. For English-language publications on the birth of Brazilian modernism in architecture, see the special issues of the *Journal of Decorative and Propaganda Arts* (Wolfson Foundation, 1995) and the *Journal of the American Society of Arts and Sciences* vol. 129, no. 2 (2000). See also Fraser (2000), Deckker (2001), Cavalcanti (2003), and Andreoli and Forty (2004). Bruand (1981), Segawa (1998), Leme (1999), and Maria Bastos (2003) are excellent accounts but have never been translated into English.
4. Now called IPHAN (Institute for National Historic and Artistic Patrimony), this agency is responsible for setting the national policy for cultural and historic preservation and for listing buildings, urban artifacts, towns, and even ecosystems for preservation—which entails protection and special rules for development and design. Although its name and placement in the state bureaucracy has changed a few times, this agency has been fundamental in implementing a preservation culture in Brazil. In 2007, IPHAN's list contained more than 20,000 buildings, 83 urban areas, and 12,517 archeological sites. See IPHAN's website at http://portal.iphan .gov.br.
5. For detailed descriptions of this important project, see Cavalcanti (2003) and Recamán (2004). Some scenes of the film *Central Station* (grand prize winner at the 1998 Berlin Festival) were shot at the Pedregulho Residential Complex.
6. A good example is the comments in Joseph Rykwert's *The Seduction of Place* (2000). See the essay by Kohlsdorf, Kohlsdorf, and Holanda (chapter 1) in this book.
7. For an account of the troubled 1960s in Brazil and the transition into the military regime see Thomas Skidmore's *Politics of Military Rule in Brazil* (1988).
8. On some of the effects of this modernist building typology on local regulations, see Macedo's essay (chapter 3) in this book.
9. The BNH has a very interesting story from the time of its conception and its noble goal of solving the housing problem in the mid-1960s to its move towards concentrating most of its resources on middle-income housing and public works in the 1970s, to its bankruptcy due to the size of its own machinery, the high rate of loan delinquencies, the inflationary economy, and the fall of the military regime (see Azevedo 1990 and Valença 1999).
10. See the essay on Salvador by Fernandes and Gomes (chapter 6) in this book.
11. On Curitiba see Irazábal (2005) and her essay (chapter 9) in this book. See also del Rio (1992); Hawken, Lovins, and Lovins (1999); and Schwartz (2004).
12. Caraíba was planned and designed by Joaquim Guedes & Associates. See *Process Architecture* 17 (1980).

13. On modernist land-use legislation and its effect on Brazilian cities, see the essay by Macedo (chapter 3) in this book.

14. Fernando Collor was the first president elected by popular vote in Brazil after re-democratization but, ironically, only two years later and following a series of scandals, charges of corruption at high levels, and street rallies, he also became the first president to be impeached through a legitimate political process (see Skidmore 1999 and MacLachlan 2003).

15. On the Cultural Corridor Project, see Pinheiro and del Rio (1993) and the essay by del Rio and Alcantara (chapter 5) in this book.

16. According to the latest national census data, in 2000 926 cities had populations of twenty thousand or more. These mechanisms for development control (such as compulsory subdivision and development of urban land, surface rights, progressive property taxes, granting cities preferential rights to purchase property, and adverse possession of urban land, see n. 23) would be regularized by the Statute of the City in 2001. (see E. Fernandes 2001, 2007 and Marcelo Souza 2003).

17. For information on the ABEA, go to www.abea-arq.org.br.

18. For information on ANPUR, go to www.anpur.org.br.

19. Barcelonization is a metaphor for the successful strategic planning process in Barcelona and the city's approach to urbanism, which became a model promoted by Spanish planners through international consulting services, as they did in Rio.

20. See, for instance, the essay by del Rio (chapter 10) in this book.

21. Information on the participatory budgeting programs in several cities was obtained from *Cidades Vivas* (special edition, 2004), a magazine published by the PT on the cities where the party holds power.

22. See the essays by del Rio (chapter 10) and Duarte and Magalhães (chapter 12) in this book.

23. Adverse possession rights allow squatters to claim legal ownership of the private property on which they live if the property owner does not dispute the claim within a specified period, which the new constitution fixed at five years for urban areas. Although this right does not apply in the case of public land, it is politically very difficult for any level of government (national, state, or local) to evict squatters if they have occupied it for a period of time.

24. Luis Cesar Ribeiro, Adauto Cardoso, and Luciana Correa do Lago (Federal University of Rio de Janeiro), interview with V. del Rio, July 2005.

25. Information from www.cidades.gov.br, retrieved on 10/26/2006.

26. See the scope of the Ministério das Cidades at www.cidades.gov.br.

Part 1

Late Modernism The Struggle to
Control City Form and Function

In the preface and introduction we discussed how deeply modernism has penetrated Brazilian culture, planning, and design. The positivist paradigm inherent in modernism still dominates most thinking, particularly through the notion that urban development is intrinsically good and represents a positive evolution, and that there is a rational order to things. As Holston (1989) and Harvey (1990) note, modernization as an ideology of development is still very appealing to developing countries and certainly to Brazil. We have also commented on how the evolution of urbanism in Brazil has helped popularize the modernist notions of urban quality, and how important these notions still are for urban development and public expectations.

This part has been titled "Late Modernism" because the essays contained herein demonstrate that modernist thinking is still alive and well in Brazilian urbanism, and is still utilized to guide city form and function towards an idealized model that is rational and good. The essays discuss examples of a shared belief that if the government would control the market and dictate development to fit the modernist model, the results would be guaranteed to serve a common public good. Also, as in modernism, late modernist practices are mostly closed to public participation processes, as the paradigm places the government and its planners in the role of paternalistically deciding what is good for the community and of overseeing and directing the behavior of the private sector.

Given Brasília's image and influence on Brazilian culture in general, and on urban design and architecture in particular, it is not surprising that the new capital is the first case study featured in this part. More that any other city in Brazil, Brasília exposes the social, economic, and cultural dualities of Brazilian society through its built environment. It continues to be one of the world's most powerful symbols of government control of urban development, and it is the only city that has been fully developed according to the principles of modernist urbanism. For that, the Pilot Plan—the area contained in Brasília's original plan—was declared a national historical monument by the Brazilian government and a World Heritage Site by UNESCO.

Although problems inherent in Brasília's modernist model do exist, such as those noted by Holston (1989), residents and visitors alike appreciate many of its qualities, some of which have been the subject of recent re-evaluations (Holanda 2000; Andreoli and Forty 2004; el-Dahdah 2005). In their essay Maria Elaine Kohlsdorf, Gunther Kohlsdorf, and Frederico de Holanda discuss how some of Brasília's original design qualities suffer from progressive degradation despite the government's efforts to preserve the Pilot Plan area and make modernism the prevailing style there. The authors discuss the Pilot Plan's *classic modernism*, which made Brasília such a strong cultural artifact, but also other morphologies that compose the urban territory of the Federal District. The settlements predating Brasília compose one such morphology, where a *vernacular* repertoire coexists with land invasions and squatter settlements that happened even before the new capital's inauguration in 1960. A third morphology appears in the infamous satellite towns of Brasília, which the authors call *peripheral modernism* because spontaneous forms and self-help design practices reproduce the disadvantages of classic modernism at the same time that they are devoid of any of its aesthetics and visual qualities. Other morphologies discussed are the old *workers' camps* built by contractors during the city's early years, the *favelas* (squatter settlements) built by poor migrants attracted to the new labor market, and the expanding *postmodern* neighborhoods and gated communities of the upper classes.

Although all these types of urban forms contribute equally to make Brasília a busy contemporary metropolis, some are recognized neither as part of the formal city image nor as part of the middle-class repertoire of desirable places. Mostly, residents are happy with the Pilot Plan's classic modernism, as it continues to represent the utopian image of urban desirability, devoid of most of the conflicts that are present in larger cities such as Rio and São Paulo. While the strong iconic meaning of Brasília's Pilot Plan is timeless and is an admirable example of modernism, the authors point out the problems that arise in a city whose symbolic core does not coincide with its morphological center. By treating these morphologies unequally, Brasília became a polynucleated metropolis suffering from a series of problems similar to those in all other Brazilian cities, from territorial social inequities to limitations in public transportation and accessibility. The authors argue that although it is important to preserve the Pilot Plan's modernist repertoire, a revision of its UNESCO's World Heritage Site status would encourage creativity, allow for more innovative design solutions, and generate more lively public spaces in a more socially inclusive city.

Another interesting example of late modernism is the design for Palmas, a new state capital built in 1990 in central Brazil. In his essay Dirceu Trindade notes that much as with Brasília thirty-five years earlier, the rationale for the creation of Palmas was to spur regional development in a backward region of the country's interior. In this respect the new city has been very successful, and development there has been astounding: the population increased from 86,116 in 1996 to 160,000 in 2003, a growth rate much higher than anywhere else in Brazil, which experienced an average growth of 3 percent for the same period.

Inspired by modernist Brasília and Keynesian philosophy, the design for Palmas established a macro-grid and general road network within which large sectors were to be handed over to private developers. The concept called for a flexible urban and architectural framework where residential and public spaces would be linked by pedestrian walkways, thus creating many opportunities for social integration. Utopia was trampled by reality, however, as the state government acted as land developer and the openness of the original design induced speculative development. In contrast to Brasília's Pilot Plan, where strict government controls persist to this date, in Palmas institutional planning turned into subdividing land and selling it under obsolete zoning legislation. Original land uses were modified—even those designated for public facilities—compromising city functions and the neighborhood scale of the original plan. Avenues designated for bus routes turned into dense commercial strips, and the wide main boulevard partitioned the city in two. Perhaps the most significant element in Palmas's late modernity is the detachment of the city core. Located on the highest elevation of an otherwise flat region, it interrupts the city-long axis of the main boulevard and holds a group of late modernist governmental buildings sited far apart from the surrounding city and from each other, in a barren plaza devoid of any use outside of office hours.

Trindade discusses how the design of Palmas demonstrates the gap between original intentions and actual implementation, and why it represents a lost opportunity to create the ecologically sensitive and sustainable contemporary city it was envisioned to be. Palmas now suffers from the problems that afflict all large cities: inadequate urban services and infrastructure, inefficient public transportation, violations of land-use regulations, large tracts of land left empty within fully serviced areas, and a growing contingent of squatter settlements. In establishing a new economic pole in the interior and in attracting a large population, however, one cannot deny that Palmas is a successful development effort with clear repercussions over the region and the entire new state of Tocantins. The new infrastructure connecting the city to the rest of the state, and the amenities proposed by the original plan—recreational and open areas, artificial beaches on the lake, and ecological parks—make Palmas different from any other frontier town and help attract development and new residents. Palmas fulfilled its mission of integrating the region and creating a new society in the midst of the savannah; it is a dynamic and promising city where "everything remains possible."

The development efforts in both Brasília and Palmas demonstrate how closely modernism in Brazil was tied to the idea of social and economic progress. As discussed before, Brasília was the dominant model of the perfect city, and modernism is still largely the dominant model for most city development control efforts and planning and urban design parameters. The effects of institutionalized late modernism on city building and particularly on São Paulo's cityscape is discussed in Silvio Macedo's study.

The models and standards adopted in both Rio and São Paolo, the cultural and economic capitals of Brazil, are highly influential in the rest of the country, and so is the typical aspect of their cityscapes: verticality. Macedo shows us how in São Paulo the verticalization process was encouraged by the land-use code of 1971 which for the first time restricted building footprints to 50 percent of the lot area, established mandatory setbacks, and forced the annexation of smaller lots to allow for the construction of tower blocks. This was also the model adopted by Rio in its 1976 code and eventually by all zoning and building codes in Brazil. Cityscapes became homogeneously determined by the modernist model of tower-in-the-green, disrespecting the pedestrian scale of development and street corridors.

As Macedo puts it, if in the initial plan density and height of buildings were to correspond to location—the closer to traffic corridors the higher and denser—this model was eventually perverted by the real estate market and land speculation. The isolated residential tower block surrounded by gardens became the hegemonic model in São Paulo and in the country. Complexes of multiple towers sited on a large parcel or occupying a whole city block would soon follow as a popular real estate solution. Zoning demands and the growing concern with security generated a sophisticated urban model much influenced by the modernist culture: residential condominium complexes composed of tower blocks, common gardens, and communal and recreational facilities in a controlled environment. In São Paulo, gated communities break up the city territory and streetscapes are marked by towers protected behind walls and fences that hold no spatial relation to the public sidewalks. Due to market demands and an increasingly less mobile society, these residential solutions became increasingly sophisticated and form islands of tranquility in an otherwise insecure and unfriendly large city.

A metropolitan area of more than eighteen million inhabitants, São Paulo was the first to pioneer this new type of urbanism where the private realm transcends the public one. In a city of large distances, low mobility, and fragmented territory, people limit their commuting, and regional and neighborhood centers become even more important than before. In this context, Gilda Bruna and Heliana Vargas discuss the importance of shopping centers as inductors of urban development and city structuring, using the city of São Paulo as a case study. Brazil ranks fifth in the world in number of shopping centers, and their growing importance in the economy has encouraged a variety of types and forms. From retail centers to discount centers to sophisticated mixed-use and entertainment complexes, Brazilian shopping centers adapted the original North American models to reflect local specificities. In 2005, according to the Brazilian Association of Shopping Centers (affiliated with the International Council of Shopping Centers), shopping centers were responsible for 18 percent of the gross sales in the Brazilian retail sector, excluding automotive and oil-related sales. In the same year, the city of São Paulo alone had thirty-nine shopping centers that received an average of 203 million visitors per month.

Bruna and Vargas point out that not only do these shopping centers reinforce secondary centers, but they also construct new centralities along growth vectors and in less densely occupied areas. This is strategic in a city as large as São Paulo, since shopping centers perform some of the functions of a central city: they help decrease the population's need for mobility; they become landmarks and important locales for socialization; and they stimulate changes in their surroundings, thus creating *places*. Of particular note in São Paulo are the recent successful shopping centers developed in the historic downtown as part of efforts to revitalize the symbolism and function of the original central city lost to regional subcenters. Stressing their importance to the urban economy, Bruna and Vargas discuss how shopping centers have become important components of urban development and how their structuring potential can be better utilized by city managers in order to induce development, direct growth, and proactively guide city building.

CHAPTER 1

Brasília Permanence and Transformations

Maria Elaine Kohlsdorf,
Gunter Kohlsdorf, and
Frederico de Holanda

The capital of Brazil since 1960, Brasília was born from a plan created by Lucio Costa and chosen in a public competition. The competition called for a Plano Piloto, a pilot or basic master layout plan, for the capital city, and according to the panel the winning proposal had indeed the aspect of a *civitas*.[1] The structure of the plan was based on the crossing of two axes, evoking the ritual of possession that was represented by the new capital's enabling the occupation of the central-western region of the Brazilian interior. The city's growth was to be controlled: once the limit of 500,000 inhabitants was reached, satellite cities would be developed in orbit around Brasília, within the borders of the new Federal District.

However, this district was formed on a "morphological mosaic" (Kohlsdorf 1985, 1996b) since Brasília was not constructed on virgin soil. Its *classic modernism* contrasted with the *vernacular* of preexisting urban nuclei (Planaltina, founded in the nineteenth century, and Brazlândia, founded in the early twentieth century) and ranch headquarters. This reality generally does not form part of the publicized image of Brasília, nor do others that we shall discuss in this text.

After the conclusion of the design competition, there were considerable changes to Costa's plan, both in the Pilot Plan itself and in the surrounding area. Most were due to housing demands which were not addressed by the plan, and they displaced the centrality of Costa's original design. The area's population was dispersed, shaping a rarefied central city where jobs and services were concentrated. The Pilot Plan did not include low-income housing, meaning that the poor who could not afford to live in the Pilot Plan area were faced with enormous transportation and infrastructure costs.

Even before the city's inauguration, satellite towns sprang up, built in a kind of *peripheral modernism* that reproduced aspects of Brasília without its aesthetic qualities. Construction companies built gigantic *workers' camps* for technicians and workers, the former clearly differentiated spatially from the latter. And vast migratory contingents, looking for opportunity in the new city and without access to proper housing, found their only alternative in *land invasions.*

Recent metamorphoses of modernism include new morphological types in central areas of the Pilot Plan still not occupied, in new middle-class neighborhoods, and in eclectic dwellings on the shores of Lake Paranoá. These new developments are distinguished from classic modernism by their shaping of public space, the structure of land use, the system of mass transportation, and their building typology. In parallel with these developments, speculative retention of land and exorbitant prices for property have pushed large groups of middle-class homebuyers far from the city center of Brasília. Gated communities arise from this perverse combination of factors, in an explicit morphological version of the *walled city.* Such developments have worsened the fraying of metropolitan space, making efficient solutions for mass transit impossible and constituting a recurring land problem that shows up repeatedly in newspaper headlines.

The Brazilian capital is a polynucleated metropolis (Paviani 1985) that has expanded beyond the limits of the Federal District (fig. 1.1). Classic modernism is restricted to the "noble" part of the "true Brasília," known as the Pilot Plan, which contains less than 10 percent of the Federal District's population of 2,383,784 inhabitants, accord-

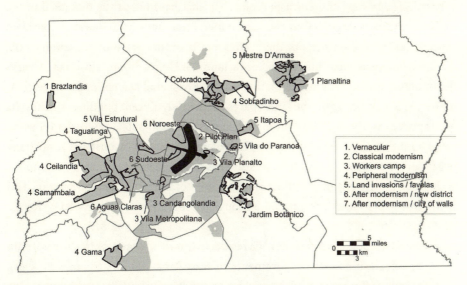

Figure 1.1. Map showing the area of Brasília's Pilot Plan and all urbanized areas of the Federal District. (Drawing by Janaína Vieira)

ing to 2003 census estimates (Kohlsdorf 1997). This area is on the UNESCO World Heritage Site list and concentrates the great majority of jobs in the Federal District, the greatest income, and the greatest benefits of urbanization.[2]

Study of the city's evolution reveals a loss of quality in the areas that bear witness to the modernist movement and documents the worsening of problems evident since Brasília's conception. However, innovations to the urban design have been relatively successful. Here, we will discuss these attempts, as well as how the city was shaped by government programs and private enterprise. Although Brazilian morphological types and metamorphoses have changed over time, our analysis concentrates on the following spatial aspects:

Functional: type, quantity, and location relative to land use;
Interactive: appropriation of city spaces by different social classes; and
Informational: orientation and visual identity of places.

The morphological types of the first period (the "ground zero" of Brasília) have been relatively well studied (Kohlsdorf 1985; Holanda et al. 2002). The morphological transformations throughout the city's history have also been studied (Kohlsdorf 1996a, 1996b; Holanda 2000). Recent studies have examined the global structure of the city and have detected a system characterized by eccentricity, dispersion, and socio-spatial segregation (Holanda 2001; Holanda et al. 2002). We shall re-examine these questions in this chapter, adding analyses of types that have developed recently.

We shall pay special attention to the changes in classic modernism, since there are urban design lessons in the Brasília Pilot Plan that have been little discussed in the apologetic texts and ignored in the critical literature. The critical literature has been sensitive to local problems, but the overall merits of the spatial organization of the city have been ignored. This is true, for instance, of Holston's remarks on the redundancy of the residential wings or on the problems of spatial perception in the Esplanade of the Ministries given the large spaces between significant buildings such as the Metropolitan Cathedral, the National Congress, and the public buildings (Holston 1989). Once one has traveled the city, however, it is easy to reconstruct it mentally because of the power of strong images such as the Highway Axis,[3] the Monumental Axis,[4] and the government buildings, generators of perfect visual landmarks. This mental image is securely constructed, although it also has perceptual problems (Kohlsdorf 1996a).

The unmistakable identity of Brasília resides in this clear structure and places it with other significant urbanistic achievements such as Paris (with its Champs-Elysées), Vienna (with its Ringstrasse), and Teotihuacán (with its Avenida de los Muertos). The winning plan was different from the other proposals in having the kind of magnitude that gives the city a strong global readability and makes it unforgettable. Costa's plan proposed this mental image for the city (Kohlsdorf 1987).

Some researchers present a falsely negative picture of what Brasília's inhabitants think of the city, as does Holston (1989), whose research is criticized by scholars from various disciplines (Machado and Magalhães 1985; Nunes 2003).[5] Furthermore, some authors even make erroneous or misleading observations about Brasília's design, as does Rykwert (2000).[6]

As we shall see, the history of Brasília is characterized by a worsening of the problems inherent in modernist urbanism and an impoverishment of the city's expressive qualities. The morphological mosaic of Brasília is characterized by movement that affects the relationships in the polynucleated complex but maintains the location of its center outside the Pilot Plan (Holanda 2002).

The Morphological Types That Comprise Brasília

The "true Brasília" is composed of various morphological types which we shall discuss according to their chronology and by comparing their major formative aspects. There are both simultaneous and sequential elements in the construction of the Brasília complex, which is characterized not only by a diversity of morphological types, but also by the transformations that these types have experienced over time. We will discuss five morphological types concurrent with modernism: vernacular, classic modernism, workers' camps, peripheral modernism, and land invasions (see fig. 1.1). We will also discuss three others that emerged in the early 1990s: transformations in the Pilot Plan, new districts, and gated communities.

The Vernacular

Until 1960, Planaltina (1810) and Brazlândia (1930s) were small cities in rural Goiás with the typical traditional spatial structure of Brazilian settlements (fig 1.2). The construction of Brasília transformed them into satellite towns where large residential areas were built for populations coming out of favelas, turning them into bedroom communities. Two groups of residents now inhabit these towns, each with its own spatial morphology implying different functional, interactive, and informational possibilities. The native population stayed in the old city, organized along vernacular patterns; the newcomers—generally migrants from the Northeast—settled in new neighborhoods analogous to official peripheral settlements.

The *vernacular* morphological type still survives in the traditional sectors of these towns, expressed in the slightly irregular road network with numerous intersections,

Figure 1.2. Aerial photo of Planaltina, one of the remaining original villages in the Brasília area. (Courtesy of TOPOCART, Brasília)

mixture of land uses, good integration of the parts, and ease of comprehension. The macro and micro subdivisions are made up of blocks of around 100 by 100 meters (109 by 109 yards) containing deep lots of various forms and sizes. Generally, buildings are built at the front of the lot, with a wall sharply delineating the home from the sidewalk, a narrow lateral setback, and a large backyard. The surviving vernacular buildings open their doors directly onto the street, facilitating street life and everyday encounters. In addition, the ranch buildings that pre-dated Brasília still remain relatively intact expressions of the vernacular, despite much of the ranchland having been sold for development.

Planaltina and Brazlândia date from the time when "tyrannies of intimacy" (Sennett 1974) and the corresponding decline in the public domain had not yet affected the urban fabric in the form of shopping centers, *blind* spaces—"dead" or "residual" spaces in Trancik's (1986) terms—or gated communities. In the traditional sectors of these towns, we find social groups similar to those that inhabit *peripheral modernist* areas, and the contrast in the use of public space between the groups in these two areas is revealing. In different morphological types, populations with the same socioeconomic characteristics use public space differently. The spatial configuration functions as an independent variable that promotes a greater use of public spaces in vernacular areas than in peripheral modernist ones (Holanda 2002).

The vernacular type in this mosaic is further characterized by the existence of robust vegetation and a harmonic relationship between the urbanized grid and natural features. In post-Brasília developments, the architectural types and morphological units of Planaltina and Brazlândia migrated toward a model of satellite towns, with specialized zoning, unused open spaces, segregation between the interior of buildings and public spaces, blind gables, and an urban landscape of visual redundancy.

Classic Modernism

Lucio Costa's Pilot Plan for Brasília is a perfect, genuine model of the modern movement in architecture, whose tenets were deeply imprinted in most of the entries for the 1956 design competition (Evenson 1973). His plan excelled because of its singular use of the modernist vocabulary, although it broke with modernist precepts in some places (Gorovitz 1995; Holanda 2002). The plan incorporated historical elements, baroque perspectives, and monumental land levelings that bow to antiquity and pre-Columbian America (Holanda 2002). It made reference to both the gregariousness of Brazilian colonial times and to international urban ideas—the ceremonial acropolis, the linear city, the garden city, and the urbanism of commercial areas (fig. 1.3).

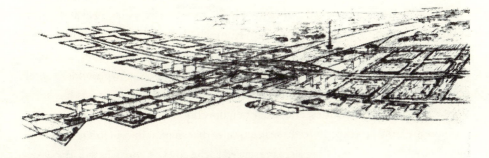

Figure 1.3. Brasília's Monumental Axis: (*above*) Lucio Costa's original sketch (Courtesy of Casa de Lucio Costa, Rio de Janeiro); (*left*) aerial view (Photo by João Facó, from his *In the Wings of Brasília* [FAC-GDF, 2003])

Selected by the jury because it was "a spatial concept adequate for a capital," Costa's design was articulated into four "scales," to use his term.[7] (fig. 1.4):

1. *Monumental*: the ceremonial territory, or *civitas*; as an appendage to the more extensive urban fabric along the Eixo Rodoviario. This east-west element would be the most extensive east-west element in the urban fabric, holding the administrative buildings of the nation and the Federal District.

2. *Gregarious*: a redoubt for the *urbs* (the urban center) as opposed to the *civitas*; it would be located in the city core and play the role of the city center.

3. *Residential* or *quotidian*: two residential wings; these would be located north and south of the city center along the Eixo Rodoviario.

4. *Bucolic*: features evocative of the natural environment; these would be present in the open areas within the city fabric and around Lake Paranoá, as well as in landscaping.

Costa expressed these ideas in the "Relatório do Plano Piloto" (Pilot Plan Report), a beautiful text that uses metaphors and analogies to other cities, as well as sketches (see fig. 1.3a). The four scales structure the Pilot Plan as two axes that meet at the gregarious scale (at the urban center or *urbs*), from which departs the appendage of the monumental scale and the two residential wings. The wings are composed of *superquadras* (superblocks) that have facilities for children (schools, playgrounds) at their center and local retail stores on one edge. Each of the four *superquadras* has social clubs, chapels, sports facilities, and other neighborhood-level facilities.

There are common aspects to these four scales that suggest they belong to the same morphological group, and they were preserved as the city was constructed. The weave of the Pilot Plan is structured by the regularity and repetition of basic elements, like a curving bundle of parallel arteries that defines the residential wings, intercepted orthogonally by another rectilinear arterial complex.

The composition is admirably harmonious, but presents challenges for internal accessibility as well as travel between the parts. Cutting through the residential wings, the Eixo Rodoviario imposes a significant separation between the superblocks to the east and west. Similarly, the Monumental Axis imposes a division between the north and south parts of the city. The macro parcels appear simple in layout, but in reality they result in complex polygons that are confusing to navigate because of numerous cul-de-sacs and parking lots. The residential buildings are sited on rectangular lots with similar dimensions, all with 100 percent land coverage but surrounded by abundant public landscaped open spaces. The visual effects of this urban design are repetitious, and the large distances between blocks (at least sixty-six feet) prevent open spaces from being clearly defined, which makes them look like residual spaces.

1

2

3

4

Figure 1.4. Examples of the four scales Lucio Costa conceptualized for Brasília: (*1*) monumental scale, (*2*) gregarious scale, (*3*) residential scale, (*4*) bucolic scale. (Photos by the authors)

Strict regulations—on land occupation, on building thresholds and heights, and on the number of stories and types of rooflines—generate architectural conformity in the residential wings that contrasts with the creativity found in the diversity of other spaces. However, the few openings between the interiors and exteriors of buildings results in many "blind spaces" and reduces foot traffic in the large open areas. These open spaces are not simply typical streets or plazas; they have been designed as morphological units such as *green area* or *esplanade*.

These features distinguish Costa's Pilot Plan from the other plans submitted for Brasília and from "an average modern city" (Costa 1995: 283). The interaction of the scales does not restrict the "dignity and nobility of intention" to the Esplanade of Ministries but "confers to the planned complex its monumental character" (Costa 1995: 283).

Immediately after the competition, the plan underwent its first modifications, requested by the jury, the federal government, and the team responsible for building the new capital (F. Leitão 2002). These changes are represented in figure 1.5:

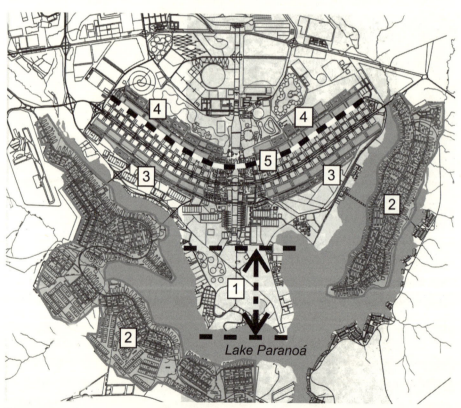

Figure 1.5. Map of major changes to Brasília's plan: (*1*) relocation of the city to the east, (*2*) reduction of the lake's western shoreline and relocation of residential areas, (*3*) added string of residential superquadras, (*4*) new band of lower-middle-class single-family residential blocks, and (*5*) transformation of W3 into a shopping strip. (Original drawing by Janaína Vieira, adapted by Vicente del Rio)

a. The city was moved about 1,650 feet to the east of its original site, decreasing the western shore of the lake. However, the design of city remained a chevron with 2.1 miles from the point to each end, creating a strong impression that the city had its back turned to the lake.

b. Reduction of the western shore of the lake and transfer of most of the single-family homes to that side, thus expanding the space for embassies on the eastern bank near the monumental axis.

c. Creation of a string of residential *superquadras* to the east (the "400s") with economical walk-up buildings with three floors and lacking *pilotis* (as opposed to the original *superquadras,* where buildings stood six stories high on *pilotis* and had elevators).

d. Creation of a band of single-family residential blocks to the west (the "700s") for lower middle-class public employees.

e. Transformation of W-3 from a road for wholesale commercial establishments into a retail shopping street that became the center of life in Brasília for years.

f. Creation of a row of blocks on both the east and west sides (the "600s" and "900s") for religious, educational, health, and similar facilities.

g. Appearance of the first satellite towns, even before the inauguration of Brasília, foretelling the polynucleated metropolis.

These transformations made Brasília denser and diluted the linearity of the original plan. They entailed unexpected and intense transverse flows of vehicles and pedestrians in the residential wings. In addition, other changes were made:

An increase in the quantity of central sectors coupled with a dispersed organization that impedes pedestrian movement between them.

A decrease in the number of loops in the cloverleaves of the Highway Axis and in its width, which, however, did not eliminate the problem of its being a major divider between the eastern and western sides of the city.

The local shops located between *superquadras* were rotated so that their main entrances faced the roads which were originally intended for service, turning their backs to the residential areas and resulting in a more urban relationship of the retail areas with the city as a whole.

Other transformations, such as invasions of public spaces and pressure from developers for changes in the city's original zoning, led to movements to have Brasília named a UNESCO World Heritage Site, a designation finally achieved in 1987. Unfortunately, this designation did not ensure the preservation of the Pilot Plan and jeopardized attempts to solve many of the city's serious problems.

Workers' Camps

Created by the construction companies hired to build Costa's project, workers' camps were meant to be temporary and to house all the employees, from engineers to laborers. The camps followed a modernist design, since their creators shared the same beliefs in modernism. Elements of the Brazilian contemporary architecture of that time were present in those timber constructions: simple building volumes, large openings, elegant façade compositions, porches, and trellises. The layout of the camps, with narrow lots, small distances between buildings, and direct relationships between residences and public space approximated this morphological type to the Brazilian vernacular. The workers' camps as a morphological type offered well-defined compositional units as well as intense social appropriation of the streets. In the first years of Brasília's construction, camps like Vila Planalto and Metropolitana were social centers for the whole city's populace.

The majority of these camps became natural solutions to the shortage of affordable housing for in-migrating workers and their descendents or relatives. Twenty years after Brasília's inauguration, some of these camps had consolidated into pleasant neighborhoods with tree-filled gardens, single-story buildings, and streets and squares of great vitality. Others, however, became large slums, as did Vila Paranoá.

When Brasília was declared a World Heritage Site, the movement to preserve these camps as testimonies to the period when the capital was built became stronger. Only two were preserved: the camp around Juscelino Kubitschek Hospital, which was restored as a center in memory of the pioneering settlers; and Vila Planalto, located very close to the Presidential Palace and now disfigured by new construction and the cutting down of most of its original trees (fig. 1.6). The other early workers' camps around Brasília were either demolished or became satellite towns, such as Núcleo Bandeirante, Candangolândia, and Velhacap.

Peripheral Modernism

According to the original plan, Brasília was to grow through the establishment of satellite towns, separated from the "mother city" by a fifteen-mile cordon of open space to preserve Lake Paranoá and the vision of the Pilot Plan. However, the government began building satellite towns even before the inauguration of Brasília in response to

Figure 1.6. Aerial photo of Vila Planalto favela (*left*), located close to the lake and the Praca dos Tres Poderes with the presidential palace (*upper right corner*). (Courtesy of TOPOCART, Brasília)

the pressing housing needs of the construction workers excluded from the workers' camps and of migrants who could not afford the expensive housing of the *superquadras*. The large migratory contingents from the Northeast, Goiás, and Minas Gerais had to choose between self-help housing in the precarious satellite towns with government financing, or squatting on land nearer to the Pilot Plan, from which they were repeatedly evicted.

Through self-help and low-income housing programs in the satellite towns, families were granted either small houses or sometimes just vacant lots no larger than 2,160 square feet. They were allowed to put up a temporary shack at the back of the lot until the permanent brick-and-mortar house had been built. Evidently, the temporary shacks typically were never demolished but simply turned into rental units to generate extra family income, thus increasing the density of these settlements. A limited number of small apartment units were also provided in four-story walk-up buildings. These self-help programs—for which engineers or architects from the public agencies sometimes served as advisors—followed the tradition of favelas. The policy implemented at the time barely met constitutional requirements by simply providing the land and the minimal housing unit. These settlements would not obtain decent infrastructure (piped water, sewers, pavement, and landscaping) until long after they had received a significant population evicted from the favelas.

The satellite towns became enormous housing complexes lacking minimal sanitation and suffering from inefficient public services and high unemployment rates. They were located in distant areas and sometimes on unsuitable land (fig. 1.1). Taguatinga, Sobradinho, and Ceilândia are all located close to springs and forests (fig. 1.7). Gama and Candangolândia are on the edge of a plain. Guará is located next to the section of the Pilot Plan designated for combustibles. The criteria for location of these towns were inconsistent, weakening the compactness of the urban complex and distorting the Pilot Plan.

The Federal District government established the satellite towns as alternatives for evicted squatters; pressured by urgent housing needs, the plans and projects followed poor modernist tenets: a hierarchical street network with only a few access roads and a large number of streets, strict zoning, and public spaces occupying residual areas. These projects resulted in towns weakened by redundant patterns in the street network, the subdivisions, and the buildings, as well as by substantial sprawl. Even though the average height of buildings is low, these settlements are dense, and the design fails to support street life even in subdivisions where buildings are contiguous rather than isolated. Modernism prevailed in the oversized circulation system, in streets that are used more for passing through than spending time, in the discontinuities of the urban fabric, and in the numerous blind walls—those containing no doors.

Figure 1.7. Aerial view of the satellite town of Taguatinga in the early 1970s. (Photo by the authors)

The early, intense "satellizing" of Brasília was its greatest transformation. Some of these satellite towns now form impressive conurbations—as do Taguatinga, Ceilândia, and Samambaia—which contained 751,933 inhabitants according to the 2000 census. In spite of deficiencies in employment and services, this agglomeration now borders on autonomy and could become the metropolitan economic center, in place of the administrative center envisioned by the Pilot Plan. Morphologically, it is not an integrated complex, and new areas are added to it haphazardly, ignoring the preexisting fabric and the natural landscape.

Land Invasions

"Land invasion" is a euphemism used in Brasília for favelas (squatter settlements), in reference to their unauthorized appropriation of land. The term does not apply, however, to the intense and illegal land appropriation practiced by wealthier groups, facilitated by the availability of lands in the Federal District and by governmental collusion.

Invasions by the poor date to the beginning of Brasília's construction. Located in the interstices of the officially planned city fabric, they helped to compress the open structure of Brasília. They became a solution to the limited availability of housing and land through official programs in the satellite towns, which were expensive and far from workplaces in the Pilot Plan area.

The initial land invasions of Brasília had the morphological character of Brazilian favelas, constructed by individual residents without planning or coordination. Built in 1957 and destroyed thirty years later, Vila Paranoá was a typical example. There, new buildings were added to the existing volumes, creating a clear overall structure: access and high traffic volume coincided in strong axes of various sizes, the longest linking the periphery to the center, thus ensuring good orientation as well as attracting retail and service establishments. In the compact fabric made up of irregular areas, streets intersected at different angles and buildings opened directly onto them, without fences or walls. Social interaction was strong in the streets and in different-sized public spaces, adequate for child and adult recreation as well as for the legibility of the Vila. The "invaders" fenced in only the amount of land necessary for a house and a small vegetable garden, weaving a complex well adapted to the topography and existing vegetation. Vila Paranoá was located on high ground with beautiful views of the lake and the Pilot Plan (fig. 1.8).vv

In spite of the precariousness of its buildings and the unsatisfactory sanitary conditions, Vila Paranoá was an unforgettable lesson in self-determined urban design. After a long struggle, the residents were evicted in the mid-1980s and the settlement

Figure 1.8. Built in 1957 and razed in the 1980s, Vila Paranoá *favela* enjoyed beautiful views of the lake and of Brasília. (Photo by the authors)

was razed by the Federal District government under the pretext that installing adequate infrastructure was too difficult.[8] Many believe that this rationale hid the real reason Vila was destroyed: its proximity to the elite mansions on the lakeshore. The strongest motivation to destroy Vila Paranoá, however, was that the existence of a morphological type that represented a backward past contradicted the "futurist metropolis" character of Brasília: from this perspective, it is impossible to see *culture* beneath the surface of poverty.

The rebirth of political representation in Brasília during the 1980s turned land invasion into an industry directed by political candidates eager to get the votes of the poor. Such was the case in Estrutural and Itapoã, where overnight invasions resulted from organized actions of politicians and their advisors. This morphological type is different from that of a genuine favela. Because land invasions have to be settled in a short period of time, they depend on centralized administration, which generally opts for a quick and easy-to-build grid pattern with perpendicular streets intersecting every three hundred feet. The natural terrain is not considered, land is subdivided following a regular geometry of lots of similar size, and shacks are built using an "invasion kit" containing sheets of plywood and flexible plastic sheeting for roofing. The political strategy of these organized communities is to resist negotiations with authorities for the time necessary to make the occupation irreversible. Once the settlement's status has been accepted by the government and there are no more threats of eviction, land prices appreciate significantly, gentrification follows, and fewer poor families move in. The invasion industry thus manufactures the embryos of new towns that serve private interests.

Morphological Types Postdating Modernism

The 1990s brought transformations in the central section of Brasília, on the banks of Lake Paranoá, and in new neighborhoods, generating the morphological types discussed in the following text.

Development within the Pilot Plan Area

Unoccupied areas in Brasília's city center still exist because of land retention by private speculators—for example, in the hotel sectors—and because the government set aside land for public uses under the original plan. In this context recent buildings are variants of classic modernism because they maintain the same relationship to public space and the same—though much impoverished—architectural vocabulary. If one compares similar old and new areas, an exaggeration of tendencies becomes clear, as is the case in the North and South Commercial Sectors (fig. 1.9). In the North Commercial Sector, a "landscape of objects" (Holanda 2002) is more evident: the spacing

Figure 1.9. An example of Costa's original modernism and an imitation of it: (*top*) An original local commercial center in one of Brasília's south-wing residential *superquadras;* (*bottom*) a later adaptation of the concept in the north wing. (Photos by the authors)

between buildings is increased, the buildings are more isolated by parking lots, and there are more residual public spaces. Business and services are internalized into shopping malls whose architecture tends toward kitsch. These features all contrast with the visual unity attained in the South Commercial Sector, which is more in accordance with the original plan.

A similar phenomenon occurs in the hotel sectors where, as in most Brazilian cities, speculators take advantage of the more relaxed zoning requirements that were meant to encourage tourism in order to build "residential hotels" that lack the amenities and parking spaces required in residential zones. In contrast to other parts of the Pilot Plan, in the hotel sector the existing infrastructure was fully utilized by private developers due to its high value and accessibility.

Hotels also occupy the Paranoá lakefront, together with apartment complexes, convention centers, multiplex cinemas, shopping malls, food plazas, and the like, following the spatial characteristics just described. Thus, in addition to the retreat of users from public areas, Brasília also suffers from the privatization of the lakeshore and the degradation of the Pilot Plan's bucolic scale.

The New Districts

In response to the housing demand from middle-class residents, new districts were created based on the Federal District's 1977 master plan, Plano Estrutural de Ocupação Territorial do Distrito Federal (PEOT; Structural Territorial Plan for the Federal District) and in Brasília Revisitada (Brasília Revisited), a report by Lucio Costa (1987). The first established guidelines for the urbanization of the Federal District and recommended the location for the new district of Águas Claras, while the second identified how the Pilot Plan could be expanded and defined new southwest and northwest sectors.

Although these three new districts were conceived as modernist projects, the private sector was a strong participant from the beginning of the design process, in complete opposition to the centralized decision-making processes typical of classic modernism. The workers cooperatives to which these buildings belonged were involved in decision making, as were the residents, who contributed design innovations. In addition, other morphological aspects also contributed to moving these projects away from typical modernism.

Surrounded by areas unsuitable for urbanization, Águas Claras is located 15.5 miles from the Pilot Plan area and near the satellite town of Taguatinga.[9] Its design evokes the Pilot Plan, although among the new districts it is the one most unlike it (fig. 1.10): In conjunction with a new form of public transportation, superblocks are built

Figure 1.10. Bird's-eye view of Aguas Claras, a planned satellite town between Brasília and Taguatinga. (Courtesy of Zimbres Arquitetos Associados)

along a subway line. Buildings preserve the high degree of separation typical of the Pilot Plan; their footprints are square (as opposed to rectangular, as in both residential wings in the Pilot Plan), and there are four apartment units per floor. Although along some streets the original design proposed retail space on the ground floor of buildings—a mixed use reminiscent of Brazilian vernacular—developers filled these spaces with garages for the residents above and built blind walls to block them off from the public space. Although in some blocks the *pilotis* of buildings were left open, the lots were fenced to increase security, thus eliminating the permeability typical of Brasília's modernist *superquadra*. Recently, part of the original proposal for Águas Claras—mixed-use buildings of up to thirty stories with residences above garages and commercial spaces on the ground floor—was resurrected. The relationship of the commercial spaces to public space is however similar to that of a closed shopping mall.

The Southwest Sector occupies an area adjacent to the Parque da Cidade (City Park) in the Pilot Plan (fig. 1.11).[10] Residential superblocks resembling classic modernist ones are organized in groups of four, on both sides of a commercial axis and with basic public facilities—such as schools—located between them. This axis is configured by the local shops of the Pilot Plan: buildings are as wide as those of the

Figure 1.11. A residential block in Brasília's newer southwest sector mimics the style of the Pilot Plan. (Photos by the authors)

Commercial Sector in the North Wing and as long as those in the South Wing. Due to the buildings' low height in relation to the wide street, however, the resulting environment looks more like a thoroughfare than a dynamic commercial boulevard.

Although the Northwest Sector remains unbuilt, it is planned to be composed of *superquadras* similar to the Pilot Plan's residential wings, arranged in groups of four and bordering a structural axis like the residential blocks in the Southwest Sector. Local shops will have a square footprint (as in the North Wing) and will be sited next to one another in continuous strips (not with multiple nuclei, as in the Pilot Plan) with a binary road system serving both sides of the buildings. Schools and other neighborhood services will be located at points of high accessibility, such as intersections, generating a healthy synergy of mixed uses.

The use of the vocabulary of classic modernism in the new neighborhoods diluted the identity of the original Brasília because it weakened the Pilot Plan's strong image of *superquadras* along the Highway Axis through the duplication of similar patterns outside their original territorial niche. The new neighborhoods are variations on modernism that maintain spatial segregation, increase legibility problems, and impoverish the symbolic qualities of the original classic modernism. Although their location may soften the dispersive characteristics, the socio-spatial segregation, and the eccentricity of Brasília, they do not succeed in changing trends (Paviani 1999).

Walled Cities

New gated communities grew up to the east and northeast of the Pilot Plan near the satellite town of Sobradinho and on the eastern shore of Lake Paranoá. They generated a growth vector opposite to the west and southwest areas favored by earlier government policies as being less environmentally sensitive and presenting fewer challenges in terms of public sanitation. Although some of the new subdivisions are unauthorized, the middle class migrated to them to escape high property prices in the Pilot Plan area, which lost residents as a result.[11] While some of these developments are still in litigation, others are in the process of being regularized.

The configuration of these neighborhoods is typical of developments carried out without the assistance of designers, and they do not comply with the requirements of the federal subdivision law (Lei 6766), which requires the dedication of 30 percent of the total area for public use, community facilities, and open space. The streets are not always organized in a hierarchical network, and their numerous identical lots are grouped into blocks that are almost exclusively residential. The only public space available is along roads linking the gated communities, roads which are bordered on both sides by interminable walls and fences (some electrified) with occasional guarded access gates. In only a few cases are there small, local retail developments along the public roads.

Conclusion

In spite of its public image, the real capital of Brazil coincides neither with its official boundaries nor with the vision that won the 1956 competition for a new capital. With regard to the area it occupies, its population, and its spatial configuration, Brasília has expanded far beyond the niche marked out by President Juscelino Kubitschek and Lucio Costa. To know Brasília implies discovering a city that exceeds the limits of the Pilot Plan district, since the real city extends through the Federal District and into the surrounding state of Goiás. It also means encountering a city that relegates less-favored classes to areas that are increasingly distant and poorly equipped. In this regard Brasília follows the typical pattern of countries with wide socioeconomic differences, as Brazil is.

But in getting to know Brasília we are also led to an aspect that makes it atypical from other cities: the exceptionally rarefied urban fabric that increases physical distances, financial costs, and social burdens. It is also atypical in the reproduction of that open layout in its newer parts and principally in its core, a form that constantly imposes barriers on human movements and constrains everyday social interactions. We may also be surprised at the diversity of morphological types coexisting in the urbanized complex, as well as at the mutability of its configuration—a mutability that tends to reduce the differences among the parts of the morphological mosaic, but that also threatens the identities of both the classic modernist districts and of the Brazilian central-western vernacular areas.

The hypothesis that problems and changes arose from flaws in the development of Brasília or from an unprepared urban administration is unsustainable under objective examination. Typical or anomalous attributes arose together with a city that has been developing along with Brazil's recent history. The fact that the *functional center* and the *morphological center* would never coincide in the capital is symptomatic of this process: the Pilot Plan has always retained the majority of jobs and services of the polynucleated metropolis, but it has never been the city's most accessible part. This fact gains weight when one observes that Brasília is the most rarefied of all the Brazilian cities studied by Holanda (2002).

The eccentric centrality and sprawling layout of the "real Brasília," added to other aspects discussed in this chapter, elevate the costs of public transportation to the highest level in the country.[12] Thus, the capital's perverse territorial structure most deeply affects those with the least buying power.

Social pressures brought some changes without changing the core of Brasília in any essential way. On the one hand, new neighborhoods have been built—albeit inside the planned greenbelt and in *non-aedificandi* areas (public domain areas), and gated communities now occupy large parcels of the Federal District without having increased its density. Their residents depend almost exclusively on private automobiles for transportation. On the other hand, as we discussed before, the tendency toward a rarefied urban fabric is not restricted to the macro scale and is unfortunately a feature of the Pilot Plan's heritage-site-listed central areas. Because of the new shopping malls and the need for a perception of security, the phenomenon of the "walled city" is not restricted to the periphery, and an anti-urban tendency is reflected in all scales of the Pilot Plan as well as in changes occurring in the other morphological types of the Brasília mosaic. The dominant morphological trend is, according to Choay (1994), the urban realm that results after the death of the city; it jeopardizes the configuration of public space and its appropriation by different social groups.

These do not seem to be problems in the eyes of many stakeholders involved with the preservation of Brasília as a World Heritage Site, however. Legitimately worried about invasions on public lands in the Pilot Plan district, these individuals are not interested in measures that could raise the quality of public open areas. The same could be said about the topics of architectural appropriateness and alleged bad taste which, though prevented in the Pilot Plan area through aesthetic regulations, are themes that should be fully debated. The process of permanently monitoring Brasília's World Heritage Site conditions should be innovative enough to encourage creativity and high design quality of individual buildings and groups of buildings, as well as of public open areas.

Preserving Brasília means, perhaps, the redeeming of dreams based on the evidence of their possibilities. One of these inherent possibilities is the significance of Brasília in the geopolitical reorientation of Brazil, insofar as it made the country start developing its interior after almost five hundred years of ignoring it. The relocation of the capital to the central plateau ranks as one of the most significant changes affecting Brazil and its society in the second half of the twentieth century. Another lesson relates to the urban design experience represented in Lucio Costa's plan, which suggests we should reflect on the transformation that occurs between design ideas and the reality that is constructed. Brasília's Pilot Plan holds an iconic meaning for modernism, and its interpretation is an admirable example of Brazilian creativity.

Notes

1. According to the competition's panel of jurors in its 1956 evaluation of Lucio Costa's plan (GDF, 1991). On the competition for Brasília see Evenson (1973).
2. In 2000, the Pilot Plan area had 198,442 inhabitants, a population decline of about 0.3 percent from 1999 (IBGE 2000; CODEPLAN 1999). Data on employment in the Pilot Plan area is controversial but estimates range from 44 percent (CODEPLAN 1999) to 75 percent (MTE 1999)of total jobs in the Federal District.
3. The Eixo Rodoviário (Highway Axis) is 7.7 miles long. The distance between residential building façades on the east and west sides of the axis is about 210 meters.
4. The distance from the westernmost point of the Eixo Monumental (Monumental Axis) to the eastern limit of the Praça dos Três Poderes (Square of the Three Powers) is 5.5 miles. If we include the extension to the shore of the lake, the total length is around 13,000 yards. The distances between the façades of the buildings on the north and south sides of the Monumental Axis range from 340 yards (on the Esplanada dos Ministérios, or Esplanade of the Ministries) to 500 yards (near its western extremity, between the Setor Militar Urbano (Urban Military Sector) and the residential area of Cruzeiro Velho. The length of the Esplanade of the Ministries, between the bus station and the National Congress, is almost 1.2 miles.
5. "Practically all those interviewed were in agreement [that Brasília should be listed as a World Heritage Site], using many different arguments, the most common being precisely that it would preserve the parks and gardens of the city, responsible for the high quality of life offered to the city's inhabitants" (Nunes 2003: 97).
6. In his recent book, Rykwert (2000: 178–79) observes that the city is a metaphor for a bird and that its body is "sometimes also called the Eixo Monumental (Monumental Axis)" whereas this is actually the official name of the place. He affirms that "the high point of the Esplanada dos Ministérios (Esplanade of the Ministries) is a 'TV tower,'" whereas it is really the National Congress, and the TV tower is actually located outside the esplanade, on the Eixo Monumental to the west of the bus station. He observes that the TV tower is "prefaced by a mastaba of white marble in the Egyptian style, the tomb of ex-president Juscelino Kubitschek"

but these two elements are really nearly 1.7 miles apart, and there are many other architectural elements between them. According to Rykwert, "the size of the city *with its satellites* was limited to 500,000," whereas this population limit was set only for the Pilot Plan area (italics ours). He adds that "the high ranked governmental bureaucrats abandoned their apartments in the superblocks as soon as they could and built houses on the other side of the lake. This led to many problems, including an increase in violent crime." In fact, however, the Pilot Plan area holds 47.05 percent of the wealthiest citizens of the federal district, whereas only 23.73 percent live in the lake area. He also affirms, "One may take a half hour or longer to go from one embassy to another," even though many of them are located next to each other and the separation of the complexes is much less than he suggests.

7. Jury's statement on Lucio Costa's entry in the Concurso Nacional do Plano Piloto da Nova Capital do Brasil, 1957 (GDF 1991).

8. During the struggle over granting permanency to Vila Paranoá, teams from the University of Brasília—particularly from the schools of architecture, engineering, and social work—supported the residents association in their fight against the Federal District government. They produced several documents demonstrating the technical viability and the sociocultural importance of maintaining Vila.

9. Following the Federal District government's decision to build a subway line in Brasília, Águas Claras was designed by Paulo Zimbres & Arquitetos Associados. The subway was a controversial decision because the PEOT proposed other, cheaper mass-transit alternatives to support the Pilot Plan's expansion towards the southeast, such as light rail on dedicated lanes. The subway line has been under construction for more than ten years at very high costs, and it still operates erratically between the Pilot Plan area and satellite cities to the south and southeast, even though the major growth vectors are in other directions.

10. The Southeast Sector was designed by Federal District government planners.

11. The use of private rather than government financing favored this process, and private developers exploited loopholes in zoning codes by subdividing well-located ranches in order to satisfy a strong but latent demand. These lands had not been annexed because they were outside the main axes for urban expansion. Even in those gated communities built on land whose ownership was in dispute, the housing prices excluded low-income residents. As in the case of planned invasions, developers bet on the new residents winning the confrontation with the government, because the massive sale of lots and the occupation of the new neighborhoods would leave the government no choice but to accept the situation. In fact, these subdivisions were regulated after 1998.

12. These data are from studies by the Morphological Dimensions of Urbanization research group in the School of Architecture at the University of Brasília, of which the authors are members. Although Brasília has Brazil's highest index of automobile use, more than half of all daily trips for all purposes are still by public transit (CODEPLAN 1991).

CHAPTER 2

Challenges for New Town Design in a Frontier Region Palmas

Dirceu Trindade

Throughout its history the Brazilian state has employed urban development in a search for progress and modernity. From colonial times, urban expansion has always been seen as necessary for the conquest of unoccupied territory in regions considered "backward": the great rain forests, the *sertão* (arid regions in the Northeast), and the *cerrado* (savannah areas such as the one where Palmas is located).[1] With independence, and later with the establishment of the republic, urbanization, the movement toward the interior, and the construction of cities came to be regarded as projects to modernize the country and transform Brazilian society. This drive to build generated first the construction of Belo Horizonte, the new capital of the state of Minas Gerais, in 1897. In the 1930s, the modernizing government of Getúlio Vargas and its "March to the West" promoted the construction of Goiânia, the new capital of Goiás state.[2] Later, the impulse was renewed under the development-minded government of Juscelino Kubitschek (1956–1960) and peaked with the construction of Brasília, the new federal capital carved out of Goiás and inaugurated in 1960.

During the 1960s population migration to the interior and a more homogenous occupation of the national territory were constant concerns of the federal government as expressed in its *planos de metas* (national development plans) and in its regional development efforts. With the return of democracy in the 1980s, these concerns were also expressed in the new National Constitution of 1988, which included the creation of the new state of Tocantins. The product of a long regional political struggle for its creation since 1821, the new state was carved out of the northern part of Goiás, and contained the poorest and least urbanized areas in Goiás, many *latifundios* (large estates), and serious land conflicts, despite its rich mineral deposits and precious raw materials, still little exploited.

The state of Tocantins is entirely located in Brazil's northern region (the Amazon River basin) and it lies in the transition zone between the *cerrado* and the Amazon forest, with flora and fauna typical of the former. The creation of the new state was an important settlement strategy for new development in a largely frontier agricultural region. Palmas was constructed to fulfill the role of capital city of this new state, and it was inaugurated on May 20, 1990.

Interestingly, starting in the final decades of the nineteenth century, Brazil had constructed new capitals every three decades—three of them in the same state—all of them resulting from efforts to direct development to the interior and to propel the country and its regions into modernity. In the case of Palmas, as we shall see, in addition to following the same modernist tenets as Brasília, its design was ecologically respectful and included sustainability concerns, particularly in the way it addressed the preservation of creeks and rivers and in its adaptation to the local environment.

In 2003, only thirteen years after its founding, Palmas already had 160,000 inhabitants, and its rapid growth was reflected throughout the region—setting a new landmark in the urbanization of the Brazilian territory. Not surprisingly, Palmas generates significant territorial, social, economic, and political effects. The study of its original design and of the implementation process helps us to better understand the effects of rapid urbanization not only on the region, but also on the everyday lives of thousands of migrants arriving from different parts of the country, many coming directly from rural areas and attracted by the construction of the city, its services, and economic opportunities.

Site Selection for the City

Wilson de Siqueira Campos, the first governor of the new state of Tocantins, directly contracted GrupoQuatro, an architectural and planning firm in Goiânia, to develop the new capital in 1990.[3] Initially the firm evaluated the potential of the candidate cities of Porto Nacional, Gurupi, and Araguaína to serve as the new capital. Innumerable political and social constraints, and the high costs involved in transforming any of these cities into an administrative center informed the governor's decision to construct a city from scratch.

Taking the geographical center of the state as a reference, the preliminary site selection area for Palmas was narrowed to a 90 by 90 kilometer (56 by 56 mile) square, the north-south dimension of which was later expanded to 112 kilometers (70 miles). The final interdisciplinary report cited four locations as particularly suitable for a new city, with different levels of appropriateness according to the following criteria: site morphology, soil quality, climatic conditions, vegetation, natural resources, spatial conditions, distance to and relationships with nearby settlements, accessibility, and potential for attracting population.

The area selected is located on the right bank of the Tocantins River. Because it was in the least developed region of the state, this area was judged most in need of development. The site's declivity is only 4 percent, and on the north it is bounded by the Água Fria River, on the south by the Taquarussu River, on the east by the Serra do Lajeado range, and on the west by the Tocantins River (fig. 2.1). Its predominant vegetation is typical of the *cerrado*, with little agricultural or pastoral development, and the small existing population was concentrated in the village of Canelas in the municipality of Taquarussu. The nearest city is Porto Nacional, sixty kilometers (thirty-seven miles) away along a local and at that time unpaved road.

A whole regional and urban infrastructure network would have to be built to accommodate the new capital. This was facilitated by the topography and by the innumerable streams and creeks that cross the site, with nearby artesian springs with great hydrologic potential. During the selection process, construction was begun on a dam and hydroelectric power station on the Tocantins River. The resulting reservoir (Lajeado Lake) greatly altered the surrounding arid *cerrado* microclimate, and it was incorporated into the design of the future capital, providing it with a scenic view toward the Serra do Lajeado in addition to various recreational and leisure opportunities.

Figure 2.1. Map of the state of Tocantins, showing the central location of its new capital, Palmas. (Drawing by Vicente del Rio)

The Plan and the Design Concepts

In addition to designing the new city and its government buildings, GrupoQuatro designed some of the public facilities. All the projects were completed in only forty days, a record imposed by political necessity since the principal elements of Palmas had to be ready within two years, the time remaining in the governorship of Wilson de Siqueira Campos, the major mover in Tocantins' creation.

GrupoQuatro sought to provide Palmas with the look of a turn-of-the-millennium city: modern, efficient, rich in its spaces and urban structure, but respectful of ecological and environmental concerns. Consonant with their desire to relate to regional culture, the designers acknowledge several influences, such as the writings and experiments of Carlos Nelson dos Santos (1985b), in conceiving of a city defined by a collection of neighborhoods, or *places,* like small towns. Goiânia, the capital of Goiás state inaugurated in 1935, inspired them for its layout with its administrative center clearly demarcated in the urban landscape, and its street network structured by traffic circles and broad avenues.[4] Brasília was inevitably another source of inspiration, and although Palmas's designers admit that they tried to avoid the spatial determinism of the federal capital, they were unable to completely remove themselves from the modernist precepts of the Charter of Athens, and Palmas, like Brasília, is dependent on the automobile for efficient vehicular circulation.[5]

The topographic limits of the designated urban area and the Tocantins River itself suggested a longitudinal north-south axis for the city form and as the main organizer of land subdivision, and an orthogonal grid was adjusted to the site's topography. This conception, continuously applied since its first use in 479 BC in Miletus, Asia Minor, appears very often in Latin America. It immediately established the efficiency, not only of subdivision grids but also of traffic flow. Another influence in this design decision was the "gigantic" urban network of the new town of Milton Keynes in England, one of the cities visited by GrupoQuatro when they were beginning their background research for Palmas. The grid as a spatial definer is also reminiscent of Brasília itself and its subdivision into *superquadras* (superblocks)—the neighborhood units—to facilitate pedestrian use and encourage social activities. In their initial studies for Palmas, GrupoQuatro expressed the following vision:

The settlement to be designed should be agreeable; it should provide its residents with a good quality of life. At the same time, the new city should keep a close relationship with the cultural and social habits of the new state; in that sense one expects a simple, agreeable urban pattern that does not appeal to monumentality. The urban functions and government activities need a setting that allows them to be performed with the desired functionality. The totality should be worthy of the beauty of the Tocantins landscape and integrate itself perfectly with it. Enjoyment of natural or constructed conditions in the urban universe and its surroundings should be available to the populace.

The Palmas city plan attempted to establish its own paradigm based on ten orienting principles: (1) a large-scale street network; (2) preservation of the natural environment; (3) an identifiable city center; (4) a public-private partnership for development projects; (5) flexibility in land uses; (6) minimization of impacts on the microclimate; (7) feasible construction costs; (8) guaranteed accessibility to the lake; (9) promotion of mixed use in order to avoid specialization of urban functions; and (10) efficient and low-cost public transportation.

Above all, Palmas is a modernist city, and as such its design is marked by a hierarchy of specific functions as outlined in the Charter of Athens, even if the spatial arrangement of these functions is diversified in the master plan, especially along Avenue Teotônio Segurado. The *residential* function was located in city blocks acting as mini-neighborhoods, provided with a minimum of retail and public facilities. The *work* function, because Palmas is primarily an administrative city, is concentrated in the Praça dos Girassóis (Sunflower Park), around it, and along Avenue Teotônio Segurado, the major north-south axis, which also attracts shopping and services. The *leisure* function is concentrated on the lakeshore, with its more than ten kilometers of beaches in specific zones. Finally, in Palmas the *circulation* function is primarily designed around the private automobile.

Despite all of its excellent objectives, an analysis of some of Palmas's design fundamentals demonstrates how the construction of the city occasionally departed from the intended paradigm, thereby contradicting several of the original design intentions. Although some of these contradictions resulted from political or market considerations in terms of speed, intensity, and manner of construction, sometimes limitations became apparent in the original concepts themselves, revealing the difficulties of designing a whole city.

The Grid as Structural Unit

The grid was the principle that generated the design of Palmas, along with the concept of organizing the city around traditional mini-neighborhoods. An urban *macro design* was established using a basic grid of 600 by 700 meters (1,970 by 2,296 feet) and limiting each neighborhood to 42 hectares (103 acres) and a target population of 12,600 inhabitants. If the actual construction had followed the master plan, the grid could have been expanded repeatedly in response to growth needs while maintaining continuity with the original nucleus; and even if vacant areas appeared, the result would always be subordinated to the general city morphology (fig. 2.2).

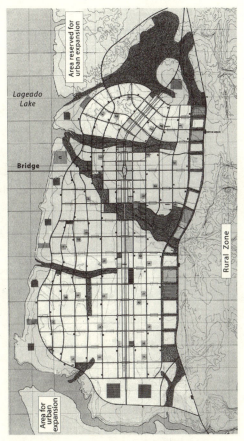

Figure 2.2. The original master plan for Palmas followed an "open grid" concept. (Courtesy of Luiz Fernando Teixeira, GrupoQuatro Arquitetos)

The *macro grid* permitted efficient zoning into sectors, with types and locations of land use responding to a set of norms and standards. Zoning followed a distribution of land-use intensities radiating out from the central axis, with the principal facilities and commercial uses being located in the city center and on the edges of the north-south axis. Neighborhood retail areas were laid out along the east-west avenues on the edges of the residential macro-blocks, and schools were to be constructed in the core of these blocks, following the usual criteria of distance and accessibility.

Traffic Circulation and Public Transportation

Based on the grid concept, the design for Palmas's original street network had three objectives: security for pedestrians, efficient circulation for people and goods, and low infrastructure costs. North-south avenues became the principal roads while the east-west avenues distributed the traffic into the residential blocks. Internal distributors and local streets complete this efficient circulation system (fig. 2.3).

Avenida Parque (Park Avenue) limits the city to the west and shields the riverfront area reserved for recreation and sports facilities. The eastern limit of the central urban grid is State Road TO-134, along which regional and supply facilities were located. Several streams run across the city from east to west, and each had a fifty-meter-wide preservation zone declared along both banks. In consideration of the site topography, the plan established clear limits to development in the buffer zones adjacent to the streams.

Like Brasília, Palmas is marked by a monumental north-south axis, the Avenida Teotônio Segurado, which has a wide planted median and a typical cross-section with 150 meters (490 feet) between buildings. This axis is interrupted only by the Praça dos Girassóis (Sunflowers Plaza), which is located at the highest elevation in the city. Situ-

Figure 2.3. Aerial view of Palmas looking west, showing the long main east-west avenue, the government center in the middle, and the bridge over the lake in the background. (Photo by Newton Paniago)

Figure 2.4. Aerial view of Palmas's administrative center. (Photo by Newton Paniago)

ated in this park, the seat of the new state government, Palácio Araguaia, became a monumental landmark visible from numerous places in the city (fig. 2.4). Because this axis was originally planned to support commercial and office uses along its length, its dimensions were conceived to permit intense vehicular traffic as well as a public transit system. The original concept design called for a system of pedestrian bridges for the safe crossing of this busy boulevard, but these were later removed from the master plan.

The city design adopted the traffic circle at the crossings of avenues, eliminating the need for traffic lights except at the intersections of Avenida Teotônio Segurado with east-west avenues. The circles organize vehicular circulation at the crossings and act as traffic mitigation, since they are only one block—about 700 meters (2,296 feet)—apart, following the plan's basic grid. It is important to note that in the original design, pedestrians were not supposed to need to cross the major avenues. Everyday needs and shopping would be taken care of by retail and service businesses located along the edges of the residential macro-block modules—called mini-neighborhoods in the plan—eliminating the need for pedestrian bridges and traffic lights along the avenues. The dimensions of these mini-neighborhoods anticipated that pedestrians would need to walk only about two thousand feet to the nearest bus stop, the element linking these blocks to the rest of the city through circular bus lines traveling along the east-west avenues.

Fundamentally modernist in its wide avenues and large distances, Palmas favors vehicular circulation and promotes the use of private transportation. This situation is reinforced by the unreliable public transportation system, consisting of buses that connect to other routes only in areas where there are high concentrations of people, creating real obstacles to the mobility of the population. This is a serious problem, particularly if one considers the dimensions of the city blocks, the empty spaces inside and around the blocks, the incompleteness of urban services, and particularly the absence of trees along the pedestrian walkways.

City Center

The original design concept called for an easily identifiable city center articulating the public and private realms and the civic and commercial functions, through federal and state government agencies, banks, offices, and shops, much like any traditional downtown. The designers envisioned that Praça dos Girassóis should assume the role of city center, and all of the city's monumentality was directed there. Covering almost 63 hectares (155.6 acres) and measuring 750 by 850 meters (2,460 by 2,789 feet) —a large area by any standard—the *praça* holds in its center the Palácio Araguaia, the state governor's executive offices. On the square's edges along Avenues NS-1 and NS-2, amidst landscaped areas, are the state secretariats, the legislature, the state courts, the cathedral, and monuments to Luiz Carlos Prestes and the revolutionaries of 1935.[6]

The city blocks around this large central square were zoned for commercial and service uses typical of an urban center, such as stores, offices, businesses, company headquarters, and banks. In the original design, the interior of these blocks would be exclusively for pedestrian use, with a *praça* surrounded by colonnades for window shopping, occasional cafés with seating, and the building entrances (fig. 2.5).

Figure 2.5. Concept sketch of the interior of the mixed-use blocks in Palmas. (Drawing by Carmen R. Silva; courtesy of GrupoQuatro Arquitetos)

The streets around these blocks would serve only to access parking and for loading and unloading. The influence of the utopian design of Brasília's *superquadras* is again evident.

Unfortunately one of Palmas's original principles—to avoid the specialization of urban functions—was abandoned during construction, when these blocks were dedicated exclusively for commercial use. The vehicular lanes and internal parks were never built, nor did land subdivision and building typologies follow the original conception. Because of the shortcomings of the public transportation system and the absence of leisure attractions and residences, these spaces are devoid of people outside business hours and are unsafe at night. The true center of Palmas—in the most traditional sense of city life with bank branches, shops, bars, and restaurants—is along Avenida Juscelino Kubitschek, which transverses the city at the Praça dos Girassóis. People are attracted there by a bus route, easy automobile access, and generous parking in front of stores in a typical strip mall layout.

For Avenida Teotônio Segurado, the city's monumental axis, the designers meant to achieve a visual composition of large architectural complexes, complemented by constant activity resulting from a mixture of public and commercial urban uses. The avenue was to be full of mixed-use clusters rather than functioning merely as a roadway. Instead, today we find along it the buildings of the municipal administration, large-scale urban structures such as the convention center, banks, large commercial enterprises, hospitals, hotels, and schools, in addition to the central headquarters of the law enforcement agencies.

Since the typical original *cerrado* vegetation was totally destroyed at the beginning of construction, landscaping in Palmas was irremediably compromised. In the median of the monumental axis, for example, non-native bushes and coconut palms were planted, and there was no attempt to provide shade. The absence of the open spaces initially planned for the commercial and residential areas also compromises one of the city's original planning principles, respect for ecology and sustainability. There have been innumerable studies and proposals for restoring the *cerrado* vegetation and environment, but this has been implemented in only a few areas, such as the park near the municipal government headquarters.

Residential Areas

In the design of Palmas, the macro-grid generates blocks, the basic unit of traditionally organized neighborhood spaces within the city. It was the planners' intention not to create small cities within the city, but to approach the scale of the individual, with the single-family dwelling as the point of departure for organizing the city. The blocks were designed for pedestrians, and their configuration sought to respond to the universe of the average citizen, for whom the referential elements are the house lot, the street, the corner, neighborhood businesses, the square, the school, bars for evening entertainment, and the church.

Following a network of winding neighborhood streets, the sort of residential block envisioned in the plan would offer single- and multifamily housing types, always surrounded by a greenbelt. The street would serve as a binding element for the populace, an interesting route to walk along, and a place for social encounters. Residents would develop a sense of belonging to the neighborhood through their identification with the neighborhood centers, which would be animated, function as meeting places, and could be developed with variable densities and building types to emphasize their identity.

In contrast to Brasília, where the state was the developer and builder, Palmas was to rely on the private sector for the subdivision and development of the city blocks. This would avoid both the monotony of Brasília-style *superquadras* and the conventional process of urban land subdivision. Residential subdivisions would vary according to market conditions, offering different forms of spatial organization and internal landscaping, with different types of residences, local commerce, and urban services. Market efficiency would help to create true mini-neighborhoods where different types of single- and multifamily residences would combine into spatially rich and varied environments that would articulate with the functionality of the city as a whole.

The plan's Memória da Concepção (Concept Report) called for the sale of city macro-blocks as single parcels that would then be subdivided by the developers according to the master plan. The original land-use legislation stated that each block should be developed as a unit, and that its internal infrastructure was the developer's responsibility. In reality this did not occur, however, and in the majority of the completed projects, developers sought to maximize the number of lots. The spatial distribution of buildings did not follow any aesthetic or rational guidelines, and lacked proper urban facilities. In most cases, streets were built with generous curb-to-curb widths of 9 meters (29 feet) but sidewalks were narrow, at only 3 meters (9.8 feet), which made tree planting impossible, hindered pedestrian movement, and impeded the construction of bicycle lanes. In other cases, zoning changes hampered the suitability of the streets for retail purposes, due to narrow lanes and inadequate parking (fig. 2.6).

The most recent problem has been caused by unpredicted urban expansion in the form of subdivisions and gated communities on the west side of the Tocantins River, outside the city perimeter. Until recently this was a rural area covered by *cerrado* veg-

Figure 2.6. A local commercial street in Palmas. Failure to implement the original master plan led to commercial streets unsuitable for both vehicular and pedestrian use. (Photo by the author)

etation, but now it is compromised by unplanned urban use without adequate infrastructure. These developments for the new middle class of Palmas were facilitated by the construction of a bridge over Lajeado Lake. The Ponte da Integração (Integration Bridge) crosses this reservoir as a continuation of Avenida Juscelino Kubitschek, the city's most important business axis, and joins Palmas to the neighboring city of Paraíso do Tocantins.

Recreation and Leisure

Recreation and leisure are fundamental activities for Palmas, not simply in defining the quality of life of its population, but also for their ability to attract visitors and new migrants from throughout the region. Besides the internal spaces for recreation and leisure planned within the residential blocks—which were never constructed—the master plan anticipated recreation and leisure uses in blocks along Lajeado Lake, between the floodplain and Avenida Parque. In this area social clubs; universities; and cultural, sports, and health facilities (such as clinics and hospitals) were to be built.

Lajeado Lake—eight kilometers wide and twelve kilometers long (4.95 by 7.45 miles)—has innumerable clean-sand beaches that run the whole length of the city. Its importance to Palmas led to a revision in the original master plan and the creation of Projeto Orla (Project Lakefront) to preserve the lakeshore, guarantee public use and access to the water, and prohibit inappropriate land uses. A specially created public-private corporation is responsible for this project's implementation.[7]

Project Lakefront made possible a great urban park system with beaches, recreation areas, sports complexes, piers for small boats, marinas, and leisure centers with places for concerts, bars, restaurants, public restrooms, parking, and landscaped gardens (fig. 2.7). In addition, the new Integration Bridge increased recreational tourism

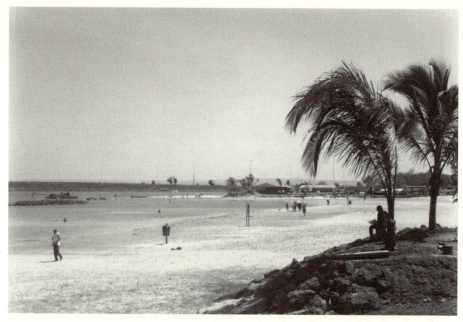

Figure 2.7. One of the beaches in a preserved area along the lakefront in Palmas, with the ramp to the bridge in the background. (Photo by the author)

coming from nearby cities. The beautiful view of the mountains counterpoints the sunsets on the lake and, as in the culture of all beachfront cities, the lakefront beaches became the city's most democratic places. This project generated profound changes in the daily life of Palmas, as the lake attracts a great number of users from both the city and the entire region, generating new social behaviors.

The master plan also specified that at least fifty meters (164 feet) alongside all streams, particularly those running east to west, should be "environmental preservation areas." Environmental recovery projects were to be developed for all these areas, allowing only public uses and small buildings in support of recreational and cultural activities, such as public restrooms and small food kiosks. Since the government was directly responsible for implementing these areas and the original design of Palmas left them totally independent of the city macro-blocks, in general their preservation has been carried out. In one of these areas, for instance, the first phase of a recreational park was built on 150 hectares (370 acres). The park takes advantage of an existing spring to create a series of interconnected pools 50 centimeters (1.6 feet) deep, connected by 1.6 kilometers (almost a mile) of waterfalls and streams, in addition to a small amphitheater for open-air shows, clusters with playgrounds and workout equipment, and a three-kilometer (1.86–mile) jogging track.

The Construction Process

Design alterations and noncompliance with plans always occur when decisions are left to elected officials and private interests interested in short-term initiatives. From the beginning of its construction, this has been the case in Palmas, which grew on its periphery due to the intense commercialization of available lots.

According to the master plan, land development was to move from the city center out, initially toward the south and always in east-west strips to lower the initial cost of infrastructure and to guarantee harmonious urban growth. The means of negotiating urban land sales—a state prerogative since the land had been expropriated—was not clearly established in the plan and the process was never respected by the politicians in power, allowing a settlement process that contradicted the original plan and led to a considerable loss of quality in the final built environment.

During the early phase of construction, the state facilities were built, followed by two state-financed residential blocks for workers and migrants who did not have the financial resources to buy the few lots put up for sale at that time. The high rate of family in-migration led to the settling of lots devoid of any urban infrastructure and pushed the state into building four low-income settlements outside the city limits. Further aggravating this situation, the state government did not know how to prepare the region and the surrounding towns for the socio-demographic impacts of rapid growth of the new capital. As a result, for example, land speculators hurried to subdivide and build in Taquarito, a village near the construction site of Palmas that already had some infrastructure. At one point the village population was larger than that inside the perimeter of the capital itself.

By expropriating rural land without establishing policies and procedures for urban settlement, the state government acted as a low-quality developer by treating the city as a large subdivision, disregarding any planning or even minimal guidelines for urban growth. In allowing speculative interests to share power, the government presided over inefficient activity and the waste of scarce resources applied in many cases to unnecessary projects: street networks expanded beyond the planned alternatives, oversized public works that met the immediate needs of state functions but were more an expression of political power than functionality, and the like. Estimates indicate that the networks that were built for the inauguration of Palmas could have satisfied the needs of a population of 500,000 although at the time there were only 20,000 residents.

The initiatives of the state government, whether due to an urgent need to accommodate new civil servants who were moving in or because of political favoritism, began the occupation of the city in blocks that were outside the master plan area, in the southeast quadrant of the city, which did not have the necessary infrastructure. However, the demand for lots exceeded expectations, which immediately led to the abandonment of the fifth principle of the plan: "flexibility in the development of land guaranteeing an orderly growth." According to this principle the original planners foresaw permitting alterations in the use of particular blocks, so long as they obeyed the implementation norms of the city.

For the in-migrating population, the founding and initially fast-paced construction of the city represented an El Dorado that fell apart when the government changed hands, bringing unemployment and lack of hope. The pace of growth, investments, and large-scale undertakings picked up again in the mid-1990s. Among these projects were the construction of the Lajeado hydroelectric plant, intended to spur regional development, and the Ponte da Integração over the reservoir, joining Palmas to the city of Paraíso do Tocantins and generating greater employment and investment opportunities. The high investments in the city by the state government, in part with resources generated by the hydroelectric project, and the arrival of new private enterprises have been augmenting urban growth and attracting a new wave of migrants from other regions of the country. Some of these resources are being devoted to improving access to Palmas, still dependent on Highway BR-153, the only link between the Amazon region and the country's south, which is in terrible condition. The local airport has already been inaugurated, and soon the state will finish constructing its section of the Ferrovia Norte-Sul (North-South Railway), which will integrate the region to other states in Brazil.

With the growth outside Palmas of illegal settlements and subdivisions lacking urban infrastructure, the state and city governments pressured the legislators to expand the city limits, incorporating the village of Taquarito and the four low-income housing projects it had built for the first migrants. Another initiative to organize the irregular and dispersed subdivisions outside Palmas is being carried out to the south of Córrego da Prata (Silver Creek), where the state is building a new urban settlement, also designed by GrupoQuatro.

This project attempts to create a new urban center—justified by the territorial expansion—and seeks to connect Palmas to the several disparate nuclei that resulted from the initial disorganized settlement. By changing the dimensions of the original block for Palmas, the designers are seeking to increase physical integration and to redeem the core of the Palmas project, with references to the Brazilian traditional small town. Their idea is to structure suburbs in a way that encourages residents to meet spontaneously on street corners, in squares, and in places for social activities. The new design promotes mixed-use corner lots and blocks, a system of pedestrian walkways, and community facilities such as cinemas, theaters, shops, and services, all with greater densities and a more intense use of multifamily typologies.

Finally, the political life of Palmas has gradually brought the government closer to the community. At Palmas's inauguration in 1990, the sociopolitical changes were immense because, in addition to accommodating the whole political and administrative apparatus of the newly created state, Palmas also absorbed the administration of the municipality of Taquarussu: its city councilors, the mayor's office, and all the municipal political and administrative structure. In later elections municipal representatives who more legitimately represented the interests of local communities were elected. Today, the population of Palmas is organized into neighborhood and community associations that strive to participate in solving city problems, particularly through public residential projects.

Conclusion

The creation of Palmas, like that of Brasília, proves that the construction of a new city is always a strong stimulus for regional development. This is especially true if we consider the recessionary economic context in which the building of the city occurred and the speed of planning and construction.

From 1998 to 2003 Palmas experienced an average population growth rate of 28.7 percent, whereas the overall rate for Brazil was 3 percent during the same period! The growth of the new state of Tocantins was not restricted to its capital, however, as the cities of Gurupi, Porto Nacional, and Araguaína also underwent dizzying growth. Hundreds of small, medium, and micro entrepreneurs were attracted from different regions of the country and even from other countries to satisfy the growing demand for services and consumer goods generated by thousands of families migrating to the newest state in the federation.

According to the IBGE (Brazilian Institute of Geographical Statistics) in 1996, only six years after its inauguration, Palmas already had a population of 86,116 inhabitants. In 2000 this figure was already 137,355, whereas the population of Tocantins state was 1,157,098. One of the reasons for the surge in population was the influx of workers attracted by the construction of the dam and hydroelectric plant, as well as the bridge over Lajeado Lake. In 2006, the estimated population of Palmas was 220,889. It is a city where everything remains possible: dynamic, stimulating, fulfilling its principal purpose of furthering integration and regional development, and creating a new society in the midst of the *cerrado*.

In evaluating the city's performance based on the accumulated experience of urban planners over the last century, one may say that Palmas did not introduce any innovations, particularly in comparison to its neighbors, Goiânia—with its culturalist design—and Brasília—the modernist national capital. The story of Palmas is a lost opportunity to create a truly contemporary city, ecological and sustainable, as outlined in the preliminary concept. Architects, urban planners, and critics, when analyzing the "late modernism" of Palmas, have denounced the utilization there of a kind of practical urban planning often used in other cities, where the idea of planning is confused with the subdividing and selling of lots, constrained only by the observance of obsolete urban legislation.

By establishing a system of 42–hectare (103–acre) macro-blocks in an orthogonal grid containing the basic urban systems, while leaving private enterprises with great flexibility to design the micro-blocks, the plan permitted, even induced, speculative development. In various residential blocks, and especially in those blocks set aside for large structures along the north-south axis, what happened in reality was a rezoning of certain lots, even those designated for institutional use that were supposed to be for public facilities, compromising the desired equilibrium of functions.

Palmas's original concept report, the document that predates the master plan, foresaw a city where the residential blocks would spur such a high degree of social integration among residents that there would be no need for walls between houses. The idea was that, as happened in Brasília's superblocks, the blocks were to be subdivided into projects designed by different architects inspired by the original concept, rather than development proceeding in the traditional lot-by-lot fashion, and that the blocks would be filled with a mix of residences and neighborhood services, linked by pedestrian walkways. This utopia was trampled by reality and by the actions of a state government that acted in the role of land speculator.

The Tocantins state government, the original sole proprietor of all land in Palmas, did not implement the plan according to its main principles and, for example, decided to award the design of nine contiguous macro-blocks to the same firm, resulting in a very homogeneous built environment. Worse, these projects were later reproduced in leapfrog developments, resulting in pockets of vacant land and inefficient public networks. This attitude from the public sector encouraged private developers to ignore the master plan and has resulted in a capital city now facing huge landownership problems and disorganized urbanization.

The new capital's major problems are similar to those afflicting other cities: in particular, incomplete public facilities and infrastructure, deficiencies in public transportation, development that ignores the plan's implementation and zoning principles, and great tracts of empty land in fully serviced areas. Problems in settling the poorest population, regularizing deeds in squatter settlements, and establishing the urban infrastructure are typical of an urbanization process that is unable to keep up with the city's pace of growth.

Between the death of the street decreed by the concepts of the modernist city and of Brasília, and the attempt to resurrect the traditional character of the city so well expressed in the Concert Report, Palmas's planners ended up developing an urban design that was efficient in serving land speculation. Throughout this discussion I have shown that, although the design principle of the macro-grid is being implemented in an efficient manner, allowing for adaptations and changes of size, the nonfulfillment of several other basic principles compromised the efficiency that was predicted by the master plan.

The experience of Palmas demonstrates the enormous distance between intention and action, and that efficient urban management will always require a constant and active planning process. One of the important lessons learned is the necessity of separating this process from executive power by putting planning and urban design in the hands of an independent citizens' council removed from petty politicking and from great sources of speculative capital, so that it can operate on behalf of the desires and needs of the population.

Notes

1. The *cerrado* is a hot and dry savannah with low-growing, scattered vegetation and small trees. It covers one-fifth of Brazil's territory in the central, west-central, and northeast regions. Brazil's northern region encompasses the Amazon River basin and those of its major tributaries, including the Tocantins.
2. See the introduction to this book and the map in figure P.1.
3. *GrupoQuatro*'s principals were architects Luiz Fernando Cruvinel Teixeira and Walfredo Antunes Oliveira Filho.
4. The plan for Goiânia was strongly influenced by the culturalist tradition and by English garden cities, both in its original design by Attílio Corrêa Lima—who also used Versailles and Washington, D.C., as models for the monumentality of the downtown—and in Armando de Godoy's subsequent alterations.
5. Located only 120 miles from Goiânia, Brasília and its modernism have been strong cultural models to the whole region and influence all architectural and urban production there.
6. These are national heroes of the communist revolt in the Brazilian army in the mid-1930s.
7. Implementation of Project Lakefront is the responsibility of Orla S/A, a company whose board of directors is formed of representatives from twenty-four civil construction firms, the Sindicato da Indústria da Construção Civil (Civil Construction Industry Union), and the Agência de Desenvolvimento do Tocantins (Tocantins State Development Agency).

CHAPTER 3

The Vertical Cityscape in São Paulo
The Influence of Modernism in Urban Design

Silvio Soares Macedo

Verticalization has become a dominant factor influencing urban form in many Brazilian cities. This essay considers the isolated tower on a lot and the complex of towers in a block as the hegemonic models that resulted from the Brazilian modernist paradigm, and discusses how they have configured São Paulo's contemporary cityscape. This verticalization process and the models they generate for private open space around the towers—with shared facilities and elaborate landscaping—have been adopted in all Brazilian cities. Verticalization introduces new forms of dwellings and a new relationship to open space and the city.

São Paulo, Brazil's largest city with a population of ten million, sets the standard for the country and most cities emulate what happens there. In São Paulo the verticalization process is based on the urban planning legislation and zoning code enacted in 1971, and also on the planning models adopted by the real estate market. These regulations began to limit radically the construction of extremely tall buildings, which required very large lots or the annexation of several small lots. Mandatory setbacks and other land-use regulations restricted a house's or tower's footprint to 50 percent site coverage in most of the city. These limitations defined a development model of a tall building standing isolated on its lot, in sharp contrast to the previous building codes, which specified little or no setbacks and allowed high lot coverage and floor area ratios.

The Vertical Cityscape: The Case of São Paulo

Verticalization is the construction and configuration of buildings with more than three floors dedicated to residential, commercial, and service activities. All buildings of more than five floors are considered towers, provided that they are separated from neighboring buildings. The Brazilian contemporary verticalization process is most generally based on the building isolated on a lot. Only in some central areas of traditional cities and in the capital, Brasília, do existing regulations permit tall buildings (of more than five floors) with no setbacks (side yards) between them.

Only in the last decade of the twentieth century did the verticalization process begin sporadically to reach suburban areas—both low- and high-income areas—sometimes achieving substantial urban networks.[1] Until the 1980s the only tall buildings that could usually be found in the suburbs were government-built low-income housing complexes following modernist precepts; these standardized buildings had no more than three stories and sat in the midst of large, unorganized open spaces, with limited retail and social facilities. In contrast, the regulation of office and apartment towers in central and elite areas of the principal cities and state capitals has been a tradition in Brazil since the beginning of the twentieth century. This type of regulation was later generalized to cities throughout the country in response to constant urban growth, to the expansion of government action over urban space and form, and to the growing demand for tall apartment buildings, until it became common in the 1960s.

Building setbacks; limits on building heights, lot coverage, and paving; on-site tree-planting requirements; and floor area ratios were the most utilized regulations in zoning ordinances in Brazilian cities, and they all promoted the modernist model of the single tower isolated on a lot. These regulations derived from the modernist paradigm that was consolidated in the country between 1930 and 1950 and was fully embraced at the time of the plan for the new capital, Brasília. Brasília's residential superblocks, with their geometric siting of buildings and the resulting cityscape, became a singular symbol of the success of modernism. This is particularly clear in Brasília's Asa Sul (South Wing) of the Pilot Plan, where the most consolidated residential sectors are located (fig. 3.1).

The modernist model was seen as a remedy to the high densities of the central areas of São Paulo and of Rio de Janeiro's Copacabana residential district, where the apartment and office towers inspired by the traditional morphology of European cities caused significant environmental problems and generated a very dense urban space with insufficient space for ventilation, sunlight, and recreation. Copacabana is perhaps the best example of the consolidation of the perimeter block pattern, with its

Figure 3.1. One of Brasília's early *superquadras,* showing the mature landscaping and the local commercial center (on the left of the photo). (Photo by the author, Projeto Quapá)

small amount of private open space and only the beachfront, a unique type of public open space, providing an escape valve for the residents.

During the 1960s and 1970s, increasing government control over urban development introduced strict land-use regulations in several Brazilian cities. In Florianópolis, the capital of Santa Catarina state, for instance, building height limits were set at twelve stories in the downtown and four in the suburbs. In Salvador, Bahia, staggered height limits were adopted, from lower heights along the seashore to higher toward the inner city. São Paulo's 1995 land-use regulations reduced the floor area ratio from 16 to 4 in downtown, making it the same as in the rest of the city. On Avenida Paulista, the city's most important business artery, rigorous legislation limited buildings to twenty-four stories and imposed restrictive floor area and lot coverage ratios, which generated a cityscape of relatively low tower blocks in comparison to Chicago's Michigan Avenue (the Magnificent Mile) or New York's Fifth Avenue, streets which hold similar functions and symbolism (fig. 3.2).

Within a thirty-year time period (from the 1960s to the 1990s) these building codes led to a national "verticalization standard" that, in fact, limits the height of towers in Brazilian cities. It is difficult to find the legal and economic conditions necessary for buildings of more than thirty or forty floors or for paired skyscrapers, a form common in Rio and São Paulo in the first half of the twentieth century. This limitation results from the high cost of urban land in areas potentially available for the construction of towers, since the real estate market tends to develop these structures in consolidated areas that are already endowed with good urban infrastructure.

Although the verticalization process is regulated by local governments, it is controlled by the actions of private agents and land developers. Eventually, it may be controlled by the state government through their agencies and low-cost housing initiatives which, in turn, have to rely on private construction companies to build their projects. Land developers influence where verticalization will occur by seeking to place apartment buildings in areas where the return will be the highest. Obviously, urbanistic concerns are not their first priority. Verticalization driven by high returns happened, for example, with the construction of the subway in São Paulo, which generated extensive verticalization corridors along the routes of all lines.[2]

In Rio de Janeiro, the government-sponsored master plan by Lucio Costa for Barra da Tijuca and the urbanization of its beachfront are other examples of the influence of land developers. In this case, in support of private capital, the city and the state of Rio built all the urban infrastructure, improved roads connecting to the rest of the city, constructed a beautiful boulevard along the beachfront, and induced the development of what is today one of the most dynamic areas of urban expansion, property development, and verticalization in Rio de Janeiro. Ample public investments were also directed to improve roads and facilitate tourism to beaches in Florianópolis,

Figure 3.2. Avenida Paulista, São Paulo's most important commercial street, where heights are relatively low due to land-use restrictions. (Photo by the author, Projeto Quapá)

Santa Catarina state, setting in place an intense process of private development and verticalization along the coast.

The cyclical variations in the property market truly direct this process, which in turn depends exclusively on the country's and city's socioeconomic situation. Times of economic crisis lead to a reduction in investments and their concentration in the most stable segments of the market—namely, development of buildings for high-income customers; meanwhile, investments in low-income housing are restricted and often limited to traditional public housing projects funded by state enterprises and agencies. The buying power of consumers, which varies over time; government action through land-use legislation and direct intervention; and the action of development corporations—all these define the location and distribution of urban verticalization in the city's territory. In central areas and their immediate surroundings endowed with good urban infrastructure—that is, in already consolidated neighborhoods of the middle and upper classes—isolated residential towers and groups of towers in gated communities have become the most common real estate development product. In contrast, state public housing agencies supply the low-income population with large-scale projects of walk-up apartments in suburbs far from jobs and most city comforts, where land is cheap. Not unusually these housing projects open new fronts for urban growth, squatter settlements, and pirate subdivisions in areas that are devoid of infrastructure such as water, paving, and electricity.

Radically altering the configuration of the cityscape, this continuously evolving process is not homogenous in space and time because it is linked to the market, its fluctuations, and the availability of land. When faced with shrinking opportunities in existing development fronts, the property market itself creates new standards of desirability through the media, marketing imaginary places and social symbols in an attempt to create new development fronts and encourage the consumption of its products. Thus, the real estate market builds value in areas of the city that are still relatively marginal to the processes of urban valuation and verticalization.

These new values are created independent of the environmental, urbanistic, and topographic qualities of a place itself. New verticalization processes then emanate from these nuclei, and depending on market conditions, may or may not consolidate. There are extreme cases where, in order to add value to his product, a real-estate developer sponsors the paving and landscaping of streets, and the painting of walls and housing around his project area.

These principal expansion fronts of the verticalization process are neither stable nor unique, because the process tends to spread out across the city's territory. In a specific moment of a city's evolution, verticalization may be concentrated in one or two places. Then it may leapfrog to new fronts, and later return to the initial development areas. This instability and flux in the process over time is relatively independent of normative and regulatory policies governing the construction of urban space.

There are few cases in Brazil, such as in Brasília and Rio de Janeiro's Barra da Tijuca, where entrepreneurial investment follows verticalization guidelines significantly predetermined in an urban plan. Lucio Costa's design for Barra da Tijuca, for instance, resulted in rigorous building codes that produced spaces where one can clearly perceive the limits of the verticalized areas, the differences in maximum allowed building heights, and the groups of skyscrapers marking the landscape (see fig. I.8 in the introduction).

Usually, existing land-use codes merely establish generic norms that generate shapeless spaces through restrictive regulations that concentrate on the lot and the building or on the territorial distribution of functions. This is true of the majority of established building codes and land-use zoning regulations. The first basically specify dimensions and habitability of buildings, while the second refer only superficially to the quality and configuration of urban space and concentrate on land-use specifications and distribution. They both ignore structures that are culturally consolidated in the community, such as morphological patterns and the architectural typology of existing neighborhoods.

The Brazilian verticalization process is directly related to the transformation and renewal of existing urban areas, whether they are located in the central city or in tourist areas. In the latter, high-rise apartments have been an important option for summer vacationers while simultaneously becoming a secure economic investment for the middle and upper classes in times of high inflation. Between 1960 and 1990 the property market invested heavily in apartment towers in cities along the Brazilian coastline, and in all of them, the traditional perimeter block design of Rio de Janeiro was abandoned in favor of the building isolated on its lot (fig. 3.3).

Figure 3.3. Verticalization and residential tower blocks in Bertioga, a costal resort in the state of São Paulo. (Photo by the author, Projeto Quapá)

New Typologies and the Market

In Brazil's large cities, the verticalization process is relatively more intense, and it is in these markets that new architectural and residential typologies are tested by private developers. Once these products have been accepted by local consumers, they are gradually "exported" to smaller cities and more diverse urban situations. Higher income groups buy into apartment blocks in neighborhoods that are considered elegant and have unique features, such as luxury towers in lush green landscaping—some of which are true landmarks. Middle-class groups move into less well-equipped towers with a greater number of apartments, emulating the rich as closely as possible. In reality, middle-class residents are spread throughout the city—living in dwellings ranging from small condominiums on the city edges to tall towers near the city center—as they seek in some way to adopt, even if in simplified form, the housing patterns of the elite. The rest of the urban population and the lower classes occupy much more modest apartment buildings, simply constructed and generally not tall, located in distant or older neighborhoods.

The diagrams in figure 3.4 represent the types of apartment buildings commonly found in Brazilian cities.

Consumer needs and demands evolve as new products appear on the market, so that solutions which were acceptable as little as ten years ago may have little appeal nowadays or may even be considered unacceptable. This is true, for example, in the efforts to market new apartment buildings in São Paulo featuring facilities that were not in demand a few years ago: the majority now contain at least a playground and a large

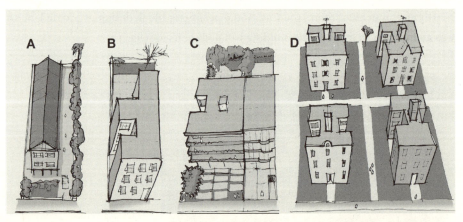

Figure 3.4. The most common types of apartment buildings in Brazil: (*A*) small apartment building on *pilotis* (columns with the ground floor open); (*B*) apartment building with small setback; (*C*) four-story building with balconies; and (*D*) the small buildings for the working classes common all over the country. (Drawing by the author)

Figure 3.5. The modernist model of residential tower blocks resulting from city building regulations and real-estate market pressures is marking Brazilian cities. This is a view from a suburb in São Paulo. (Photo by the author, Projeto Quapá)

landscaped area for recreation, and a large number offer a sports field and a swimming pool. All are surrounded by a perimeter wall or fence with guarded entry gates.

The development process is flexible and responds to the changing needs of the moment and to the availability of technologies and capital. Little by little, it alters the final configuration of the housing products that are offered. As new construction technologies are introduced, buildings rise in height and new political pressures lobby for increases in indexes for urban land use. In contrast to the first skyscrapers built in São Paulo in the 1920s—few of which had more than ten stories—nowadays apartment towers twenty, or even forty, stories high are fully accepted by consumers. Verticalization now is typified by the variety of heights of new apartment towers (fig. 3.5).

This process of urban transformation results in new cityscapes and new ways of configuring and using urban space. For the majority of the population, it generates new ways of looking at housing. It induces new forms of living and different ways of using open spaces, creating new patterns and whole neighborhoods, altering lifestyles and social habits,.

Inside the lots, these new typologies generate new relations to the street space. The access to the apartment building and the dwelling units is now privatized and highly guarded, and the elevators, parking areas, gardens, and other amenities become social spaces because they belong to a group of families—the condominium residents.[3] In these developments, neighborly interactions—such as the traditional chat over the garden wall or on the sidewalk—are extinct and the possibility of an individual altering the open space next to his or her dwelling is almost nil since the development belongs collectively to all the owners as a shared property. Throughout these new urban spaces, the resulting built form follows rigid standards, and each site is closed in on itself and subdivided into functionally adequate areas following a more or less pre-established arrangement. These arrangements are similar in all parts of the city, differences being determined by the available credit of consumers (residents), producers (developers, financial institutions, and so on), and landowners.

Each city has some unique standards for the vertical arrangement of buildings on a lot. These depend on municipal land-use regulations, which are always a product of an ideal model of livability, as well as of the variations in the local property market. What may be observed in all medium-sized and small cities across Brazil is however an extrapolation of the model and land-use standards of large cities. Even in distant places such as Belém (state of Pará, Amazon region) or Cuiabá (state of Mato Grosso, in the central region), one sees residential developments whose architecture and landscaping are designed by São Paulo or Rio firms as they would be for these markets.

São Paulo: A Model of Verticalization

In contrast with Rio, where in the 1920s verticalization spread from the city center out to the neighborhoods along the valleys and the southern coastline, in São Paulo and in the other large Brazilian cities, tower blocks were concentrated in the downtown area until the 1940s. Verticalization then started to appear in specific locations in other districts, particularly those of the upper classes, such as Avenida São Luís, in the Higienópolis neighborhood.[4] Unlike in Rio de Janeiro, where building styles were inspired by traditional European urban architecture, in São Paulo the model for siting an apartment block on its lot and for the open space around it was the stand-alone tower on *pilotis* surrounded by beautifully landscaped gardens.

First adopted in high-income areas such as Higienópolis and the "garden" districts, this model eventually caught on and led to verticalization in other parts of the city, particularly the southwest. Tower blocks were first allowed in restricted areas and along arteries until market pressures expanded the verticalization process across the city. As large urban areas were renovated, old structures and spaces were replaced, new cityscapes were configured, and new standards and forms were established and disseminated. In these lots, open spaces are standardized functionally and formally by the city codes and the patterns defined by the market, even though a large part of urban daily life flows through them. As a result, nowadays São Paulo has a homogenous cityscape and a predictable morphology within which foci of renewal and mutation appear relatively unpredictably in relation to norms and regulations.

The design fundamentals for the siting of built forms, particularly of apartment tower blocks, are based on an idealized lot, not surprisingly following a modernist approach to urbanism that is responsive to market demands. The land subdivision is the sole physical support driving design, whereas topography and site configurations—such as slopes or horizontal and vertical planes—are only marginally considered. As the idealized lot for vertical buildings is always perfectly flat, the real estate market and the land-use regulations seek to impose this ideal model across the city.

In verticalized residential development open spaces tend toward spatial fragmentation and sophisticated specialization of use that depend on the buying power of residents. An increasing percentage of the population is closing itself off from the city by buying into walled projects and gated communities, a phenomenon spurred by urban violence, which has increased significantly in São Paulo since the 1980s.[5] This situation favors an imbalance in the treatment and availability of public open space, and favors higher-income neighborhoods.

At the same time, impelled by the property market and favored by legislation, large gated communities are built throughout the city. Referred to in planning jargon as "residential complexes," they facilitate the private appropriation of public space: the street becomes a space for the exclusive use of the residents, and the development re-creates the appearance of a closed, private mini-club. Large gated communities respond to the need for public open spaces for recreation—such as the traditional public squares or parks—by providing these facilities within the controlled private environment. This decreases the demand for new open and publicly accessible spaces for recreation among an increasing segment of the population. The new residential model re-creates spaces for "socialization" and recreation inside its restrictive walls. The resulting open spaces tend toward a dispersed, fragmented, specialized, and privatized design, since the city regulations are too general to control their specific design. It is the property market itself that creates the new models of the cityscape (fig. 3.6).

In São Paulo, as well as in many other Brazilian cities, the verticalization process adds to the destruction of the existing physical structure, natural site, and vegetation. The stain of verticalization sprawls through the most diverse locations; buildings with

Figure 3.6. In São Paulo, as in all major Brazilian cities, large, vertical gated communities are a popular residential option and provide many amenities within the confines of their walls. (Photo by the author, Projeto Quapá)

similar height and form can be seen all over, from floodplains to mountain ridges and steep slopes. From the spurs of the Serra da Cantareira range on the north to the edges of the reservoirs on the south, every residential tower block carries the same siting precepts, whether on flat or sloping terrain, on lowlands or hills.

Articulation between Buildings and Open Spaces

The opposition between public open spaces and private open spaces (those contained within a lot) appeared with the construction of the first apartment buildings and skyscrapers. In the beginning of the verticalization process, between 1920 and 1950, open spaces resulted from patios or shafts that provided ventilation and natural lighting to windows and terraces. More luxurious buildings had parking provided at the back of the lot in a patio or backyard. The building footprint would cover the largest possible percentage of the lot, with walls coinciding with property lines and touching the neighboring buildings.

The street space was defined by continuous vertical planes of buildings—long stretches of juxtaposed façades interrupted only by street intersections. This was the model favored by the first land-use regulations, which led to the intensely vertical configuration of the residential districts. Good examples are found in São Paulo, Rio de Janeiro, and most Brazilian cities, where verticalization occurred through renovation of residential districts into higher-density development following a pattern that radiated outward from the city center.

This process started earlier in Rio de Janeiro, beginning in the downtown, moving next to the waterfront, then consolidating a vertical cityscape along the valleys and the shore. Copacabana, a popular neighborhood from the 1920s to the 1940s, is the prototypical result of this process, with its rows of attached high-rises that make streets look like canyons. In Copacabana, the disadvantages of this high-density model are compensated for by the proximity of the beach—a truly linear park of sand and water—around which city life flows.

In São Paulo the process was slower, expanding to the residential neighborhoods immediately around the central area only in the 1950s and 1960s, when the new land-use models were already being adopted. Slowly, the model of the building as a solitary tower block inside the lot set back from the street and the property lines—in contradiction to the old city patterns—became the rule. By this time, the whole country was embracing the modern movement, which would see its peak in the formal synthesis represented by the construction of Brasília in 1960.

From the 1950s, landscaping began to be used as a design element in front of the buildings in upper- and middle-class neighborhoods of São Paulo, a pattern that was to spread to the rest of Brazil. Nowadays, it is hard to find an apartment building that does not offer at least a modest front garden since consumers like this feature. This model was generated by the front setback mandated in the current land-use code, which applies to most of the city. In addition, setbacks are recommended—and mandated in many areas—for the sides and back of the lot, which reproduces the model of the isolated building on a lot.

The sizes of building setbacks—and therefore of open spaces—vary according to the size and configuration of the lot, the zone of the city, and the standards of the property market. Influenced by the minimum setback requirements in the land-use code, around the 1970s a new trend slowly appeared: in addition to the gardens, a series of outdoor recreational facilities began to be provided by developers. Initially, playgrounds became popular, then tables and benches, and now swimming pools are considered almost indispensable. Today, the majority of residential real-estate developments under construction in São Paulo have swimming pools. A panoply of other facilities have followed, such as multi-sport fields and tennis courts, jogging tracks, kiosks, gazebos, pergolas, covered pools, fountains, and so on (fig. 3.7). Each of these new items is first introduced and tested in verticalized areas for high-income customers, before it is slowly adopted throughout the city and in areas where the verticalization process is still expanding.

Between the 1970s and 1990s in São Paulo, a new urban model started to con-

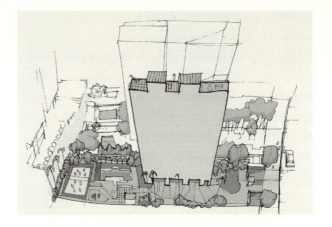

Figure 3.7. Diagram of a typical residential tower in the middle of a lot in São Paulo, showing the private amenities and landscaped spaces. (Drawing by the author)

solidate: the "lot-block"—a large vertical condominium complex occupying a whole city block or most of one. Within the complex, buildings are designed more freely as the model does not require them to face the street or to parallel the lot boundaries. These condominiums are truly superblocks or "neighborhood units" in the modernist sense, and the market expects them to provide open space and all sorts of facilities, which most do. This model emerged first in only a few specific areas of São Paulo, but now it can be found everywhere.

Norms, Codes, and Spaces: The Case of São Paulo

Based on the official model implied in the land-use code of the 1970s, the minimum unit for urban land subdivision is the building lot. Laws that govern land use influence the lot development and the habitability of the building. One would expect that the same code would also guarantee the quality of the open spaces; however, it guarantees only the *existence* of open space through indexes such as floor area ratios, mandatory setbacks, and maximum lot coverage, which in reality standardize the open spaces.

The code guarantees that a minimum amount of open space exists in all lots—the standard being 50 percent of the lot area. If developers opt to provide more open space and recreational facilities, the code allows them to build higher. However, the quality of these open spaces is not regulated. Such land-use codes derived from the modernist model and the design of Brasília, but they are nothing more than a fragmented interpretation of the capital's buildings sited in superblocks amidst landscaped areas. The residential towers in São Paulo and most Brazilian cities represent a distillation of this ideal model adapted to the market and to the traditional urban grid. Because the verticalization process of Brazilian cities expanded after the 1950s, it is easy to identify the direct influence of the modernist spatial patterns and design solutions of Brasília in mid- and high-rise neighborhoods and city sectors throughout the country.

The construction of Brasília promoted the building isolated on the lot as an ideal model for urban development and influenced all types of buildings—commercial, industrial, and residential. However, although it has been continuously adapted to the conventional city, Brasília's original modernist model places value on and is integrally designed to coordinate with the surrounding open spaces, as well as valuing the quality of the final urban landscape, even if it negates the traditional city.

The Plano Diretor de Desenvolvimento Integrado do Município de São Paulo (PDDI; Integrated Development Master Plan of the Municipality of São Paulo), adopted in 1972, clearly shows this contradiction in its major goal: "To create and maintain an urban environment that provides the population with access to urban functions of life, mobility, work, and development of the body and spirit." Like all the others, this goal is obviously modeled on the Charter of Athens and the principles of modern urbanism. And although the plan places the preservation of the environment as a fundamental starting point for urban development, it never really defines what that environment is, and consequently this ideal is never reached. In 2003, more than thirty years after the adoption of the PDDI, it is easy to observe the high degree of transformation in the city and its environs, and how and where environmental considerations have been neglected.

The plan employed two basic instruments for implementation: zoning—used in São Paulo for the first time—and indexes to control the placement of the building on the lot. The notion of the opposition between built and unbuilt spaces was also present in these instruments. One of the PDDI's resulting regulatory mandates explained the concept of zoning as the process "orienting and controlling the localization, dimensioning, intensity, and the kind of use of lots and buildings, as well as the control of relationships *between built spaces and unbuilt spaces*" (my italics) (Law 7668, 1971).

This control of relationships is accomplished through two principal standards of occupation: the coefficient of lot use and the rate of land occupation, both of which vary according to the usage zone in their locations. These two indexes determine the obligatory setbacks, based on the idea of guaranteeing in each lot the existence of 20 to 88 percent open space.

The setbacks merely orient and direct the spatial organization inside the lots. Like other indexes, they do not contain any specifications that would guarantee the quality of the open space. An analysis of the formal definition of the objectives of urban setbacks clearly reveals the necessity to regulate the quality of open spaces, independently of but complementary with these indexes. In the legislation, the stated purposes of setbacks are "to guarantee adequate conditions of aeration and illumination; to avoid one building's encroachment on another; to provide security for children in their play area; to give space to adults for entertainment; to reduce risks and fires; to ensure space for trees, vegetation, and gardens; and to provide a healthy and secure environment." The spatial boundaries of the lot are established on these principles.

After enactment of the PDDI, the city of São Paulo was first divided into eight land-use zones, then redivided into eighteen the following decade. Each had its own characteristics and specific rules for the treatment of lots, including setbacks, occupation rates, and indexes of usage. The cityscape is divided into two types of areas: horizontal and those subject to verticalization.

Horizontal Areas

High-income housing is consolidated and regulated in four types of residential zones restricted to low-density use where apartment buildings are prohibited. This zoning includes the "garden" neighborhoods of the early twentieth century, where single homes or duplexes sit on lots of at least 2,000 square meters (21,600 square feet), artesian springs are protected, lots are well landscaped, and, in general, tree-lined

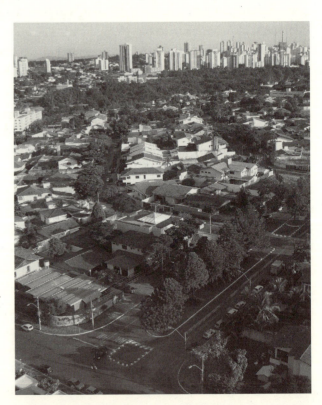

Figure 3.8. Strict land-use restrictions preserve Jardim Europa, one of São Paulo's garden districts, from the verticalization process occurring around it. (Photo by the author, Projeto Quapá)

streets have wide, landscaped sidewalks. Districts of this type are extensive and concentrated in the south and west of the urban complex and in the Serra da Cantareira, the mountains north of the city. Figure 3.8 shows one of the most famous and consolidated high-income neighborhoods of the city, which is surrounded by completely verticalized areas.

This zoning category also includes industrial areas that occupy extensive flat areas along the principal valleys and rivers that shape the city: Tamanduatei, Tietê, and Pinheiros. The industrial zones are crisscrossed by rail lines connecting the city with the interior and the coast. Here, housing is practically nonexistent, and tall buildings are the exception.

Areas Subject to Verticalization

This category accounts for the remainder of São Paulo's city perimeter, including the great majority of zones in which land use ranges from predominantly low-density residential to predominantly industrial, where housing may exist only under municipal control.

Areas without Direct Controls on Building Height
In these zones, the construction of apartment towers is permitted and maximum heights are dependent on the availability of land and on market conditions. Here, controls are exercised only indirectly through floor area and lot coverage ratios. Setbacks are valued by the real estate market since the modernist model is popular with consumers. Throughout the city, the new zoning legislation would lead to entire areas being exposed to urban renewal and severe transformations, even where pre-existing morphologies were clearly identical to those of the high-income garden neighborhoods.

Transition Zones
Created by the zoning legislation as formal buffers between zones occupied by horizontal neighborhoods and other zones, the transition zones are the only ones where verticalization is allowed but building heights are controlled and limited to twenty-five meters or nine stories. These are typically residential zones, although a variety of other uses are permitted, such as retail, service, and institutional uses.

Even in areas where the maximum height of buildings is not specifically defined, the verticalization process is regulated indirectly through a maximum allowed floor area ratio, which is 4. Consequently, due to high land and construction costs and the limitations of the consumer market, developers will rarely build high towers since the size of lot necessary for such a building makes it a risky and costly endeavor. Thus, apartment and office towers in São Paulo tend to be limited to thirty floors, with only a few exceptions.

These zoning mechanisms and indexes favor the institutionalization of a building standard: the tower block that is set back from the lot boundaries, if not on the ground floor, then at least from the third floor up. Replaced by this new model, the attached buildings and the morphologies of the traditional city are left behind, symbols of another legislation and of a distant past.

Created Scenarios

The standard model today is a tower or a complex of apartment buildings—two, three, or more—amidst landscaped areas with ball courts, swimming pools, and other recreational facilities, and surrounded by walls, gates, and guard towers. Formally, some situations stand out:

The tower block set back from the lot edges from the second floor up, on top of a ground-floor parking garage that covers the whole lot surface. Open spaces for leisure, services, and so on, may be placed on top of this platform or at street level.

The tower block completely isolated on the lot and set back from all neighbors with the resulting unbuilt spaces occupied by access ways, patios, and gardens; all building façades are parallel to the sides of the lot.

The tower block isolated on its lot but whose façades are not necessarily parallel to the property boundaries; open spaces and natural lighting conditions vary with the site.

Innumerable variations of these three basic models exist, but the design of the resulting open spaces in the lot will always tend toward the following patterns:

Distribution of space in corridors for access and vehicular circulation, leisure, and services, and patios for recreation, services, gardens, and so on.

Sectioning off of specific areas for leisure and recreation. An example is the formally defined playground, separate from the front garden and other recreational areas.

Maximum occupation of the lot, with parking underground, behind the building, or often along the sides and back of the lot.

Landscaping of the verticalized lot became the rule in São Paulo and in the rest of the country. Since the building's internal architecture is generally standardized, the façades and open spaces become fundamental in increasing a development's market value. Landscaping as scenery, in the manner of old European gardens matching the buildings' architectural blend between Italian and French neoclassic, for instance, has strong consumer appeal. Pergolas, fountains, gazebos, and topiaries are placed alongside facilities such as swimming pools, sports courts, and playgrounds. Postmodern porticos, romantic lawns, and vaguely English-style flowerbeds are also common.

Open spaces may also be landscaped in what might be called a tropical style, with lush vegetation and pavements with colored cobblestones set in wavy or geometric patterns. Prevalent throughout São Paulo and the rest of the country, this kind of landscaping is a formal and conceptual derivation from the modernist projects of the 1960s and 1970s, a time when romantic and classical ornaments were deemed unfashionable.

In any case, these examples are no more than a reflection of a current urban phenomenon. As the density and verticalization of the city increase, streets lose their traditional qualities as spaces for leisure and social encounters, and become primarily used for circulation and parking, and for pedestrian and vehicular access to the apartment blocks. Public squares and parks and open spaces within private parcels are then expected to make up for the loss of the street as a social space. In São Paulo parks and public squares are few, poorly distributed in relation to demand, and concentrated in only a handful of neighborhoods.

To some extent unbuilt spaces in verticalized lots compensate for this situation but they solidify the privatization of collective recreation into the interiors of blocks, lots, and gated communities, stripping the street of its multiuse character and recasting it as a mere conduit for access and circulation.

The Vertical Landscape and Growth Vectors

The skyline of any city divided into generically defined zones, as São Paulo is, will always be difficult to understand through simply studying any one zone. Each zone may take on a form—a specific spatial configuration—as a function of the different tendencies of urban development. In the city of São Paulo, simple observation and even a superficial study will not allow us to distinguish the different forms of spatial organization that characterize specific zones. A pattern is clear only when one enters a garden neighborhood whose spatial structure is characterized by predominantly low-density residential use in a horizontal and profusely landscaped cityscape. In other areas differences are more subtle and the cityscape seems to be the same. The basic difference lies not in the structures themselves but in the possibilities that they offer for functional diversity. Even variations in lot coverage and floor area ratios are often difficult for a layperson to perceive.

In its verticalized landscape, São Paulo presents three basic types of skylines:

A skyline where tower blocks stand out—these are areas where the morphology is strictly characterized by tall buildings.

A skyline where one- and two-story homes prevail—areas where the verticalization process is still incipient.

A mixed skylines, typical in areas under transformation or urban renewal. Constituting the majority of recently verticalized areas, these areas are characterized by a highly fragmented urban fabric as structures from different epochs coexist side by side.

These profiles are structured around some forms of spatial arrangement and tower blocks:

Residential developments set homogenously on their lots. Typical in the suburbs, this arrangement is composed of low buildings with fewer than five stories, with similar volumes and small setbacks.

Mixed profiles with towers of different heights—for example, four, eight, and twelve stories. Like in the previous type, buildings are isolated from one another. These first two types are common throughout the suburbs.

Tall residential buildings developed in clusters of two, three, or even four, which are found throughout the city in all types of neighborhoods.

Tall residential buildings developed in large clusters of more than five units, which generally occupy an entire city block.

Large, solidly built streetscapes composed of isolated units. These are typical of the densely verticalized areas of the city, such as the neighborhoods of Jardins, Moema, Itaim, Perdizes, and Tatuapé.

In the city as a whole, the rows of towers aligned side by side for block after block form large morphological structures where the building—the individual unit—loses its identity to the whole. These aggregations extend through extensive areas of the metropolis and occur in two basic forms:

Verticalized stains—groups of verticalized city blocks that spread out in all directions.

Verticalized lines, where the development of tower blocks follows a linear pattern along one or more streets—often along a ridge that defines a growth vector. These lines are unstable, however, because as the development process consolidates, the high buildings themselves tend to foster the construction of new towers around them, forming verticalized stains (fig. 3.9).

Figure 3.9. A verticalized line in São Paulo's cityscape, following a major artery. (Photo by the author, Projeto Quapá)

Conclusion

More than three decades have passed since the approval of urban legislation regulating verticalization in São Paulo in 1972. This legislation influenced the city's spatial organization by generating ample and generous private open spaces, fostering construction of shared facilities in such spaces, guaranteeing side and front setbacks that allow sunlight and ventilation to reach residential and commercial units, encouraging the creation of corporate plazas, increasing parking, and discouraging excessively tall buildings.

On the other hand, most of the urban territory was left open for verticalization, regardless of the parcel's location, the capacity of street access, the characteristics of the neighborhood, or the existing physical structure. In such areas, legislation allows more than 80 percent of the lot surface to be impermeable and allows the natural elements of the site to be destroyed. The various urban areas where development is well consolidated show similar and homogenous morphological configurations. And it is the property market that in fact decides where and when verticalization will occur.

During these years there were constant alterations in the zoning legislation, including the opening of new areas to verticalization—with height controls—on the edges of garden neighborhoods and horizontal residential areas.

Radical changes in the development process were implemented with the new legislation, which replaced the old planning standards that had favored high towers and did not privilege open spaces for gardens, recreation, and leisure inside the lots. The isolated tower block became the new planning model, and zoning was the tool for its implementation.

The gains were considerable and the same model was adopted in the majority of cities in Brazil, although usually with fewer limitations on building height or with smaller setbacks. In small- and medium-sized cities in the states of Rio Grande do Sul, São Paulo, and Paraná, buildings are very close together and overbuilding has caused severe environmental problems. In coastal cities such as Recife, the capital of Pernambuco, apartment towers along the beachfront reach up to forty floors and shade the beach in the afternoon. Nevertheless, living in tower buildings has become a common and desired lifestyle in the Brazilian urban context, one that is fully accepted by all income groups and has morphologically structured extensive urban areas in the whole country.

The urban mechanisms to regulate high-density housing in Brazilian cities were primarily created during the second half of the twentieth century, and one can argue that they are the most enduring and well-realized expressions of the modernist paradigm. As the case of São Paulo has demonstrated, these mechanisms need to be revised. If they were adequate for major functional and environmental improvements in the 1970s, by the end of the twentieth century they were already quite out of date in terms of the current property market, existing urban demands, and in particular, environmental needs.

A city's spatial morphology is still underappreciated in Brazil, and it has been regulated only in special situations, such as in the plans for Brasília and for Barra da Tijuca in Rio de Janeiro, both of them government endeavors in times of highly centralized decision making processes. The verticalization processes that act upon Brazilian cities demand a re-evaluation of their morphological and social effects, which have historically been segregation, excessive privatization of open spaces, and significant environmental problems. Control of urban development and the verticalization of the cityscape in São Paulo are clear examples of these pressing needs.

Notes

1. It is important to note that development patterns of suburbs in Brazil are quite different from those in the United States. The peripheries of cities have been developed in a more haphazard and uncontrolled manner, and are largely occupied by low-income groups. Uncontrolled development, lack of urban services, and pirate land subdivisions mark the Brazilian suburban environment. Only in the last decades of the twentieth century have middle- and upper-income groups started to move into gated communities and subdivisions in the suburbs of big cities.

2. In 2004, the São Paulo subway system had three lines in operation along more than fifty-seven kilometers (thirty-four miles), with fifty-two stations, many of which are multimodal—integrated with train and local and regional bus stations (see the São Paulo state government site at www.metro.sp.gov.br).

3. Editors' note: The *condomínio* is a traditional form of property in Brazil, where owners have exclusive ownership (and use) of individual units and share the rest of the property. Popularly, the word *condomínio* is applied to a gated community.

4. Editors' note: See the essay by Bruna and Vargas (chapter 4) in this book, which in part discusses Higienópolis.

5. See Caldeira (2000) on violence and spatial segregation in São Paulo.

The Shopping Centers Shaping the Brazilian City
Two Case Studies in São Paulo

Gilda Collet Bruna and

Heliana Comin Vargas

In only about forty years, since the first one was inaugurated in 1966, shopping centers have become a dominant feature of the Brazilian urbanscape. In Brazil, shopping centers took the form of large retail complexes—which normally include anchor stores—under a single roof and with dedicated parking facilities. Now, after four decades, we can start evaluating their importance to city development and to urban design. In this essay we analyze the Brazilian version of the shopping center through two significant examples built more than thirty years apart in the city of São Paulo: Iguatemi (1966) and Pátio Higienópolis (1999). We will analyze their roles in contributing to new growth vectors within the city structure, in defining new poles of development, in generating changes in land use, and in appreciating surrounding land values, as well as their effects on the morphology and the vitality of the city.

Brazil is among the top five countries in number of shopping centers, although it still lags far behind the countries that head the list (Clemente 1997). More than the number of existing enterprises, however, the rapidity of this phenomenon since the mid-1980s and the volume of investments dedicated to the sector—which is out of proportion to the growth in Brazilians' buying power—point toward a change in the direction of property investments away from the residential and toward the retail and service sectors. This move occurs not only because of a true expansion of these sectors, but also as a result of an increase in income and buying power of the population.

The diverse types of retail complexes that claim the status of shopping center make a quantitative analysis of this sector difficult. The two important retail trade associations representing shopping centers in Brazil define "shopping center" differently. According to the Brazilian Association of Shopping Centers (ABRASCE) there were 346 shopping centers in Brazil in 2004, whereas the Association of Shopping Center Store Owners (ALSHOP) registered 579 in operation and another 51 under construction.[1] According to ALSHOP, by far the heaviest concentration of centers (33 percent) is located in São Paulo state, and the city of São Paulo alone has thirty-three centers. Whichever association's figures we consider, these numbers demonstrate the great influence that this type of enterprise exercises on the structure and dynamics of Brazilian cities.

Independent of the numerical and conceptual differences in definition, an analysis of the effects of shopping center development on urban structure and design is a fundamental consideration for the quality of the environment. However, complex situations such as these with strong impacts on the urban landscape are difficult to measure properly, in part due to the multiplier effect of the transformations, which cumulatively produce new configurations in the urban fabric.

In any case, we can say that in Brazil shopping centers stimulate several alterations in their surroundings and generate new centralities in the city environment. On the other hand, the great competition among them in the face of a stable or declining consumer market has led them to successive transformations and adaptations in order to satisfy different types of consumers and their new demands.

Shopping Centers in Brazil

Although the Brazilian model incorporates all the concepts of contemporary and global retail, it also promotes its own features adapted to local specificities. The first great difference that arises in Brazil is a result of the lengthy time gap between the appearance of shopping centers in the United States and the construction of the first one in Brazil—the Iguatemi shopping center, which opened in 1966. This alone led Brazilian shopping centers to incorporate a series of innovations from more recent generations of the American and European versions. Interestingly, the Iguatemi shopping center was also a pioneer in renovating and expanding, in order to try to maintain its status as the most profitable and sophisticated center in São Paulo. Only recently has it apparently found a worthy competitor in Pátio Higienópolis, our other case study.

Our discussion is centered on the city of São Paulo not only because of the pioneering nature and the intensity of the shopping center phenomenon there, but also because the city's huge consumer market of more than ten million people is the largest of any city in the nation (SEADE 2000). Thus, São Paulo offers a well-set stage for retail development. The magnitude of its commercial sector allows it to absorb quickly the various forms that its retail outlets assume, permitting us to consider their landmark effects in Brazilian retail development (Vargas 2004).

Before comparing the features of our two case studies, it is relevant to consider a simple typology of the phenomenon of the shopping center in Brazil. We will discuss it as a type of enterprise, its insertion in the urban context, its type of architecture, and its status as a facility that serves the public.

Types of Shopping Centers

Although some aggregations of stores and retail arcades claim shopping center status after they are built, planned shopping centers as they are now known did not result only from an innovation in retailing but also from a promising new vision of property development. Gruen (1962) observed that this vision began when the term "shopping center" was chosen, indicating that the emphasis is on the consumer and not on the seller (store owner), in which case the more appropriate term would be "selling centers." Thus, when shopping centers appeared in Brazil, they adopted the American model of a property development enterprise for shopping.

It is also interesting to observe that, in parallel with shopping center developments in the United States, mixed-use enterprises (combining offices, hotels, apartments, and recreation) started to be developed in the 1930s, the Rockefeller Center (1943) being perhaps the most representative and widely imitated example. As the name implies, however, these enterprises did not focus on retail.

This mixed-use retail typology would reproduce the European modernist concept of the planned buying centers that were built after World War II and as part of the new-town policies: a property development that sought self-sufficiency based on the creation of centralities within the building complex itself. In São Paulo an important example is the Conjunto Nacional on Avenida Paulista, designed in 1955 and inaugurated in 1958 (fig. 4.1).

Insertion in the City Context

In the international context there are three major types of shopping centers in terms of their relationship to the city: (a) out-of-town, (b) downtown, and (c) within-town. The first shopping centers in Brazil were of the last type, built within the consolidated urban fabric and generating the most popular location model, particularly in the São Paulo metropolitan region (Vargas 2001). While these developments were outside the downtown area, they were not located near consumers residing on the peripheries of the city fabric, nor next to highway interchanges, as they are in the United States.

Figure 4.1. The popular Conjunto Nacional on Avenida Paulista in São Paulo. This 1950s modernist project consists of an office tower on top of a shopping arcade that includes restaurants and movie theaters. (Photo by Heliana Vargas)

As a matter of fact, in developing countries such as Brazil, middle- and high-income groups do not reside in the suburbs, which are occupied by low-income families. Only recently and in a new type of suburban development based on gated communities are some middle-class residents moving to the suburbs the way they have in the United States (Caldeira 2000).

The first shopping centers in São Paulo were located either within the urban fabric and near regional centers (as were Iguatemi, Eldorado, North Center, West Plaza, and Penha) or on the urban fringe (as were Continental, Morumbi, Interlagos, and Aricanduva) (Vargas 1992). The first in both these categories—Iguatemi (1966) and Continental (1975)—were built as speculative developments, and it took a number of years (and various business and marketing strategies) for consumers to acquire new purchasing habits and turn them into enterprises successful enough to stimulate new investments. The increasing population density in the surrounding areas and improvements in traffic circulation and in the road system also favored these shopping centers, which were then able to generate their own centralities (Vargas 1992).

Although these first centers experienced a difficult beginning, probably because the city did not initially possess the necessary conditions for their success, in the second half of the 1980s, there was a rapid expansion in the number of shopping centers throughout Brazil, starting in São Paulo (table 4.1). One must bear in mind that although table 4.1 shows the evolution of the sector during the period it does not reflect the true intensity of the phenomenon because it includes only shopping centers affiliated with ABRASCE. Much higher numbers appear in data from ALSHOP. In March 2004, São Paulo state had about a third of the total shopping centers in Brazil—91 in São Paulo versus 253 in the country (according to ABRASCE), or 195 in São Paulo versus 579 in the country (according to ALSHOP).

Table 4.1. The growth of shopping centers in Brazil (1966–2004)

Year	1966	1971	1976	1981	1986	1991	1996	2001	2004
Total shopping centers	1	2	8	16	34	90	147	294	346

Source: ABRASCE website at www.abrasce.com.br; accessed on 07/18/07.

Out-of-town shopping centers with regional characteristics started to be built in the hinterland of São Paulo state only in the late 1980s. Located next to highway junctions, they would attract both travelers and consumers from towns in a wide catchment area. Good examples are the Valley Center in São José dos Campos (1987) and the Galeria in Campinas (1992), both important cities close to São Paulo. Whereas the Valley Center was installed in a converted former factory on the road linking São Paulo to Rio de Janeiro, the Galeria was built on vacant fields because the developers had already discovered the potential for shopping centers to induce urban development. Shopping center developers now promote the shopping center as a destination, foster the appreciation of land in the surrounding areas, and then carry out additional real estate ventures in a new and more valuable urban market.

The location of shopping centers in medium-sized cities such as São José dos Campos and Campinas generates a shift in their centralities and is partially responsible for the deterioration of their central areas. As a matter of fact, these malls offer such amenities as playgrounds and movie theaters, providing a safe and comfortable environment for a variety of activities and leading consumers to prefer them as places of consumption and leisure, to the detriment of traditional leisure centers.

In the case of within-town shopping centers, their location is more heavily dependent on the availability and price of land than on the catchment area, defined in terms of demographics, density, purchasing power, and travel time isochrones. Because of their large size and business strategies these establishments acquire the capacity to create their own privileged locations (Vargas 1992). Many of these developments are coupled with other types of real estate developments from the beginning; for example, residential subdivisions in the cases of Iguatemi and Ibirapuera (1976) shopping centers. Others, controlled by groups of landowners, are located on the periphery of urban areas in order to exploit the resultant appreciation in land values in the surrounding areas. Still others are established in areas that are already undergoing a process of land-use change, such as in old industrial warehouses or department stores.

Unlike in the United States and Europe, where family income is higher and more homogeneous, one can find in Brazil a type of shopping center specifically catering to low-income groups. This type of shopping center started in São Paulo in 1984. Generally anchored by a supermarket or mega-market, its architecture and facilities are of lower quality to cut down on construction and operation costs—for example, by using cheap finishing materials and by not providing air-conditioning in the common areas.

Recently, in the downtowns of São Paulo and other Brazilian cities, more compact shopping centers have started to appear, either through replacing old buildings or through renovating historic buildings. Although the majority of shopping centers still have large parking lots and are oriented toward customers with motor vehicles, in these recent cases accessibility for pedestrians and public transportation—subway and bus lines—also becomes an important factor.

On the other hand, shopping centers in central locations in consolidated parts of the city with greater population densities or near facilities that attract large numbers of people—such as schools and universities—will naturally draw significant numbers of pedestrians. This is the case with Pátio Higienópolis shopping center, one of our case studies, which initially faced a lot of community opposition to its location but eventually became an attractive meeting place for people who live or work in the area.

Shopping Center Design

In terms of construction standards, there are accepted typologies for a mall: covered or uncovered, open-air or enclosed, and with one or more floors. Brazilian shopping centers followed the typology of the third American generation of malls, which closed themselves from the exterior and bore no relationship to their environs. Not only were they surrounded by parking lots—which in time became multistory structures—but they also avoided windows to the outside, even store display windows at street level. This type of "boxed" enterprise, as Vargas (2000) calls it, is common in São Paulo, although the two case studies presented in this essay differ a little from this norm.

Iguatemi shopping center, perhaps because of its excellent design in the first phase, was well integrated with its surroundings, more like downtown centers built for local customers. Nevertheless, as we shall see, its design has been undergoing major modifications in order to respond to consumers' new demands and strong competition from new enterprises. Unfortunately, these modifications are making it more and more similar to all the other "boxes" (fig. 4.2).

In the case of Pátio Higienópolis, because local neighborhood associations strongly opposed its construction, developers sought a dialogue with the community before construction permits were obtained. This led to a design that blends into its surroundings through architectural elements, careful landscaping, and permeability between inside and outside, with bars and restaurants opening to the sidewalk (fig. 4.3). Taking advantage of the site's topography, its multistoried design provides exits to two streets, for both pedestrians and vehicles.

This enclosure of São Paulo shopping centers is partially explained by the low quality of public spaces and the lack of a welcoming natural environment. In other cities, such as Rio de Janeiro, Salvador, and even cities in the interior of the state of São Paulo, open and unenclosed centers are more common. The Downtown shopping center in Rio de Janeiro, for instance, attempts to reproduce an "unplanned" city space with retail spaces, movie theaters, and services in separate buildings with a variety of façades (fig. 4.4). The Aeroclube center in Salvador is an open-air mall that enjoys beautiful views to the sea (fig. 4.5). The Parque Don Pedro shopping center in Campinas, an important city close to São Paulo, was one of the largest ventures in Brazil in 2004 and included several partially uncovered areas. Evidently, all these

Figure 4.2. The Iguatemi shopping center, São Paulo. The postmodernist façade and the parking structure on the left resulted from the last renovation and expansion. (Photo by Gilda Bruna)

Figure 4.3. Pátio Higienópolis shopping center, São Paulo. The surrounding historic buildings and community pressures generated a design that is relatively open to the outside, with restaurants and landscaped areas. (Photo by Gilda Bruna)

are attempts to add to the mall's attractiveness through differentiating architectural projects.

Functions of Shopping Centers

At first shopping centers were dedicated almost exclusively to retail and consumer services. Anchoring was provided by department stores and supermarkets, which attracted the customers, directed their flow inside the mall, and increased the overall profitability of all mall tenants. Later on, in order to keep the return on investment high, it became important to maintain rigid control over the tenant mix (number and type of stores) in accordance with retail and marketing theories being developed in the United States.

The growing competition among shopping centers demanded better location studies, more precise definition of the catchment areas, and better identification of

Figure 4.4. The Downtown shopping center in Rio de Janeiro mimics a small town ambiance with a variety of faces and landscaped pedestrian walkways and fountains, with most of its parking located underground. (Photo by Vicente del Rio)

Figure 4.5. The Aeroclube open-air shopping center in Salvador is located by the beach; its design integrates interior and exterior spaces and takes advantage of the beautiful views. (Photo by the authors)

the target consumers' purchasing power and consumption habits in order to better plan the appropriate size of the development. Constant modifications in the design and in the tenant mix also became fundamental for mall success. The need for ongoing change introduced many new attractions, which even became the real anchors in some shopping centers. In their own controlled environment, these attractions try to reproduce the dynamics of a city and the high vitality of urban retail areas: recreation, food plazas, theaters, and fitness centers mix with offices, hotels, and apartments, all surrounded by green areas as well as other community attractions in order to compete for a niche of the market and increase the attractiveness of the mall (Vargas 1992). In some Brazilian malls, the strategy is to offer high-quality goods and services, an exclusive tenant mix, specialization, or even a specific theme.

These attractions become a way of increasing impulse buying, when people buy without noticing that they are consuming and without feeling like they are being induced to spend. These strategies and innovations are quickly replicated but also become obsolete very quickly, the reason for the difficulty of maintaining the vitality and profitability of malls. In the face of the proliferation of malls and the competition among them, innovations are designed to extend the center's life span, and this is when the architectural design becomes an important aspect. Brazilian shopping centers have been introducing these innovations and are mutating into large public spaces and meeting places for the population.

Shopping Centers as Poles of Attraction and Urban Growth

In Brazil as a whole, and particularly in São Paulo, shopping centers were located in existing urban areas, attracting consumers and generating new land uses and occupation patterns. When the Iguatemi shopping center was built (the first one), there weren't any specific urban regulations for this kind of development. It was only in 1971, when the new lei de zoneamento (zoning law) was approved,[2] that the construction of shopping centers began to be analyzed. Under the 1971 legislation, shopping centers could be located only in zones that allowed diversified activities with more than 250 square meters of built area. Under the more recent 1992 building codes, mega-centers are required to get a special license for construction due to their great urban impact (Moreira 1997).

These developments alter the urban space, strengthening or reorienting some urban expansion vectors, changing the land use and occupation of the neighborhood and its environs, increasing traffic congestion, and interfering with the urban dynamic and landscape design. The two study cases presented here illustrate details and peculiarities of this process, and their basic construction aspects are compared in table 4.2.z

Iguatemi Shopping Center

Inaugurated in November 1966, Iguatemi was the first shopping center in Brazil and in the city of São Paulo, as previously mentioned. Responding to trends in the property market, it was located on Avenida Faria Lima (formerly Rua Iguatemi), the primary axis for the southwest expansion of the city, and it was designed to serve the highest-income customers (fig. 4.6). It would struggle until the end of the 1970s, when its success started drawing away the customer base of Rua Augusta—a nearby traditional commercial street—which went into a slow decline. When the center first opened, Iguatemi was largely devoted to shopping, as shown in column 2 of table 4.2.

Its expansion and renovation in 2004 brought in new types of anchors and new satellite stores specializing in famous brands, as well as a new multistory attached parking structure. The large shops of the original design had their square footage reduced, which allowed for more tenants, more shops, more variety, and consequently a

Table 4.2. Main characteristics of the Iguatemi (1966 and 2004) and Pátio Higienópolis (2004) shopping centers

	Iguatemi 1966[a]	Iguatemi 2004[b]	Pátio Higienópolis 2004[b]
Total land area (sq. ft.)	529,032	463,312	166,667
Built area (sq. ft.)	358,849	1,182,935	774,194
Gross rentable area (sq. ft.)	n.a.	404,677	258,065
Parking spaces	576	1,850	1,350
Floors	3	3	5
Anchor stores	2	4	3
Satellite stores	75	320	220
Food courts	0	2	1
Cinemas	2	5	6
Theaters	0	0	1
Restaurants	2	9	5
Fast-food eateries	2	34	18
Video game arcades	0	0	1
Customers per month	n.a.	140,0000	120,000
Type of consumers	58% high-income	58% high-income	high-income

[a] From Fava (2000).
[b] From Associação dos Lojistas de Shopping Center (ALSHOP website: www.alshop.com.br (retrieved April 3, 2004).

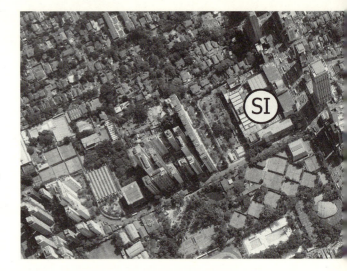

Figure 4.6. Aerial view of Iguatemi shopping center (SI); this center dictated most of the development of its surroundings and of one of São Paulo's growth vectors. (Courtesy of Base Aerofotogrametria e Projetos S.A., São Paulo, Brazil)

stronger pull factor. New children's play structures and food courts were introduced, and the movie theaters were modernized. On the other hand, Iguatemi lost its semi-open character and relatively good dialogue with its surroundings, and these alterations that reinforced its boxlike aspect were marked with a postmodern façade.

From a business perspective, the renovations and expansions in Iguatemi were driven by stiff competition created by the growth in the sector, as other shopping centers began offering new attractions with different characteristics (Bruna 1982; Bruna and Ornstein 1990; Vargas 1992, 2000, 2004; Masano 1993; Nobre 2000).

Iguatemi also spurred the transformation of Avenida Faria Lima from an area occupied by one- and two-story buildings into a high-rise area with buildings of twelve to fourteen floors, predominantly housing retail commerce and offices, in keeping with the 1971 zoning law.

Along with Iguatemi the same group of developers built a complex of high-income residential buildings that have almost direct access to the shopping center through the parking lot in back. Most of the remaining district, though, is composed of low-density single-family homes occupied by high-income families and protected by the zoning law as exclusively low-density residential. The population living in this district forms an important consumer market for Iguatemi.

Iguatemi's main façade is located on Avenida Faria Lima. Zoned as a commercial corridor, until 2001 the avenue allowed mixed uses, medium density, a floor area ratio of 3, and 70 percent lot coverage, which led to intense land development. In addition, since Iguatemi's inauguration, the avenue had its traffic area doubled; it was extended in both directions, and it gained new access loops coming from different directions in the city. These expansions attracted new investments in property development, generated a multiplier effect, and induced the shopping center's polarization in the 1980s.

Thus, coinciding with the establishment of the shopping center, an important axis for urban expansion was consolidated through the intensification of the tertiary sector, real estate investments in the surrounding area increased, and denser residential uses were implemented. Data presented by Masano (1993) show that, between 1980 and 1990, there was a 17 percent growth in the built area in Iguatemi's direct catchment area, 52 percent of which was dedicated to commercial use. Meanwhile, the floor area ratio increased from 1.13 to 1.32, residential uses decreased by 3 percent, and a process of transformation from lower to high-rise commercial and service buildings began. Masano also shows that in São Paulo the areas directly influenced by shopping centers experience increased density and an intensification of commercial and service uses compared to the rest of the city. Shopping centers appear to be generators of associated commercial spaces that, in turn, provide more customers for the centers.

In the 1990s land prices in Avenida Faria Lima and its environs increased more than those in Avenida Paulista, São Paulo's main business and financial axis. This situation was soon to change, however, when a new centrality was defined along two newer avenues farther to the southeast, leveraged by the construction of two new shopping centers.

Pátio Higienópolis Shopping Center

Opened in 1999, the Pátio Higienópolis shopping center is located in a consolidated residential area made up predominantly of apartment towers that by the early 1940s had replaced the original mansions belonging to the rural aristocracy of the end of the nineteenth century (Macedo 1987a). At first, upper- and upper-middle-class families occupied these large apartments, often one per floor. As the buildings aged and became inadequate for modern lifestyles—because, for example, they did not have recreational facilities or offered only one parking space per family—and the competition from more prestigious areas got stronger, the neighborhood declined and some streets became commercial corridors oriented primarily to office use.

Later, because of the area's central location and dropping real estate values, these residential buildings started to attract new buyers, mainly singles, seniors, and middle-class childless couples. This spontaneous neighborhood revitalization, in turn, attracted property investment and higher-income residents, which led to greater densities and more dynamism in retailing and consumer services.

Unlike Iguatemi, Pátio Higienópolis was built in a consolidated area with a high-

Figure 4.7. Aerial view of Pátio Higienópolis shopping center (SPH), which was inserted in a highly consolidated residential area of São Paulo. (Courtesy of Base Aerofotogrametria e Projetos S.A., São Paulo, Brazil)

density population that had time and money to spend and that clamored for places to socialize and for diversified shopping in a safe and comfortable environment (fig. 4.7). It is also important to note that within walking distance are the campuses of a private university, two public colleges, a private school, and several small private educational institutions, which generated a big consumer market and ensured this shopping center immediate success.

At the time of construction, zoning around Pátio Higienópolis permitted four different land uses, with residential uses prevailing.[3] One of these zones allowed medium density, two others medium-high to high densities, and the fourth mixed use with floor area ratios ranging between 2.5 and 3.5. Zoning also permitted neighborhood retailing and services, so that many eateries and restaurants had opened in the area.

It may be too early to observe significant changes in the surroundings of this shopping center, but certainly the existing high-density, consolidated neighborhood and numerous protected historical landmarks in the area will tend to diminish the center's impact or make the changes less evident. However, more intense pedestrian and vehicle flows are already occurring.

Positive effects of Pátio Higienópolis are the reorganization of local businesses and the fact that it generated a centrality in the district, which previously had none. These changes further increased the flow of consumers who walk to the shopping center. The fact that its design had to comply with the existing city zoning requirements in terms of respecting historic buildings and integrating with its surroundings was a positive feature. Two historic residences on the lot next to one of the shopping center's entrances were preserved and adapted for community-oriented activities.

Finally, Pátio Higienópolis's contemporary design—by one of São Paulo's leading architects—was also part of the strategy to satisfy market demands (see fig. 4.3). The shopping holds a theater, several stores catering to the extensive Jewish community in the neighborhood and, unlike other malls from this period, it allows pets and has pet stores. Its success led to the addition of another floor with two new areas for stores selling daily necessities, perhaps to attract more students from the nearby universities and schools. In any case, due to the short time since its inauguration, a careful analysis of its effects and the transformations it has led to in the district has not yet been carried out.

Conclusion

Due to its enormous metropolitan area and its eighteen million inhabitants whose mobility is restricted by a chaotic transit system and limited mass transportation, São Paulo is a compartmentalized territory. People tend to limit their commuting within specific sectors, thus reinforcing certain regional centers at the expense of the downtown; this tendency is strengthened by the existing shopping centers.

The early shopping centers in São Paulo were located near existing secondary centers in the central area and only later did they start to reinforce centralities in less densely occupied areas. By structuring new urban centers, shopping centers have become an alternative for a population experiencing constantly decreasing urban mobility, and these urban centers turn into pull factors themselves. They become important locales and landmarks, stimulating changes in the land use and density of their surroundings, in sharp contrast to the effects of traditional unplanned retail developments.

In the first of our cases, the Iguatemi shopping center and the commercial corridor where it is located ended up emulating the functions of the central city, and the users they attract expect the same diversity of functions they would find there. In the case of Pátio Higienópolis, it brought a significant increase in the flow of pedestrians due to the power it exercised in an area that lacked an attraction of this sort and due to the large student population in its vicinity. In generating safe and comfortable semipublic spaces, shopping centers change the habits of consumers, who end up preferring to shop and spend time there rather than along city streets, which normally results in negative effects on the traditional commercial areas.

On the other hand, cities can use shopping centers to support downtown revitalization and urban redevelopment programs, consolidate new centralities, and achieve a more balanced distribution of goods and services to the population. The several city and state government revitalization programs that target São Paulo's traditional

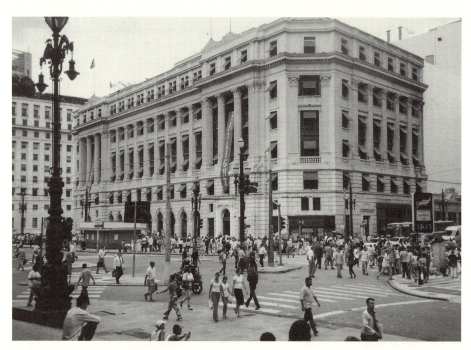

Figure 4.8. The new Shopping Light center in São Paulo. The renovation of this historic building into a new retail hub is an integral part of the city's efforts to revitalize the downtown. (Photo by Heliana Vargas)

downtown, for example, are encouraging the establishment of shopping centers to attract different groups of consumers. One example is Shopping Light, a 184,000–square-foot shopping center installed in a renovated 1929 six-story historical landmark building that used to be headquarters of the São Paulo Tramway Light and Power Company. Close to a subway station and a bus terminal, it opened in 1999, holds two department stores, one hundred shops including eateries and four restaurants, two hundred parking spaces, and receives more than thirty-five thousand visitors a day (fig. 4.8).[4] However, because of recent business difficulties, the building might be renovated once again by its owners, perhaps into a college or university use.

It is important to point out, though, that planners could make better use of the power of shopping centers to structure urban areas (Omholt 1998; Vargas 2003). Thus, the capacity of shopping centers to induce urban development, to direct growth, and to alter urban design can be utilized positively and can improve the quality of urban environments if properly used. Shopping centers could be initiated as public-private partnerships with a strong potential to revitalize decaying areas, thus becoming key factors in urban development.[5]

Notes

1. ABRASCE is affiliated with the International Council of Shopping Centers and counts as shopping centers only members of its organization. Under their definition, a shopping center is a development under centralized ownership and management, with anchors and satellite stores and on-site parking facilities. ALSHOP includes among its members a wide variety of types of retail complexes, regardless of their administrative structure.

2. There were practically no restrictions on development in São Paulo until 1971, when the master plan and its accompanying implementation laws (governing subdivision and land use) were approved (Nascimento 1997). Until then development controls were basically restricted to the central area and to residential zones. Under this new legislation, the floor area ratio was limited to 4 (one could build up to four times the lot area), and limitations on heights and minimum setbacks were established for different zones in the city. Requirements have been changed over time for some zones until the new master plan was approved in 2002. (See the essay by Macedo, chapter 3, in this volume.)

3. Pátio Higienópolis was built under the previous zoning law, which allowed higher densities. The new 2002 São Paulo Strategic Master Plan is more restrictive to development.

4. See http://sampacentro.terra.com.br/textos.asp?id=105&ph=22 (retrieved on March 3, 2008).

5. The 2002 São Paulo Strategic Master Plan introduced the concept of *operações urbanas consorciadas* (associated urban operations), which allows for case-by-case relaxation of zoning regulations for specific projects if the developer agrees to provide public investments as determined by the city.

Part 2

Revitalization The Struggle to Make
the Best of the Existing City

In the 1980s the country's return to democracy, the serious economic crisis, and the changing international development paradigms were reflected in increased community participation and in a demonstration that the modernist model was not the only possible one for planning and urban design. Officials in large Brazilian cities realized that they should focus some of their planning efforts on their downtowns, where deteriorating and underutilized buildings, urban blight, and vacant areas; antiquated modernist zoning regulations; and overambitious road projects were common problems. It is important to note, however, that unlike North American cities, which generally have few downtown residents, most Brazilian downtowns still have a significant number of residents, besides being heavily utilized by riders of public transportation, who use central hubs daily to go to their jobs elsewhere in the city (del Rio 1997).

By the mid-1980s, planners and politicians had realized that caring for the older parts of town, and particularly for the downtown, was a good idea not only because of their functional, social, and symbolic importance, but also because of growing pressure from community groups. In the last two decades of the twentieth century, several revitalization programs and preservation projects were developed in major Brazilian cities, most of them with a heavy bias on creating public spaces with cultural and recreational uses. Representative examples are projects developed in Rio, Salvador, São Paulo, Porto Alegre, and Belém.

The most important such project is Rio de Janeiro's Cultural Corridor Project, the first inner-city revitalization program in Brazil, discussed by Vicente del Rio and Denise de Alcantara. Initiated in 1982 and covering four large noncontiguous areas in Rio's historic downtown, the Cultural Corridor started by replacing the existing modernist zoning laws with a new set of regulations and guidelines aimed at preserving the area's historic heritage, promoting social and economic revitalization, and renovating the cultural role of the downtown. Through a specific design review process, public education, tax exemptions, and building incentives, the project encourages the rehabilitation of historical structures, the maintenance of traditional uses, and new infill development with buildings that reinterpret history through contemporary vocabularies. Having broadened its scope over time, the Corridor Cultural Project now includes signage control, streetscaping, and the promotion of public cultural activities.

By 2005, 75 percent of the more than three thousand buildings in the Cultural Corridor area had been partially restored, and nine hundred had been totally renovated. In addition, the area now has twenty-five new cultural centers, theaters, and museums that are intensively used by the entire city population. Del Rio and Alcantara discuss how the success of the Cultural Corridor results from harmonizing planning and design goals with social, cultural, and economic revitalization, and from a well-balanced mix of preservation and redevelopment, public and private participation.

The success of the Cultural Corridor inspired other Brazilian cities to preserve their historic architecture and revitalize their central areas. One such city was Salvador, the first capital of Brazil during the colonial period and now capital of the state of Bahia. Ana Fernandes and Marco Filgueiras Gomes discuss a large project launched by the state government in 1992 to revitalize the Pelourinho, a district in Salvador's historic center. Named a World Heritage Site by UNESCO, Pelourinho is the district most representative of Salvador's rich cultural history: it contains one of the most important collections of colonial buildings and baroque churches in Latin America, and it is a center for the country's Afro-Brazilian culture. The authors show how earlier, unsuccessful attempts to renovate this once-decaying area led the state of Bahia to adopt a radical, large-scale operation in the early 1990s in order to give the district a strategic role in national and international tourism development.

Fernandes and Gomes discuss the significant transformations that this controversial top-to-bottom project introduced in the Pelourinho. Residents were evicted, and original uses and spontaneous practices were changed and were sometimes institutionalized into tourist attractions. The historic urban fabric was ruptured by new access corridors to the interior of blocks, which transformed what had been private yards into semipublic areas with restaurant seating and arenas for shows, not uncommonly surrounded by pastiche architecture. New cultural centers and museums operated by the public sector now help promote cultural gentrification as part of the new urban spectacle. Nevertheless, however controversial, the project did manage to restore the Pelourinho to its extremely important place in Brazil's cultural history, make it safer and more attractive for tourists, and facilitate proper maintenance of the historic architecture. Despite the area's gentrification and tightened government control, perhaps the passage of time will bring a gradual return of some of the original social practices to the Pelourinho.

Next, Simone Seabra and Alice Rodrigues discuss the results of efforts to revitalize the riverfront in the central area of Belém, one of the most important cities in the Brazilian Amazon, founded in the sixteenth century by the Portuguese to safeguard the mouth of the Amazon River. Until recently, most government efforts and urban development in Belém had not paid much attention to the quality of public spaces downtown, and both physical and visual access to the river was taken for granted; but in recent years both the state and city governments have been implementing projects there, although not always in a coordinated manner. The authors analyze three of these projects, which treated the riverfront as an amenity, implemented multiple public uses and stressed recreation and leisure, and tried to re-create the historic symbiosis between city and river.

Starting with the city's 1993 ambitious master plan, municipal efforts were directed to the promotion of environmental and aesthetic quality and territorial organization, and tourism development and the creation of better public spaces became high priorities. The *Ver o Rio* (See the River) program started to develop parks and small recreational areas along the riverbanks, all eventually to be interconnected and lead to downtown. The city also renovated the Ver-o-Peso complex, a traditional open-air market by the river and one of Belém's main tourist attractions, building new stalls for the merchants and rehabilitating the public spaces and surrounding historic architecture. Meanwhile, because Belém is the state capital, the state government also implemented two large revitalization projects directed at the tourism industry: the Estação das Docas (adaptive reuse of three protected historic warehouses into a retail and restaurant complex), and the Núcleo Cultural Feliz Lusitânia (revitalization of part of Belém's historic core, including the restoration of colonial buildings and churches to serve as new museums).

Seabra and Rodrigues show that although not always integrated and sometimes geared to tourists rather than the local population, these state and city efforts have helped to turn Belém back toward its riverfront and have opened up a new perception of the river and its importance to city life. By promoting public use of the riverfront through new parks, recreational areas, shopping, and entertainment, these projects have raised public expectations and set higher standards for the quality of the public realm. The authors also show how the designs of these projects try to harmonize with the Amazon regional culture and address issues of sustainability.

Lastly, Lineu Castello discusses a brownfield revitalization project that was planned and implemented entirely by the private sector and that had important positive repercussions for the public. Located in the central area of Porto Alegre, capital of the southern state of Rio Grande do Sul, the Navegantes Commercial District (Distrito Comercial Navegantes) is now a very popular outlet shopping center in the former garment district. Unlike most postmodern developments, which fabricate a false identity, this project capitalized on the area's historic industrial architecture, centrality, and accessibility by public transportation. The Navegantes Commercial District is an excellent example of the successful creation of a place in an area that previously did not really have an identity in the public's imagination.

In this revitalized brownfield–turned–shopping center dozens of shops and eateries were installed in rehabilitated buildings and new additions, and well-landscaped semipublic areas hosting public events generated a simple and attractive mix of uses. Since this project's first phase, other private developers have jumped on the bandwagon by converting surrounding buildings, creating more attractions, and further revitalizing the area. It was only after these developments proved successful that the public sector started to support the initiative through streetscape improvements and a small pedestrian precinct for street performances. Castello points out that the Navegantes Commercial District—although based in the creation of a place by replicating its original images—was able to use an efficient place-marketing strategy that values the existing qualities of the area as an effective way to attract the public. The project also stands out as perhaps the only example in Brazil of a successful urban revitalization that has been entirely planned, funded, and implemented by the private sector.

CHAPTER 5

The Cultural Corridor Project Revitalization and Preservation in Downtown Rio de Janeiro

Vicente del Rio and

Denise de Alcantara

Conceived at the beginning of the 1980s as the first revitalization project for downtown Rio de Janeiro, the Cultural Corridor represents a landmark in the planning and development of Brazilian cities. Both a pioneering and an integrative effort, the project includes not just the preservation of the city's historical and cultural heritage, but also the recovery and renovation of its urban and architectural works, together with their social and economic revitalization.

From the moment of its conception by the city, the Cultural Corridor Project has enjoyed the total support of property owners, merchants, and the community. Its successful trajectory can be explained by considering four fundamental aspects of urban revitalization: history, memory, preservation, and community participation. By harmonizing historical-architectural models with economically and structurally feasible implementation, the project avoids the exaggerations and rigidities of purist restoration. In addition, infill development is encouraged with new buildings that reinterprets historic structures using contemporary vocabularies.

The Cultural Corridor Project integrates development control, special design guidelines, streetscape embellishment, tax exemptions and incentives, community education and participation, cultural programs, and public events. The sustained effort of the city government over more than two decades has been fundamental to the success and effectiveness of the project objectives. As of September 2002, of the more than three thousand buildings included in the project area, 75 percent had been partially restored, including painting and the installation of new signage, and some nine hundred had been totally renovated. In addition more than twenty-five new cultural centers, theaters, and museums had been erected.

The Historical Context of Downtown Rio de Janeiro

Historically, the urban development of Rio de Janeiro has been characterized by fragmentation and discontinuity of the territory, especially because of the city's geomorphological site. In particular, Guanabara Bay, adjacent swampland, and various hills limited the development of the historical core, until these features were overcome through removal, dirt fills, and total or partial leveling. The city's structure has always responded to social and economic factors, particularly after the Portuguese royal family and court, fugitives from the Napoleonic wars, moved to Rio de Janeiro in 1822. Rio's transformation into the Portuguese empire's capital and later into Brazil's capital until the inauguration of Brasília in 1960 were definite political factors in molding the city's morphology and architectural models. The neoclassicism of the 1800s and the eclecticism of the republican period at the turn of the century are the urban and architectonic types that characterize the historical center.

In the first decade of the twentieth century large-scale public sanitation works and beautification projects, expansion of the port, and improvement of roadways and public transportation transformed the city. Inspired by the works of Georges Haussmann, the designer of modern Paris, and with the total support of the federal government, Mayor Pereira Passos dedicated himself to the modernization of the capital from 1903 to 1906. In one of history's first city marketing operations, he sought to construct a new international image for the city to compete with its main rival, Buenos Aires.[1] Additionally, public sanitation projects and public health initiatives led to the eradication of endemic illnesses—like typhoid—whose epidemics had decimated the population and frightened away international commerce.

The adoption of an international cosmopolitan model along French lines demanded the transformation of the city's antiquated colonial morphology by means of a spatial reorganization that reflected capitalist logic and permitted the consolidation of property values. The opening of new avenues resulted in new transportation axes and new modes of access, notably the Avenida Central, a Parisian-style boulevard where the upper classes of the time strolled and which even today is the heart of the city's business district. In this period, innumerable streets and alleys were widened, old colonial houses were torn down, expansion of elegant residential boroughs was consolidated along the seacoast south of downtown, and an eclectic mix of public squares and buildings emerged in the style of the French belle époque. The government evicted the poor to the outskirts of town, eradicated urban epidemics, embellished urban spaces, and redesigned streets and buildings in the downtown area (Pinheiro 2002). Dislodged by public works and by new restrictions on hostels and tenement houses, lower-income groups were pushed toward the hills and the *favelas*—squatter settlements—that would later become a trademark of the Carioca landscape.[2]

In the 1920s the city began preparing for the arrival of industrialization with the total renovation of a vast area in the city center for the celebration of the centenary of Brazil's independence and the construction of the International Exposition of 1922, which resulted in the leveling of hills and eliminated even more pockets of low-income families remaining from earlier reforms in the historic downtown. In 1930 the city concluded the Agache Plan, Rio's first master plan, inspired by the beaux arts tradition, which proposed the creation of a monumental, functional, and efficient capital that sought social transformation by means of physical remodeling, beautification, new garden suburbs, and "scientific" zoning (see figure I.2 in the introduction).[3] Although not totally implemented, certainly because of its high economic and social costs, this plan led to a new office sector in the city center and is still evident in land-use regulations and urban design features such as mandatory pedestrian arcades and the types and volumes of buildings. In the following decade the federal government built the Avenida Presidente Vargas, a new monumental traffic axis that required bulldozing an area two city blocks wide and more than three kilometers long, expelling even more low-income families from the downtown.

Although the architecture and the urban structure of Rio de Janeiro's historic center were in effect consolidated by the beginning of the 1950s, city growth still caused negative effects, particularly through the expansion of the real estate market. In addition, as in the rest of the world, the 1950s and 1960s were marked by decisions related to traffic engineering, with priority being given to the needs of the automobile: roads were widened, sidewalks narrowed, and new expressways and viaducts built, demolishing the urban fabric and impinging upon the landscape. The 1970s were marked by the construction of the metro system, which, although largely underground in the downtown area, generated the renovation of various areas along the lines and around the stations.

In the historic center, various public and private properties and significant spaces survive side by side with the skyscrapers of modernism as testaments to past periods (fig. 5.1). On the other hand, reflecting a pattern that can be seen throughout Latin America, downtown Rio de Janeiro maintains a strong financial and service center and is the hub for the transportation system that links the whole metropolitan region, factors which explain its vitality. In addition, the area still has a significant fragment—now diminishing—of the low-income residential population at its edges, 79,108 people in 2000.[4]

In spite of all the assaults upon it and the emergence of important new subcenters throughout Rio de Janeiro, the city center is still an intense and active component in the city life, as a functional political, social, and symbolic nucleus (del Rio 1997). In contrast to North American metropolises, Rio's downtown never lost its formal and informal economic and cultural momentum, and maintains itself as a reference point for the population of the whole metropolitan area, which totals more than nine million. This function as a vital attraction point with pluralistic and differentiated characteristics has intensified since the implementation of the Cultural Corridor Project, a catalyst for the process of renovation and revitalization of the center of Rio de Janeiro.

The Cultural Corridor Project

The Cultural Corridor Project was conceived at the end of the 1970s, a historical moment when Brazilian society was initiating a return to democracy that culminated in 1985 with the abolition of the military regime imposed on the country in 1964. Carioca society began to question the quality of urban life and environmental degradation. Various social movements and the press, taking advantage of new freedoms, pressed the government to act against the excesses of urbanization and real estate speculation and development. Particularly in Rio, people became interested in preserving the city's natural beauty and significant architectural- historical heritage.

In 1979, a team of local government planners developed an inventory of historic buildings in the city center that had resisted urban renovation. They proposed the Cultural Corridor Project as an attempt to reconcile preservation with economic development and various political, social, and cultural interests.[5] The project was feasi-

Figure 5.1. Aerial view of downtown Rio de Janeiro, showing areas of the Cultural Corridor Project. (Photo by Denise de Alcantara)

ble only because it obtained total political support from the mayor, from community groups devoted to historical and cultural preservation, and from the general population. Support from retail business owners who operated in the project area and had been organized into commercial associations since 1962 was particularly important, since most were tenants not property owners, and understood that the project would protect them against the threat of large commercial and real estate operations. Since then, the movement for the rehabilitation of downtown Rio has been the result of a process of combined actions by various groups, under the direction of municipal power.

While the debate over preservation issues in Rio and the Cultural Corridor Project were still in their early stages, the city government instituted a technical council composed of various influential personages and intellectuals in the cultural arena, such as writers, journalists, and musicians. The council's role was to instigate debate about and ideas for the city as a whole, as well as for architectural, environmental, and cultural questions related to the downtown. Its importance was enormous; it provided the project with insights and practical contributions, in addition to giving it great prestige as the press and the public came to recognize it as an important effort outside the government. The preservation of the city center gained a new image, that of the protection of an atmosphere, of a heritage you cannot touch but can feel, a concept more poetic and flexible than any that planners and architects had proposed up until that time.

The Cultural Corridor consists of an area of almost 1.3 million square meters (14 million square feet) in the historic center of Rio de Janeiro and includes three thousand buildings with diverse levels of protection. The original project subareas represented different periods of public administration: Colonial Brazil (Praça XV and surroundings), Imperial Brazil (SAARA),[6] and Republican Brazil (Lapa and Largo de São Francisco) (fig. 5.2) (Sisson, 1986). With their different histories and traditional functions, these urban fragments possess very distinct characters but complement each other very well in their sociocultural and morphological relations. The Central Business District permeates these central areas, where tall, modern skyscrapers, wide avenues, and renovated spaces coexist with historic pockets and eclectic antique buildings that have resisted urban renewal.

The Implementation Process

In Rio de Janeiro, all master planning, zoning, and subdivision regulations are typically promulgated by the city government and sanctioned as laws by the legislature. However, land use is governed through three major instruments that do not depend

Figure 5.2. The original boundaries and subareas of the Cultural Corridor Project, Rio de Janeiro: (*1*) SAARA, (*2*) Largo de São Francisco, (*3*) Praça XV, (*4*) Lapa. (Courtesy of IPP)

on the legislature: the Building Code, the Street Alignment Projects (Projetos de Alinhamento, PAs)—which define rights-of-way and sections of streets, front setbacks, and sometimes the height of buildings along streets—and the Subdivision Projects (Projetos de Parcelamento, PALs)—which refer to specific areas and their subdivision into lots. The Cultural Corridor was first implemented through a mayoral decree in 1983 that modified the previously existing PAs and PALs for the area, later to be followed by legislation declaring it a Special Zone with a specific set of guidelines in January 1984. This process gave the project teeth, since all urban or architectural modifications in the area would have to obtain approvals at both the executive and the legislative levels.

In succeeding years, the incremental implementation of the Cultural Corridor allowed for new design guidelines to prevail over old zoning regulations and building codes in a viable manner, not simply in order to preserve historic buildings but to integrate them with the renovation of areas using good architectural and urban design practices. For instance, the relaxation of parking requirements for new construction and the prohibition of parking structures in the area—due to easy access by public transportation—were fundamental new zoning elements. The combination of legal and fiscal instruments with an innovative process to accomplish projects and new construction in the Cultural Corridor guaranteed the success of the project and the compatibility of new development with the preservation of the cultural heritage.

Project implementation followed four complementary approaches that will be briefly discussed in this essay: (a) a special process for project approvals and a set of design guidelines; (b) the actions of the Cultural Corridor executive committee; (c) tax deductions and fiscal incentives; and (d) community participation.

Preservation Types and Design Guidelines

The Cultural Corridor Project, with its specific requirements, guidelines, and the role and functions of its executive committee, was superimposed on the city's traditional project approval process. Any work on a building in the Cultural Corridor had first to be analyzed and approved by the Cultural Corridor executive committee. Depending on the building's architectural characteristics, the analysis originally followed one of three broad categories with different sets of guidelines: preservation, reconstruction, and renovation.

A large proportion of the more than three thousand buildings in the project area pertain to the "eclectic period" of Carioca architecture. Of these about 1,300 were classified for *preservation* because the architectural, decorative, and artistic features of their façades and roofs were largely intact and in a good state of conservation. For these properties, any renovation of the existing building or its physical adaptation to new uses had to follow strict guidelines for what, in practical terms, was analogous to a historic registry (fig. 5.3).

The *renovation* category encompasses lots and vacant areas, recently constructed buildings, and those not considered in need of historically accurate reconstruction. Initially, very strict directives were imposed on projects in this category, including maximum building volumes, types and patterns of façade elements (principally voids and decorative elements), and construction elements such as overhangs and crown-

Figure 5.3. A building in the Cultural Corridor: (*left*) before (Courtesy of Maria Helena McLaren, collection of the Escritorio Técnico do Corredor Cultural, Prefeitura do Rio de Janeiro); (*right*) after renovation (Photo by Denise de Alcantara). Its original architectural features and color palette were recovered.

ing. These requirements were found to be too restrictive, however, and at the time of this writing, only the basic dimensions of the building envelope are mandated—always as a function of the existing surrounding buildings—while other aspects such as patterns and compositional elements of the façade are only recommended, always in such a way as to achieve a "contextual design" and integrate the new building with its surroundings (fig. 5.4).

The last category, *reconstruction*, encompassed damaged buildings of historical and cultural importance whose original architectural elements could still be rebuilt. Because this category proved to have very limited application, however, the Cultural Corridor Project discarded it in 1987.

To educate merchants, property owners, and architects about the objectives, the process for getting projects approved, and the design directives of the Cultural Corridor, the manual *Como Reformar, Renovar, ou Construir seu Imóvel no Corredor Cultural* (How to Recover, Rebuild or Construct Your Property in the Cultural Corridor) was published in 1985. This manual also contains rules for the installation of signs and awnings, as well as technical instructions for verifying the stability of foundations and for structural repair of roofs. A series of other works and projects were contracted or developed by the Technical Office; a few were published, such as *Cores da Cidade* (Colors of the City), which identified a palette of original colors for façades and allowed contractors and property owners to work with greater freedom in the restoration of their buildings. Another important, extensive work was *Como Preservar a Sua e a Nossa Herança* (How to Preserve Your and Our Heritage), which addressed fire danger. All of these studies are very pragmatic and aim at direct practical application.[7]

The Technical Office

Established by the initial legislation in 1984 to lend assistance to the community, regulate redevelopment, propose changes to existing legislation, and oversee the completion of projects, the Cultural Corridor executive committee—also called the Technical Office—was certainly one of the key factors in the project's success. The pioneering nature of the project and limited previous experience with an enterprise of such specificity and breadth made the creation of a technical team necessary. The team was made up basically of young architects who learned on the job, through intense analysis of projects and daily work in the field. In overseeing the projects and in their interactions with community members and property owners, the team repeatedly formulated solutions to problems as they appeared, which resulted in several modifications to the original Corridor Cultural guidelines over the years.

Figure 5.4. A commercial street in the Cultural Corridor with restored historic structures and a new building (*white, center*) conforming to the design guidelines. (Photo by Denise de Alcantara)

A fundamental prerequisite for the team's work was to have an iconographic register and catalog of buildings in the Corridor, and to document their compositional and typological characteristics, history, designer and builder, and previous or current uses. In one study commissioned by the Technical Office, 800 two-story houses were photographed in the SAARA area and classified as to their degree of importance and architectural sophistication. In this busy and traditional popular commercial area, the team searched for historical and cultural references, not just for the building itself, but to increase awareness of the value of old buildings, registered or not. This database allowed them to contextualize the building to the larger scale of the city block and the street, permitting special directives for each new construction project. For example, given the enormous variation in existing building heights in these areas, it is preferable to define the different patterns to be applied on a case-by-case basis than to establish a single allowable height for the whole zone, as is typically done in a city's land-use legislation.

Another relevant aspect of the project is the value it attributes to the "fifth façade"—the rooftop. Over time, a large number of rooflines had been modified, significantly altering the spatial characteristics of these historic buildings. In cases where the original roof and skylights had been replaced with corrugated roofing, property owners had to return the building to its original characteristics using timber structures, ceramic tiles, and skylights. It is also important to note that the technicians always oriented new projects to avoid a "pastiche" of ornamentation, railings, and other decorative elements, in a manner that ensured an appropriate reinterpretation of historical conditions through the use of contemporary language and materials.

The restoration of antique houses and the fabrication of ornaments and decorative elements for buildings placed on the historic register or undergoing renovation prompted the formation of a new group of professionals and artisans who had worked on the earliest projects. With the aid of the technicians who accompanied them daily on the construction site, these workers today have become specialized laborers whose activities and profits are tied to this practice.

Fiscal and Economic Incentives

The economic implications of the Cultural Corridor Project were another decisive factor in its success, and particularly the incentives conceived at the municipal level. Fundamentally, renovated properties and well-maintained historic buildings in the project area were exempted from property tax and other city fees. This potentially permanent exemption is contingent on the continued maintenance and conservation of the property, which is periodically verified by the Technical Office. Other incentives exist at the federal level, such as the Rouanet Law, and the recent (2000) grant by the Inter-American Development Bank for the renovation of public spaces and historic buildings in the Praça Tiradentes historic district.[8]

The Technical Office is aware that fiscal incentives are extremely efficient instruments for implementation and that it would be difficult for the project to succeed without these benefits. As soon as the Cultural Corridor was implemented, various merchants took advantage of the incentives to repair their properties, and many famous chain retail stores—some previously located only in shopping malls—opened branches in the area. Retailers perceived that the maintenance of Rio's cultural heritage and urban environment adds value to their properties and helps attract a wider clientele.

In a study of the economic implications of the Cultural Corridor in the SAARA area, David Rodrigues (1999) demonstrates that although the exemptions from property taxes and other municipal fees resulted in a significant loss of revenues to the city, they also freed the city from the direct burden of restoring and renovating historic properties. At the same time, the project fostered more intense commercial and tourist activities which, in turn, generated new and alternate revenue streams to the city from other forms of taxation, indirectly compensating the city for the tax exemptions that had been granted.

Appraising the cost of renovating a historic property is an almost impossible undertaking: data are specific to each case and to the difficulties encountered in the construction. The property owners or tenants undertake the projects in various stages, but unfortunately there are no surveys or official data on costs. Because the directives of the Cultural Corridor Project are aimed at original building mass, façades, and roofs, normally the work begins with the exterior. In July 2003, we estimated a cost of between R$25,000 and R$30,000 (US$8,000 to US$10,000) as the average for a simple renovation of the façade, the roof, the wiring, and the mechanical systems of a typical old building in the downtown (assuming it is in a good state of conservation).[9] Since the total municipal taxes for a typical old building in the city center are between R$10,000 and R$15,000 per year (of which 70 percent is in property taxes alone), the owner could recover this investment in three years.

Although the value of property as heritage is undeniable, it is evident that the country's economic fluctuations affect return on investment and that not all that is invested, even with tax incentives, returns directly to the entrepreneur. Another difficulty in adhering to the project concerns responsibility for building maintenance and the payment of taxes when properties are later transferred to tenants since, especially in periods of major economic difficulties, there is no security in investing in the restoration of buildings one does not own.

Community Participation

Finally, one of the major ingredients in the successful implementation of the Cultural Corridor Project was the consistent and active participation of the community. It should be emphasized that a major demand for the preservation of properties came from store owners, in a growing movement of organized associations that fought against the loss of their properties to large property owners, such as the religious orders, who threatened to dislodge them.[10]

In this sense, an interesting characteristic is the particular culture of the area. In the SAARA area, for example, there are significant populations of Jews and Arabs who immigrated at the end of the nineteenth century and the beginning of the twentieth; these groups build upon a very strong past with rules of kinship and friendship and family histories that generate profound ties of cultural identity (fig. 5.5). The result was groups of people unwilling to leave the properties that served as the foundations for their commercial establishments. The project was well received by these strategic groups, and their interest in permanence came to have new significance as a standard by which their properties were to be restored. The restorations generated new respect for the properties and for the rich, ornamental façades that were revealed behind the awnings and signs that had covered them.

The project also aimed at sensitizing the population to the importance of preservation, not simply because of the visual appeal resulting from the restoration of the façades, but also because of the relationships that developed between the community, the architects and builders contracted by the property owners, and the technicians of

Figure 5.5. A commercial street with traditional uses and renovated buildings in the Cultural Corridor's SAARA area. (Photo by Denise de Alcantara)

the Technical Office during everyday work. Many renovation solutions were arrived at by common agreement, and numerous public meetings were held where commercial associations and the community could discuss and share ideas and proposals that would directly affect building users. Today the Corridor has been incorporated into the downtown culture that the community recognizes and values. The term "cultural corridor" has become synonymous with revitalization.

Partners in Revitalization: Complementary Cultural Projects

From the beginning, the project also included stimulus for and investment in cultural, tourist, and leisure activities. The project promotes and supports activities in the arts, music, dance, and theater, many of which use the streets and squares of downtown as stages and backdrops for performances and shows. An important aspect of the Cultural Corridor is the reconditioning of buildings and historic houses for cultural activities or new cultural centers, and the renovation of existing museums. The downtown was revitalized as a major social destination for after-work and weekend recreation, principally because of the numerous museums and cultural centers established in the last few years.

Numerous buildings that were listed on municipal, state, or federal historic registers have been renovated and are maintained by the public sector and by historical endowment funds or even through private incentives with the support of cultural incentives laws. In various locations in the Cultural Corridor—particularly around these new cultural poles—restaurants, bars, and nightclubs have multiplied. In 2003 these initiatives, which are basic to the revitalization of the historic center, totaled twenty-five cultural buildings—museums, theaters, cultural centers, and the like—twenty-three of which are located in historic buildings registered at the federal, state, or municipal level. Of these, eight buildings have been renovated and modernized, but maintain their original cultural function, while fifteen were restored and converted to new uses.

One example is the area around Praça XV, where until the nineteenth century the Pharoux Dock was the principal point of arrival to the city. Of great historical significance, the area also includes the Paço Imperial—an early eighteenth-century government building renovated as a museum in 1989—the 1789 Mestre Valentim fountain, which provided fresh water for arriving ships, and the Arco do Teles complex, a 1716 elegant, arched gateway under a building leading to an alley flanked by late nineteenth-century commercial buildings. The gateway and alley connect Praça XV to another group of historic buildings, also renovated for public use as cultural centers: the old Bank of Brazil and Post Office headquarters, the National History Museum, and an 1820 building originally designed as the first trade exchange by Grandjean de Montigny, the architect who arrived with the first French artistic mission and started architectural education in Brazil.

Lapa, which used to be the traditional domain of bohemian Cariocas in the mid-twentieth century, is now totally revitalized and holds numerous bars, dancehalls, and cultural events. Framed by the arches of an aqueduct built in 1750, the pioneer in this revitalization was the popular Circo Voador (Flying Circus), which became an important landmark of 1980s and 1990s pop culture by sponsoring weekend dance nights and nurturing various new bands. The circus now occupies a new, award-winning permanent building inaugurated in the summer of 2005. Next to it, a large center for concerts and cultural events was built from the remnants of the Fundição Progresso—a late nineteenth-century iron foundry. Both were private initiatives supported by the public sector and were pivotal in revitalizing Lapa and in attracting other private investments.

Private investors, many times in partnership with the public sector and in response to government actions, soon realized the existence of a consumer market that was very supportive of cultural enterprises. Historic buildings renovated into cultural centers generate large influxes of people; increase daytime and evening pedestrian traffic; and stimulate the development of bars, restaurants, and nightclubs around them in a "new urban phenomenon yet to be studied by our academics and entrepreneurs" (Pinheiro 2002, n.p.). Increasing numbers of visitors and tourists are attracted to the downtown during business hours and on evenings and weekends, drawn by national and international art exhibits, shows, and the buzz from new cultural and arts centers, or simply by the crowds of people in multiplying bars and cafes.

Reverberations and New Tendencies

The Cultural Corridor Project has expanded far beyond the rehabilitation of historic buildings, promoting urban renewal, innovative development projects, and cultural events and attracting new residents to the city center.

Renovation of Public Areas

Soon after the implementation of the Cultural Corridor, the Technical Office realized that architectural renovation alone would not be sufficient for urban revitalization, which largely depends on the quality of public spaces. Street infrastructure and streetscapes have been renovated, and more pedestrian-friendly areas were created in the downtown, encouraging more intense and diverse public use and increasing the public dimension of the historic core. Although anticipated from the start of the project, these developments only started to occur five years after the renovation of historic buildings began, when the city responded to pressure from the local merchants who realized that their newly restored buildings were surrounded by streets, squares, and plazas in disrepair or by bus terminals, parking lots, and other uses that were unattractive to their clientele.

Figure 5.6. The revitalization of Lapa included a new street layout, renovated public spaces, and new cultural and nightlife-oriented uses. An amphitheater fronts on the old city aqueduct, and just behind it are the Circo Voador (Flying Circus), Fundição Progresso cultural center, and the cone-shaped metropolitan cathedral. (Photo by Jean-Pierre Janot)

Several recent city initiatives for the renovation of public spaces can be cited as complementary to the architectural objectives of the Cultural Corridor. Avenida Rio Branco—the main artery through downtown—was renovated through the Rio Cidade urban design program in 1995,[11] and Praça XV—the most important historic complex in Rio, described earlier in this article—was entirely renovated in 1998. This ambitious project included the construction of an underground street that permitted bus routes and vehicular traffic to be redirected, and the creation of a large landscaped pedestrian precinct integrating the square and the historic imperial government house to the waterfront and docks. The areas of Praça da República and SAARA—where street grids maintain much of their historic features—had their original curb lines and cobblestone paving restored, while Largo do São Francisco and Praça Tiradentes squares were renovated for general public use. The Lapa area, which had been seriously damaged by bad street design in the 1960s, was totally renovated and now features large sidewalks and a median with imperial palm trees connecting to an amphitheater with the historic aqueduct as a backdrop, and to the Flying Circus just behind it (fig. 5.6). Large crowds are attracted by the public performances in the amphitheater on Easter, Christmas, and other holidays.

Residential Use: Synonymous with Life

Restrictions on the remaining existing residential uses and the prohibition of new residences, and even of hotels, were probably the single gravest problem posed by the zoning laws affecting the Central Business District and the Cultural Corridor area. As in other metropolises, the absence of a resident population resulted in an almost total absence of life and traffic outside business hours in the city center, where the majority of uses are commercial and institutional. Residences are mostly occupied by low-income families and concentrated in fringe areas and on hillsides such as Santa Teresa and Morro da Conceição, which contains a significant number of small houses dating from the early 1900s as well as squatter settlements—historical remnants of the workforce from the docks and of families evicted from inner-city slums. This situation began to change in 2002, when the city council approved important changes in the city master plan, and the city government issued ordinances and zoning changes that provide for residential uses throughout the business district and adjacent areas. By encouraging the construction of new buildings with small studio apartments (300 square feet) and the conversion of vacant and underutilized commercial buildings to residential use, and by waiving many of the normal parking requirements for residential buildings, the city hopes to provide the Cultural Corridor with residents, the missing ingredient for a complete revitalization of the downtown.[12]

Recent proof that this new vision has been embraced by the market is the success of the first large-scale residential development in Lapa, geared to lower middle income buyers. In 2006, a former beer brewery was converted to thirteen apartment buildings with 668 residential units of one and two bedrooms, some located over shops. The complex included landscaped areas, sports courts, playgrounds, a spa, cultural facilities, and even a bowling alley for residents. Surprising even the biggest optimists, sales broke a record: all the apartments were sold in only a day.[13]

New Ideas

New ideas for downtown and the Cultural Corridor constantly appear, including proposals to expand the project to include innumerable other buildings from different historical periods and styles, which do not always make up homogeneous urban areas. Between modern towers of the international, eclectic, and art deco styles, and even those representing the "heroic" phase of modernism—the 1930s and 1940s—stand badly preserved buildings, outdated and threatened by urban redevelopment. However, the Cultural Corridor staff is aware of the political difficulties of overextending the project and understands that the preservation of these buildings is not always essential, since many other examples have already been protected in more homogeneous areas. Their idea is that the city should provide flexible and specific directives and incentives for their preservation, but as a response to the dynamics of market demands: these buildings would be entitled to tax exemptions as long as their historic architectural features are respected and well preserved.

An example of the feasibility of this idea is the recent restoration of a twelve-story art deco office building in Cinelândia, an area that still holds some of the city's old movie theaters and where the Municipal Theater (1906), the Fine Arts Museum, and the National Library (1905) are located. This corner building with its elegant yellowish façade and its restaurant and tables on the sidewalks had become a traditional meeting place and a cultural landmark in the downtown. In 2001 it was successfully renovated and retrofitted into modern offices by a private developer, who retained the restaurant on the ground floor and referred to the building in his marketing flyers as an "architectural jewel" which "was preserved by municipal ordinance, in a beautiful setting of great historic value and intense cultural activity."

There are many cultural reverberations of the Cultural Corridor over the whole downtown area, and a recent episode demonstrates well the spirit of the project and its impact outside its area of direct influence. Recently, the merchants of Rua do Lavradio—a traditional street mostly composed of antique and used-furniture stores—decided to sponsor an antiques street fair on Saturdays, which, set against the

Figure 5.7. Rua do Lavradio, a street of antiques stores in downtown Rio de Janeiro. The buildings were renovated and public spaces revitalized with new cultural and social activities, such as sidewalk bar seats and street dancing, after local merchants began a street market on Saturdays. (Photo by Denise de Alcantara)

eclectic façades of the old buildings, injected a new charm into the locale and attracted large numbers of people. The area's sidewalks and storm drainage were in deplorable condition, so the city government responded to the street fair initiative by renovating the street infrastructure and the public spaces. Since then, new cafés and small cultural centers have been built in the old buildings, sharing space with antiques, and the renovated street environment resulted in an attractive and animated new place in downtown (fig. 5.7). This street is not within the Cultural Corridor Project area, which demonstrates the contagious spirit of the Cultural Corridor and of the city's support for revitalization.

Conclusion

As noted by Augusto Ivan Pinheiro, the main city planner behind the Cultural Corridor since its inception, "experience has demonstrated that the past and present, preservation and renovation, culture and tourism, leisure and business, can and should coexist, and that, better yet, together they produce riches, work, economic and social development, good health, and self-esteem and become a new culture for cities" (Pinheiro 2002, n.p.).

From a social point of view, the Cultural Corridor Project proved to be sensitive to different constituent groups, respecting their interests and involving them in the decision-making process. From an economic point of view, it maintains the dynamism and diverse commercial activities of small businesses, protecting them against large-scale developments and improving the quality of their spaces. From an ideological viewpoint, it differs from the totalitarian/public health approaches of earlier planning efforts, by emphasizing the symbolic value of buildings, spaces, and existing activities. And, from the cultural viewpoint, the project recovers the value of the city and its downtown as a cultural resource.

Throughout the implementation of the project, but especially at the beginning of the process, developing awareness and educating the merchants and users of the Cultural Corridor's protected area were fundamental for the preservation of historic buildings. The project not only guaranteed the maintenance of existing commercial activities but also provided for their expansion through fiscal incentives, such as reductions or exemptions from property taxes, and the Technical Office's provision of expertise and support to property owners who were restoring their buildings and renovating the façades.

The increasing importance that the city center has gained in the imagination and life of Cariocas is due to the Cultural Corridor Project, the herald of this change. The project defined a new paradigm for the downtown: to preserve, conserve, recycle, renovate, and modernize, taking advantage of the synergy between these activities (Pinheiro 2002). It achieved a stimulating effect beyond buildings, and has accomplished the transformation and refurbishment of "places."

On the other hand, renovation outside the Cultural Corridor should always be regarded as a fundamental aspect of preservation, because without constant reinvestments in architectural modernization and retrofitting, the downtown will continue to lose its centrality to newer areas of the city, such as Barra da Tijuca. Enlarging the concept of protecting cultural heritage to encompass the ongoing renovation required of a dynamic city will ensure that the downtown continues to be the *center of reference* for the city. The Cultural Corridor succeeded in preserving what needed to be preserved and encouraging new construction that is respectful of its context, but there are still areas in need of renovation: the city must continue to offer strategic opportunities for new development.

In the twenty years of the project's existence, much has been learned about the revitalization of the historic center of Rio de Janeiro, but there is still much to learn and to do, for the process of renovating a living downtown is occurring within a city in constant evolution: its customs change, its interests diversify, and its inhabitants develop new perceptions and new relations with the environment in which they exist. According to Augusto Ivan Pinheiro (2002), based on his long experience as an initiator and major articulator of the Cultural Corridor Project, the overall value of the twenty-first century city will be determined by a combination of diverse concepts of value: historic, architectural, property, symbolic, environmental, and cultural values.

Notes

The authors would like to thank architects Augusto Ivan Pinheiro, Maria Helena McLaren, and Andre Zambelli for granting interviews and providing information for this chapter.

1. On the transmission of European urban models to Brazil in this period, see Almandoz (2002) and Outtes (2002); on the modernization of Rio de Janeiro, see Evenson (1973), Sisson and Jackson (1995), Leme (1999), and Pereira (2002).
2. *Carioca* means a native of or something pertaining to Rio de Janeiro.
3. The Frenchman Alfred Agache was one of the founders of the garden city movement in Europe and one of the biggest names in international urban planning. See the introduction to this book and also Underwood (1991) and Leme (1999).
4. The annual census data for Rio de Janeiro show that the residential population in the central region decreased by 36 percent between 1980 and 2000. The city has been struggling to reverse this trend through zoning alterations and incentives to convert vacant or exclusively commercial buildings to moderate-income residential use.
5. Architect Augusto Ivan Pinheiro has been the major planner behind the project since its conception. He coordinated the original team and continues to act as a leading city official in the project's implementation and in the city efforts for revitalization. The name "Cultural Corridor" plays on the once-fashionable urban planning jargon of "transportation corridors."
6. SAARA stands for Sociedade Amigos das Adjacencias da Rua da Alfandega (Association of Friends of the Neighborhood of Rua da Alfandega), formed in 1962 by the merchants in the area.
7. Unfortunately, some of these studies were never approved by the city for implementation, such as the inventory of existing well-maintained building interiors and the proposal to place them on the historic register (Vasconcellos 2002). This resulted in the irrecoverable loss of many historic interiors.
8. The Rouanet Law, approved in 1991, allows partial exemptions from income tax for individuals and companies that invest in cultural projects, such as in the renovation and construction of museums and cultural centers.
9. Estimate by Maria Helena McLaren, director of the Technical Office of the Cultural Corridor, in an interview with the authors.
10. SAARA and SARCA (Association of Friends of Rua da Carioca) are two of the strongest and most active of central Rio's commercial associations.
11. See the essay on the Rio Cidade program by del Rio (chapter 10).
12. See Secretaria Municipal de Urbanismo, Instituto Pereira Passos, *Macrofunção: Habitar o Centro*. Coleção Estudos da Cidade Rio Estudos no. 105, June 2003. Rio de Janeiro: Editora Sextante. Available online at www.armazemdedados.rio.rj.gov.br.
13. See http://veja.abril.com.br/vejarj/290306/p_012.html (retrieved March 29, 2006).

CHAPTER 6

Revisiting the Pelourinho Preservation, Cultural Heritage, and Place Marketing in Salvador, Bahia

Ana Fernandes and

Marco A. A. de Filgueiras Gomes

Tourism has been a goal in the development plans of the Brazilian northeastern state of Bahia since 1959. Bahia is where the first Portuguese arrived in 1500 and where they founded the city of Salvador in 1549, which was to become Brazil's first capital during most of the colonial period—from the sixteenth to the eighteenth centuries. The *recôncavo bahiano*—the region of the state where Salvador is located—became Brazil's most dynamic urban network of the colonial period (CLAN/OTI 1970).

In the late 1960s, a Brazilian national policy linking historic preservation to tourism development was delineated to overcome economic stagnation and reverse urban decay, particularly in cities directly linked to the colonial economic cycles. This move encouraged state initiatives such as Bahia's Plano de Turismo do Recôncavo (Tourist Plan of the Recôncavo) in 1970, and at the national level the Programa de Cidades Históricas (Program of Historical Cities) in 1973. This important program promoted projects and investments for recovering historic urban and architectural complexes with tourism potential, beginning with the centuries-old cities of the Brazilian Northeast. Within this context Salvador held an exceptional position for its rich colonial architectural heritage, its extensive beachfront, and its powerful and complex culture (religious practices, festivals, music, cooking, and the like).

Therefore, policies concerning the preservation and renovation of Salvador's historic heritage have been in development for more than forty years; a particular target of these efforts has been an area in the old center known as the Pelourinho. The name originated in colonial times, when it referred to the pillory, a stone column located in a prominent plaza where criminals and rebels were publicly shackled and punished. In time, the name came to refer to the plaza—Largo do Pelourinho—and to its surroundings. Since the Pelourinho is the popular designation for the area, we refer to it by that name, avoiding other terms with a strong dose of ambiguity such as "traditional center," "old center," or "colonial center." The city center is constituted of a *low city* where the port and commercial and banking facilities are concentrated, and a *high city* where administrative, retail, and service establishments prevail. The terms *high* and *low* are literal, since the high city is located atop a cliff that overlooks the harbor, or low city (fig. 6.1).

Several different types of government interventions from the 1950s to the 1980s were unsuccessful in reversing the Pelourinho's social and physical deterioration, despite its rich historical and cultural character. In 1992, however, in a burst of national and local publicity, the state of Bahia announced a huge operation to revitalize and rehabilitate the area. The project succeeded in promoting economic, social, and

Figure 6.1. Aerial view of the Pelourinho and the historic center of Salvador, Bahia. (Photo by José Carlos de Almeida Filho)

physical redevelopment on a scale never before seen in the area, with effects that we are only now beginning to understand.

In the first part of this essay we explain why Salvador's historic center and the Pelourinho area were never successfully integrated into the development projects implemented since the 1950s, and we discuss the policies, interventions, and cultural practices used in attempts to renovate the historic areas. In the second part we discuss the process and major elements of the 1992 project for the Pelourinho, which was in its seventh stage in 2004. Finally, we analyze the project's role in urban revitalization and in contributing to Salvador's cultural consumption, and we conclude by discussing the limits of cultural strategies for urban revitalization within contemporary urban planning.

Preservation Policies in the Traditional Center

A constituent of Salvador's center located north of the high city, the Pelourinho area constitutes one of Brazil's greatest urban and architectural complexes of the colonial period and the nineteenth century. Totaling approximately 31.2 acres, it experienced its greatest prominence through the mid-nineteenth century when a significant portion of the urban residences of elite families from Salvador and the surrounding region were located there, in addition to religious institutions, services, and small retail shops. Since its apex, the area has deteriorated significantly, but its historic architectural aspects have always attracted a significant part of the city's tourism.

From the late 1950s on, the city of Salvador experienced a rapid increase in economic activities and began regaining its importance in the national urban network. The Pelourinho, in contrast, shared the fate of traditional city centers throughout

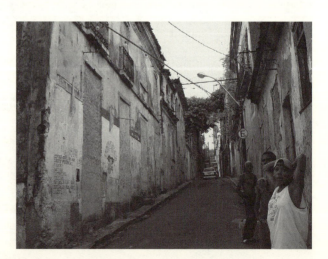

Figure 6.2. A deteriorated street in the Pelourinho before renovation, with windows and doorways boarded up. (Photo by Griselda Kluppel)

Brazil, experiencing accelerating stagnation and loss of economic power in spite of various public attempts to reverse this trend. As its high-income residents gradually started to move out, middle-income and low-income residents were left sharing space in the Pelourinho. Beginning in the 1940s, new middle-class housing elsewhere in the city would lead to an exodus of these residents, further impoverishing the area as only the poorest remained; they made their living from informal or insecure economic activities—if not crime or prostitution. The old colonial two-story houses, divided and subdivided, became an important housing alternative for this population, which would come to depend on the area's centrality for their survival (fig. 6.2). In the 1970s, when the first public redevelopment effort began in the Pelourinho, data indicated that it had 1,170 properties and almost seven thousand inhabitants (Bacellar 1979).[1]

The Deterioration of Central Salvador

Economic stagnation dominated Bahia and Salvador between the 1920s and the 1940s, but in the 1950s new opportunities arose for integrating the city into the capitalist network controlled by São Paulo and Rio de Janeiro.[2] Salvador became a capital-attracting magnet for the Brazilian Northeast, and starting in the 1960s and over the next two decades, a new economic dynamism would completely transform the city in appearance and the way it operates.

On the purely urban level, three processes sustained these immense transformations. The first was the privatization of public lands, which made possible the full commercialization of urban land in Salvador and consequently the full development of the real estate and construction sectors (Brandão 1981).[3] This change allowed the city to grow beyond its existing limits and redirected its expansion.

Second, a significant transformation of the city's urban structure and the expansion of its roadway system would contribute to the fragmentation of its city center. The rapid growth of the circulation grid then produced a system of avenues running along the bottoms of valleys, in strict synchrony with the land privatization process, whereas historically the city's expansion had essentially occurred along the hilltops. This circulation system, implemented in the 1960s and 1970s, still determines to a great extent the current growth pattern of Salvador.

The third process contributing to the fragmentation of Salvador's city center was the relocation of different institutions and structures beginning in the 1970s. Perhaps the greatest change was caused by the construction of the state's Centro Administrativo (Administrative Center) to which all state government facilities were relocated. Located fifteen kilometers (nine miles) from the downtown on vacant land, this center was a move by the state to generate a catalyst for the formation and expansion of a new city center. To access it a new road was built, and more than 10,000 hectares (25,000 acres) were incorporated for private development, which at the time corresponded to approximately two-thirds of Salvador's total occupied urban area (Santos Neto 1991: 87). In addition, the state transferred important public facilities—such as the bus terminal—to the outskirts of the consolidated city and into this new expansion axis, and the private sector was encouraged to build a large shopping center there, which because of its impact, lent its name to its surroundings. Together with the previously cited processes, these structures would foster extremely rapid land development in this new urban expansion area.

These new territorial dynamics placed downtown in a double bind, in the sense that on top of the existing restrictions on its growth, the new areas offered better conditions for development: availability of large plots, easy accessibility and circulation, and in particular, appropriate conditions for the full development of the real estate market. The downtown, which at the end of the 1950s already demonstrated "an ever increasing marginality in relation to the rest of the city . . . and was, in relation to it, 'perfectly eccentric'" (M. Santos 1959: 117–18) had its area of dominance further restricted.

The displacement of retail stores, the fragmentation of administrative and service activities, and the reduction in importance of Salvador's port would generate a crisis in the city center which resulted in an accentuated loss of dynamism and deterioration of its physical condition. At the same time, the city center, particularly the part around the Pelourinho, became the target of policies ostensibly designed to integrate it into this new territorial logic.

Attempts to Reverse the Deterioration of the Pelourinho

A local discussion, even if initially quite limited in scope, about the destiny of the old city center was restarted in the 1950s.[4] It began with a press campaign against the prostitution that was established there, arguing for the need to recover the area for other functions and another population, and to redeem its "past splendor" (Bahia 1969: 18). The campaign was marked by a moralistic tone, nostalgia for the past, and especially desire for a change in the area's social structure by bringing the city's historical heritage into the political dispute over crime in the area (Gomes 1984). Conditions for the renovation of Salvador's old center were facilitated at the national level by the redefinition of Brazil's preservation policy between 1960 and 1970 and its articulation in the country's new policy for tourism development, in which the Programa de Cidades Históricas (Historical Cities Program) played a prominent role.

Attention then concentrated on the city center and particularly on the Pelourinho,

Figure 6.3. Largo do Cruzeiro de São Francisco, one of the first areas to be renovated in the Pelourinho. (Photo by Griselda Kluppel)

which had been declared a National Heritage Site for Preservation in 1959 (fig. 6.3). This new status resulted in limitations on property rights in the area which, together with the unequal development of city infrastructure and the area's exclusion from the main urban development vectors, ensured the permanence of its physical structures albeit in increasing states of decay (Gomes 1984).

To rehabilitate Salvador's downtown, the state government created the Fundação do Patrimônio Artístico e Cultural da Bahia (Foundation for the Artistic and Cultural Heritage of Bahia, now transformed into an institute called IPAC), which focused on creating the necessary conditions for the development of tourism. The first idea, probably derived from the heightened public concern about prostitution at the time, was to radically change the area's social makeup through a "deportation operation," although the first recovery project in 1970 spoke of "safeguarding the prestige of the sector, with a minimum of social justice." This project assumed that by rehabilitating the heart of the most deteriorated area (Pelourinho Square) and the access roads to the district, the state would be able to unleash private development in a transformational dynamic that would spread to the whole district. The fact that the Fundação established its own headquarters in the area was significant in terms of what the project was attempting to do and helped reduce the stigma attached to that part of the downtown.

This first project was only partially implemented, did not succeed in attracting the expected reinvestments, and generated very minor changes in the area. Then during the three final decades of the twentieth century, more than twenty projects were carried out by agencies at various levels of government (national, state, and city), almost all having in common a concern with promoting tourism. Some of these projects were abandoned in the draft stage, others were partially executed, but all tried with little success to impose a new dynamic and new aesthetics on the area. In addition to their short-term nature, which reveals the fragility typical of government actions in Brazil, innumerable other obstacles would impede the idea of restoring the traditional center and sanitizing it for tourist consumption.

The extreme poverty of the area's resident population was the first of these obstacles. Legislation and financial resources were directed at salvaging isolated buildings considered historic monuments, despite the need to comprehensively rehabilitate a building stock that in some areas was totally deteriorated or even in ruins, a broader challenge that the government had no success involving private property owners in addressing. The very nature of the available resources—which were earmarked for public properties—would result in an increasing dependence on public funds that made large-scale operations impossible, especially during Brazil's cycle of economic crises starting in the early 1980s and the contraction of resources for the cultural area (Gomes 1984).

Because private investors did not respond with improvements in the area, as the government had expected, the situation got even more complicated. This was due to at least two factors: first, listing the area as a National Heritage Site, which limited property rights, was a disincentive to private investment; second, there were better investment opportunities in other areas of the city. Also, as revitalization attempts had not been able to eliminate the reputation of the area around the Pelourinho as a center of criminality and prostitution, this further discouraged a more upscale clientele.

The gradual reduction in public resources for large-scale projects, the organization of a protection movement by the residents, and the area's unattractiveness for private investors were primary factors responsible for reinforcing the "social option" of containing the poor population within the Pelourinho throughout the 1980s. Nevertheless this increasingly paternalistic option would coexist with a lasting vision to transform the area through tourism. This implicit agenda led to a number of the renovated historic buildings being dedicated to public, commercial, or service, rather than residential, uses, consequently reducing the number of available residences. Property owners would allow their buildings to fall into disrepair in order to pressure the government to buy them, since the restrictions imposed by historic preservation frightened off private buyers. This situation reduced even further the Pelourinho's potential as a residential space. Thus, paradoxically, in spite of the different plans, projects, and interventions, buildings became increasingly deteriorated and further subdivided into new tenements.[5]

Mistakes at the political level of these operations became supplemental obstacles that impeded full project implementation: there was never effective articulation among the different levels of government (federal, state, and municipal) acting in the area, nor was this very complex urban question ever attacked in a long-term way that extended beyond each change of state or municipal administrations. Finally, from the fundamental concepts behind these projects, it is clear that they were never able to identify the problems of the old city center comprehensively and address them in a way that could integrate the area with the dynamic of Salvador as a whole.

In the 1990s Salvador's general policies for rehabilitating the Pelourinho were not related to the broader efforts to restructure the dynamic of the city center other than in a fragmentary way. However, an intense process of cultural revitalization and cultural production in the city would be superimposed onto this extremely deteriorated building stock, anchored in several initiatives but especially in popular practices.[6] Through a reinterpretation of local traditions, this area's role as a territorial anchor for these new cultural manifestations was reinforced.

Symbolic Reinvestment in the Pelourinho

Independent of any institutional project, a powerful cultural force emerged in the Pelourinho in the second half of the 1980s, due in part to the opportunities fostered by tourism and in particular to the visibility it brought the area. This "collective investment in place construction based on ethnic symbols" (Morales 1991: 73) would requalify the spaces in a way contrary to the government policies to that time, and would generate a slow but continuous affirmation of black identity in Salvador.[7]

Due to its historical conditions and its longtime status as the colonial capital, Salvador is strongly marked by Afro-Brazilian culture—blacks account for 85 percent of the city's population. Both politically and socially, the city was in the center of the black social movements that characterized the 1970s and 1980s. In this period, for instance, Afro-Brazilian Carnaval groups multiplied—leading to the largest mass celebration of Carnaval in the city since the 1950s (Santos Neto 1991). Composed almost exclusively of blacks, these groups publicly renewed the African traditions that strongly characterize local culture. In a short time several of these groups were formed in different city neighborhoods, uniting different social classes.[8]

This process combined with the explosion of the national and international cultural industry in the 1980s and its search for novelty and exotic combinations. Bahia, traditionally a font of artistic talent (in literature, cinema, and principally in music), saw an opportunity to satisfy this market niche and the hunger of the cultural industry. This happened especially through popular music, an ephemeral cultural phenomenon that must be rapidly recycled to remain novel. Each summer, when preparations for Carnaval are happening nationwide, Salvador responds by providing the rhythm and dance that will dominate the year throughout the country. International cultural contacts and exchanges between Salvador and artists worldwide multiplied, injecting new elements into the black and exotic traditions of the colonial city.[9]

Unlike the purism and immutability that characterizes traditional architectural preservation and revitalization movements—which essentially attempt to re-create the past—the preservation of culture simultaneously valorizes tradition, its contemporary interpretation, and its value as a cultural product that should circulate in the market and that uses the media as a vehicle for its dissemination.[10] In this way the combination of a potent movement affirming black identity, a new relationship between the defense and the marketing of culture, and the reinforcement of tourism as the main economic enterprise of the city, especially in its old center, would form the basis of the process of cultural explosion at that moment in Salvador.

Consequently, the city saw the appearance of a strong and explicit network of territories structured around the formation and multiplication of cultural groups. The Pelourinho would progressively become the hub of this network. Its long history, the investments during two decades of state intervention, the tourism industry that imposed its own cycles on this area, its central location, and its role in the city's cultural network combined to accomplish what new investments alone could never achieve: the possibility of reversing the deterioration of the Pelourinho.

An Effective Urban Operation: 1992–2004

Building on the earlier revitalization attempts and with the benefit of new cultural investments the Pelourinho had received in subsequent years, the longstanding idea of transforming the area into a cultural and tourist center was vigorously renewed in mid-1992, and again Pelourinho Square and its surroundings were targeted because of their centrality. Promoted by the state government through IPAC and CONDER,[11] the new project aimed at an almost complete renovation of all the buildings in the area in seven operational stages targeting various areas which were extremely deteriorated (fig. 6.4). The pace of work was surprisingly fast until the fourth stage: the first and second stages were inaugurated in March and November of 1993, and the third and fourth in March 1994, renovating a total of 366 properties with some US$25 million in state funding.[12] The fifth stage was completed in 1997, and the sixth was under way in 2004, at the time of writing this essay, while the seventh was in the planning stages. A total of 747 buildings are involved in the operation, representing public investments of around US$80 million (Sant'Anna 2003: 101–2).

Some aspects of this initiative are worthy of comment. In a record time of 150 days, the first stage renovated 104 properties, which were converted into 463 new units, 60 percent for retail and 40 percent for services and housing. In order to create semipub-

Figure 6.4. Largo do Pelourinho (Pelourinho Square): (*top*) looking south (photo by Griselda Kluppel); (*bottom*) north (photo by Vicente del Rio).

lic spaces with the character of commercial squares in the heart of some of the renovated blocks, the project eliminated all annexes and additions to the buildings and destroyed the traditional morphology of the city blocks (fig. 6.5). Now more than ten of these spaces hold stages for musical and theatrical performances, attracting a large clientele to the surrounding bars and restaurants. In aesthetic terms, these typological alterations in the block cores altered the buildings and their façades, artificially reinforcing their colonial character and often producing a pastiche effect (fig. 6.6). Architectural details were highlighted and a supposedly original color palette used in an attempt to provide some unity to the whole and increase its visual impact, particularly in comparison to their previous condition and to the areas of the center that are still rundown. The other stages followed the same principles and were executed in the same way, although after the fifth stage, the speed of renovation slowed down.[13]

Over the entirety of the project, significant investments have been made in modernizing and expanding the infrastructure, particularly water, sewer, electricity, and telephone services, which raised the potential market demand for the area. These public works were carried out by private firms, hired and supervised by the state agencies responsible for the project. By hiring firms with great experience in con-

Figure 6.5. Largo Tereza Batista, a "public" space in the core of one of the Pelourinho's historic blocks, is an example of inappropriate changes to the historic morphology. (Photo by Griselda Kluppel)

trolling schedules and managing labor, the state was able to meet the deadlines the politicians had set for the various stages of the project. However, the scale of the work and the short timelines resulted in low-quality construction and obliged the new occupants to redo or complete much of the work, particularly in spaces designated for commerce and service activities. Three public parking structures were inserted into the redesign of blocks, in order to facilitate the access of private vehicles to the area, which had always been one of the greatest problems it faced (Fernandes and Gomes 1995b).

To facilitate project implementation, the ownership of properties was transferred to the state government through either *comodato* contracts (transfer of property to the government for up to ten years) or eminent domain whenever opposition interfered with implementation.[14] This process concentrated in government hands a substantial portion of the properties to be renovated, transforming the state into a giant landlord that decided who could rent property in the area and controlled all rental contracts. This mechanism accentuated the centralized control of the operation and enabled a client-driven political relationship with those interested in relocating to the area.[15]

The rapidity with which private investors responded to the government's initiatives, even given the substantial incentives it offered them, signaled large-scale adherence to the government's vision of increasing tourism in the area and particularly to the reversal in its traditional social uses. The occupation of the new retail and service spaces, which occurred practically immediately, the rapid sequencing of the project phases, the increase in tourism resulting from the marketing campaign, and especially the highly conspicuous police patrols, worked together to dismantle what had been the greatest obstacle to promoting the area as a cultural and tourist destination: its image as dangerous and full of criminals.

In addition to the political desire to establish unequivocally and quickly a definitive change in the Pelourinho, other elements distinguished this intervention from those that preceded it and facilitated its completion. The amount of public money and the way it was invested—in concentrated spurts within each phase—permitted a great number of buildings to be renovated at the same time and increased the project's credibility. It also created a larger supply of units—particularly commercial ones—that could be placed on the market at the same time, stimulating real estate sales and diminishing the time required for return on investment. On the other hand, the concentration of property in state government hands ensured that activity would conform to the project's policy goals because it could control the destiny of the different units. The *comodato* contract system allowed property appreciation generated by the project to be attenuated and relocation incentives to be offered to storeowners, reducing the initial property tax burden on new businesses. In exchange for low rents, the state required tenants to invest in their units by completing the renovation process.

This concentration of investments in a short period of time, the speed of private responses to the state efforts, and the mute desire of middle-class intellectuals for the area's renovation were translated in political terms into support for "a govern-

Figure 6.6. European tourists in one of the Pelourinho's over-rehabilitated streets with an artificially colonial ambiance, under the discreet protection of the police officer on the left. (Photo by Griselda Kluppel)

ment that works," increasing the chances that the project would succeed. Regarding the expectation for change nourished by intellectual segments of the middle class confronted by the increasing threat that the Pelourinho would become irreversibly ruined, it is symptomatic that in spite of the dire effects of the operation on those who lived there, no wider attempt was made to discuss the project's direction or to propose alternatives. The silent demand of these social sectors was transmuted into a passive acceptance of the intervention as its results began to be revealed.

Residential use was overtly excluded from the first six stages: 91 percent of the resulting units were dedicated to commercial and service uses, and only 9 percent to residential purposes (Fernandes and Gomes 1995b: 48). Each family among the original residents of the Pelourinho was offered two alternatives in individual negotiations: (a) monetary compensation if they freed up the space they occupied; or (b) relocation into one of the units renovated for residential use.[16] As the large majority of residents were extremely poor, the first option was the most attractive for them.[17] "Operation deportation"—a dream since 1967—was then largely accomplished, and 2002 estimates indicate that only about 2 percent of the original population remained in the area (A. Oliveira 2002: 124).

From a social point of view, the residential question was always confronted only partially up to the sixth stage of this operation, and was characterized by a radical abandonment of the guiding rationale of maintaining the resident population that had characterized IPAC's action from its founding, and which had at times assumed specifically populist and pro-resident dimensions (Magnavita 1995: 152). The lack of community political mobilization and the residents' inability to organize themselves facilitated the eviction of a large number of families, particularly those considered most undesirable by the project managers, thus increasing the square footage available for commercial use. The few remaining residents were relocated to new units within the area itself or in the area yet to be renovated; while their numbers were not enough to preserve the Pelourinho's original social profile, their presence contributes to the maintenance of a certain way of life that confers "authenticity" to the renovated historical center.

The Crisis of the Model and the Seventh Stage

Fifteen years after the beginning of the operation, the majority of the renovated buildings are now fully operational with retail and service tenants whose main clientele are visitors and tourists. Eateries, bars, restaurants, shops selling local crafts and souvenirs, and art galleries predominate (fig. 6.7). The Pelourinho was never able to recover its dynamic urban life, however, and it continues to demand significant

Figure 6.7. A renovated street in the Pelourinho with a high concentration of restaurants and bars. (Photo by Griselda Kluppel)

investments by the state government, which has retained the responsibility for maintaining building exteriors (façades and roofs). There is also a high degree of turnover among the businesses there, and even some of the most culturally oriented have left the area (Sant'Anna 2003). Today, with rare exceptions, the area has an ambiguous character between a tourist center and a popular center, which still feeds its fragile, uncertain, and decreasing urban dynamics. According to statistics from the Programa Pelourinho Dia e Noite (Pelourinho Night and Day Program), in spite of enormous efforts to produce daily events, public attendance has dropped dramatically, except for during Carnaval and the June festivals.[18] Sant'Anna (2003) points out that between January and December 2002 almost US$900,000 was invested to promote 1,546 events that involved 13,134 artists and attracted an audience of more than 2,800,000.[19]

Having realized that the conceptual model of rehabilitating the area as a great open-air shopping center with a constant parade of heavily promoted events clearly was not sustainable in terms of urban dynamics, in 1999 the state started discussing the insertion of housing into the Pelourinho. Four new factors reinforced this idea: (a) new programs by the Caixa Econômica Federal, Brazil's major housing financing agency; (b) new national programs for the revitalization of city centers, particularly the Projeto Monumenta with resources from the Inter-American Development Bank (IDB); (c) the new budgetary constraints of the state government, which up to 1999 had almost exclusively used its own resources; and (d) the necessity of attracting external funding to continue with the operation.[20]

These new factors conditioned the conception of the project's seventh phase, which targeted an extremely deteriorated, impoverished, and marginalized area. In this phase a total of 134 properties were identified for renovation for predominantly residential use, along with the restoration of some historic monuments and the construction of parking. Although the inclusion of residences increased the potential for making the area more dynamic, very little truly changed in terms of social policy. On the one hand the government still continued to compensate or relocate the remaining 1,647 resident families without offering them the alternative to remain in the Pelourinho, because the new residents attracted to the area were primarily state and municipal employees (Sant'Anna 2003: 86). On the other hand, because of the difficulties with negotiation that had characterized the earlier stages, and with the support of nongovernmental organizations and politicians, the residents sued the state government in an effort to stay in the area.[21] However, their vulnerability against the conditions imposed by the negotiators has not changed.

With great emphasis on cultural consumption—the departure point for the renovation of the Pelourinho and its urban dynamics—the heritage-tourism binomial would now be complemented by another element: housing, even if only on the edge of the project area. The seventh phase seeks to bring the urban vitality resulting from consumption and service activities in daily life, as well as to reduce dependence on direct state intervention to maintain the operation.

Moreover, it is interesting to observe that, paralleling the state's commitment to create housing, some leading-edge local private developers took the initiative of investing in Salvador's historic center by investing in the renovation and adaptive reuse of old buildings. These developments aim to transform the city center into a great hub of cultural and social events, once again reinforcing the unidimensional and cyclical rhythm that experience has already demonstrated to be inadequate.

Conclusion: Tourism, Culture, Heritage, and the City

Many aspects of the intervention in Salvador's old center are similar to those found in several projects around the world, particularly in terms of the way that city history, urban restructuring, and tourism interconnect. Other similar aspects include the fundamental role of tourism development in the city economy as a whole, the use (even if only hypothetical) of historical precedents to inform the project, and the abandonment of large-scale projects in favor of more specific and localized interventions as a mode of public action in the city.

The issue of tourism is still central to understanding the process under way in the Pelourinho. A shrinking economic sector in Bahia at the end of the 1980s, tourism became a priority for the state government in 1991, which implied defining "tourist attractions." Salvador was considered to be strategic not only because of its unique historical, cultural, and scenic assets, but also because its airport is the principal entrance for tourists to the Brazilian Northeast. Salvador was given the role of a magnet for cultural tourism, events, and nautical activities for which a modern infrastructure was created, including marinas in Todos os Santos Bay.

The Pelourinho's renovation is part of a series of cultural revitalization initiatives and urban planning interventions that seek to associate history and culture with entertainment for the purpose of tourism development (fig. 6.8). Cultural institutions were given new vitality and requalified, as culture was perceived as a means to promote the state economically in a globalized world. Public spaces of high visibility and those strategically located with regard to tourism were also the object of specific projects. Interventions of greater or lesser design quality were carried out in parks, gardens, and avenues to enhance their intended role as "image-synthesizers" of the city, serving as catalysts for approval and consensus among influential segments of public opinion. Like in other cities, in Salvador place marketing not only tries to attract outsiders and "sell the city" to tourists, but it also has an important role in influencing the local population, creating political legitimacy, and giving the illusion of solidarity and social cohesion in a city that is increasingly fragmented and segregated.

Therefore, the recovery of the Pelourinho is part of a much broader strategy designed to sell the city as a tourist product alongside other methods of place marketing, such as the promotion of events and urban design. In the first case, history and culture became essential elements for the creation of an attractive image of the city, associated to other characteristics attributed to people from Bahia, such as their taste for partying, their hospitality, and their informality, in addition to the self-proclaimed dynamism of their political leaders. In terms of history, the strategy is aimed not at promoting an outmoded and museum-like past, but at staging it as a spectacle and form of entertainment that is continuously recycled with contemporary values.

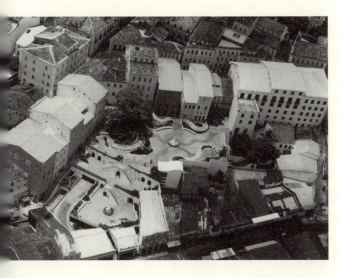

Figure 6.8. The award-winning Quarteirão Cultural and Praça das Artes e da Memória, the Pelourinho. This complex of eighteenth- and nineteenth-century buildings was successfully renovated into two theaters, art galleries and studios, a dance company, a public library, and three small museums; the sloping terrain allowed for a parking structure under the plaza. (Photo by Claudiomar Gonçalves)

Thus, another fundamental aspect of the strategy is the promotion of city events such as the Carnaval and other music festivals, street markets, art exhibits, national and international conferences, and the like.

No event exceeds the Carnaval in scale, external visibility, or economic importance. Perhaps more than any other Brazilian city, Salvador provides an interesting example of these new urban strategies. If Carnaval is an excellent expression of the Salvadoran population's love of music and festivities, it has also been exploited as a fantastic export product that generates important resources and is a direct or indirect source of jobs for thousands of persons. Each year Carnaval channels hundreds of thousands of tourists to Salvador, privatizes public spaces, subverts the city's functioning, and transforms many of its places into stages for festivals and parties.

In terms of the political level it is important to emphasize that together with the preservation of Salvador's traditional center, several other public initiatives have been designed to provide the city with a "cultural" label, including all the diversity this notion implies. Since the early 1990s this effort has also included the recovery of important cultural buildings, Salvador's competition against other Brazilian cities to attract the Brazilian branch of the Guggenheim Museum, and more recently the (questionable) decision to build a branch of Paris's Rodin Museum in the city—a high-cost investment that will certainly harm other cultural institutions by drawing away much of the available resources.

In spite of having cultural preservation as its basic foundation, the intervention in the Pelourinho district had a negative impact on important local cultural spaces such as the Afro-Brazilian bars that had developed there at the beginning of the 1980s. Frequented by an Afro-Brazilian clientele, these bars catalyzed the effervescence of the area over a significant period of time. Each of them used to be run independently and drew clients to themselves and their competitors alike through their sheer presence, resulting in an animated locale where Afro-Brazilian music attracted an enthusiastic population that spilled out of the bars and into the streets. Today, these bars have been confined to a space previously occupied by a vacant lot, which was improvised into the Praça do Reggae (Reggae Plaza), where each bar's music interferes with the others because they share a common space, and access is limited by an intimidating fence and a ticket window (fig. 6.9).

From the point of view of heritage conservation policy, there is no doubt that the operation was a response to a strong public demand to halt the accelerating deterioration of an important urban heritage site, although the approach chosen carried a high social cost. The neglect of other parts of the old city demonstrates the same narrow understanding, which is allowing very important areas to deteriorate or to experience rapid changes in their morphological, functional, and social aspects by private-sector

Figure 6.9. The Praça do Reggae replaced a dynamic group of bars that used to be a traditional meeting place for the Afro-Brazilian community. The uninviting design and its isolation from the public realm show the high level of control imposed by the state. (Photo by Griselda Kluppel)

redevelopment. The poor design quality of the completed works in the Pelourinho coupled with the authoritarian tenor of the operation show the project's disrespect for IPHAN (National Institute for Historic Preservation) guidelines, to which any intervention in a federally listed heritage site should adhere, and tarnish the richness of the Brazilian experience by re-creating its historical heritage.

From the point of view of urban policy, we wish to point out some mistakes and contradictions in the quest to revitalize the Pelourinho. There were three fundamental mistakes: relying for too long on a single function (cultural) while practically eliminating new residential uses in the area, conceding total priority to tourism in spite of its seasonal swings in Salvador, and practically eliminating the area's traditional residents. Among the contradictions, we can point out the project's disarticulation from policies and programs for the city as a whole, and most important, the focusing of all efforts on the Pelourinho in detriment to other parts of the old city, some of which have equally important architectural and urban complexes.

The only exceptions to this panorama of neglect in the rest of the city are the neighborhoods of Carmo and Santo Antônio, bordering on the Pelourinho. Developed in the eighteenth and nineteenth centuries on a pattern different from the Pelourinho, these areas hold mostly small single-family residences built on the front and sides of their lot, along with a small number of two-story houses. Although the areas never experienced any significant public intervention, and perhaps because of its morphology, its middle-class residents were able to stay and take good care of their properties, although they did introduce substantial changes that dramatically changed the neighborhood's character. Yet because they maintained a certain architectural and urbanistic integrity along with an authentic "neighborhood life," and because of its proximity to the Pelourinho's cultural attractions, the social profile of Carmo and

Santo Antônio is rapidly being transformed. Property values have shot up, hotels and inns have multiplied, and the poorer segments of the original middle-class residents are being replaced by a more intellectual population and a significant number of foreigners who reside or have a second residence there.

Therefore, the recent transformations in the Pelourinho confront us with three fundamental issues with regard to the type of urban revitalization that is now under way. The first concerns the fact that these processes take a long time to mature, and their effects on urban dynamics can only be accurately evaluated in the long term. The second issue relates to the necessity for articulation between rehabilitation projects targeting specific areas and the urban processes that led to decay in the first place. The exaggerated focus on particular phenomena diminishes the possibility of understanding the broader logic and the mechanisms that produce them, resulting in actions of limited scope. Finally, the lack of success of the authoritarian projects in the Pelourinho renews our hope in the legitimacy of democratic negotiation as a road to urban recovery that is longer lasting, has more vitality, and adheres more closely to social justice.

Notes

This essay is an expanded and updated version of "O Passado tem Futuro? Os Descaminhos da Requalificação do Pelourinho," a paper presented at the 1995 national meeting of ANPUR (the National Association for Post-Graduate Research in Urban and Regional Planning).

1. These data are only estimates, since there is no reliable information on the area. Only a handful of socioeconomic surveys exist, and their methodologies are, in our view, questionable.
2. The discovery of oil in Bahia in the 1940s gave the state the necessary financing to implement the nationally mandated development plans successfully. An industrial park was built near Salvador in the 1960s, and an oil refinery was built in the 1970s.
3. At the time 11,750 acres (4,700 hectares) of public lands were privatized, and according to Mattedi et al. (1989) by 1978 the titles to 6,000 acres (2,400 hectares) of property had already changed hands.
4. Preservation efforts in Bahia began in 1917 with the creation of a municipal commission to protect works of historical or artistic value. In the 1920s and 1930s a public debate about the demolition of a sixteenth-century diocesan church increased public awareness of Salvador's heritage. The church was demolished in 1933 to make way for a trolley line (Fernandes and Gomes 1992).
5. The decrease in housing units in the area caused them to be disputed over by an ever-increasing number of tenants, in spite of the overall population decline in the area as a function of the factors mentioned in the text (Gomes 1984).
6. Examples are A Cidade é Nossa (The City Is Ours), a movement started by Salvador's merchants' association (Clube de Diretores Lojistas), and collaborations between businessmen

and institutions in the low city aimed at its economic, cultural, and symbolic revitalization. Cultural and community organizations have participated in these efforts (see Fernandes and Gomes 1995a, 1995b).

7. In this chapter we do not try to analyze the complexity of this movement in Salvador, but merely to situate its importance in the symbolic reinvestment in the Pelourinho.

8. Among the most prominent groups are the internationally known Olodum (based in the Pelourinho and composed basically of blue-collar workers); Filhos de Gandhi (formed in the 1950s by dockworkers and also based in the Pelourinho); Ilê Ayê (in Liberdade neighborhood, composed of a large number of workers from Camaçari petrochemical plant), and Araketu (in Periperi, a suburb of Salvador) (Morales 1991).

9. Among the several international politicians and artists who visited Salvador, it was perhaps Michael Jackson who garnered the most attention by shooting a music video directed by Spike Lee there in February 1996.

10. These movements cultivate the relationship between the cultural industry and tourism at the same time that they defend their cultural traditions without seeing any inherent contradiction between these two goals.

11. IPAC is the state of Bahia's Institute for Artistic and Cultural Preservation, while CONDER is the state Urban Development Agency.

12. The amount in U.S. dollars is only an estimate due to various changes in the Brazilian currency and the fluctuating exchange rate during the period.

13. The election of a new state governor, albeit one from the same political party, resulted in the slowing of projects (A. Oliveira 2002).

14. *Comodato* is a legal term that comes from the Latin *commodatum* and is similar to a lease, except that the property is transferred with no monthly payments for a predetermined period of time.

15. For more details, see Fernandes and Gomes 1995b.

16. See interesting statements by former residents in Augusto Oliveira (2002).

17. Studies done in 1997 by the Institute of Artistic and Cultural Patrimony cited by Sant'Anna (2003), indicate that in stages one to five, 1,855 families were indemnified at an average of R$1,222 (about US$1,000) per family, which was clearly not enough to really solve anybody's housing problems, even if they relocated to distant neighborhoods.

18. Statistics for Carnaval are difficult to analyze because of the enormous variation in numbers from year to year, from one-half to one million persons, which probably reflects different methodologies for gathering data. However, they indicate the importance of this event in the Pelourinho and in the city as a whole. St. John's Day, in June, a traditional celebration in rural areas and small cities, has been gaining importance in Salvador.

19. Events include dances, shows, Carnaval group rehearsals, theater, children's activities, performances, and *capoeira* shows. Statistics graciously provided by Projeto Pelourinho Dia e Noite (IPAC/Governo do Estado da Bahia).

20. For a detailed discussion see Sant'Anna (2003).

21. The 2002 video documentary *O Avesso do Pelô* (The Other Side of the Pelourinho) shows some of the residents' testimony and documents their wish to continue living in the Pelourinho.

CHAPTER 7

Riverfront Revitalization in the Amazon The Case of Belém

Simone Silene Dias Seabra

and Alice da Silva Rodrigues

Over the last decade several of Brazil's port cities have been experiencing projects intended to improve the quality of their built landscape, not only in order to reestablish closer relations with their unique historical, geographical, and cultural qualities in response to community pressure, but also to make themselves more competitive in regional, national, and global markets. Many of these projects are based on the recovery of the symbiosis of the urban network with the bordering body of water—ocean, bay, river, or lake—and also with the older port, commercial, and residential zones. In the majority of large cities, shorefronts near the downtown were associated with criminality as a consequence of the port activities that had originally occurred there, and later because of the degradation caused by alterations in port functions and their removal to more modern installations in new ports far away. Emptied of their function and their financial base, these obsolete urban and architectural structures would end up abandoned or neglected by city administrations. This situation has changed in the last few years, however, because of the discovery of the great scenic, cultural, and symbolic potential of central city areas near waterfronts. These have been recovered and revitalized as new places, contributing to the redesign of their city's maps.

This process also occurred in Belém, the capital of Pará state, located on the banks of the Guamá River and Guajará Bay. The old structures there, however, had not been totally abandoned but were underutilized or were converted to new uses. For example, in addition to freight they now handled passengers. In response to the growth of the city, the development of the waterfront prioritized economic activities linked to transportation and manufacturing, which occupied the whole riverfront corridor without any sort of regulation by city government. There was no concern for ecology nor any incentive for the installation of tourist and recreational facilities, in spite of the region being known worldwide for its wild rivers and vegetation. Various commercial activities also developed spontaneously along the bayshore and the river, in small shoreline communities, and in the archipelago that makes up the delta part of the municipality. This contributed to the installation of innumerable passenger ports along Belém's continental shore.

It was only during the 1990s that the Belém government began to direct special attention to urban design projects that focused on rehabilitating specific spaces along the shore. Generally located in the historical center of Belém (the original nucleus of the city), these efforts have sought to preserve and enhance the natural environment, giving priority to creating new functions for buildings significant to the history of the city and to the creation of spaces for culture and recreation. Belém's urban design—which was disdained by the modern movement—turned out to be a useful instrument for changing the character of the local urban landscape. It has helped reestablish parameters for visual quality that seek to enhance the city's panorama and the relationship between old and new architecture, and to generate new spaces that draw the city population back to enjoy the river edge. Besides discussing some of the results achieved by these urban design projects, this chapter evaluates how well they met their initial goals, and how well they linked with traditional sociocultural practices. Finally, we discuss the new possibilities that are open to the city of Belém through urban design practice.

The Inextricable Connection of Belém and the River

Belém owes its urban and economic development to its geographical position on the estuary of the Amazon River, and its development has always depended on the rivers. From its foundation in the early sixteenth century until 1960, when the Belém-Brasília Highway was inaugurated to integrate the Amazon region with the capital and the rest of Brazil, the rivers were the city's only connection with the rest of the country and with some cities in the interior of the state. And as far as foreign commerce is concerned, the rivers continue to be the principal means of exporting regional and local produce. In Belém riverfront development reflects the city's social and economic development.

The foundation of Belém resulted from Portuguese efforts to reorganize their territorial policies for Brazil, a much-needed response to increasing Spanish, French, and Dutch attacks and attempted invasions. Strategically located between the mouth of the Guamá River and Guajará Bay—access point to the Amazon—the city was founded in 1616 with the construction of a fortification (Forte do Presépio, or Forte do Castelo). The fort marked the perimeter of the settlement, defined the street grid, and shaped the first urban nucleus, the Cidade Velha (Old City, now a district of Belém). In 1688, to control the export of produce to other countries, the Portuguese crown built scales in a cove of Guajará Bay, where the famous Ver-o-Peso (See-the-Weight) pier would be built some years later (E. Rodrigues and Meira 2004). By then two other forts had improved Belém's defensive system, one of them the São Pedro Nolasco, close to Ver-o-Peso pier (Cañete 2003).

Before the eighteenth century the city's growth was slow and restricted to the Old City and Campina districts, which were separated by the Piry marsh, a swampy area that impeded unification between the two nuclei (Belém 2000a). City development would be significantly increased by the end of that century, however, when the crown founded the Companhia do Comércio, a company with a monopoly on trade in the region that was responsible for a major increase in regional exports to Europe. The boom to the local economy was reflected in the growth of Belém, the construction of a number of new mansions and sumptuous buildings, and several urban improvements, such as street paving and construction of a new dock and private warehouses (IPHAN 2003).

By the turn of the nineteenth century, the waterfront was being built up hazardously, with a large number of small private and government-owned wharves and warehouses. Two great city improvements transformed the natural context of the original settlement. First, the Piry marsh was drained and filled, allowing the expansion of the city and the interconnection of the Cidade Velha and Campina districts. Second, the filling in of the land between Ver-o-Peso pier and Mercês Church created a new section of the city that jutted into the bay (Belém 2000a). By the mid-nineteenth century, Belém was becoming the world's largest exporter of rubber, which had a decisive impact on the city's spatial reorganization and particularly on its connections to the port. At the end of the nineteenth century more urban improvements were carried out, one of the most significant being the construction of Boulevard Castilhos França along the waterfront, which eventually became a major access route to the shore.

In 1909 the first phase of the wharf and the first warehouse of the new publicly controlled Companhia das Docas do Pará (CDP; Pará Docks Company) were inaugurated. Despite the importance of rubber exports to the region and the country, the new port was finished only in 1913, after several private piers and warehouses had been expropriated. The port consisted of 1,860 yards of shoreline and fifteen warehouses (Trindade 1997; CDP 2004). At that time, two landmark buildings were built: the annex to the Recebedoria de Rendas (Customshouse), now the Solar da Beira cultural center, and the Mercado de Ferro (Iron Market), prefabricated in England

and assembled at Ver-o-Peso pier. Next to the pier, the Mercado Municipal de Carne (Municipal Meat Market) was expanded, and the Praça do Relógio (Clock Square) was built on the landfill over the Piry marsh (Rodrigues and Meira 2004).

The construction of the new port totally changed the riverfront and consolidated the major city works there. Ironically, its completion coincided with the end of the rubber boom in the early 1910s and, inevitably, the city plunged into economic decline and the port activity slowed. Because of the increasing size of modern ships, the constant need to dredge the river, and modern operational requirements, in 1985 the Companhia das Docas do Pará began transferring some port activities to more adequate facilities in a neighboring municipality. At that time three warehouses were closed and two were adapted to handle small containers, bulk cargo, and passenger ships.

In spite of the decline in Belém's port activities, retail sales on Ver-o-Peso pier got stronger, and this traditional area of the downtown became the major retail and service center in the region. The geographical position of the city favored access to small riverside communities, and Belém's commercial center became the primary supplier in the state of Pará. Properties located in neighborhoods around the original city core that had good infrastructure and services greatly appreciated in market value.

The dynamism of retail is fundamental for the permanent vitality of the historical area and the emergence of small-scale private port operations, such as small moorings for cargo and passenger boats. Therefore, despite the center having undergone economic decay in recent decades, primarily because of the construction of shopping malls in other parts of the city, it survived because of the popularization of its commercial activities and the growth of the informal market. The recent economic revitalization of the historic center and some of the surrounding areas coincided with the new urban projects that added value to the waterfront.

Redesigning the Riverfront

The strong presence of the rivers, forests, and riverside dwellings in the urban ecology of the Amazon comes from the coexistence of its inhabitants with their habitat. Although the gigantism of these natural elements reaffirms the supremacy of nature over humans, historically Belém's cultural and social activities were kept away from the river margins and restricted to the city squares. Only in the 1990s, with the first public projects for restaurants and bars at the riverfront, was the river reestablished as a destination and the population alerted to the importance of the waterfront for social gatherings and events.

The first step toward revitalizing downtown and the waterfront was taken with the 1993–2013 master plan, Plano Diretor Urbano do Município de Belém (PDU), approved by a city council ordinance (Belém 1993). This innovative plan introduced new planning tools in service of its major goal, the promotion of environmental and landscape quality through a series of different environmental programs, physical planning, and control over the aesthetics of the natural and built landscapes. The plan also aimed at promoting tourism through direct investments, rehabilitation, and a process of continuous management of key attractions such as the riverfront and other public areas.

The PDU gave special attention to the unique elements of the city, especially those that represented its historical and cultural heritage such as the river, the bay, the channels between islands, and the mango trees (the city's symbol). It gave priority to the recovery of public use of the banks of the Guamá River and Guajará Bay for leisure and recreation. Guided by these objectives the state and municipal governments began to establish revitalization projects and to create new cultural and recreational spaces along the shore, especially in Belém's historical center. However, these initiatives were not sufficiently coordinated to create continuous and complementary spaces, even though the majority were located in contiguous areas, as we shall see.

When the master plan was approved, there was little interaction between the different spheres of government that have jurisdiction over the city territory—the city functions simultaneously as capital of the state and of the municipality, in addition to being an important federal port. Differences in policy orientation between state and municipal governments led the former to implement projects that sought to insert the city into national and international business and tourism, whereas the latter directed its actions toward community-based needs such as recreation and open spaces. Furthermore, the lack of an integrated vision of the urban realm compromised initiatives, which often supported projects isolated from their surroundings and the communities of users.

In 2000 the city developed the PRO-BELÉM Plan for Restructuring Belém's Riverfront (Plano de Reestruturação da Orla de Belém), which followed the PDU's guidelines, in order to integrate the various public and private actions along the river (Belém 2000a). These guidelines establish that areas along the shore should be set aside for environmental protection, and provide incentives for the establishment of cultural and recreational facilities. To recover environmental quality along the river and the bay, enhance the public image of these areas, and attract users, PRO-Belém seeks to integrate the different city and state government projects already under way, to identify and set aside areas along the shore for future projects of public interest, and to establish criteria for these initiatives. Although PRO-BELÉM gives only general guidelines rather than specific policies for the riverfront and ignores important questions such as how the area should be administered, it does help constrain indiscriminate appropriation of space, such as land invasions by individuals, and contributes to a new institutional and political posture in relation to the use of those spaces.

In this context, public initiatives on the riverfront have been undertaken since 1997, when the state government began construction of the Núcleo Cultural Feliz Lusitânia (Happy Lusitânia Cultural Nucleus) and Estação das Docas (Dock Station). The former project sought to rehabilitate several historic buildings and public spaces in Cidade Velha. The latter involved the creation of a tourist attraction through conversion of three vacant port warehouses (Warehouses 1, 2, and 3) and the rehabilitation of their immediate environs for public use.

Paralleling this effort, the city government gave attention to recovering degraded areas along the shoreline with the Ver o Rio (See the River) project to the north of the central city. According to the official description, the project attempted "to open windows on the river," a phrase that reflected the intention of the municipal government to create spaces for public use and recreation, redirecting the type of use that had prevailed on the shore until that time. At the same time, the municipality began an ambitious collection of urban reforms and revitalization projects in the area that became known as the Ver-o-Peso Complex. Work began in 2001 with the restructuring of the market and the renovation of the Mercado de Ferro.

In the next sections, we discuss some of the specific rehabilitation projects in the city center and on the riverfront. Although the success of these projects was mostly limited to the local scale, they represent important steps forward and have generated spontaneous transformation of their environs, contributed to improving Belém's urban aesthetics, and altered social habits and the population's perception of the riverfront (fig. 7.1).

Ver o Rio

The Ver o Rio project consists of a series of integrated actions to be implemented in several phases in order to renovate degraded public and private areas along Belém's riverfront. The goal is to create open spaces for recreation and leisure and to provide new vistas of the bay and the river (fig. 7.2). The project started in 1998 with the declaration of eminent domain and expropriation of private properties, piers, and drydocks, and as of 2004 two phases had been completed.

The first phase of the project encompassed an area of 50,000 square feet and included walkways, seating areas, kiosks for food vendors, two small bars, and a playground whose structures simulated local folk toys made of *miriti*—raw material from

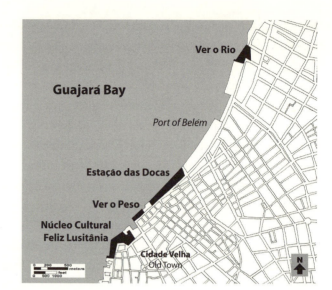

Figure 7.1. Belém's central area, showing the project sites. (Drawing by Simone Seabra, adapted by Vicente del Rio)

Figure 7.2. View of the Ver o Rio project at the Belém riverfront, showing the lake and main landscaped areas. (Photo by João Ramid, www.joaoramid.com.br)

a palm tree native to Amazon region (CTB 2003). In 2001 a 75,000–square-foot park was added, with an artificial lake, a boardwalk, and two memorials—one honoring native peoples and the other, black people—two ethnic groups that together with Europeans gave birth to Brazilian cultural manifestations (Belém 2000b).

The project design was inspired by nature and utilized meandering pedestrian walkways and park equipment laid out amidst gardens and palm trees. Only a limited amount of angled street parking is provided along the avenue that links the area to the downtown and will be expanded northward along the waterfront in future phases. A bike path was built along the whole project area, which eventually will link with a larger bike system that the city expects to construct in the near future.

In the next stage of the Ver o Rio project, sports facilities, a new anchorage for boats, and an amphitheater are planned, but construction has been delayed because the land designated for it is in litigation. The major challenge the project area faces, however, comes from its present environs, where large-scale industrial and commercial uses, warehouses, shipping firms, and small industries still predominate and dominate the cityscape. Besides, if one wants to travel to the project area by bus—a large number of city dwellers do not own cars—the closest stops are two blocks away beyond high walls, blind spots, and intimidating industrial buildings. This makes the project unattractive and even unsafe for a large segment of the population, and the city has yet to come up with initiatives to make these surroundings more supportive of Ver o Rio.

PRO-BELÉM envisions redevelopment along the whole riverfront avenue, and around 20 percent had been completed as of 2007. This reduced the possibility of establishing municipal incentives for land-use changes in the surrounding areas to support the project. This issue could be addressed through the implementation of useful and flexible planning tools that already exist in Belém's master plan—such as the transfer of development rights or special interlinked operations.[1]

Estação das Docas

In 1998 the state government converted three practically abandoned port warehouses for retail, cultural, and recreational uses, turning them into a new tourist attraction, Estação das Docas. The buildings had been prefabricated in England and assembled in Belém at the turn of the twentieth century, and because of their historic and cultural importance were under the protection of the Instituto de Preservação Histórica e Artística Nacional (IPHAN; National Institute for Artistic and Historic Preservation. This 230,000–square-foot project also incorporates the archaeological remains of the old Fort of São Pedro Nolasco as part of the design, which includes a public plaza, an amphitheater, and pedestrian walkways along the riverfront leading to the renovated warehouses. A smaller warehouse was restored to serve as a terminal for passenger hydrofoils, and a floating pier was added for boats offering tours along the river (fig. 7.3).

The historic warehouses were renovated following a simple but effective architectural solution that restored the historical elements and provided comfortable interiors protected from the Amazonian heat and high humidity. Interior and exterior spaces are harmoniously integrated, and new metal marquees attached to the original structures provide shaded restaurant verandas where patrons can sit and enjoy the view. Warehouse 1, renamed Boulevard das Artes (Arts Boulevard), holds a permanent exhibit of artifacts recovered from the old fort, shops and stands selling local and regional crafts and produce, and eateries and bars with indoor and outdoor seating (fig. 7.4). Warehouse 2 became Boulevard da Gastronomia (Gastronomy Boulevard) with five restaurants on the ground floor and fast-food locations in the mezzanine space. Warehouse 3, the Boulevard da Cultura (Cultural Boulevard), now houses a 450–seat theater, a space for cultural events, and traveling exhibits. The three warehouses are linked by covered passageways that allow ample views to the river and the bay, and old cranes are placed along the pedestrian walkways as reminders of the original port functions.

Figure 7.3. Aerial view of Estação das Docas, showing one of the converted warehouses and the pier for tour boats. (Photo by João Ramid, www.joaoramid.com.br)

Figure 7.4. Pedestrian walkway and a renovated warehouse at Estação das Docas. (Photo by Simone Seabra)

Although the state government achieved its goal, and the Estação das Docas is a major regional and national tourist attraction and leisure area for the upper and middle classes in Belém, the project faces some urban design problems. First, the architecture of the project is off-putting to lower-class patrons—the majority of the city population—who feel they cannot afford to go inside. Second, the project is totally oriented on the river, it does not integrate well with its urban surroundings, and it is visually unappealing from the outside. Parking spaces, protective fencing, and uninviting gates are visual and physical barriers that separate Estação das Docas from the street sidewalk. The area is also separated by a grate from the contiguous Praça do Pescador (Fisherman's Square) in Ver-o-Peso, the next riverfront project built by the city—a clear sign of the disconnect between state and city actions. Finally, from a wider urban design perspective, the interesting historic buildings immediately across the street hold uses that do not complement the project, accentuating the status of Estação das Docas as an isolated destination rather than a part of the city fabric.

The Ver-o-Peso Complex

The largest of the projects in the present study, known as Ver-o-Peso, encompasses an area of about 350,000 square feet that stretches 745 yards along the riverfront in the historic downtown, the city's busiest business and retail core. The project was meant to integrate the existing street markets and renovate public spaces, piers, and streets, in addition to restoring the main historic buildings within its boundaries. Because of the area's heavy daily use and because it connects to other central spaces, special attention was dedicated to the improvement of all pedestrian spaces, linkages, and circulation, and to enhancing the principal gateways to the project.

As we have noted earlier, the Ver-o-Peso complex is Belém's major physical and cultural heritage area; it encompasses the old dock and buildings representative of

Figure 7.5. The Ver-o-Peso complex, showing the renovated Mercado de Ferro, the Solar da Beira, and the new tentlike structures of the public market. (Photo by João Ramid, www.joaoramid.com.br)

military, religious, and commercial architecture from different historical periods since the eighteenth century (fig. 7.5). They include the Mercado Municipal de Carne, Mercado de Ferro, Relógio and Pescador squares; the Solar da Beira (Shore Manor), and private buildings along the waterfront. The area is in constant use due to the open-air markets of Açaí and Ver-o-Peso—among the most diverse in Brazil—which have long been local tourist attractions.

The Ver-o-Peso complex is a marketplace selling produce (fruits, medicinal herbs, fish, meats, and so on) and handicrafts coming primarily from the interior of the state, among other things, as well as having a food court where traditional dishes are sold. Because it holds the most diverse and representative forms of culture in the state of Pará and because it is flavored by the mysticism of the Amazon, Ver-o-Peso is strongly embedded in the popular imagination and has become the city's best-known image. Large crowds of shoppers from all parts of Belém and Pará intermingle daily with tourists from other parts of Brazil and overseas.

The city government decided to intervene in 1998 by renovating the Praça do Pescador and its parking area in order to provide better views of the water and begin reestablishing the longstanding relationship between city and river. National competitions for the rest of the area followed in the same year, and four phases of construction were planned, two of which have been concluded as of 2004. In the first phase 10,210 square feet of the market's produce section was renovated, and the façades of the Mercado de Ferro were restored. Built with cast-iron components imported from England in 1901, this building is a major tourist attraction and one of Belém's best-known postcard images.

In the second phase the Solar da Beira, an eclectic building that once was the regional customshouse, was restored and converted into a cultural center with educational facilities and stalls selling regional crafts (fig. 7.6). Another 11,540–square-foot area of the market was renovated into stalls serving food and selling groceries, industrial products, ironwork, and plants. In the third phase, which began in 2003, another 4,030 square feet of the marketplace was renovated to include more food stalls plus areas for crafts, ceramics, fruit concentrates, and fish. In this phase, the interior of the Mercado de Ferro was restored and modernized for commercial fish sales. The fourth and last phase, which is yet to be undertaken, will encompass 140,290 square meters, including the Praça do Relógio, the Ver-o-Peso pier, the Açaí Market, and Ladeira do Castelo—a steep street leading to the old fortress and the first to be built in Belém—which links the market to the Núcleo Cultural Feliz Lusitânia, the adjacent revitalization project overseen by the state government.

Once rehabilitation is completed, the open-market will be totally integrated with its surroundings: the Praça do Pescador, the parking lot, the two market buildings, and the Solar da Beira. The project generates a continuous space that provides for

Figure 7.6. The tentlike structure of the public market with the Solar da Beira and the Mercado de Ferro in the background. (Photo by Simone Seabra)

the different specialized activities, prioritizes pedestrian traffic, and is coherent with preexisting traffic flows (pedestrians, vehicles, buses, river transports, and cargo hauling). The open-air market was arranged so that the views of the river from cross streets were maintained, which enhanced its integration with the rest of the central city.

During project implementation, several changes to the original plans had to be made to accommodate conflicts, particularly those caused by the proposed spatial distribution of some market activities and because the project did not anticipate the exact number of stalls necessary to house all vendors. The original design—tensile canvas on a tentlike metallic structure covering each individual stall—was modified to accommodate Belém's climate of intense sunlight and high rainfall. Now a common roof covers the entire area, better protecting stalls and shoppers from rainstorms. The resulting silhouette stands out in the cityscape, making an interesting contrast with the surrounding historic buildings.

Two of the principal challenges of Ver-o-Peso were to modernize the infrastructure of the open-air market without interfering with its existing uses, and to preserve and revitalize the area's historic buildings. Intervening in the market space was certainly the greatest challenge because the market represents a very complex social dynamic that involved, in addition to the legitimate activities there, criminal activities such as trafficking in wild animals, drugs, and juvenile prostitution. As part of the rehabilitation efforts, the city attempted to clean up the area by relicensing the vendors and increasing police activity.

The positive fallout from the project was already evident in 2004, when the last phase was being implemented. Improvements in landscaping, general aesthetics, and the infrastructure of the stalls influenced the behavior of vendors, improving the quality of their service and their attentiveness to customers. Ver-o-Peso continues to be one of Belém's most memorable images, but the market has now won a new status and attracts new and more affluent customers.

Núcleo Cultural Feliz Lusitânia

The Núcleo Cultural Feliz Lusitânia is a state government project that revitalized a 500,000–square-foot area along the riverbank in part of Belém's original historic core adjoining the Ver-o-Peso pier. The project encompassed buildings and spaces that form the traditional Largo da Sé (Cathedral Square), which together with the Catedral da Sé (Diocesan Cathedral) and the Praça Frei Caetano Brandão (Fray Caetano Brandão Square) constitutes one of the city's most representative cultural spaces and the starting point for the Círio de Nazaré, a yearly procession on Our Lady of

Figure 7.7. The Casa das Onze Janelas, one of the historic buildings converted to a cultural use in the Núcleo Cultural Feliz Lusitânia, where public spaces were also renovated. In the background is the Ver-o-Peso complex. (Photo by João Ramid, www.joaoramid.com.br)

Nazareth's feast day, Pará's most important religious festival, which attracts large crowds.

The project began with the restoration of Igreja de Santo Alexandre (Church of St. Alexander) and the former Palácio Episcopal (Episcopal Palace) and their conversion into the Museu de Arte Sacra do Pará (Pará Sacred Art Museum). Later, more buildings were restored and adapted to new uses: eight private residences were converted into a small museum on the Our Lady of Nazareth festival, an ice-cream parlor, and a crafts shop; the Forte do Castelo was restored and converted into the Museu do Encontro (Encounter Museum); and the Casa das Onze Janelas (House of Eleven Windows), built as a private mansion in the mid- eighteenth century and converted into a military hospital in the same century, was remodeled to hold the administration of the state museum system, the state government's collection of contemporary art, and a public eatery (fig. 7.7).

The buildings in the complex were integrated through the design of the public spaces with new landscaping, renovated sidewalks and pedestrian walkways, sitting areas, and viewpoints to the shore and the city.[2] In the third of the project that included Forte do Castelo and the Casa das Onze Janelas, several buildings and additions that were erected during the time the building was a military hospital had to be demolished to restore the original historic buildings. The design enhanced the area between the fort and the Casa das Onze Janelas with gardens, viewpoints, walkways, an amphitheater, and a pier for tour boats. Excavations revealed remains of the old fortification and its original moat, which now form a public open-air museum. The wall that used to border Ladeira do Castelo, judged of little historic value, was demolished in order to allow more views of the fort. However, this decision disrupted Largo da Sé's morphology and its original urban character, since expanding the open spaces around it destroyed the visual framing of the square (figs. 7.8 and 7.9).

The Feliz Lusitânia project was clearly inspired by the "spectacle of space," in that its design sought maximum impact in service of marketing the city and creating a new landmark in Belém (Lima 2004). The result was a gentrification of the area through a design that appeals to tourists and offers increased comfort and security, but that ignores the interests of the majority of the population, who are less affluent. The museums are mainly geared to visitors who do not know the city and its history. Nevertheless, the renovated public spaces facing the bay, primarily the Guamá Esplanade and the Lembrança (Memorial) lookout, are visited by a broad segment the population, particularly in comparison with the Estação das Docas, which as we said before, is a clear example of social and spatial segregation.

Figure 7.8. The old fort, the cathedral, and the Casa das Onze Janelas are the main renovated buildings around the revitalized main square in Feliz Lusitânia. The street and open space in the lower left-hand corner have now also been renovated and connect to the Ver-o-Peso complex. (Photo by João Ramid, www.joaoramid.com.br)

Figure 7.9. Demolition of a wall opened new views from the Feliz Lusitânia plaza down to the Ladeira do Castelo and the river. (Photo by Simone Seabra)

Lessons from Belém

The urban interventions carried out along the riverfront in Belém are imbued with political objectives that seek to ratify it as a public social space through the quality of its landscape and the redemption of the different historical phases of the city's evolution. However, the ideology that is reflected in the very conception of the projects does not always promote public access and the enhancement of local culture, a clear problem with Estação das Docas. Instead, this project is closer to models directed toward international tourism such as Puerto Madero in Buenos Aires, Port Urba in Barcelona, and Pier 17 in New York City.

On the other hand, it is necessary to change the historically constructed relationship between the population and the Belém waterfront—which has always been the basis of the population's transportation and economic well-being—given the enormous demand for green spaces and recreation sites, especially in the neighborhoods along the shore. The initiative that best addresses this objective is the Ver o Rio project, which seeks the expansion and linkage of public recreation areas along the water's edge. Countering this vision are the Estação das Docas and Núcleo Cultural Feliz Lusitânia, which seek to promote cultural heritage primarily for tourists, leading to spaces with fragile economic and social sustainability because they are irrelevant to the daily lives of the majority of the population. Finally, the Ver-o-Peso complex is notable for having helped to rehabilitate the area while maintaining a balance of its multiple commercial, social, tourist, and circulation uses. This project's main merit is that it was able to upgrade the area while maintaining the traditional uses and characteristics of the spaces.

These results of these projects in Belém reveal that the renovation and revitalization of specific city spaces cannot be accomplished merely by physical interventions. As Jacobs (1961: 24) observed decades ago "it is futile to plan a city's appearance, or speculate on how to endow it with a pleasing appearance of order, without knowing what sort of innate, functioning order it has. To seek for the look of things as a primary purpose or as the main drama is apt to make nothing but trouble" such as the abandonment and depredation of the public heritage. Public policies and wider complementary actions are necessary in conjunction with urban design and physical interventions in order to involve the various stakeholders that have interests in the urban spaces. Such a process would result in places that effectively reflect the social, economic, and cultural expectations of the city, and thereby promote its potential for tourism. Urban design could then become a fundamental tool in the service of a greater goal: bringing about new planning perspectives for Belém.

Notes

1. Editors' note: The National Constitution of 1988 introduced a series of innovative planning instruments for city master plans which were later regulated in the Estatuto da Cidade (Statute of the City) a national law approved in 2001. Cities can choose to use these instruments, such as the "special interlinked operation," a public-private partnership in which the private partner agrees to invest in another area of the city in exchange for a zoning change in the project area (see the introduction to this book).
2. The landscape design was by Rosa Grena Kliass, of São Paulo, founder of ABAP, the Brazilian Society of Landscape Architects.

CHAPTER 8

Redesigning Brownfields in Porto Alegre

Lineu Castello

After a period of rapid industrial development and accelerated urbanization in the last half of the twentieth century, by the turn of the twenty-first century Brazilian society was fully aware of the negative consequences of these processes and of the finite nature of the country's environmental resources. However, even though growth has slowed in comparison to previous decades, cities have continued to grow centrifugally, towards peripheral suburbs—which in Brazil are marked by accentuated levels of poverty. And although social behavior in big cities displays signs of ever-growing consumerism, the transition to full democracy has translated into increasing levels of community participation and preoccupation with the quality of life that cities offer to their citizens.

Urban design in Brazil has also started to share many of the same concerns as in other parts of the world; it has experienced significant conceptual changes and has become another effective means of transforming Brazilian life. Consequently, urban action no longer seeks complete products—whole cities, morphological objects designed to function rationally—as extolled by the modernism that culminated in Brasília. Moreover, the general plans which encompassed the whole of a city were infrequently implemented and even became discredited. The a priori vision of the whole was replaced by projects that value an a posteriori vision that concentrates on particular aspects of that whole. That is to say, as in what is becoming known as the "Barcelona paradigm,"[1] planning no longer deals with the level of an entire city, but rather with the design of a complex of places that marks human existence in this more complex city. Consequently, the city acquires a polycentric structure with a diversity of simultaneous events that are, likewise, offered in a diversity of places.[2]

The city of Porto Alegre is a clear reflection of these aspects, two of which will be discussed in this chapter: (a) the appearance of vacant sites and buildings in the central city and the corresponding tendency to convert elements of the urban heritage to new uses; and (b) the creation of new spaces dedicated to consumption and to practices associated with it which are potentially capable of generating new places in the urban structure. These two aspects are typical of what is conventionally called *post-modern urbanism,* reflect concepts recently introduced to the field of urban design, and represent development operations that are becoming common in contemporary Brazilian cities.

Sustainability in Urban Brazil

Brazilians are still proud that they hosted the 1992 United Nations Conference on Environment and Development (UNCED), known as the "Earth Summit" or "Rio-92." In that year Brazil was also the site of the 1992 Global Forum, a series of simultaneous events that enabled all sectors of society, even the poorest, to express their views about the growing problems in the human-environment relationship. Concern for environmental sustainability—and the international prestige that the subject seemed to bring—was such a fertile concept in the minds of Brazilians that supporting sustainability became almost a national behavior.

Sustainability is a concept with admittedly diverse definitions, sometimes focused on the urban and sometimes on the natural aspects of the environment. In this chapter, I primarily address sustainability with regard to the built environment and only indirectly with regard to the natural environment. When I do discuss the natural environment, I focus on ways to keep rural lands free from urbanization. This has an obvious, direct relationship with the concept of sustainability, since the conservation of land in its natural state prevents the soil from being covered by structures, hence contributing to a sustainable urban development. Therein lies a novel way of thinking about the city and its design in Brazil, where there has been unceasing growth outward from the center. Containing the growth of a city, the expansion of major transportation axes, the endless growth of the infrastructure network, and the centrifugal nature of urbanization are all viable strategies for a policy of sustainable urban development.

The very concepts of urban planning underwent substantial changes at the end of the twentieth century to reflect heightened concerns with sustainability. A new thinking moved traditional urban design towards alternative visions, which started to be considered and employed in Brazilian urbanism. One such conceptual change derives from the argument that it is always more economical to invest in services in a compact city, rather than to extend expensive infrastructure to the urban periphery. Growth without expansion came to be seen as one of the most important contemporary concepts in urban development. This approach is in direct opposition to the philosophy of traditional Anglo-Saxon urbanism, which once prevailed throughout Latin America, including Brazil. In this philosophy, expansion toward healthier suburban areas and the creation of new garden cities were seen as the best antidotes to the polluted industrial city. Later, the urbanization process came under North American influence, leading to the construction of freeways and the development of large, polarizing regional shopping malls. Today, it is common to find both Britons and North Americans advocating the infill of central urban spaces, as part of the new concept of promoting environmental sustainability. Expanding the city is unthinkable because "only an extraordinarily rich country could even contemplate such a possibility, and it still seems improbable. The replacement costs of buildings, roads, and utility services . . . would be higher than its total assessed valuation plus its entire capital debt" (Barnett 1996: 9). Regarding the metropolises of emerging countries, there are additional strong social arguments that support the idea of reusing vacated central areas: the relatively lower mobility of the population and the need to lessen the length of commutes to and from work.

In addition, new ethical concepts in planning highlight the convenience of reusing vacant city spaces. Barnett (1996: 181) observes that the concept of sustainability brings another important change to the philosophy of planning when it argues that people should manage their environment in a way that serves future generations, not just their own immediate interests. In commenting on how many metropolises in the third world are compromising their natural environment by following the example of North American urbanism, Rogers (1997: 33) does not hesitate to affirm that "the 'dense city' model can bring major ecological benefits . . . [and] can be designed to increase energy efficiency, consume fewer resources, produce less pollution and avoid sprawling over the countryside." Similarly, even theorists favor the compaction of large cities as a strategy for sustainable development. Jencks (2000: 129) postulates four main probable paths for the future of today's metropolises, one of which is precisely the reurbanization of brownfields.

In addition, sustainability is closely related to the maintenance of traditions and social practices associated with the cultural origins of a given population. An aspect that is frequently overlooked, however, is area studies, in spite of their crucial importance for the achievement of any effective policy aimed at the sustainability of the human environment. In fact, it is not enough simply to guarantee the permanence of natural and built elements: it is also fundamental to protect the *psychological environment* generated from the uses human beings make of these elements in their daily lives. In this regard another emerging concept in urbanism is the employment of methodologies of environmental perception in support of a more contextual urban design, since they allow clearer identification of the landscape elements responsible for environmental images that are meaningful for the community. Consequently, these are the elements truly responsible for conferring meaning to the landscape. This concept is especially true of industrial landscapes, since they directed the social values and patterns for many twentieth-century societies.

Brownfields in Urban Brazil

Brazilian urban development presents peculiar features. Some of the large cities, particularly those in metropolitan regions, reveal subtle differences in their levels of urbanization. Whereas some of them are mere urban agglomerations, others show high levels of urban development and exhibit postindustrial landscapes resembling those in the most advanced industrial societies. It is precisely in the latter Brazilian metropolises that the phenomenon known as brownfields may be found: vast portions of urban land occupied by structures that have become obsolete as the city surrounding them has evolved. Examples of brownfields include old railway stations, abandoned docks, and especially, large expanses of land in city centers filled with abandoned factories and other structures. The continued presence of underutilized land in city centers generally provided with good infrastructure causes significant losses of revenue and consequently affects the social function of the land.

The twentieth century ended with the tacit recognition of the serious effects of the Industrial Revolution on earth, water, and air, and of the excessive paving over of the natural environment caused by the expansion of the built environment. This, of course, leads to several questions, such as, What should be done with the urban brownfields that abound in the city centers of Brazilian metropolises? How should city planning face the new circumstances of urban environments in post-metropolitan conditions? Where should we find the space needed to accommodate the demands created by new behaviors in postmodern society? What kind of urban design will be able to accommodate these demands appropriately? Where do we find space: through increasing residential densities, infill, or even promoting *exurbia*?

The Concept of Place in Urban Brazil

Place, as traditionally interpreted in urbanism, is a qualified space that the public recognizes because it contains profound meanings represented by strong referential images. For precisely this reason, physical and psychological factors go into its creation, factors that have as much to do with the design of the urban morphological configuration as with the interactive behavior adopted by the users of that configuration (Castello 2005). These places are fundamental to the psychological-spatial processes of the urban phenomenon, to the simple fact of living in a city. I call these spaces "places of urbanity," where urbanity is understood as linked to the dynamics of the existential experiences people have through the use they make of the urban environment. In other words, urbanity exists by means of the quality that the system of public spaces in cities tends to bestow on its users, and through the capacity for interchange and communication it contains (Castello 2000b).

When however one considers the most recent *place-making* projects (Carr et al. 1995, Carmona et al. 2003)—particularly those that some authors include in the so-called postmodern urbanism (Ellin 1999; Nesbitt 1996)—the concept of place refers to the construction of images that seek to create an imaginary contextual reality or even to break with it in order to promote a *place-marketing* (Hannigan 1998; Castello 2000a). Thus, the design of a place either reinforces and reproduces an image already perceived in that reality or tries to introduce an image that intentionally represents a fantasy. This is why I like to refer to this kind of urbanism as "meta-urbanism."

In Brazil today it is possible to recognize two predominant types of *places*: (a) those that mimic contextual elements and seek to reconstruct them by using forms that best represent the cultural identity of that context; and (b) those that build new elements by using forms that operate as consumer "brands" of that environment and are used in marketing strategies. Both types of places derive from a cloning process that simulates forms which may be either contextual or totally extraneous. In both cases, these places represent what I call "places of cloning." It is however important to distinguish genuine cloning operations from the immediacy of interventions that are merely cosmetic. The latter are limited to beautifying the ugliest aspects of an urban brownfield, as "in an age when industrialization becomes chic, when former factories are converted into apartments and power stations into national museums . . . a disused abattoir might easily be perceived as a potential art gallery" (Leach 1999: 15). The case study presented in this chapter is a typical example of these new concepts, as it is a place where the cloning process was astutely conceived as contextual from the beginning.

Porto Alegre, a Southern Brazilian Metropolis

Porto Alegre is the capital of the state of Rio Grande do Sul, the southernmost state in Brazil at 30 degrees south latitude, which makes for a temperate climate with well-defined seasons (see fig. P.1 in the preface). It occasionally snows in winter, especially in the mountains. The state has international frontiers with two countries, Argentina and Uruguay, and Porto Alegre is situated practically equidistant from the capitals of those countries (the cities of Buenos Aires and Montevideo) and the principal Brazilian metropolises, São Paulo and Rio de Janeiro.

This situation in itself confers peculiarities to Porto Alegre, such as a dual cultural heritage, one Portuguese—like other Brazilian cities—and the other Hispanic. The ethnic type of the Brazilian *gaúcho*, as residents of Rio Grande do Sul are called, is like that of those who live in the interior of Argentina, also called *gauchos* (but without the accent). The state of Rio Grande do Sul also enjoys strong ethnic diversity, as it received one of the most intense flows of immigration in Brazil. Wave after wave of immigrants to the state, mainly Germans and Italians, contributed their own cultures, which were very distinct from that of the rest of the country. All these factors give the state a subtly special character in Brazil.

Porto Alegre is approximately one hundred kilometers (sixty-two miles) from the Atlantic Ocean on the shores of the Guaíba, a large lake everyone calls a river (Rio Guaíba). The city center is on a peninsula extending along the "river," where a group of approximately forty couples from the Azores Islands founded the first settlement in 1752. Once the third-largest Brazilian city in terms of population, Porto Alegre was one of the first to attain relative population stability, in contrast to the rapid demographic growth that generally characterizes third world cities. Today it is the eighth largest Brazilian city, with 1,360,590 inhabitants and an annual growth rate of 1.35 percent (IBGE 2000). In Brazilian terms, it has enviable socioeconomic indicators, such as a life expectancy of 71.4 years and a literacy rate of 96.7 percent; 99.5 percent of its population has access to piped drinking water, and the average income is R$6,861 per capita (in 1999–2000; IBGE 2000; Porto Alegre 2003).[3] Today, Porto Alegre is the center of a prosperous metropolitan region formed by thirty different municipalities with more than 3,600,000 inhabitants.

Porto Alegre also has special characteristics in terms of urban planning. It was the first Brazilian state capital to have a master plan (1914), and since then the city has always continued the tradition of regulating its urban development.[4] The current plan incorporates some of the new urban concepts mentioned in this text, especially by favoring planned decentralization, establishing foundations for sustainable development, seeking recovery and improvement of underutilized or degraded areas, and favoring the control and the rehabilitation of areas for the preservation of cultural patrimony.[5]

The turn of the twenty-first century did not see abundant urban developments in Porto Alegre. With the exception of some road projects, like the construction of a third ring road to improve traffic flow and surface paving of the main roads in poor neighborhoods, there have not been any outstanding changes in the area of urbanism. Perhaps the most important development occurred in the city administration with the election of a mayor and a majority of city councilors from the Labor Party. New government practices mobilized intense popular (and populist) movements and a new decision-making process, apparently grounded in the selection of particularly charismatic leaders to speak at public assemblies and influence public opinion.

In fact, Porto Alegre's vigorous political activity over the past decade has made it one of the most controversial cities in Brazil, and perhaps in the world, since it has become a living laboratory for ideological-administrative experiments. Most notable is the "participatory budget" process, which has been cited frequently, even by eminent scholars such as David Harvey, who says that "in cities like Porto Alegre . . . some highly innovative means have been found to enhance popular empowerment and democratic forms of governance. . . . We have much to learn from them" (Harvey 2000: 187).[6] In fact, participatory budgeting generated a movement that has tried to establish a dialogue between municipal government and the whole of the population and that became emblematic of the city's administration. Delegates elected from sixteen regions within the city decide spending priorities and allocation of municipal resources in public assemblies.

There have been mixed results from these policies. Critics point out the negligible number of delegates who participate effectively in the regional assemblies, the excessive number of public works that are assigned but never completed, and the interference in the functioning of the city council and public administration. Finally, there are complaints that the Labor Party made intensive use of the participatory budget as an instrument of partisan indoctrination and urban marketing.

Styling itself the "Capital of the Participatory Budget," Porto Alegre fits quite well into the framework discussed in the first part of this text, since its administration adopted extreme policies of political and city marketing of the type that has become common throughout the world. The city has experienced intense politico-social movements that have brought it unexpected worldwide notoriety, for example, by hosting the World Social Forum, an international event put on by developing nations and socialist leaders as a counterpoint to the World Economic Forum of the developed nations.[7] In any case, it is possible to recognize in Porto Alegre some examples of postmodern urbanism that correct some of its weaknesses. One of these cases will be discussed here.

Reuse of a Brownfield and the Concept of Place in Sustainable Postmodern Urbanism

A few years ago the private sector in Porto Alegre implemented an urban design experiment grounded in postmodern urbanism and architecture that effectively

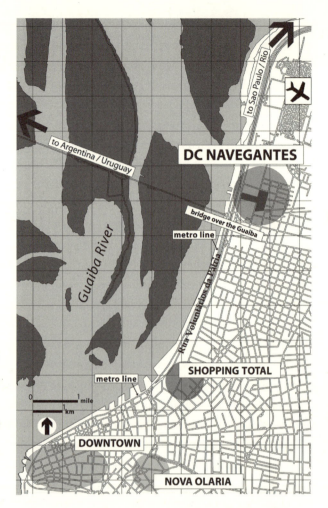

Figure 8.1. Map of central Porto Alegre, showing the three projects discussed in this chapter. Close to the city center, they are well served by various modes of public transit and by public facilities. (Map courtesy of Iára Castello, Regional Development, Planning, and Environmental Administration Research Group [CNPq/UFRGS. Adapted by Vicente del Rio)

synthesizes the conceptual changes previously mentioned. This project is a privately developed shopping district located in a region that is popularly called Navegantes (Navigators) and comprises three old industrial districts.

The morphology of Navegantes and its neighboring districts is marked by important remnants of the city's industrial past, including the best examples of industrial architecture, which are located along a former structural artery, Voluntários da Pátria, which parallels the Guaíba.[8] Although the area's street network follows the regular grid pattern typical of urban industrial areas, physical disruptions in the grid generated a mix of large and small blocks. In addition to its abundant road network, several modes of transportation serve Navegantes. A commuter light rail line, the railroad, and a complex of federal highways and freeways cross the area; there are several docks along the riverside and the international airport is close by (fig. 8.1).

The behavior of Navegantes industrialists naturally changed in consonance with the important changes occurring in Brazil's industrial sector as a whole. The whole area went into decline as a result of a major exodus of large industrial plants to more favorable metropolitan locations where either property costs were lower or access to communication networks was better. At this time the region is characterized by depots, wholesale warehouses (either built as such or adapted to this use), and commercial services. Freight haulers and small manufacturers remained, and some even improved their premises, but the area has many empty lots and vacant buildings.

Research projects I carried out in the area led to a somewhat surprising conclusion from the point of view of environmental perception.[9] In spite of severe urban decline in some locations and a high rate of building vacancy, the visual power of some elements of this industrial landscape seem to have persisted vividly in the minds of the majority of our survey respondents. The prevailing perceptions of city residents are a reasonably homogeneous collection of images from the time when the area's industrial production was at its peak. Results clearly indicate that there was a lifestyle typical of the industrial era, and respondents singled out as icons numerous monuments marking important events in the area's past and celebrating its former industrial grandeur. These icons ranked high among all three groups of respondents to our field research (residents, workers, and passersby).

A significant number of landmarks are concentrated in the Navegantes area and near the Guaíba, including the river itself and its islands, the entrance to the city for those driving on the main national highways or coming from the MERCOSUL countries, the confluence of several modes of transportation (river, rail, subway, and airline), and the church of Nossa Senhora dos Navegantes (Our Lady of Navigators), Porto Alegre's patron saint, from which a procession of boats departs during one of the city's most important yearly religious celebrations. These elements are charged with the highest degree of symbolism in the region and offer the area the potential to generate a new place in the city structure.

The Navegantes Commercial District

The Navegantes Commercial District (Distrito Comercial Navegantes, or DC Navegantes) is a shopping mall situated on the banks of the Guaíba River just two kilometers (almost 1.2 miles) from the downtown area (fig. 8.2). Resulting from the adaptive reuse of old industrial buildings formerly belonging to the Renner factory and the addition of a handful of new buildings, it spreads over three blocks comprising approximately fourteen acres.[10] Established in 1916, Renner was a textile manufacturer involved in spinning, dying, and weaving, and it rapidly became one of the largest industries in the state. As the company gradually modernized its operations and began

Figure 8.2. The Navegantes Commercial District was an adaptive renovation of the Renner industrial complex. Old buildings were converted into retail and administrative uses, and new buildings were added. It is located on a major entry route to the city, next to a highway, a rail line, and the bridge over the Guaíba River. (Photo by Henrique Amaral Studio, adapted by the author)

relocating to new buildings elsewhere, it also began implementing a project to create a shopping center in its former installation. Marketing studies recommended the creation of an outlet mall, so the historic buildings were remodeled for that purpose, and warehouses were subdivided for small retailers that operate as factory outlets (fig. 8.3). Inaugurated in October 1994, the project started winning awards in 1995 and has experienced ever-increasing success.[11]

By recycling the old industrial buildings and integrating them with new buildings, the Navegantes Commercial District inaugurated a new shopping concept with an urban dimension that succeeded in maintaining the dominant industrial imagery.[12] The "spirit of the place" is embodied in the converted buildings, and their adaptive reuse binds together the most expressive topological and psychological referents of the region and city (fig. 8.4). The design strategies were effective, in spite of (and perhaps because of) being unpretentious. As its authors explained when describing the project,

"The existing architectural heritage . . . had great potential. . . . The conservation of the buildings was one of the premises of the project, which was directed toward redeeming the district, reurbanizing the area, and making the structures suitable for the demands of an outlet. . . . We needed a unifying strategy strong enough to integrate different blocks containing different buildings with varied languages and typologies into a single context. We worked with design elements such as access porticos, canopies, towers, lighting devices, urban furniture, and visual communication. These elements assumed specific languages which were repeated throughout the space in order to integrate it and to ensure the necessary unity."[13]

In September 1996 with city approval, the Navegantes Commercial District turned an underutilized thoroughfare into the Events Street. Closed to vehicular traffic, the street extends for one block from the structural axis of the complex. Used for outdoor public events, it is managed by the shopping center, which calls it "a permanent cultural space, free, and public" (fig. 8.5).[14] Soon thereafter, public activity expanded beyond the limits of this street to encompass previously vacant warehouses, which now host frequent public events, such as the MERCOSUL Art Biennale and international art and dance performances.[15] In addition, the Navegantes Commercial District expanded its own attractions to include a theater, ethnic restaurants (such as *churrascarias*, selling Brazilian barbecue), and various permanent cultural events and fairs that animate the place year-round. Today, the area also houses a university campus.

The Genesis of a Place

Even if one considers its small scale—and the carefully calculated modesty of its objectives—the Navegantes Commercial District project advances our understanding of the genesis of a place in the postmodern city. The area's *re-architecture*—possibly inspired by a combination of the public perception of the surrounding environment

Figure 8.3. This building of the former Renner industrial complex, located on a public street, was converted to retail uses. (Photo by Lineu Castello)

Figure 8.4. The pedestrian mall along the Navegantes Commercial District serves as its structural axis and evokes the ambiance of a small town. As an extension to this axis, the street in figure 8.5 was closed to vehicular traffic and now hosts outdoor events. (Photo by the author; courtesy of the Environmental Perception and Urban Design Research Group, CNPq/UFRGS)

Figure 8.5. This pedestrianized street serves as an extension of the shopping center's main pedestrian mall; it is used for outdoor public events as are some of the buildings around it. (Photo by the author)

as significant and the physical and psychological contextual landmarks that existed there—gave the area the status of an urban *place* within the overall city structure.[16] Revitalization is affecting the Commercial District's surroundings, where new buildings are being erected on previously vacant lots and old buildings are being converted for commercial use. Interestingly, these projects are trying to replicate the district's morphology.

Residents of neighboring areas recognize that the Navegantes Commercial District has improved their quality of life: they have better accessibility through new bus lines, better public safety and more effective policing, more opportunities for socialization, and improved public services. The attractiveness of the new place now extends beyond its immediate neighborhoods. Perhaps the essence of its design concept—revolving around the idea of a traditional small-town main street—is responsible for the magic that it now enjoys. Customers are "transported" to the "good old days" where they can enjoy a comfortable and agreeable stroll and shop in peace, just like in a small town. They can experience a reality that exists only in their imagination, amidst the bustling commercial centers of the capital.

The Navegantes Commercial District's management strongly emphasizes this point in its marketing, which highlights the escape from reality offered by Navegantes but not other city shopping venues. Low prices are not advertised as much as one might expect for a factory outlet; rather, marketing invokes the pleasure of shopping outdoors in a natural setting, with the possibility of seeing the sky or a sunset, feeling the proximity of the water, listening to the breeze blowing in the (natural) palm trees, and walking on the (natural) grass. In 1996, shortly after its inauguration, the Navegantes Commercial District received the Top Marketing Award from the commercial association as one of that year's best performing commercial enterprises in the state.

Although the design of the Navegantes Commercial District may be labeled as minimalist, it proved to be surprisingly rich because it is expressed in many ways and with a diversity that encompasses sensory, historical, preservationist, experiential, and, of course, commercial dimensions.

Sensory because the project was able to incorporate the industrial atmosphere that permeates the local environment. Also, it is welcoming to diverse social groups, so that a variety of patrons feel entirely at ease on its premises, which offer an environment (not just cloned scenery) where they can replicate spontaneous practices and behaviors that they usually adopt in familiar places. This dynamic is demonstrated, for instance, by the fact that students from the nearby campus and workers from surrounding factories both use the complex for recreation and behave as if they are on public sidewalks in front of their own houses.

Historical because the project uses the contemporary and increasingly widespread public esteem for symbols of the past, and is able to manifest the essence of an urban memory.

Preservationist because the project is committed to popularizing the new environmental ideals that value regaining contact with natural elements in the urban milieu—taking advantage of the fact that the area is near the river. In addition, it promotes the regaining of contact with the city's cultural elements by reusing the historic industrial architecture.

Experiential because the project recognizes society's new values and behaviors with regard to leisure and shopping. It generates a public place for cultural expression, particularly through Events Street; the special events; and the pavilions for shows, performances, and art exhibitions outside the city's formal museum circuit.

Commercial because the project exposes and rejuvenates the powerful commercial nature of the region in all its latent potentiality, keeping it alive in the continuing evolution of the city.

Conclusion

The road paved by the re-architecture of the Navegantes Commercial District adds a success story to experiments that employ a new concept of place-making, even in spaces with limited attractions such as urban brownfields. All signs indicate that this trend still has much to offer in the evolution of Brazilian urban design and that it can withstand the new challenges of the postmodern era, such as sustainability.

Along the same lines and at the same time as the Navegantes Commercial District was being developed, another space important to Porto Alegre's cultural memory was inaugurated. The Nova Olaria Commercial Center is an old brick factory that was remodeled to house retail shops, restaurants, cafes, and movie theaters, with a design that connects well to the street scale and integrates perfectly with the surrounding context. This commercial center successfully provided a new anchor to what is today a highly diversified and attractive entertainment district in Porto Alegre, a focal point for bohemian life (fig. 8.6).

More recently, in 2003, a brownfield holding one of the city's oldest breweries became Shopping Total, Porto Alegre's newest commercial complex (fig. 8.7).[17] Located between the Navegantes Commercial District and downtown, this project is laden with affection and memory. The converted old structures and the new buildings will hold 557 retail stores, five restaurants and fourteen fast-food places, five movie theaters, a bingo hall, a genuine German beerhouse, and a wine museum designed to resemble a wine cellar and located in a network of underground tunnels discovered accidentally during construction. Reflecting the community-oriented goals of con-

Figure 8.6. The conversion of a former small brick factory into the Nova Olaria shopping center provided a new place for socializing and events. (Photo by the author)

Figure 8.7. The former Brahma beer brewery was converted into Shopping Total, which houses a mix of retail and cultural activities and has helped to revitalize a city district. (Photo by the author)

temporary Brazilian urban design, the mall also features a new public plaza serving the local community and will soon host a public library—certainly a very unusual presence in a shopping center—and the headquarters of the Porto Alegre Symphony Orchestra.[18]

The success of the Navegantes Commercial District seems to derive precisely from its ability to combine a whole set of environmental values in a single place, all of them with strong connections to the city memory. These values match those advocated by even the most demanding postmodernist critics such as Huxtable (1997: 36), who cites three absolutely essential conditions for the conservation of urban memory: "the manner in which the historical setting accommodates change, the degree to which style and identity support authentic functions, and the frequency with which destruction is avoided by legitimate continuity through an appropriate role in contemporary life and use."

Clearly, the Navegantes Commercial District and the more recent Nova Olaria and Shopping Total suggest a path to follow in the design of the postmodern Brazilian city. That path seeks to promote a new generation of *places* that value the city memory, preserve its environment, and avoid uneconomical and unnecessary expansions to the urban fabric. Simple variations around a commonly perceived theme—such as the industrial memory of a region—are likely to provide a useful direction for urban projects searching to create true urban *places*. Using the displacement of memory from one historical period (the era of the city's industrialization) to another (the era of large shopping centers in cities) as a fundamental design principle may help generate successful and contextual urban design.

Notes

I would like to thank everyone who in one way or another collaborated in the research for this chapter, with special thanks to my wife, architect Iára Regina Castello, for her help with the images. I also wish to thank Henrique Amaral and his team (*hastudio@terra.com.br*) for the use of their photos, and architect Adriana Hofmeister Fleck for the use of material on DC Navegantes.

1. This phrase makes reference to the revitalization efforts in Barcelona, Spain, especially following the big investments for the 1992 Olympic Games, when several public works and urban design interventions were carried out alongside historic structures and sites, introducing a network of new urban *places*.

2. It is interesting to note the apparent analogy that emerges between "places" in a city and what some authors have been calling "events," which are scattered in the large contemporary metropolises, as do, for example, Bernard Tschumi in *Event-Cities* and Paul Virilio in *A Landscape of Events*.

3. The exchange rate in February 2004 was US$1 = R$2.90.

4. The João Moreira Maciel Plan dates from 1914 and its directives on traffic were partially implemented. The Gladosch Plan followed in the 1940s, but the 1959 plan was the first to have effective legal enforcement. The 1979 plan introduced comprehensive planning and combined social, economic, and physical directives. Since 2000, Porto Alegre has followed the II PDDUA (Master Plan for Urban and Environmental Development).

5. In Brazil, preservation has evolved from considering elements and areas for their "historic" and "natural" values to a wider and more comprehensive approach based on their "cultural" values, which is determined with considerable public input.

6. On participatory budgeting see, for instance, Abers (2000) and Goldsmith and Vainer (2001).

7. The World Economic Forum meets each January in the Swiss city of Davos. In January 2001, Porto Alegre launched the World Social Forum as a left-wing response to the traditional global capitalist summit. Curiously, in 2003 the recently elected president of Brazil, Luiz Inácio "Lula" da Silva, attended both forums, delivering the message that "in another world, less inhumanity and more solidarity are possible" (see www.forumsocialmundial.org).

8. Two of these buildings stand out: the Moinho Chaves (Chaves Mill) and the Moinho Rio-Grandense (Rio Grande Mill). Among the first examples of modern architecture in the city (dating from 1915 and 1919, respectively), they are highly ranked in the urban heritage register.

9. Research conducted by the Research Group on Environmental Perception and Urban Design, headed by myself, in the School of Architecture, Federal University of Rio Grande do Sul.

10. Project by Adriana Fleck (principal), Rosane Bauer, and João Carlos Ferreira. Technical data: site area: 65.963 square meters (712,400 square feet); built area: 49.400 square meters (533,520 square feet); leasable space: 24.070 square meters (259,956 square feet). To the 120 retail stores of the first phase (October 1994), 80 were added in the second phase (April 1995).

11. The project received an award from the third Biennale of Architecture of Rio Grande do Sul (1996) and the Young Architects prize from the Institute of Brazilian Architects–São Paulo Section (1997).

12. Although the factory utilized chemicals in the washing and dying of textiles, there is no record of any tests for environmental contamination prior to initiation of the project.

13. From an interview with the authors in *Revista Arquitetura & Urbanismo* 74, 1997).

14. According to the local newspaper *Zero Hora* (December 15, 1996, p. 8), by December 1996—four months after the opening of Events Street—more than one hundred exhibitions had already been held there, six million people had visited the mall since its inauguration in 1994, and every weekend the area received an average of fifty thousand visitors.

15. MERCOSUL is an economic free-trade zone encompassing Brazil, Argentina, Paraguay, and Uruguay.

16. *Re-architecture* is one of the research areas at the graduate program where I teach. It refers to the contemporary redevelopment of cities in keeping with their preexisting functions and morphology.

17. Shopping Total occupies 13.5 acres of what used to be the grounds of one of the city's oldest and most famous breweries. Four of the shopping center's seven buildings are converted brewery structures that—together with the original chimney and boilers—had been designed in 1911 and were listed on the city's historical register. The shopping center was inaugurated with 450 of the planned 557 retail stores, represented an investment of US$45 million, and was expected to generate 2,500 direct jobs.

18. Regarding the design of shopping centers in Brazil, see the essay by Bruna and Vargas (chapter 4) in this volume.

Part 3

Social Inclusion The Struggle to Make
a Better City for the Community

This third and last trend of Brazilian contemporary urbanism concentrates on promoting social inclusion. In the introduction we discussed the evolution of Brazilian urbanism and how it achieved an important role in responding to the social agenda set forward by the 1988 National Constitution and the country's re-democratization. By subordinating the property rights of private landowners to the social function of that land and by including a chapter on urban development, the Brazilian constitution paved the way for a socially responsive urbanism. We have also discussed how crucial the constitution and its follow-up, the 2001 Statute of the City, are in the struggle to achieve social equity and a just city for all through the quality and equitable distribution of public spaces, amenities, infrastructure, and services, particularly transportation. Urbanism in Brazil can be an effective tool for accomplishing full enfranchisement and for lessening the gap between rich and poor.

Over the last twenty years, a significant number of government efforts have been geared toward the renovation of the existing city—or at least parts of it—in order to extend public, social, and cultural amenities to a wider portion of the population. These efforts recognize the importance of design in making the city more accessible and livable for all segments of the population. Various such efforts are discussed in the next chapters, illustrating different ways of addressing the struggle to make a better and more inclusive city for its communities of users through interventions in the public realm.

The most internationally recognized of these efforts has been happening in Curitiba since the 1970s, and it is only natural for us to start this section with a discussion of what that city has done to promote a more socially inclusive environment. Clara Irazábal examines the planning model, major urban design projects, and citizen involvement in Curitiba, and underlines the reasons why over the past decades this city has been frequently referred to as an environmentally sustainable "model city" and as a remarkable example of an effective planning process. Indeed, there are many reasons why the city deserves praise: efficient mass transit, historic and cultural preservation, a revitalized and pedestrian-friendly downtown, effective environmental programs, and a series of urban design and architectural catalyst projects.

However, Irazábal also argues that although Curitiba deserves praise, there are urban governance and planning problems that ought to receive closer attention and scrutiny. The author points out that most of the planning decisions are in the hands of a small group of planners, and questions whether there is an adequate qualitative and quantitative level of citizen involvement. She argues that Curitiba is an instance where insufficient and poorly managed public participation can delegitimize the decision-making and implementation process that had a brilliant start in the 1960s and outstanding success in the 1970s.

The second case study of socially inclusive urbanism is Projeto Rio Cidade, discussed by Vicente del Rio. This citywide program for remodeling and revitalizing Rio de Janeiro's commercial cores began in 1993 as part of the city's new strategic plan. The project targeted the historic centers of city districts and their most important retail areas and vehicular arteries, all of which were physically deteriorated and unfriendly to pedestrians. Sidewalks and open spaces were poorly maintained, and street vendors and illegal parking had invaded most pedestrian areas. The renovation of these areas not only provided them with a stronger image and identity and made them more comfortable for public use, but also attracted new private investment and revitalized retail activity, thereby helping the city to recover some of its national and international prestige.

Del Rio observes that Rio Cidade was unique in its objectives and scope, in the way it was implemented, and in its political and economic repercussions. From 1993 to 2004, several design teams were hired to address almost fifty project areas around the city from the downtown to distant poor suburbs. The design teams concentrated on increasing the quality of public spaces through streetscaping (including landscaping and the design of new street furniture), signage, parking, and pedestrian and vehicular circulation. The city coordinated the various projects and public service providers. Important infrastructure improvements included constructing storm-water drainage and sewage systems, and burying utility lines underground in some areas. By 2004 about half of the planned projects had been implemented, and their effects on the quality of public spaces are evident and are helping Rio regain some of its positive image.

São Paulo, a world megalopolis, has also implemented important urban interventions, ranging from large scale to local. Carlos Leite discusses some of São Paulo's efforts to transform its postindustrial spaces and try to overcome the territorial fragmentation caused by *terrain vagues*, highways, meaningless modernist open spaces, and illegal subdivisions and favelas in preservation areas. Through the analysis of three case studies—an intervention in the city center, the upgrading of a favela in an environmentally sensitive area, and a project for restructuring a town center—Leite argues that urbanism can operate within the limits of the possible even in such a complex and globalized metropolis.

The results of the projects in São Paulo show us the importance of an urbanism that creates meaningful public spaces and reaches for a new articulation of territory through the use of empty spaces as opportunities for new social and physical connections. Leite notes that, fundamentally, projects in post-Brasilia São Paulo have to promote a judicious reading of the geography of a place, reflect pressing global and local demands, and respond to the social function of the city.

Lastly, Cristiane Duarte and Fernanda Magalhães discuss Favela-Bairro, an innovative and successful favela upgrading program by the city of Rio de Janeiro. Unlike most previous policies that considered favelas as places of marginality, this program recognized the long-term social and capital investments that squatters have made in their communities and took the position that favelas should be helped to integrate into the formal city both physically and socially. Analyzing four different projects of the Favela-Bairro program, Duarte and Magalhães discuss how physical improvements combined with community development programs and occasional new housing units and community buildings.

As in the Rio Cidade program, in Favela-Bairro private firms were hired to carry out projects for almost one hundred small- and medium-sized favelas throughout the city. The authors argue that the design and implementation processes played fundamental roles, not only because each favela is a complex sociocultural and spatial reality, but also because at any given time projects entailed dozens of simultaneous operations at various stages of execution. The city and the design teams had to gain the cooperation of local strongmen and drug lords, and participatory processes helped engage communities in decision making and implementation. In 2005, the city estimated that more than 500,000 people in 143 settlements benefited from Favela- Bairro. The program has proven to be a huge success: it has been expanded to include the regularization of land tenure, other communities have demanded to participate, and research indicates that residents are investing more in the quality of their buildings. Favela-Bairro received much international praise from the Inter-American Development Bank (1998 Project of the Year) and from the 2000 Hannover World Exposition (Best International Project), and it was recognized by the United Nations as a model in its 2006–07 world report on cities.

CHAPTER 9

Urban Design, Planning, and the Politics of Development in Curitiba

Clara Irazábal

Over the past several decades, Curitiba, Brazil, has been referred to as an environmentally sustainable "model city" and as a remarkable example of both a successful urban planning process and a large array of urban design projects that are attractive, innovative, functional, cost-effective, and replicable. This chapter examines urban design and planning projects and processes in Curitiba since the 1960s, and shows many reasons why the city deserves praise: an effective and continuous planning process has guaranteed efficiency in public transit, historic and cultural preservation, a revitalized and pedestrian-friendly downtown, effective environmental programs, and a series of urban design and architectural catalyst projects.

This chapter also discusses some political and institutional factors that have facilitated the development of Curitiba's planning process, and some current urban governance and planning problems the city is facing. Curitiba's planning process has been shaped by the accommodation of diverse interests around a political project, the media dissemination of a particular city image, and the permeation of material gains to the lower income classes. Conversely, some factors that are challenging the city's governance model and threaten to subvert the future of planning processes include increases in urban problems and inequalities across the municipalities of the metropolitan region, deficiencies of institutional structure and coordination at the level of metropolitan planning and governance, and inadequate responses to the increasing challenges to government and planning institutions from citizens demanding greater accountability and participation. I argue that the institution of more effective citizen involvement in Curitiba's decision making is the way to relegitimize and continue the processes of urban design and planning that had such a brilliant start in the 1960s and a commendable implementation record from the 1970s to the early 1990s.

Planning and Urban Design in Curitiba

Curitiba has a six-decade-long history of formal urban design and planning.[1] It started with the Agache Plan in 1943, designed by the French urbanist Alfred Agache, when Curitiba had 120,000 inhabitants.[2] Through the restructuring of the street network, this plan established guidelines for concentric growth of the city and provisions for land-use zoning, sanitation measures, distribution of open spaces, and allocation of areas for urban expansion. The plan also proposed the construction of cultural and government buildings and centers, one of which—the Civic Center, housing local, state, and federal public agencies—was constructed beginning in 1952 and was designed according to the tenets of modern architecture.

Curitiba's population reached 180,000 inhabitants at an annual growth rate of more than 7 percent in 1950—more than what the Agache Plan had anticipated. To address this massive growth, Curitiba's first zoning act was passed in 1953 and the first mass-transit system plan in 1955. By 1960, the population had doubled to 361,309 inhabitants, and the rapidity of urban growth increased the need for its management. This growth, together with the planning and building of Brasília as the new capital city of Brazil in the late 1950s and early 1960s, created a renewed impetus for the fields of urban design and physical planning in Curitiba as means to direct growth and achieve progress and modernization. Curitiba continued a process of significant growth through the 1960s, maintaining one of the highest growth rates in Brazil— an average of 5.36 percent a year—demanding more urban planning.[3] In the 1960s, the Agache Plan remained only partially implemented and required updates and adjustments.

In 1965, the municipality of Curitiba opened a public competition for a new *plano diretor* (master plan) and selected a planning firm from São Paulo led by architect-planner Jorge Wilheim.[4] Developed in conjunction with city officials and elite groups, the plan was approved in 1966. By this time, Curitiba had almost 470,000 inhabitants and an annual growth rate of 5.6 percent. Unlike the Agache Plan, which was based on concentric circles, the *plano diretor* envisioned urban growth occurring in radiating axes outward from the city center and employed integrated public transportation and mixed land-use principles (fig. 9.1). Other pillars of the plan were management of growth, promotion of industry, and improvement of the environment and quality of life in the city.

The *plano diretor* called for major physical interventions in the city, including a

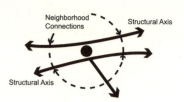

Figure 9.1. Diagram of growth
alternatives for Curitiba.
(Illustration by Vicente del Rio
based on Curitiba's master plan)

number of significant urban design projects. The greatest of these was the creation of five "structural axes" of public transportation radiating from the center of the city to guide the direction and concentration of growth. The structural axes plan combined massive public transportation infrastructure with zoning that allowed mixed uses and significant density. Although zoning had begun under the old plan in the 1950s, the new plan instituted creative approaches to shaping the urban fabric; channeling growth; and defining the establishment of specific zones such as the Central Zone, Structural Sectors for business and other services, and Residential Zones. Residential growth was encouraged near streets with concentrations of public transportation infrastructure and other services. In addition, Special Interest Preservation Units were established to restore buildings of historical significance.

The need for economic support for a city that was growing at rates higher than 5 percent a year in the 1960s led to the creation of Cidade Industrial de Curitiba (CIC, Curitiba Industrial District), and Special Connecting Sectors were designated to effectively integrate the Industrial District into the rest of the city. The CIC was designed with suitable urban infrastructure, providing basic services, housing, preservation areas, and integration to the urban transit system. The municipality also passed legislation restricting the establishment of polluting industrial plants.

The epitome of Curitiba's urban policy—achieving great benefits for a small investment—has been the transportation system (Cervero 1995; Rabinovitch and Leitman 1993). The main structural mass-transit axes began to operate in 1974, in 1980 the Rede Integrada de Transporte (RIT, Integrated Transportation Network) started providing an efficient bus rapid system with different types of bus lines integrating all parts of the city. (figs. 9.2 and 9.3). There have also been further improvements in bus boarding and vehicle characteristics.[5] Significantly, the transportation system has been used to promote development along the structural axes.

In 1974, a new street system created Priority Avenues and redirected vehicular traffic away from downtown by establishing connector streets between neighborhoods and major avenues. Also at this time new streets were built to connect established avenues, and new traffic circulation patterns were established. The Trinary System was also established, composed of an exclusive bus lane dedicated to mass transit bordered by two lanes for slow-moving and local traffic, a solution that provides access to businesses and homes, while two additional fast lanes in each direction into and out of the downtown area allow through traffic to flow.

The transit network has evolved since 1974, and today the RIT extends to other cities in the metropolitan area. Thanks to the RIT, the government estimated that gasoline consumption in Curitiba was 30 percent lower than in eight comparable Brazilian cities in 2004.

One of the institutional proposals derived from the new *plano diretor* was the creation of the Instituto de Pesquisa e Planejamento Urbano de Curitiba (IPPUC; Institute of Urban Research and Planning of Curitiba) in 1966 to implement the plan and to develop all complementary projects. IPPUC established a team of planners

Figure 9.2. This aerial view of Curitiba clearly shows the structural axes and the higher densities along them. (Courtesy of IPPUC)

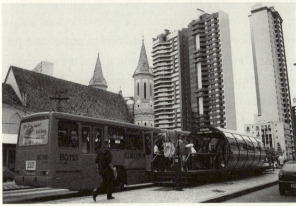

Figure 9.3. A bi-articulated bus and a tubular shelter on one of Curitiba's structural axes. (Courtesy of IPPUC)

Figure 9.4. Rua XV de Novembro, the first pedestrian street in Curitiba, showing the old streetcar used for child care and special events. (Courtesy of IPPUC)

working outside the city's established institutional framework, so that they were able to respond quickly to development pressures. Since its founding, IPPUC has efficiently led the planning process and the transformation of Curitiba's physical structures, designing projects and overseeing their implementation.

IPPUC is also dedicated to the preservation of the city's history and the enhancement of its identity. Its first Revitalization Plan for the Historic District dates back to 1970. In 1971, the Heritage Sites Preservation policy was also established, resulting in the creation of cultural facilities as well as the rehabilitation of historic buildings. Old, abandoned, or underutilized buildings became homes to orchestras, art workshops, theaters, and museums—for example, a former army headquarters facility was transformed into the Curitiba Cultural Foundation; a historic gunpowder depot became the Paiol Theater; and a former glue factory became the Creativity Center. In 1972, the city's main street—Rua XV de Novembro—became Brazil's first pedestrian mall.[6] Its popularity made it a model emulated in other cities. Furthermore, its success in attracting more people to shop in the downtown changed the minds of shop owners, who originally had opposed the idea, and they requested expansion of the pedestrian precinct (fig. 9.4).

Zoning for specific purposes and occupation parameters guided public and private investments and projects. A 1975 law further defined land use in the city, creating areas for residential, service, manufacturing, and rural activities. The law also defined structural sectors, pedestrian areas, natural and riverside preservation areas, parks, and the Historic District. To address environmental problems in fragile areas, special land-use and occupation sectors were created through specific legislation. These laws contributed to the preservation of green areas and protection of floodplains along rivers, transforming them into recreational sites. A system of parks was implemented that simultaneously addressed recreation, flooding, and sanitation issues. The Municipal Decree for Riverside Areas Preservation in 1976 became a pioneer intervention and land-use control instrument, providing an environmentally sensitive and cost-effective alternative to the engineering works that were customary elsewhere at the time. According to IPPUC estimates, today there are more than twenty-six parks and woods in Curitiba, which together with plazas, gardens, and pocket parks make for thirty-six square meters of public green area per inhabitant.

Curitiba's accelerated growth also demanded new housing solutions as the city entered the 1970s with 609,000 inhabitants and a population growth rate of 5.36 percent per year. By 1980, Curitiba's population was above one million inhabitants, and its growth rate remained high at 5.34 percent. The growth was even more significant in the surrounding municipalities, where annual rates were as high as 14 percent. In 1976, the Slum Relocation Plan was developed to assist families living in squatter settlements in risk areas. Discarding the notion of building large housing complexes far from the city, the Companhia de Habitação Popular de Curitiba (COHAB-CT, Public Housing Company of Curitiba) began diversifying the types of housing it provided (from single-family houses to walk-up apartment buildings) and the number of housing units available in each complex, aiming at full neighborhood integration and conurbation. Some of these areas also received public health and day-care centers, as well as educational, sports, and recreational facilities. By 1989, the Bairro Novo integrated development project was built in one of the city's remaining vacant areas, providing housing for approximately twenty thousand families.

Expansion and improvement of the RIT continued in the early 1990s. IPPUC-designed and -manufactured high capacity, bi-articulated express buses that carry up to 270 passengers went into operation (fig. 9.5). The capacity of these buses is comparable to light rail systems for a minor fraction of the cost, and they circulate along the dedicated lanes of the transportation axes, encouraging higher-density development along them. Presently, the RIT includes more than six different types of buses and bus routes in the city: express links along the transportation axes connect neighborhoods to one another, to the downtown and to nearby towns; provide direct connections between specific places; circulate within the downtown; serve students with special needs; connect to city hospitals; and connect tourist attractions and parks. It was also during this period that Curitiba's Trade Bus Line was established: retired buses were recycled as mobile units to reach out to communities, offering education and training in traditional trades and service jobs.

In the 1980s, specific legislation facilitated the creation of preservation areas through incentives and land-use controls. The mapping of preservation areas began undergoing regular updating, serving as a land-use instrument and as a way of monitoring preservation activities. Several new parks and wooded areas were created, to-

Figure 9.5. Aerial view of a structural axis, showing the dedicated bus lanes, express buses, and tubular bus shelters. (Courtesy of IPPUC)

taling more than eight million square meters of public preservation areas, and IPPUC dubbed the city the "Ecological Capital of Brazil." One of the most important incentive instruments for growth management—the Transfer of Building Rights Act—was created in 1982. This law gave impetus to the process of preservation of the city's historic, cultural, architectural, and natural assets, by allowing development rights of culturally significant buildings or natural/open spaces to be transferred to other areas of the city. Also, new transportation alternatives were created with the implementation of bike paths. The Bike Path Network now has approximately 120 kilometers of bike paths integrated into the urban system along certain streets, railway lines, and rivers.

Curitiba entered the 1990s with 1.3 million inhabitants. During that decade, the population growth rate was approximately 2.29 percent per year, significantly lower than in previous decades. The city had grown to occupy most of the available land in the municipality, and growth spilled over into other municipalities in the metropolitan area. During those years, Curitiba hosted several national and international planning events, and the city began winning awards for its urban projects. Innovative solutions to issues of environment, transportation, housing, health, education, job creation, and generation of income were continually pursued and acknowledged.

In 1990, the Fundo Municipal de Habitação (FMH, Municipal Housing Fund) was created, with the purpose of providing financial support to housing programs for low-income populations. Since then, the FMH has been a source of financial support for implementing land-tenure regulation and low-income housing construction. The fund's resources come from the transfer of municipally owned real estate, budget appropriations, and income from development incentives (for example, the transfer of development rights). Job creation and the linkage of jobs to housing were also important goals of specific programs in Curitiba in this decade. For example, the city sought to ensure the vitality and continuance of traditional trades through the creation of the Vila dos Ofícios (Village of Trades) Program, implemented in 1995, creating live-work units where people can both reside and work. In addition, a concerted effort among all municipal government agencies coordinated by IPPUC in 1997 created the Linhão do Emprego (Jobs Line)—a program aimed at providing the necessary structure for creating jobs and generating income for fifteen peripheral neighborhoods.

In the 1990s the city concentrated on facilities to help revitalize local culture and leisure. Two important structures were the Ópera de Arame (Steel-Frame Opera House; fig. 9.6), built on the site of an abandoned and inundated quarry, and the Rua 24 Horas (24–Hour Street) shopping arcade, where forty-two stores, eateries, and a restaurant are open around the clock (fig. 9.7). The Universidade Livre do Meio Ambiente (Unilivre, Open University of the Environment) was created in 1993 as a

Figure 9.6. In a new park replacing an old quarry, the steel-framed Ópera de Arame was built on stilts over an artificial lake (Photo by Vicente del Rio)

Figure 9.7. The Rua 24 Horas is an arcaded row of shops, eateries, and bars; built on a public right-of-way, it stays open around the clock. (Courtesy of IPPUC)

research, educational, and consulting center for environmental and sustainable practices. Since its inception it has served as a model for similar institutions in Brazil and elsewhere, and has demonstrated the potential of partnerships to promote urban sustainability among public, private, nonprofit, and community organizations, and through national and international collaboration.

In 1995, the historic downtown area was further revitalized through the restoration of the original façades of historic buildings, and the Cores da Cidade (City Colors) project returned them to their original colors. In the same year, public access to learning was extended with the inauguration of the first of forty Farois do Saber (Lighthouses of Knowledge)—small neighborhood libraries built near public schools, open to students and the community (fig. 9.8).

Also in 1995, the first of five Ruas da Cidadania (Citizens' Streets) was inaugurated. Functioning as a mix of community center, transit hub, and headquarters for the city's regional administrative centers, these complexes concentrate public social service, retail, cultural spaces, and sports and arts facilities (fig. 9.9). In 1996, the Curitiba Memorial Cultural Center was inaugurated, and one year later the Rua XV de Novembro pedestrian mall was remodeled. In the late 1990s the city also witnessed the opening of the Brazilian Popular Music Conservatory; the Novelas Curitibanas Theater, the Dadá Theater, the Casa Vermelha; and the Casa dos 300 Anos—all in celebration of Curitiba's three hundredth anniversary. Parks, thematic wooded areas, and ethnic memorials were also created that decade throughout the city to pay homage to the numerous ethnic groups that contributed to Curitiba's demographic history and current makeup—such as the Ukrainian, Arab, German, and Japanese memorials, and the Portuguese and Italian parks.[7]

Another area in which Curitiba has won recognition is the management of solid waste. Curitiba deals with solid waste without expensive mechanical garbage-separation facilities. According to government estimates, Curitibanos recycle nearly two-thirds of their garbage through programs that make the city cleaner and provide jobs, income for farmers, and food and transportation benefits for the poor. The Garbage That Is Not Garbage and Garbage Exchange programs involve curbside pick-up and disposal of recyclables sorted by households. In less accessible areas, such as *favelas*, the program gives out food stamps or transit tickets for low-income families that col-

Figure 9.8. One of the Lighthouse of Knowledge public libraries. These small libraries have become neighborhood social and physical landmarks. (Photo by Vicente del Rio)

Figure 9.9. One of the Citizens' Streets that serve Curitiba's low-income outlying districts; it integrates a bus terminal, public social services, and educational and sports facilities. (Courtesy of IPPUC)

lect and sort their garbage. Trash is taken to a plant built of recycled materials, where it is sorted by retired or unemployed persons and recovered materials are sold to local industries. Curitiba's selective garbage collection system now extends to twenty-four surrounding municipalities.

The *plano diretor* has guided development in Curitiba ever since its inception, and it was not revised at all until 1998. At the end of 2000, after a two-year period of technical studies and public input, a zoning law was approved that aimed to address the new metropolitan conditions of Curitiba. This new law formulated metropolitan growth management policies, created an axis of metropolitan integration and development (BR-116), designated new axes of urban density and areas of environmental preservation, and promoted economic development and job creation.

During the 2001–2004 mayoral term, the following projects were part of the government agenda:

Nossa Vila (Our Village), aimed at upgrading and securing land tenure of squatter settlements, promoting community development, and preventing new land invasions;

Viver Junto (Live Together), aimed at expanding and upgrading public schools with facilities for sports, recreation, the arts, and cultural activities open to the community;

Aprender (Learn), which sought the creation of new physical and virtual educational spaces throughout the city for lifelong educational opportunities;

2000 Plan, aimed at developing—in partnership with communities—new sidewalks, road paving, landscaping, and lighting in selected areas;

Nova Rebouças, aimed at implementing new recreational and cultural uses in a neighborhood as sources of income and jobs;

Linha Turística (Tourist Line), which sought to consolidate a tourist axis through a combination of environmental conservation and economic and cultural development;

Curitiba Tecnológica, which emphasized innovation of urban and ecological technologies

Ambiente (Environment), aimed at enhancing the city's environmental conditions, emphasizing waste management and watershed protection; and

Cidadãos em Movimento (Citizens in Movement), which implements and enhances engineering, management, control, regulation, and education programs related to transportation systems to improve efficiency, safety, and quality.

The current administration, led by Mayor Beto Richa (2004–2007), has continued these programs and added a few others. These projects are at different stages of implementation and their degrees of success remain to be seen. The breadth of planning objectives that they manifest are however indicative of the robustness of planning activity in the city.

In 2007, Curitiba had approximately 1.8 million inhabitants, and its metropolitan area had 3.5 million. The city has done much in the last four decades to maintain and improve its urban quality and address issues of urban transportation, land use, and sustainability in innovative, efficient, and cost-effective ways, to the extent that it has achieved worldwide recognition, and is held up by many as a model of urban planning and management.

Elements Shaping the Urban Development Process

The development of Curitiba's planning project since the mid-1960s has been mainly shaped by the conjunction of three elements: (a) the accommodation of diverse dominant interests around a single political project; (b) the massive media dissemination of a particular city image; and (c) the permeation of some material gains to the lower income classes.

Accommodation of Diverse Interests

First, the consensus and convergence of the interests of the business, planning, and government elites around a single political project constitutes the very origin of the planning transformation in Curitiba since the 1960s, and has become the basis for successive design and planning decisions to this date. The cohesion and survival of the planning process have been strategically supported by the political continuity that the government and planning elites of Curitiba have enjoyed since the beginning. The administrative continuity in Curitiba's government is unique in Brazil and rare in Latin America, and was made possible by at least three concurrent factors: (a) the role played by the economic elites of the city in the definition and implementation of the plan; (b) a series of mayors and governors who were supportive of the plan; and (c) institutional mechanisms that forged and maintained the political project within the government (D. Oliveira 1995, 1998).

First, the *plano diretor* and its subsequent reforms were at all times exceptionally compatible with the interests of the business elite of the city, particularly those in the industrial, real estate, construction, and mass-transit sectors. These sectors influenced formally, through their professional organizations and political representatives, and informally, through personal relations and lobbying, the definition of the *plano diretor* and its process of implementation and change.

The second factor was the succession of mayors and governors committed to the realization of the plan. There cannot be a better example of the unity of political and planning leadership backing the *plano diretor* than Jaime Lerner,[8] who has emblematically personified those roles continuously since the 1960s. Lerner, the first president of IPPUC, was appointed mayor of Curitiba by the military regime for the first time in 1971, when he was able to launch the implementation of the *plano diretor* (Rabinovitch and Leitman 1993). Since then, Lerner has thrice been mayor of Curitiba and twice governor of the state of Paraná. Even during his terms as governor, members of his inner circle, who had a compatible party affiliation and planning philosophies, served as mayor of Curitiba: Rafael Greca and Cassio Taniguchi, the latter serving two mayoral terms (1997–2004). The current mayor was also endorsed by Lerner, but is not professionally associated with him.

The last key factor supporting the continuity of the planning process in Curitiba was the creation of an ingenious institutional structure to support the implementation of the plan. This key element made it possible to avoid the political entanglements that complicated or completely stalled planning processes of other Brazilian cities.[9] Of particular importance was the creation of IPPUC in 1965, which provided a political means for injecting flexibility and dynamism into the planning process. IPPUC was able to bypass the bureaucracy of city departments in order to enhance the city's appearance and prepare it for the future through a functional technocratic planning under the watchful eye of the military regime (del Rio 1992).

With the creation of IPPUC, planners came to dominate the municipal government. Because the framework of the military dictatorship was still in place and was backing IPPUC, they could make decisions with relative autonomy. The success of the initial transportation and land-use plans implemented by Lerner and IPPUC gave them leverage to continue making innovations. The IPPUC Administrative Council included representatives of all the government bureaucracy, thus establishing functional links with all other agencies. When IPPUC was created, all its members shared the same political inclination, had participated in the development of the *plano diretor*, and were appointed by Lerner. IPPUC was further vested with authority over all other government agencies. Having survived political changes and transformations since its founding in 1966, IPPUC continues to be the major planning agency in Curitiba.

Image Making and City-Marketing Processes

City-marketing strategies are used to select and edit urban images, and to direct citizens' perceptions of their city and the way they view their relationship with it and, to a certain degree, their own identity (del Rio 1992; Sánchez 1996, 1997). Curitiba is an example of resourceful use of the media to enhance the city's image and the citizens' sense of belonging. The media have been used to disseminate a particular city image and create a hegemonic urban imaginary. Sharing a unidimensional, uncontested image of their city as a place that has already solved its problems, many Curitibanos have not become active in the city development process. They have limited themselves to the role of passive recipients of city-provided services or commodities.[10]

The rhetoric of political and planning discourses has constantly renewed the locally, nationally, and internationally positive assessment of the city through three main strategies: (a) inserting its discourse into the major thematic planning debates of the time—for example, promoting the "Ecological Capital of Brazil" as a theme of the 1990s (Sánchez 1997); (b) mystifying the role of planners; and (c) promoting a hegemonic, homogeneous reading of the city through media messages and the suppression of dissent.

The privileged means for deploying these image-making strategies have been architectural and urban interventions. These visible works are easily charged with constructed meanings. The marketing strategy for each new urban product—building or space—is meticulously designed to distinguish it from its predecessors, and to maintain momentum and public excitement regarding the continuous process of architectural and urban interventions.[11]

These buildings were planned to have such strong iconic power that they started to be part of the urban imaginary of the citizens and together constructed a strong image of Curitiba—an image that differentiated the city from the rest of Brazil. Citizens have been portrayed by the media as happy contributors to the well-being of the city, and thus pressured to show approval for the design interventions. Curitibanos have responded positively to these campaigns, turning out in large numbers to appropriate and enjoy the public spaces of the city. With its rise to international fame, Curitiba has also become a destination for planners, politicians, and environmentalists from around the world. Curitiba's image of high quality of life and "environmental correctness" is a factor in attracting investments, new industries and services, and a quality workforce. However, the insistence on discourses that promote "a city of and for the people" hides the social contradictions existing in that contested terrain, homogenizing the city and its social fabric through manipulations of the urban image (Sánchez 1996; M. Santos 1987).

Provision of Material Gains to Lower Income Classes

If the popular sectors were not allowed to have direct or even represented participation in the definition of the *plano diretor* in Curitiba, they certainly gained from its implementation. In Curitiba, the planning model has percolated enough material benefits to the population at large to guarantee that residents have an overwhelmingly positive assessment of the city and the planning process. Examples of these benefits are the RIT and the programs for the purchase or exchange of recyclable garbage for material goods such as food and transit tickets (D. Oliveira 1995).

Indeed, programs such as the RIT make large sectors of low-income groups feel that they are participants in a commonly implemented city project, and grant substantive relief to their budgets and improvements to their quality of life. An example is the integration of bus terminals in 1980, when a single fare was implemented. The short-distance trips—which mostly served the middle and upper classes—subsidized the longer routes. Users can transfer between buses in many of the stations without paying an extra fare. Besides time savings and accessibility, this transit system brings economic benefits for the citizens, given that according to a 1992 report, they spent only about 10 percent of their income on transportation, one of the lowest rates in Brazil (Margolis 1992). This transit system has reached capacity, however, and the city is exploring the creation of a complementary light rail system. Meanwhile, bus ridership is decreasing and private automobile usage is increasing.

Factors Undermining the Governance Model and Planning Practices

At least three factors are causing stress in the governance model of Curitiba, threatening to undermine some of the successful urban programs enacted or otherwise to subvert the future progress of planning processes. These include (a) exacerbation of urban problems and inequalities; (b) deficiencies in institutional structure and coordination at the level of metropolitan planning and governance; and (c) inadequate responses to the increasing challenges to government and planning institutions from citizens demanding greater political accountability and democratic participation.

Exacerbation of Urban Problems and Social Inequalities

The first factor undermining the governance model and planning practices in Curitiba is increasing urban problems and social inequalities. Probably the major problem is the great disparity in resources that exists between the municipality of Curitiba and the other twenty-five municipalities within the legal boundaries of the Curitiba Metropolitan Region (CMR).[12] These disparities are starting to cause dysfunctions in the central city, such as increases in unemployment and crime rates, a collapse of infrastructure, and environmental degradation. In order to preserve the urban quality within Curitiba, the broader metropolitan region has to be brought within the scope of planning. Recently, under the leads of Curitiba mayors Cassio Taniguchi and Beto Richa, planning and government officials at the metropolitan level have started to address the problems of the discrepancies between center and periphery with several plans addressing the entire metropolitan region.

Deficiencies in Institutional Structure

The second factor that is critically impeding the effectiveness of planning and governance in Curitiba is deficiencies of institutional structure and coordination for planning and governance at the level of the CMR. A recent city government plan has defined three basic guidelines, two of which prioritize metropolitan issues; namely, shared management and metropolitan integration.[13] However, despite recent attempts by IPPUC, COMEC,[14] and ASSOMEC[15] to pursue such goals, there has been little progress.

Additional institutional constraints make metropolitan planning difficult in Curitiba. Only municipal and state governments in Brazil hold legal decision-making authority. The state legislature is the organ that governs legally defined metropolitan regions.[16] Therefore, metropolitan-level entities such as COMEC and ASSOMEC have only advisory but no legal authority. A proposal was presented for the creation of a metropolitan council with political authority where municipal councilors could meet and deliberate upon metropolitan issues, but vested political interests resisted it. There has not been the political will to confront the power structures of the neighboring municipalities in order to accomplish some sort of metropolitan government or effective inter-government coordination. Instead, fragmentation of the CMR into more municipalities and incorporation of new municipalities into the metropolitan region have happened frequently in recent years, making attempts to coordinate across city governments ever more difficult.

In the current state of affairs, the only other institution capable of taking over metropolitan leadership is IPPUC. Yet today, IPPUC's actions do not have the same all-encompassing impact they had during the first periods of the design and implementation of the *plano diretor*. This is mainly due to the fact that the major planning actions called for in the *plano* have already been implemented. There has been a clear shift in the role of IPPUC since Lerner's last term as mayor of Curitiba, from an emphasis on structural urban planning to keeping architectural and landscaping projects on schedule.[17]

IPPUC has been recovering its leadership during the last two mayoral administrations, which have emphasized urban planning at the level of the metropolitan region. In effect, ASSOMEC is respecting IPPUC's own goals, and some IPPUC personnel are devoted to metropolitan projects and are addressing the integration of neighboring municipalities with Curitiba. Since IPPUC is a municipal agency, however, there are some institutional constraints on what it can do in the area of regional planning beyond Curitiba city limits. These institutional problems are somewhat ameliorated by the fact that some municipalities, lacking technical capacity, are contracting with IPPUC or with professionals from this institution to provide consulting services as they develop their municipal *planos diretores*. Municipal-level decision making remains in the hands of individual mayors, however, who may or may not comply with metropolitan-region plans.

The effect of these conditions is that nowadays planning at the level of the Curitiba Metropolitan Region is occurring reactively rather than proactively—that is, it is not structuring the growth of the city as it once did, but is attempting to remedy some of the functional deficiencies resulting from unplanned growth. The fact that the government and planning officials have chosen until recently to shelve the problems of the metropolitan region, and in particular the demands of the low-income sectors of the population, has made it even more difficult for them to deal with and provide solutions to those problems now. Social problems such as lack of affordable housing; substandard education and health services; and increases in crime, violence, homelessness, and unemployment have sprouted in both urban and suburban areas, and have become critical signs of a deteriorating urban environment.[18]

Demands for Democracy and Citizen Participation

The third factor causing strains in the technocratic governance and planning model of Curitiba is the increase in planning and political consciousness among the citizenry in the last decade. This has led to growing challenges to what are perceived as unresponsive government and planning institutions from citizens and groups demanding greater political accountability and democratic participation.

Since the reestablishment of democracy in Brazil in 1986, local governments have been incrementally forced to turn to their constituencies for legitimacy and support. Curitiba's government, however, has been slow in adjusting its urban planning and management models to accommodate truly democratic participation. Thus, public participation in Curitiba today is still largely hampered by the hegemony of government power and the burden of the popular myths that the planning elite has "made everything all right" and has already planned a wonderful city that should not be interfered with. The national political context has changed, however, and citizen awareness and involvement in planning and management are growing in many Brazilian cities. Therefore, an autocratic corporate government in Curitiba can no longer sustain the relatively smooth and efficient urban planning and implementation process that has occurred in the city since the 1960s.

My claim that there currently is a wave of citizen participation which could provoke changes in the model of planning and governance in Curitiba is supported by empirical observation of concerned citizens and groups lobbying ceaselessly for discussion of alternative views of the city's future. Sectors of the population are becoming better organized, coordinated, and outspoken, seizing opportunities to propose alternative visions for city development.[19] Heightened citizen consciousness and participation is focused on several areas: the growing dimension and complexity of urban problems; the contradictions between the actual and promised performance of government and planning representatives; the increasing recognition and testing of popular influence in the planning process; and the greater disclosure, diffusion, and discussion of knowledge about alternative political projects that have created more socially equitable urban transformations in other cities in Brazil and around the world.

In the political arena, several Brazilian cities have implemented participatory budgeting programs that allow citizens to give input into and make decisions about the distribution and administration of their metropolitan budgets. In contrast, Curitiba's city council rejected a proposal to create such a mechanism put forth by the political opposition, the Partido dos Trabalhadores (PT, Labor Party).[20] In 1999, the PT promoted through the city council a set of seminars in which the master plan of Curitiba, adopted in 1966, was publicly discussed and challenged for the first time in more than three decades; this series of major metropolitan events took place over a period of two months.[21] Despite broad public interest in the seminars and the fact that, prompted by both law and public pressure, IPPUC did indeed begin revising the plan, the revision process was mostly carried out behind closed doors. Finally, in early 2000, the revised *plano* was declared law and made public, and since then professionals and scholars have been critically examining its implications.[22]

In summary, civil society in Curitiba has shown a much greater capacity to change, adapt, and take advantage of a new age of democratic governance than has the city government bureaucracy, which has for the most part entrenched itself in the old top-down technocratic mode. This model was effective in the past but is being increasingly contested in the present and shows signs of rapidly losing legitimacy. A number of intellectuals and activists have committed themselves to promoting analyses and discussions of the current state of affairs in the city, and are pressing for changes. They are acting within academia, planning and government institutions, grassroots movements, and nongovernmental organizations. In addition, low-income and middle-class communities in the metropolitan region are reacting, albeit slowly, to the problems they face and their lack of opportunities for inclusion in the decision-making processes at the city level.

Conclusion

Curitiba can justifiably be considered a model of urban design, planning, and management within Brazil, and even internationally, because of the creative, effective, and cost-effective ways the city has dealt with the creation and enhancement of public spaces, urban transportation, land use, and sustainability. In effect, attractive urban design projects and creative land-use or transportation strategies have facilitated the creation of cultural, social, recreational, and educational facilities; the preservation of natural areas and buildings of historic or cultural significance; and the promotion of housing and employment for all income classes. In combination, these projects and policies have positively transformed the physical realm of Curitiba and garnered national and international recognition for the city.

The top-down politics involved in Curitiba's urban design and planning processes and some of the paradoxical results on the spatial and social fabric of the city, however, have not received adequate attention and are yet to be critically assessed (Irazábal 2005). Notwithstanding Curitiba's fine accomplishments in the areas of urban design and planning, an analysis of the politics of development in Curitiba provides some evidence that insufficient and low-quality opportunities for public participation are starting to delegitimize the planning process. Indeed, in current local governance practices, the interaction between government leaders and citizen groups has not yet generated a creative, respectful, and productive dialogue. Curitiba's government must involve citizens in the planning process in a more thorough way before the city's development dynamics lose momentum. Arguably, those dynamics have already begun a process of decline and delegitimization. Thus, Curitiba could rapidly become an example of a brilliant planning process that ran out of steam and prestige if the current local practices of poor interaction between government leaders and citizens persist and if more attention is not paid to social and spatial inequalities.

Hence, at the dawn of the new millennium, Curitiba is at a crossroads. The city could rest on its laurels, complimenting itself on the successes of its *plano diretor* and other urban design and planning initiatives implemented between the 1960s and the 1990s. But it would do so at the risk of losing vitality and becoming outmoded. Or, conversely, the city could try to maintain the innovative profile and dynamism that has characterized it so far, searching for new ways to develop a competitive advantage and strategically position itself within the regional, national, and international networks of the new global economy, while addressing the growing challenges of democratization, regional urbanization, and social and spatial justice at the local and metropolitan-region levels. A new set of participatory and economic premises and development paradigms is needed in order for the government, planning agencies, and citizenry in Curitiba to reevaluate and renegotiate their governance and urban development priorities. Open discussion should be fostered among the entire population so that they can explore together the real potentialities of the city and construct new, more sustainable and equitable development paths for the future.

Interviews

Barz, Elton Luiz. Historian and PT city council member's assistant. Interviewed by the author, September 17, 1998.

Moura, Rosa, and Maria de Lourdes Kleinke. "Avaliação de Experiências em Planejamento de Cidades. Entrevistas Curitiba." Instituto Pólis. Curitiba, 1998.

Oliveira, Dennison de, Ph.D., UFPR. Professor of History. Interviewed by Moura, Rosa, and Maria de Lourdes Kleinke. "Avaliação de Experiências em Planejamento de Cidades. Entrevistas Curitiba." Instituto Pólis. Curitiba, April 8, 1998.

Santos Neves, Lafaiete, Ph.D. Political activist. Interviewed by Moura, Rosa, and Maria de Lourdes Kleinke. "Avaliação de Experiências em Planejamento de Cidades. Entrevistas Curitiba." Instituto Polis. Curitiba, April 2, 1998.

Urban, Teresa. Environmentalist. Interviewed by Moura, Rosa, and Maria de Lourdes Kleinke. "Avaliação de Experiências em Planejamento de Cidades. Entrevistas Curitiba." Instituto Pólis. Curitiba, April 8, 1998; also interviewed by the author, August 13, 1998.

Notes

1. For a more detailed discussion of planning and development in Curitiba, see Irazábal 2005; for the history of planning in Curitiba and a description of particular projects see IPPUC (2003).
2. There had been many city plans and projects in Brazil before the Agache Plan for Curitiba—for example, in São Paulo, Rio de Janeiro, and Porto Alegre—and even the design of two new state capitals—Belo Horizonte and Goiânia. The Agache Plan for Curitiba however was one of the first comprehensive master plans in the modern sense.
3. Population growth at this time was mainly a result of migration from the hinterland following the mechanization of agriculture, which displaced many workers.
4. The military regime that came to power in 1964 created the National Housing Bank (BNH) and the Serviço Federal de Habitação e Urbanismo (SERFHAU), a national agency charged with overseeing urban policies and master planning. Municipalities were mandated to have a master plan in order to receive federal funds for capital improvements, for which SERFHAU and the BNH would offer loans. See the introduction to this volume for a brief account of these institutions.

5. When it was inaugurated, the bus system carried only 54,000 passengers daily, whereas by 2006 it was carrying 2.3 million. The system has inspired many cities around the world, including Bogotá, Colombia; and Los Angeles, California.

6. The pedestrian mall was built on a weekend to prevent shop owners who opposed it from taking any legal action to halt it until it was too late. Then, children were invited for a painting fair in the middle of the street, further preventing any action against the work. Curitiba's mayor convinced opposing groups to give the project a try, while the children's fair became a successful weekly event that helped to consolidate the pedestrian activities.

7. Although city officials decided what ethnic memorials to build and where to locate them with no community participation, the ethnic groups have generally been receptive to the products, have appropriated them for cultural events, and have created partnerships with the city for their maintenance. For a detailed discussion of the ethnic memorials see Irazábal (2004).

8. Jaime Lerner is an architect, urban planner, and savvy politician who has led Curitiba's planning through all its important modern stages. In addition to his skills, Lerner enjoyed good fortune in his political career. He was the president of IPPUC when appointed mayor by the then military government to a term (1971–1975) that coincided with the prosperous phase of national development known as the "Brazilian miracle"; thus, he could count on abundant resources and no opposition to his mandate. After the return to democracy he was Curitiba's first elected mayor (1979–84) and was reelected in 1989–92, when he enjoyed the broadening of municipal resources and power granted by the new 1988 National Constitution. (He administered a city budget of $R850 million, $R600 million more than his predecessor's.) He went on to be elected governor of Paraná in 1994 and re-elected in 1998.

9. The cases of Rio de Janeiro and São Paulo are paramount examples of these political entanglements in Brazil (see D. Oliveira 1995).

10. It is relevant to mention that at the time of the creation of the *plano diretor* and until recently, a significant portion of Curitiba's population—and the most politically powerful one—was middle class and composed of descendents of European immigrants. These conditions made the city a relatively homogenous and conservative market socially, economically, and culturally. These factors led the planning and political processes to be conservative, to create consensus, and to promote the myth of the "good planner."

11. For example, before it was actually built, the Rua 24 Horas project was the object of an intense marketing campaign in which Curitibanos were depicted as active agents who demanded the project and, consequently, received it with great anticipation. Meanwhile, before this project was complete, the city started marketing another project, the Ópera de Arame, positioning Curitiba once again in the national and international news. Because of its impressive landscaping and architectural style—a light transparent steel-frame building with ample glass panels (see fig. 9.6)—this building became an obligatory tourist stop, despite its limited usefulness due to bad acoustics.

12. One comparative datum suffices to demonstrate the degree of this polarization: in 1998, the municipal budget of Curitiba was R$1,000 per person, whereas the budget of the neighboring municipality of Campo Magro, within the CMR, was only R$15 per person (interview with Elton Barz, 1998). Hence, there are strong disparities in almost all urban services between the central municipality of Curitiba and its surrounding metropolitan area.

13. The first objective is job generation.

14. COMEC (Coordenação da Região Metropolitana de Curitiba, or Coordination of the Metropolitan Region of Curitiba) is a technical planning agency for the metropolitan region created in 1974, restructured in 1994, and regulated in 1995. It has no lawmaking powers.

15. ASSOMEC (Associação dos Municípios da Região Metropolitana de Curitiba, or Association of Municipalities of the Metropolitan Region of Curitiba) is a political council composed of the mayors of all the municipalities within the CMR, with the mayor of Curitiba as president. It was created in 1997 and has no lawmaking powers.

16. There were nine such legally defined metropolitan regions in Brazil, one of which is Curitiba, currently composed of twenty-six municipalities. The other metropolitan regions are São Paulo, Rio de Janeiro, Belo Horizonte, Porto Alegre, Recife, Salvador, Belém, and Fortaleza (see the introduction to this book).

17. During Lerner's last administration, several architectural icons were created—for example, the Rua 24 Horas, the Ópera de Arame, and the Botanical Garden, among others. During the Rafael Greca administration that followed, architectural works such as the Farois do Saber, the ethnic monuments, and the Ruas da Cidadania were built. Under Mayor Taniguchi, IPPUC embarked on the enlargement or creation of new parks, such as Parque Tangüa, and the revitalization of some streets and boulevards, such as the Rua Comendador Araújo.

18. In 1998, unemployment was 12 percent in Curitiba and its metropolitan region, only 5 points lower than in the troubled metropolis of São Paulo (interview with Lafaiete Santos Neves 1998).

19. The variety and growing number of neighborhood associations, religious, environmental, professional, political, and academic groups in Curitiba is evidence of the increasing sophistication and organization of civil society, and the types of bottom-up pressures from citizens striving for a more inclusive urban planning and management process, and consequently, a more inclusive city.

20. The orçamento participativo (participatory budget) has been successfully implemented by Labor Party–led local governments in several cities such as Porto Alegre, Belo Horizonte, Santos, Londrina, and more recently, Brasília (see Abers 1998, 2000; also see Lineu Castello's essay in chapter 8 for a discussion of participatory in Porto Alegre).

21. "Plano Diretor de Curitiba: Uma Abordagem Metropolitana," municipal seminars, May–June 1999.

22. For a discussion and critique of the new plano diretor, see Moura (2000) and Firkowski (2000).

CHAPTER 10

Reclaiming City Image and Street Livability

Projeto Rio Cidade, Rio de Janeiro

Vicente del Rio

Rio Cidade is a program begun in 1993 to revitalize commercial corridors and neighborhood centers as well as the image of Rio de Janeiro through urban design interventions. Each of its component projects aimed at making these areas perform better both functionally and socially by renovating public spaces and making them more pedestrian-friendly. Rio Cidade is notable not only because of its results but also because they are representative of the wider and more intense collection of urban design actions in Rio since the city's public health and beautification works of the early 1900s.[1]

Projects included streetscaping, vehicular circulation, landscaping, street furniture and public lighting, and signage, and in spite of the breadth of the problems addressed, results were extremely positive. By 2006, thirteen years after being conceived, Rio Cidade encompassed sixty areas of intervention in different districts throughout the city, including the downtown. Despite various technical and political changes, its original vision has survived different mayors and city administrations. This vision still guides city actions in improving urban design aspects that affect communities and the image of the city.

In this essay I discuss the concepts behind Rio Cidade, as well its major effects on the city and the lessons learned from it. I will illustrate the discussion with two successful projects from Rio Cidade's first phase, which intervened in almost diametrically opposed socioeconomic and urbanistic contexts of Rio de Janeiro.

Introduction: Project Background

In order to better understand the scope of Rio Cidade, it is important to note its historical and political role in the city's development. After the transfer of the country's capital to Brasília, Rio de Janeiro was incorporated into the state of Rio de Janeiro and suffered a long period of indefinite political status and financial loss. In the 1960s and 1970s the development of a nucleus-periphery model was strengthened and the spatial structure of the metropolitan region favored the city center and a few neighborhoods, at the expense of the rest of the urban network. On one hand, the development paradigm and the country's approach to economic growth encouraged this spatial model, and public policies concentrated investments, implemented sector-specific actions, performed selective urbanization, and pursued simplistic functionalist solutions. High investments in the roadway system, for example, responded to the consolidation of the automobile industry, and in Rio in the 1960s, the attempts to accommodate the urban space to the automobile represented "a fever for the construction of viaducts and new avenues" (Abreu 1987: 133).

The economic model resulted in stratification of the city and real estate speculation promoted by exaggeratedly modernistic land-use legislation that was based on a rigid model, ignored the idiosyncrasies of neighborhoods, and imposed a nearly identical architectural typology over the whole city. Spatial conflicts were intensified with the zoning and city building works code of 1976, instituted at a time when Rio's municipal government had the prerogative of legislating urban matters by decree without the approval of the city council, and was constantly modifying the "rules of the game" in favor of political and economic interests.[2]

Intensified by the development model adopted by the national government and by the economic crisis of the 1980s, this situation contributed to a profound urban crisis in Rio; its results are clearly visible in the city's spatial structure and the quality of its places. The social and spatial conflicts that resulted from this political and economic model were particularly profound in Rio, a city blessed by its geography and natural setting, by the collection of its neighborhoods, and by the identity of its urban design. Yet within this context was a long list of city governments that were disinterested in the social, environmental, and physical quality of the public realm. The increases in poverty, in criminality, and in residents' feelings of insecurity completed the scenario in the city of Rio de Janeiro at the beginning of the 1990s. The city had lost its title of "Marvelous City" and had acquired an extremely negative image nationally and internationally. Even hosting the International Earth Summit in 1992 and carrying out some high-visibility projects (a new expressway linking the city to the international airport and the redesign of walkways along the beaches of Copacabana, Ipanema, and

Leblon) had little lasting effect, and the quality of life and of public spaces in Rio, in fact, was minimally affected.

A Strategy for the Recovery of Rio de Janeiro

The return of democracy to Brazil and of direct elections for mayor of Rio de Janeiro allowed the city to undergo a true urbanistic revolution at the turn of the millennium, particularly because of the development of a new city master plan in 1992 and of the strategic plan between 1993 and 1995 (Rio de Janeiro 1996a, 1996b). Former mayor Cesar Maia justified his strategic plan by stating that "the city was in a process of accelerating deterioration, generated by the impoverishment of its population, by the disorganized occupation of public and private spaces, by the deterioration of public services, and by the flight of financial and human capital. A city without defined vocations, with a distorted image in a growing process of disintegration . . . reversing this situation demanded a greater effort than the individual will of the city government" (Rio de Janeiro 1996b: 10).

With strong support from the private sector, particularly the Associação Comercial (Chamber of Commerce) and the Federação das Indústrias (Federation of Industries), and backed up by a consulting firm from Barcelona, the strategic plan had an executive committee, a board of directors, and thirty-one working groups with more than two hundred participants, including technicians, professionals, and community members. The planning process also included interviews with innumerable stakeholders.[3]

Despite criticisms—particularly for its neoliberal model and its relative independence from the city master plan approved by the previous government in 1992—the strategic plan was approved by the city council in 1996 and became an important tool in integrating efforts and public policies, and in directing programs and private and public investments in the city. On the other hand, strategic planning helped the city to overcome the static vision and the ambitious programs that dominated the centralized planning and technocratic model of previous years. The plan established seven strategies, each with its own set of objectives, to which 161 projects were appended. Of this total 70 percent were already underway in 1998, with the municipal government being responsible for 40 percent of them, the state for 14 percent, the federal government for 11 percent, private enterprise for 12 percent, and public-private partnerships for 23 percent.[4]

The Projeto Rio Cidade was part of "Strategy 2: Welcoming Rio," whose goals are to improve the relationship between the community and the environment, to strengthen the quality of social life in neighborhoods, and to improve public spaces. The important Cultural Corridor Project—started in the early 1980s—was a component of "Strategy 4: Integrated Rio," which seeks to develop new centralities and revitalize downtown, to revise urban legislation, and to increase accessibility.[5] This strategy also incorporated Favela-Bairro, a program begun in 1994 to upgrade *favelas* in the city through the enhancement of public spaces and development of new infrastructure and public facilities.[6] The strategic plan also addresses widening community participation through channels that go beyond organized public interest groups to include the common citizen, and seeks to strengthen cultures and values of the different parts of the city, aspects which Projeto Rio Cidade responded to.

The Foundations of Projeto Rio Cidade

Projeto Rio Cidade was an innovation for the city government in various ways. First, it tried to reclaim the city's image through a series of coordinated urban projects. Second, it chose to reinforce the polynucleated character of Rio de Janeiro and the specificity of its urban morphology of valleys and mountains by favoring commercial streets, by strengthening the identity of neighborhoods, and by investing in the self-esteem of local communities (Rio de Janeiro 1996b, 1996c). Finally, in order to generate new ideas and context-specific solutions, and to permit the simultaneous implementation of many projects, the city government adopted a new policy of hiring project teams through public competitions.[7]

In an open call for proposals, Rio Cidade was described as a project that would, according to the mayor, "act to structure sections of the city's image, revitalizing the concept of the street and returning it to the citizens under conditions appropriate for its use, comfort and security" (Rio de Janeiro 1996b). The competitive bid process was innovative in soliciting not specific project proposals but "methodologies for urbanistic intervention," and competing teams were free to give examples of how their concepts and ideas would be implemented in the project areas indicated by the city. The bid parameters also demanded that teams be multidisciplinary and include at least an architect/urbanist, a graphic/product designer, a landscape architect, and a traffic engineer.

In October 1993, in the competition for the first phase of Rio Cidade (Rio Cidade I), seventeen teams were selected, and in July 1997 twenty-seven were selected for the second phase (Rio Cidade II). All were contracted and managed by the Instituto Pereira Passos (IPP, the municipal foundation for city planning), which determined the area to be assigned to each team and the amount of each contract. A few areas were contracted through a call for proposals strictly from private firms while others were designed by teams within IPP itself; by 2004 there around sixty projects in Rio Cidade.

The intervention areas of Projeto Rio Cidade are distributed all over the city, from the downtown to the southern districts and the northern and western suburbs. These areas suffered from problems that are very common in Brazilian cities, such as dangerous public spaces; narrow, ill-equipped, and deteriorated sidewalks; complicated vehicular circulation and antiquated streetscapes; lack of trees and street furniture; invasions of public spaces and other abuses by peddlers; and visual pollution. To respond to these challenges, the contracted firms were to deal with all types of issues and projects that directly affected the quality of public areas, since the city wanted projects that could be built in the short term.

Although as varied as the working teams and the neighborhoods affected, the projects shared common objectives: (a) to improve the perceived aesthetics and the security and comfort of pedestrians through the renovation of public spaces, street furniture, and landscaping; (b) to improve vehicular circulation, parking, loading and unloading, and comfort for bus users; and (c) to integrate project interventions. In addition, the interventions included the rehabilitation of infrastructure networks (drainage and sewers), the burial of aerial utility lines, and the suppression of peddling on sidewalks. Some teams also proposed complementary projects such the preservation of historic buildings and changes in bus routes and terminals.

In 1996, only three years after the launching of the first competition, fifteen projects of the first phase had been built in a total investment of around R$220 million (1996 values), 60 percent of which was dedicated to infrastructure projects. In 2004, out of all sixty areas within Projeto Rio Cidade, twenty-three were already built, four were under construction, and the rest were on the drawing boards.

Following I shall discuss the Rio Cidade projects for Méier and Leblon not only because they were typical of the program, but also because the communities they served represent two very different socioeconomic realities in the city. In addition, these were the first Rio Cidade projects to be carried out, providing us with enough distance for objective evaluation. My analysis considers not only the appropriateness of the design solutions but also the overall Rio Cidade program as an expression of a twofold city policy: on one hand to deliver visible environmental improvements to stakeholders, and on the other to carry out an immense city marketing operation intended to improve the city's image.

Project Rio Cidade Méier: Functionality and Comfort

Located less than six miles from downtown, the Méier district is a typical example of how urban growth occurred in Rio de Janeiro. The area was once a large orange plantation belonging to the Meyer family, who migrated from Germany in the nineteenth century. Facing falling agricultural prices and the city's pressing demands for growth, and taking advantage of a new railroad station on their land, they started selling off their property. Development around the station and along the new streets occurred in piecemeal fashion, ignoring topographic conditions, and was accelerated by trolley lines built in the mid-twentieth century. By the 1950s Méier, nicknamed the "Capital of the Suburbs," had a busy commercial core and was one of the preeminent residential neighborhood suburbs for the middle and lower middle classes. Because it is on the only route between the city center and neighborhoods farther north, thousands of people pass through on their daily commutes to and from work by train, bus, or private vehicle, making it one of Rio's busiest retail and service centers—a "functional subcenter" in Rio's planning jargon.

Rapid development and neglect from previous city governments had resulted in very poor environmental and functional conditions, loss of identity, and deteriorated public spaces in Méier. Lack of regulation over development, increasing use of sidewalks by street vendors, and a chaotic traffic circulation and parking situation were also among the evident problems the district faced (fig. 10.1). The haphazard subdivision process had generated an urban fabric of low continuity, a problem aggravated by the physical barriers imposed by the railway.

The project concentrated on Rua Dias da Cruz, the main street into Méier from downtown and the train station, and an important access route to neighborhoods beyond. This busy artery is always packed with pedestrians and vehicles because of its high concentration of businesses and services. On both sides, eight-story mixed-use buildings are lined up side-by-side, and in many the retail area on the ground floor resembles a mini–shopping center. The importance of this commercial artery

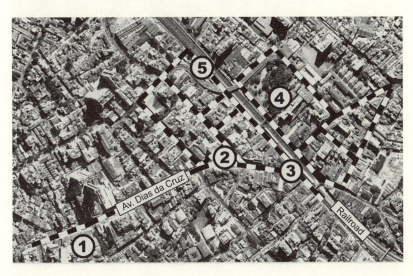

Figure 10.1. The center of Méier district and the boundaries of the Rio Cidade project: 1. Méier Shopping Center. 2. Agripino Griego Square. 3. Largo do Méier Square. 4. Jardim do Méier Park and Municipal Hospital. 5. Bus terminal. (Courtesy of IPP)

is illustrated by its having received the largest movie theater in Latin America in the mid-1950s, With a two thousand-seat capacity, the famous Imperator was adapted into a music hall in the 1980s and now holds a religious temple. In 1965 the street also attracted Brazil's first attempt at building a modern shopping mall, which continues to attract a large clientele (del Rio et al. 1987).

The four lanes of Rua Dias da Cruz were incapable of handling the existing two-way traffic, which included more than forty-five bus routes. Varying lane widths; irregular parking; lack of pullouts for bus stops, loading or unloading; lack of lanes for left or U-turns; and complicated intersections contributed to the overall chaos (fig. 10.2). Pedestrians competed with vehicles, and more than two hundred peddlers elbowed for room on the narrow, poorly maintained sidewalks devoid of trees, street furnishings, or signage.

Figure 10.2. Looking west along Rua Dias da Cruz, showing the chaotic vehicular and pedestrian traffic before renovation. (Photo by Mariza Almeida)

Beginning in December 1993, Project Rio Cidade renovated thirteen acres of Méier's commercial core on both sides of the railway, focusing on Rua Dias da Cruz.[8] In addition to the study of traditional planning and urban design issues, the methodology for Rio Cidade Méier included research on community expectations and on the evolution of the area's morphology; surveys of visual, cognitive, and behavioral concerns; and studies of how public spaces were being appropriated by street vendors and others.[9]

The redesign of Rua Dias da Cruz was a priority, and the solution achieved a significant increase in pedestrian comfort and vehicular flow through a uniform street cross-section with a constant curb-to-curb width, a new median with a row of palm trees and street lights, wider sidewalks lined with trees and pedestrian lighting, pull-outs (for bus stops, taxis, and loading/unloading), the prohibition of parking along the street, and the diversion of some bus routes to a new bus terminal (fig. 10.3). Vehicular traffic along Rua Dias da Cruz is now banned on Sundays, when the area becomes a pedestrian-only "leisure street" where local residents socialize, stroll, play, and participate in community events.

A system of pocket parks was created throughout the project area, wherever the width of sidewalks and the surrounding uses permitted. These spaces received special landscaping, including elaborate paving, seats and tables, and provisions for future kiosks for the selling of flowers, foods, and beverages. One of the larger of these pocket parks resulted from landscaping a vacant lot left over after the construction of the ramp to the auto bridge crossing the railroad tracks. The space was remodeled into a playground and a roller-skating rink, which made it instantly popular with youngsters. Another important pocket park was created as a gateway to Rua Dias da Cruz for those arriving by car from the city center, and its design included a new monument of vertical slabs inscribed with the word "Méier." This monument is laid amidst a metallic grid through which water jets up, highlighted by spotlights.

Agripino Grieco Square, located along Rua Dias da Cruz, was totally remodeled thanks to the reorganization of vehicular circulation in the project area and the relocation of bus routes that terminated at one of its edges. The new design included colorful paving materials in a geometric pattern, new trees and planters, an amphitheater, a small playground, tables and benches, and spaces for kiosks. Linked to one of the park's edges was a new pedestrian precinct with wider sidewalks, raised pedestrian crossings, and abrupt lane diversions for traffic calming, in order to revitalize existing restaurants and bars and draw more patrons during happy hour.

The square and the new pedestrian precinct were even further animated by another design intervention. The existing pedestrian bridge linking the two sides of the project area to the train platforms was extended over the street and renovated with

Figure 10.3. Rua Dias da Cruz and Agripino Grieco Square after renovation. (Photo by J. D. Tardioli/ AEROCOLOR-Rio)

new ramps, a colorful fiberglass roof, and new lighting. The bridge now leads to a new pocket plaza that connects to a previously existing shopping arcade and to Agripino Grieco Square (fig. 10.4). The bridge became a landmark for those passing through Méier, increased the spatial continuity between the two sides of the railroad tracks, and provided a direct pedestrian link from the train platforms to Rua Dias da Cruz (fig. 10.5). These changes fostered the revitalization of the existing retail uses and increased pedestrian comfort.

Paving for sidewalks and public spaces followed a consistent and colorful geometric design formed of colored concrete scored in stripes and with patches of small cobblestones. Intended to reinforce the spatial continuity between the two sides of the railway and to confer a strong identity to the project area, this design was inspired by the colorful aspect of Carioca culture. The new design was also intended to guide peddlers to install their stalls in an organized manner along the sidewalks: the paving geometry was such that some patterns outlined the dimensions of a vending stall and were marked with the peddler's city registration number.[10]

Concern for the needs of users with disabilities marked all design solutions: ramps were provided throughout, and all sidewalks had a consistent width free of physical barriers and urban furnishings. An important project element was a series of "service islands": simple shelters shading public telephones, area maps, trash containers, benches, and a mailbox. With small variations, the same basic design was used for shelters for bus and taxi stops. Easy to spot and distributed over the entire area, these service islands increased the comfort and safety of pedestrians using the facilities.

Finally, a visual communication system was implemented for both pedestrians and drivers, which included the placing of special totems at all intersections labeling the street names and directions, and the adoption of a consistent color palette and symbol on the street furniture. The team decided that street furniture should be functional, simple, and easy to construct and maintain, which led them to adapt and improve on elements from the existing city catalog whenever possible. This approach was completely different from that used in all other areas of Rio Cidade, where teams proposed new and exclusive designs that were expensive and difficult to replace. This was the case in Leblon, discussed and illustrated later in the chapter.

Work began in December 1995 and the project was officially inaugurated in the following September, but the part of the project on the far side of the railway from the main commercial zone was not undertaken until 2003. The total cost of the work completed was approximately US$15 million (based on the exchange rate at that time), including infrastructure. The project included 10.4 square miles of paved roads, 10 square miles of sidewalks, 0.85 miles of storm-water drains, 206 garbage receptacles, 19 bus shelters, 359 streetlights, and 460 trees. As in all other project areas of Rio

Figure 10.4. Agripino Grieco Square and the pedestrian precinct. The mixed-use building with the shopping arcade and the new pedestrian overpass leading to the train station is in the upper part of the photo. (Photo by J. D. Tardioli/AEROCOLOR-Rio)

Figure 10.5. Partial view of Rio Cidade Méier, showing Agripino Grieco Square and the pedestrian precinct, the pedestrian bridge over the railroad tracks, and the gateway plaza in the lower right-hand corner. (Photo by Vera Tângari)

Cidade I, all electrical lines were buried underground, guaranteeing a truly clean visual appearance that was welcomed by the population.

After project completion, significant improvements in traffic patterns were observed; the sidewalks were more intensively used and more convenient; conflicts between vehicles and pedestrians were minimized; public areas were more intensively used, even by children; and there was a clear enhancement of commercial locations, which in turn led to new commercial investments. This was especially true along Rua Dias da Cruz and around Agripino Grieco Square with the consolidation of "Baixo

Méier" as an area for nightlife (the nickname is inspired by the traditional bohemian areas in Leblon and Gávea, in famous Carioca "south zone"). Bars and restaurants were renovated, new commercial locations were opened (such as a second branch of McDonald's in the neighborhood), and an old cinema was renovated for showing commercial films.

Project Rio Cidade Leblon: Aesthetics and Landscaping

The Leblon district developed along the seashore south of Ipanema and has always been occupied by high-income residents (Abreu 1987). In the 1950s, when living along the seashore became desirable and the popularity of Copacabana had peaked, the district experienced a property boom. Today, it is one of the wealthiest areas in Rio, and it enjoys a high index of green areas, plazas, and relatively well-kept and landscaped streets.

Leblon's intense and selective commerce, restaurants, bars, and office buildings are concentrated along Avenida Ataúlfo de Paiva, its main artery which runs parallel to the beach and two blocks inland from it. Crossing the neighborhood longitudinally for almost one mile, the avenue starts at the base of a mountain on the south and connects to Ipanema and Copacabana on the north. The avenue suffers from busy vehicular traffic including several bus routes running along it, from difficult parking, and from the presence of high-density mixed-use buildings (averaging ten stories) lining both sides. Commercial galleries and small shopping centers, various bank branches, two McDonald's restaurants, the traditional Leblon two-screen movie theater, a Catholic church and its attached school, and the important Antero de Quental Square are some of the elements along the avenue. At Leblon's south end, an area stretching for a couple of blocks known as Baixo Leblon is a lively focus of bohemian nightlife with a number of cafés, bars, restaurants, bookstores, newsstands, and drugstores, some of them open around the clock.

As expected, the city government designated the full length of the Avenida—which totaled sixteen acres—as the focus of the Rio Cidade project for Leblon, (fig. 10.6). Unlike the Méier project, where the design approach focused on improving functionality and practicality, the Leblon project focused on improving aesthetics because that neighborhood already enjoyed a high level of environmental quality. Here the design team chose to upgrade streetscaping to even higher levels, principally through the quality of detailing and diligent attention to landscaping and street furniture.[11] The specific objectives of the project were to support the local trend toward leisure activities, to expand pedestrian areas, and to improve the comfort of users (Rio de Janeiro 1996c).

Figure 10.6. Aerial photo showing the Rio Cidade Leblon project boundaries and main project areas: (1) "Baixo Leblon" bohemian area, and (2) Antero de Quental Square. (Courtesy of IPP)

The avenue was redesigned along its whole length through the reorganization of on-street parking and the provision of pullouts at bus stops and for loading/unloading. Sidewalks were widened, wheelchair ramps were installed at all pedestrian crossings (in some cases the whole corner was ramped), sidewalks were flanked with benches and generous planters, and their paving gained a sophisticated mosaic of curving patterns in white, black, and red cobblestones in a typical Carioca style (fig. 10.7).

Two significant areas along the avenue were considered for exclusive pedestrian use. In Baixo Leblon, a traditionally bohemian area on the extreme east end of the project area, starting from an existing small park, the designers proposed to close a side street to vehicular traffic and turn it into a two-block pedestrian mall, redesigning it to provide outdoor seating for patrons of the existing bars and restaurants. Although it reinforced the area's character, this idea was discarded due to opposition from both local residents and business owners who did not want the street closed to vehicles. At the far west end of the project area, at an intersection where the 45–degree orientation of the buildings and curbs evoked the Barcelona style, sidewalks were widened to form traditional square street corners. This design allowed extra room at the four corners, which were treated as pocket parks with planters, trees, benches, and kiosks selling flowers, newspapers, and magazines.

Along the avenue, the traditional Antero de Quental Square, which occupied an entire city block, received special attention from the designers. The project team wisely chose to maximize the potential of the square, which has always been an important recreational area for the neighborhood. It was already well equipped, full of trees, and very much used all day, every day, its heavy use reinforced by bus and taxi stops along its whole perimeter. Existing uses were maintained but reorganized and better separated through landscaping. Surrounding sidewalks were elevated above street level to better separate pedestrians in the square from the busy surrounding vehicular traffic. Shaded tables and seats, a new playground, elegant stone planters, new benches and appropriate lighting, and shelters for bus and taxi stops were added. A florist's kiosk with a large red concrete pergola became very popular, and a second similar pergola was added at a bus terminal on one of the square's edges.

Rio Cidade Leblon stands out from all the other projects for the attractiveness of the landscape solutions, particularly the paving of the sidewalks and the elegant, contemporary design of all urban furniture elements, which earned national and international prizes. The new streetlights, for example, provide differentiated lighting for vehicles and pedestrians, and diffusing plates on them guarantee indirect and homogenous lighting over the sidewalk. On street corners, four of these poles incorporate traffic signals and signage for motorists (names and traffic direction of streets, numbering of buildings in each block, and so on); designated pedestrian crossings are similarly illuminated, ensuring well-lighted crossings, augmenting pedestrian and

Figure 10.7. Sidewalks in Rio Cidade Leblon with cobblestone mosaics, niches for benches, landscaping, and special pedestrian lighting. (Photo by Vicente del Rio)

motorist safety, and emphasizing their structuring role in the urban fabric (fig. 10.8). Attached to some of these poles, an unusual small tubular shape shelters a public telephone, with Plexiglas sides to allow light to enter (fig. 10.9). At taxi and bus shelters, the same style of light pole supports an elegantly curved, light roof made of perforated sheet metal and polycarbonate (fig. 10.10).

Great care was taken with the detailing of the new elements; for example, in the elaborate paving design with colored cobblestones and in the use of white granite slabs for pedestrian ramps bordered by large concrete spheres to prevent the incursion of vehicles. All curbs were also cut out of white granite. All sidewalks contained raised paving to alert blind pedestrians to barriers and street crossings.

Construction on the Leblon project began in February and was completed in December 1996, at a cost of approximately US$11 million (at the 1996 exchange rate). The project involved the repaving of 10 square miles of roads and the renovation of 10.8 square miles of sidewalks; as well as the installation of 0.4 miles of new stormwater drains, 467 light poles, 561 trees, 8 bus shelters, and 121 trash containers. The result was quite positive since the project was able to upgrade an already privileged neighborhood while maintaining its Carioca character through visually attractive streetscaping. The sidewalks—widened, well illuminated, and shaded with trees, with attractive pavement mosaics, benches, and planters—pleased residents and visitors alike. The improvements became a point of reference for the community, which was pleased to see its public space more comfortable and secure and better adapted to the evening use of bars and restaurants.

Lessons from Rio Cidade

Today, fifteen years after the conception and launching of Rio Cidade, the projects can be evaluated objectively and judged successful. Because of its objectives and method of implementation, Rio Cidade was an innovative program of urban interventions in the Brazilian and even the international context, revealing itself as a true "urban planning laboratory" for the redesign of the city. In the face of great deterioration in the city's image and infrastructure, the Rio Cidade project focused on quickly completed, localized actions that produced highly visible, attention-getting results and generated social and economic multiplier effects in both the short and medium terms.

However, Rio Cidade should also be evaluated as a municipal policy of implementing a series of urban projects targeting specific areas of the city. When Rio Cidade was launched, many citizens questioned the appropriateness of the government funding localized urban projects without justifying its choice of areas, particularly because many areas were already privileged within the range of necessities in the Carioca ur-

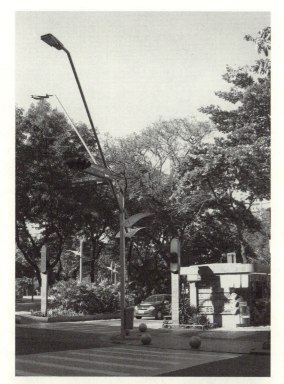

Figure 10.8. The pedestrian crossings and intersections in Rio Cidade Leblon are marked by elegant poles that integrate vehicular and pedestrian traffic lights with street and directional information. (Photo by Vicente del Rio)

Figure 10.9. New public phone booth attached to pedestrian lighting in Antero de Quental Square, Rio Cidade Leblon. (Photo by Denise de Alcantara)

Figure 10.10. Elegantly designed bus shelter with its information panel and attached trash container, Rio Cidade Leblon. (Photo by Vicente del Rio)

ban context. The program was also accused of providing a simple makeover of these areas, in which resources were spent on superficial aesthetic improvements without identifying the underlying problems from a more traditional prism of integrated planning. Moreover, the government was accused of neoliberal bias, in that short-term, opportunistic projects were used to mask deeper, long-term structural concerns. An underlying question was whether it was appropriate to intervene in specific parts of the city at the expense of the whole.

The municipal government's response to these concerns argued that a traditional planning process of identifying neighborhoods and priority areas would take too much time given the pressing, emergency status of Carioca public space. The government defended itself by saying that in allocating projects to the most important commercial axes and segments of the city's neighborhoods it was following a "natural" prioritization of interventions. Further, although the projects would not lead to significant structural changes (albeit that a few proposed altering traffic circulation, as was done in Méier, for example) all would raise the levels of vehicle and pedestrian security and comfort. They would also promote the renewal of infrastructure networks like drainage, sewage, and public illumination.

Regarding the development of Rio Cidade, we raise some methodological considerations. First, selecting teams through methodological and conceptual competitions did provoke public debate and encourage a healthy exchange of ideas, but it also risked contracting inexperienced teams. This danger was reflected in the municipal government's efforts to oversee the projects in order to guarantee their final quality. Second, the short time frames specified in the contracts for the development of the projects, particularly for the diagnostic and preliminary studies (generally only three months were allotted), created a risk of improper design solutions, either because the project team did not have time to identify the relevant urban phenomena and specificities of the context and its users, or because details were overlooked to meet deadlines.

In this sense, the experience the municipal government gained by simultaneously managing different teams and firms stands out. In this process the government also learned to be more prompt in evaluating and responding to proposals, and in clearly defining the objectives of each urban project without unduly interfering with the teams and their creativity.

The multidisciplinarity of Rio Cidade raised several important considerations. On one hand it was important for the government to require that the contracted teams be multidisciplinary and coordinated by architects, since this led to richer, more integrated solutions. On the other hand, one of the greatest difficulties confronted by the teams, particularly in the first phase, was precisely in persuading the city's administrative machinery and service providers to adopt an interdisciplinary posture. Difficulties arose primarily in the resolution of problems with multiple cross-disciplinary considerations, for example, in attempts to resolve conflicts between pedestrians and vehicles.

Not unlike in the majority of Brazilian cities, the different city departments and public companies, the urban service providers, and their technical teams were accustomed to acting independently, each with its own practices and particular objectives. Further, some providers are in the orbit of the state government, as are water, sewer, and telephone utilities. During Rio Cidade I many of these public entities did not even have any established criteria or clear technical norms for guiding or evaluating projects, some were unreceptive to innovation, while others were defensive of their respective areas of expertise. For example, the engineers responsible for traffic circulation and public transportation sometimes made unreasonable demands of the project teams, or were even antagonistic to professionals from other fields.

Although disciplinary barriers are longstanding and have always characterized public activity, they can be overcome through integrated project practices and by the collaborative advance definition of common objectives by the various responsible agencies under the coordination of the city government. The municipal executive branch relearned during Rio Cidade I how to coordinate an integrated public works project that involved multiple agencies and levels of government. During the development of Rio Cidade II this situation was considerably improved, because the mayor's office and city agencies had a more integrated vision, and had prepared for phase two by better defining a set of general directives and norms that they distributed to the contracted teams up front.

A very serious problem confronted by the project teams was the lack of a tentative budget for the projects in each area. If, on the one hand, as the city government argued, the freedom from budgetary constraints tended to generate more creative solutions in the development of the proposals, on the other hand it left the teams unsure of their own project limits and with no basis for making decisions about details, execution, and maintenance—which is certainly the greatest problem affecting Rio Cidade, particularly regarding custom-designed elements and street furniture.

The uniqueness of the projects led to greater individualization of the areas in the context of the city. Yet the use of nonstandard solutions for street furniture, traffic signals, and streetscaping is expensive and very challenging. If any of these original elements breaks down or malfunctions, the city will be tempted to replace it with a much cheaper, standardized product. Moreover, idiosyncratic design elements have confused pedestrians and drivers, who expect a certain homogeneity in urban systems, messages, and functions in a circulation corridor, a region, or even the whole city. As proof of this difficulty, several furnishings—such as the shelters for bus stops and public telephones—were later replaced and standardized throughout the city.

Regarding implementation, low-quality materials and poor construction characterized the majority of the projects. Once the construction firms were contracted by public bid, the project teams were kept on only in an advisory capacity. The construction firms not only had to comply with a very tight public budget but also had to complete the projects on schedules driven by the electoral calendar. In Rio Cidade I, for example, the mayor wished to use the projects as an electoral platform to help his party's candidate succeed him in office. Therefore, he used the first years of his term to raise capital funds, while the projects and works had to be contracted and executed in the last two years of his mandate. This meant that in spite of their complexity, the urban projects were planned in less than nine months (Méier and Leblon), the complementary projects implemented in six months, and the construction completed in three months!

Finally, Rio Cidade showed the necessity of channels for input from communities and users into the project process, and of changing the long tradition of excluding public participation in the decision-making process of urban projects in Rio de Janeiro.[12] In its first phase, because of the unprecedented nature of the program, the short time frame for planning and implementation, and the fear of political opposition, the mayor's office did not even permit the teams to directly contact community members and involve them in project planning. Public input occurred only through the data-gathering methodologies adopted by some teams, as in the case of Méier, or through formal meetings with local community associations sponsored by the mayor's office.

In Rio Cidade II the municipal government offered expanded opportunities for community participation in an attempt to make the results more consonant with local expectations. Although participation was still limited to a few meetings with the communities affected by the projects and their representatives, some suggestions actually led to changes in projects, even while construction was under way. This experience demonstrated that a fuller participatory process and more open channels of communication allow the population to appropriate the project as "owner" and thereby collaborate in controlling its use, limiting of vandalism, maintaining it, and keeping it clean. Those Rio Cidade projects with which the communities most identify are the same ones that the population most values and that experience less vandalism.

Conclusion

There is no doubt that Rio Cidade was an urban design program with positive results and repercussions in Carioca daily life, in spite of its rapid implementation, its unusual methodology, and the negative aspects discussed previously. It was successful as an instrument of the city strategic plan to improve the image of Rio de Janeiro and to promote the renovation of public spaces and commercial avenues in the centers of neighborhoods. The repercussions of the individual projects were very positive, particularly in the context of the city's need for development.

Rio Cidade achieved four great improvements:

The consolidation of the role of public urban space in providing sites for recreation and socialization. This function has become increasingly important with the expansion of private areas, and is particularly important in poor neighborhoods with needy populations, which historically have lacked green areas and quality public spaces. The population, in effect, took full advantage of the renovated and more functional spaces, and felt that their leaders cared about their needs.

The attention given to commercial axes that assume multiple centralities in terms of their function, place in the public imagination, and potential as spaces for socialization. The city's geography and history generated very distinct neighborhoods with populations that feel a strong sense of belonging, and the projects capitalized on that.

The recognition of the importance of urban design interventions in revitalizing the power of places, recovering the city image, and attracting private investment. In all the project areas, residential and commercial property gained in value and the business owners invested in improvements to their stores. Rio's image changed for the better both nationally and internationally, which translated directly into an increase in tourism.

The promotion of a "culture" of urban projects that revitalize and transform the urban image, which was reflected in the population at large and in the administrative machinery of the city. Urbanism once again became an important issue to the public, and laypersons exchanged opinions about solutions for different neighborhoods. Staff from the different government agencies gradually adopted a more integrated and multidisciplinary vision of the project, and occasionally, even without contractual obligation, they consult the original project teams.

The spirit of Rio Cidade has survived changes in municipal administrations, with new administrations continuing to support efforts to improve daily life in the city's neighborhoods and enhance the city's overall image. By 2006, the city was undergoing diversified kinds of urban intervention, rehabilitation, and special projects—such as constructing parks, bicycle paths, and community centers. The present efforts to revitalize the port area, for instance, make it clear that the city learned important lessons from Rio Cidade: whereas in the former there was sometimes a lack of direction or clear project parameters, in the port area all proposals must conform to an overall revitalization plan approved by the mayor's office.

The most recent chapter in Rio de Janeiro's planning and urban design revolved around various projects that prepared the city to host the 2007 Pan American Games. Next, they will possibly revolve around Brazil's winning proposal to host the 2014 World Soccer Cup and its candidacy to host the 2016 Olympics. These efforts are part of its broader strategy to participate more fully in the global tourism market and attract investments. Rio Cidade will certainly be a fundamental contributor to stimulating an urbanism that strengthens the public realm and revitalize communities.

Notes

I am grateful for comments and materials provided by Vera Tângari and Denise de Alcantara (Universidade Federal do Rio de Janeiro), and by Sergio Bello and Solange Cintra (Instituto Pereira Passos).

1. See the introduction to the Cultural Corridor case study by del Rio and Alcantara (chapter 5); see also Pereira (2002).
2. A peculiarity of Rio de Janeiro should be noted. Until the approval of the master plan of 1992, the city council relegated control of use and occupation of urban land to the mayor's office, which acted through decrees, a bizarre form of coexistence of an "independent" technocracy with special-interest groups. Even though the 1988 National Constitution clarified the role of municipalities and city councils over land use, Rio has inherited a crazy-quilt urban legislation that is certainly one of the most complicated in Brazil.
3. It should be noted that strategic planning in Barcelona, as well as its urbanistic accomplishments, strongly influenced the municipal government of Rio de Janeiro at that time, including the city's application to host the 2004 Olympics.
4. See www.rio.rj.gov.br (retrieved on February 15, 2004).
5. See the essay by del Rio and Alcantara (chapter 5) in this book.
6. See the essay by Duarte and Magalhães (chapter 12) in this book.
7. Competitions were sponsored by the Empresa Municipal de Informática e Planejamento (IPLANRIO, Municipal Information and Planning Corporation, today renamed Instituto Pereira Passos, or IPP) and by the Instituto de Arquitetos do Brasil (IAB, Brazilian Institute of Architects). On Projeto Rio Cidade and the interventions in its first phase, see Rio de Janeiro (1996c).
8. Project by Mayerhofer & Toledo: Luiz Carlos Toledo (partner in charge) and Vicente del Rio (associate; project director and urban design). The team was composed of Vera Tângari (landscape architecture) and architects Simone Neiva, Mario Ferrer, Lilian Nóbrega, and Luiz Claudio Franco.
9. The methodology was based primarily on Kevin Lynch's work (for example, Lynch 1981) and on del Rio 1990.
10. Although this idea received much support from the local vendors and the city officials in charge of controlling the use of public space, it was dropped in the final project because the mayor passed a resolution prohibiting peddlers in any area of the Rio Cidade project.
11. Project by Índio da Costa Arquitetura: Luiz Eduardo Índio da Costa (partner in charge, architecture), Fernando Chacel (landscape architecture), Luiz Augusto Índio da Costa (graphic and product design).
12. Public involvement has been changing significantly in recent years because the new city master plan and related legislation require community participation during all phases of a specific plan or urban project, through permanent and temporary commissions, community organizations, working groups, public hearings, and so on.

CHAPTER 11

Reshaping the Metropolitan Territory
Contemporary Urban Interventions in São Paulo

Carlos Leite

São Paulo, Brazil's largest and economically most important urban area, is a city of incredible contradictions. Although the Greater São Paulo metropolitan area produces more than 25 percent of the country's gross national product, little has been done to regenerate deteriorated urban spaces. With this in mind, this chapter seeks to answer a set of broad questions: Can a metropolitan territory in a process of accelerated transformation be influenced by local actions? Can urban design, without creating scenic simulacra, rescue immense degraded historic areas? Can large urban projects rearticulate a fragmented urban territory of such a large scale? Can the rehabilitation of the illegal but omnipresent city be planned and managed? Finally, how can urbanism confront wastelands—*terrain vagues*—without becoming an instrument of power and repression but rather one of change and territorial weaving?

After briefly analyzing the contemporary city's process of territorial transformation and the new possibilities for urban intervention and design, I discuss three recent complementary urban interventions. Urbanism becomes a new fundamental praxis in the rehabilitation of the central city, as demonstrated in piecemeal projects for the Luz district and Praça Júlio Prestes, as well as Praça do Patriarca in São Paulo's downtown. The possibilities of large-scale urban interventions are discussed through the program to upgrade favelas and rehabilitate the environment in the Guarapiranga reservoir area, and the plan for a public esplanade and multimodal transport center in Mauá, both on the periphery of Greater São Paulo.

São Paulo: Global City, Metropolis in Transition

There is a worsening conflict between local space—that which is shared by all of us in our daily lives—and global space, which represents a logic and an ideological content beyond us. For this very reason *the great contradictions of our time play out through the use of territory.* (Santos, Souza, and Silveira 2002: 15)

São Paulo is the paradigm of a local metropolis in a global world. It is simultaneously a world city linked to global networks and a local city with low-quality spaces that are ignored by local authorities. According to Sassen (1998), São Paulo is one of ten "world cities" integrated into the network of global cities. In truth, the city presents opposing, contradictory realities. On one hand, there are spaces defined by new financial capital and linked to new information technologies which in turn are tied to the global economy. On the other, so-called banal spaces in the fragmented territory reveal neglect and social pathology. We are dealing with a "glocal" metropolis, the repository of an urban area that faithfully portrays contemporary society, with all the contradictions of our time (Peixoto 1998).

We are living an era of accelerated transformations, and São Paulo manifests all urban contemporary mutations within its metropolitan territory. The territorial dynamics are dramatic and subject to rapid change, and the consequences of these rapid transformations in the postindustrial metropolis are varied and heterogeneous. In this context, urbanism and architecture suffer in all of their dimensions, and the fragmented metropolis lacks an urban consciousness. Deteriorating spaces characterized by vacant lots, urban dysfunctions, poor maintenance, and lack of safety emerge as residues of older productive areas. According to Nelson Peixoto (1998), São Paulo's architectural transformations are contained in the territorial environment and vice-versa.

At the scale of individual buildings, the transformation is in terms of their functions. Adaptations in the surrounding territory are demanded and generated by the local society. Outdated historic buildings are recycled and converted to serve new uses, as I shall discuss later in the case of the conversion of the old Júlio Prestes train station into an important concert hall.

In the realm of cities, at the present time existing spaces are being adapted and transformed in contrast to past eras when the changes resulted from the imposition of renovation processes (such as the tabula rasa approach of modernism) or from revitalization through historicist or pop projects (such as the postmodernism of the 1970s and 1980s). Contemporary urban dynamics generate a much more complex and rich situation for territorial change and adjustments.

Functions, uses, and spaces are being transformed in a dynamic and unprecedented way. Spaces once thought to be consecrated are being recycled. The long-term processes of large-scale development are being replaced by smaller projects with shorter completion times. Immense, historically shaped environments lose their traditional functions, historic centers are emptied, and industrial spaces suddenly become inadequate. Whole neighborhoods are subjected to speculative transformation. Leftover spaces are reconsidered and reenergized through property development. Luxury residential areas emerge in previously devalued land at the edges of the city, sitting within closed walls in high-quality islands amidst areas devoid of public facilities. Environmentally protected land is illicitly occupied and reurbanized as the illegal city imposes itself on the legal city. Urban legislation is obliged to catch up with the illegal reality and to face urban mutations (Rolnik 2000).

Amidst all this, global society is entering the twenty-first century with unparalleled concerns for sustainability, environmental preservation, and the recycling of existing resources. The United Nations Agenda 21 places new demands on the territorial realm, and environmental changes—on the scales of both the territory and the building—have to occur within a framework for sustainable development.[2] Like any other resource, the built environment cannot go without recycling and transformations: it is wiser to transform existing and underutilized spaces than to ignore and replace them.

Today, São Paulo reflects such conditions in its more than 1,500 square kilometers (570 square miles). The city has been reconstructing itself for nearly five hundred years through a painful process of historical negation—a territorial palimpsest where the new was always built upon the already existing,[3] making the territory mutable and polynucleated. Now, however, the city is confronting the challenge of restoration.

Within this extremely complex situation, urbanism, urban design, and architecture are fundamental alternatives for the transformation of the territory as essential instruments for physical and spatial change. As Meyer (2001) observes, the challenge to contemporary architecture is to confront the existing city, beginning with its infrastructure, without negating it. Planning and design professionals have been developing this concept, both in academic circles and in the development of new urban projects.

Whereas many cities around the world promoted the large-scale redesign of downtown areas, São Paulo rejected this path until recently, when its leaders decided to improve and enhance its center. The delay isn't without its advantages: urban improvements in São Paulo can now address contemporary reality more coherently and avoid the errors of earlier efforts elsewhere.

Finally, the impossibility of completing a comprehensive urban redesign in a metropolis of such a scale as São Paulo now seems clear: its territory is immeasurable. Today, the greatest opportunity for governmental intervention is to use urban design to stitch together new territorial logics and to link disconnected public spaces and facilities. This process would make urban connections possible and link fragmented metropolitan territories by redeveloping empty spaces that articulate the territory and by carrying out urban restoration.

Incomplete Urban Design: Renovating and Strengthening the City Center

In São Paulo's continuous reconstruction of its territory, the city center has been mutable. The Old Center is the sixteenth-century Portuguese nucleus, morphologically structured by European design, where a handful of colonial buildings mix with eclectic architecture of French neoclassical derivation (fig. 11.1). From the 1940s, Brazilian modernism started to dominate in the central area, generating new spaces, emptying the old, and producing the New Center. Occupied by a new elite—the emerging industrial bourgeoisie that was culturally "enlightened" in opposition to the old and archaic elite—the New Center started to become the object of new urban and architectural references.

Modern Brazilian urbanism and architecture would pursue an ideal New Center, and important emerging modern architects had a chance to participate in constructing this innovative piece of the city. They experimented with an urban architecture where the city's ground level was dedicated to public use (buildings on *pilotis*, sometimes over retail, service, or recreational spaces), in search of a pluralistic and democratic ideal. Today, these buildings in the New Center are models of this type of urban quality; good architecture that evokes a clear idea of what a city should be like: the Copan building (Oscar Niemeyer, 1951) and the Metrópole building (Cândia and Gasperini, 1960) are examples of such architectural masterpieces inserted in a frank dialogue with the urban fabric, close to the streets and generating good pedestrian spaces.

The 1970s marked a shifting of centrality in São Paulo. This was a time when the New Center was functionally emptied and began its decline and deterioration, a process that the Old Center had already experienced. Away from both the Old and New Centers, Avenida Paulista and its environs became the new financial and business center. In the absence of plans to rehabilitate the central area, it was emptied of people and jobs, its physical infrastructure deteriorated and, beginning in the 1990s, it was taken over by the informal economy (street vendors and illegal activities), which appropriated public spaces in an uncontrolled and disorganized way.

Figure 11.1. Praça da Sé and the cathedral, one of the most important places in São Paulo's traditional center. (Photo by Nelson Kon, www.nelsonkon.com.br)

Planning and urban design were timid, ineffective, or altogether nonexistent during this period, and the city government ignored the importance of public space. Innumerable architecture and urban design competitions addressing downtown spaces were held, but very few projects were actually carried out. Among the exceptions, the first great attempt to rehabilitate the city center merits attention: the project for the Vale do Anhangabaú which forged an important connection between the Old and New Centers.

Winner of a national competition in 1981 and built in 1988, this project included an immense cap (fifteen acres in size and 1,650 feet wide) over a highway that bisects the city center.[4] On this platform, an enormous area dedicated for pedestrian use, public events, and leisure was landscaped with a design based on geometric motifs (fig. 11.2). In spite of its interesting design and the large open space that it created in the heart of the downtown, the project was criticized for not having correctly interpreted the historic and geographic dimensions of the place: instead of resolving the differences of height in the valley in a subtle way that would resuscitate the link between the upper and lower cities, the platform simply made the valley disappear (Bucci 2004).

By itself, this project was not enough to halt the abandonment of the central area, which continued until the mid-1990s when the nongovernmental organization Associação Viva o Centro (AVC; Association Hail to the Center) was formed with strong support from BankBoston, whose headquarters are in the Old Center.[5] By means of workshops, events, studies, and projects, AVC was able to generate intense public debate on the immediate necessity to revitalize the city center. This effort led the city government to launch Operação Urbana Centro (Operation Urban Center) in 1997, when specific zoning changes were made to encourage redevelopment in the area, including more flexible land uses and indices and fiscal incentives to attract new activities and private investment. Unfortunately, the new legislation was not enough to attract capital and revitalize the area.

It was not until the late 1990s that the federal, state, and municipal governments directed their attention and investment policies toward recovering São Paulo's central area. In spite of the absence of a much-needed general action plan for rehabilitation, over a twenty-year period several programs and projects to revitalize the central city have been implemented. These include efforts in areas such as culture, public trans-

Figure 11.2. Projeto Vale do Anhangabaú, São Paulo. A landscaped concrete slab spans the valley above the highway, connecting the two centers of downtown. (Courtesy of Rosa Kliass)

portation, and renovation of public spaces, including renovation of the Pinacoteca do Estado (São Paulo State Art Museum) by the state and federal governments (US$9 million, 1998); conversion of the historic São Paulo Tramways Light and Power Company building into a shopping center by private developers (US$23.7 million, 1999); renovation of the Sé Cathedral by private donors and the Catholic Church (US$7 million, 2002); renovation of the Central Market by the city (US$6.8 million; 2004); and the renovation and expansion of Estação da Luz, the central train station, with federal, state, and private funds (US$10.3 million; 2006). There were other concurrent projects such as the Corredor Cultural, the creation of the Júlio Prestes cultural complex, and the renovation of Praça do Patriarca; these last two interventions will be discussed next as part of ongoing programs: the Monumenta project for the rehabilitation of the Luz district (funded by the Ministry of Culture and the city), and the Ação Centro (city-funded).

Regenerating Downtown

The redevelopment and revitalization of São Paulo's center is occurring through two major programs: the federal Monumenta (Monument) and the city-funded Ação Centro (Central Action). These programs reflect Brazil's changing understanding of how to address aging central areas in terms of intensifying their uses, attracting different groups of users, and increasing property values.

Monumenta is a program run by the Ministry of Culture to rehabilitate historic areas in Brazilian cities with financial support from the Inter-American Development Bank (IDB) and technical assistance from UNESCO.[6] It is the first program that provides funding for sustainable historic preservation and rehabilitation on a nationwide basis, amassing more than US$200 million for the implementation of its first stage. In São Paulo, Monumenta has concentrated on the area around Estação da Luz, the city's most important train station. Built in the early nineteenth century by the English company São Paulo Railway with materials imported from Glasgow, Scotland, the station is an important cultural and architectural landmark. In addition to restoring various historic buildings in the Luz district, Monumenta is working to make the area more pedestrian friendly and to control visual pollution from inappropriate private advertising. The program coordinators quickly realized, however, that the projects they envisioned were too extensive for the available funding from the IDB, and they managed to attain collaboration from the state—which owns most of the buildings in the area—and the city government, as well as to enter into various partnerships with private institutions.

Since the 1990s, several public and private historic buildings in the Luz district have been restored, including the Museu de Arte Sacra (Sacred Art Museum) and São Cristóvão Church. The former Liceu de Artes e Ofício (Arts and Crafts School) from 1896 was converted into the Pinoteca do Estado (State Art Museum) in an award-winning project by Paulo Mendes da Rocha.[7] The historic Parque da Luz (Luz Park), São Paulo's first public park, built in 1798 when Brazil was still a colony, was restored. The Luz Station building is currently under renovation with private funding, and part of it will house the Museu da Língua Portuguesa (Museum of the Portuguese Language), also designed by Paulo Mendes da Rocha.

Paralleling Monumenta and encompassing a much larger area, AVC developed the São Paulo Centro project at the end of the 1990s, to promote "the dynamism of collective life as a means of recovering urbanity, that is, balanced convivial relations between the population and its surroundings" (Meyer and Izzo 1999: 143). The project adheres to three guiding principles: to articulate a network of public, to promote pedestrian linkages between public areas and facilities, and to create pedestrian-only areas in greater harmony with the daily functioning of the city. Toward this end, urban design assumes the role of reorganizing public spaces while restoring the architectural heritage. AVC is also aware of the importance for viable contemporary urban revitalization of partnerships among entities at different levels of government, nongovernmental organizations, and the private sector. The partnership involved the São Paulo state government, the telephone company, Nossa Caixa Bank, and BankBoston, with the support of the federal Ministry of Culture.

The Monumenta program collaborated with AVC on the Pólo Luz Cultural, a project to rehabilitate the area around the Luz Station. This project established two important and complementary lines of action to improve multimodal transportation and to make the area more pedestrian-friendly.[8] First, more than five kilometers (three miles) of the railway embankments are to be enhanced with wide, tree-lined public walkways connecting the Luz Station to the Memorial da América Latina (Latin American Memorial, a cultural and events complex).[9] Second, the project refrains from investing in road projects, concentrating instead on upgrading the pedestrian realm, since the area is served by a good and integrated public transportation network (subway, trains, and buses).

The different stages of technical and financial preparation for the Ação Centro program have spanned two different municipal administrations. The program was expanded beyond the Luz district, initially targeted by the Monumenta program, to encompass the whole city center—both new and old.

EMURB, the municipal planning agency, is administering US$168 million for this program: US$100 million from an IDB loan and US$68 million in municipal matching funds. Several projects costing a total of US$100 million are being timed to coincide with the city's celebration of its 450th anniversary. Resources have been allocated proportionally (60 percent from the IDB, 40 percent from the São Paulo city government); 26 percent of the resources are directed toward urban infrastructure, 25 percent to housing, 23 percent to urban projects, 23 percent to public transportation and roadways, and 3 percent to illumination and security.

Besides the renovation of Praça do Patriarca (Patriarch Square), concluded in 2005, the main projects under way in the area are the Corredor Cultural (Cultural Corridor, modeled on the project of the same name in Rio; see chapter 5); the rehabilitation of Ramos de Azevedo, Dom José Gaspar, and Xavier de Toledo streets; revitalization of the Mercado Municipal (municipal market); refurbishment and expansion of the Biblioteca Mário de Andrade (municipal library); conversion of the Palácio das Indústrias (the former city hall) into a municipal museum; and renovation of Praça da Sé in the city center where the cathedral is located (see fig. 11.1), Praça da República, Praça Roosevelt, and Parque Dom Pedro II (a large urban park). According to coordinator Nádia Somekh, this is "the greatest program ever financed by the IDB, so important it has become a world standard" (in an interview published in *Revista Arquitetura & Urbanismo* 44, 2004).

Projeto Pólo Luz Cultural was envisioned as a conglomeration of numerous projects that would serve as a catalyst for redevelopment of the Luz district (fig. 11.3). Unfortunately, the project was not fully implemented, and the only component completed was the award-winning conversion of the historic Estação Ferroviária Sorocabana (Sorocabana Train Station) and the renovation of the small Praça Júlio Prestes (Julio Prestes Square) to serve as an entry to the building.[10]

Built in 1938, the Sorocabana Train Station is a good example of Paulista eclecticism. In 1999 the state government funded an impressive project for renovating and adapting the building to house the São Paulo State Symphony Orchestra. It now contains the Sala São Paulo, a splendid concert hall which seats 1,500 people (the largest of its kind in Latin America), a smaller hall for chamber music, a recording studio, practice rooms, restaurants, and a parking structure for six hundred vehicles (fig. 11.4). The acoustics of the concert hall are outstanding, especially considering that the railway line and a train station continue to operate immediately next to it.

In spite of the success of this architectural conversion, the question remains whether an opportunity was lost to implement a wider urban design project that might have regenerated the area as a whole, as had been originally proposed. Located in one of downtown's most decayed areas, famous for its prostitution and drug trafficking, the project stands out as a splendid exception to its degraded surroundings. A chance was lost to revitalize the area, integrate this important new cultural center with its context, and reconnect the train station with the surrounding public spaces.

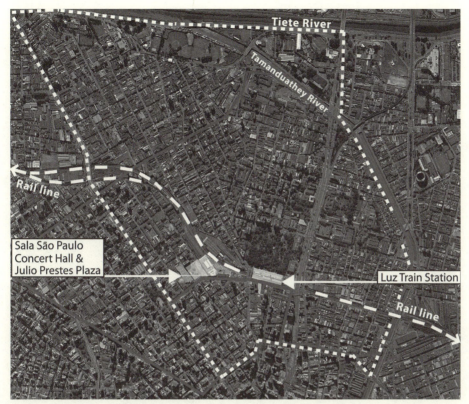

Figure 11.3. Map of the intended interventions in the Projeto Luz Cultural. (Illustration by the author)

Intervention in the Praça Patriarca

I now turn to an important urban design intervention focused on integrating two older urban areas with historic value. The Praça Patriarca (Square of the Patriarch) was built in the early 1900s as a symbolic place on the border between the New and Old Centers of São Paulo. The space connects the different elevations of the central area and, below the square, the old Galeria Prestes Maia provides an underground pedestrian walkway to the previously mentioned Vale do Anhangabaú project (see fig. 11.2). Over the years the area had become degraded with many bus terminals and badly maintained public spaces. In 1992 the city government decided to revitalize the square, redeeming its image and its strategic function as a downtown landmark.

Through a careful design, a minimalist approach, and precise tectonics, the project by Paulo Mendes da Rocha has restored the place, making it meaningful to the public realm once again. A large, white steel canopy over the plaza creates a new urban environment and forms a new gateway between the New and Old Centers. Spanning 39

Figure 11.4. Area da Luz, São Paulo, with the Estação Ferroviária Sorocabana converted into a music hall and the renovated Praça Júlio Prestes in the foreground. (Photo by Nelson Kon, www.nelsonkon.com.br)

meters (128 feet) and composed of 138 tons of steel, the canopy shelters the entrance to the Galeria Prestes Maia and highlights the sculpture of José Bonifácio, the patriarch of Brazilian independence for whom the plaza is named (fig. 11.5). The project also utilized pictorial documentation to reconstitute the beautiful historic paving, an arabesque mosaic made of colored "Portuguese stones."[11] The subterranean pedestrian passage was restored and revitalized with a new branch of the São Paulo Art Museum (MASP) that stages small exhibits and houses a café and gift shop.

In a city so little accustomed to planned urban interventions, any project generates debate. In this case, polemics came from several stakeholders: professionals, the general public, and the media. They argued that the new canopy obscured the cityscape, was oversized for the place, and obstructed the views of the sixteenth-century church of Santo Antônio, a historic site. Yet the design of the great metallic piece and its placement in such a complex site were carefully considered by the architect. The foundations were placed outside the limits of the underground passageway and its surrounding maze of water, light, gas, and telephone cables and pipes. The canopy is supported by only two pillars to avoid obstructing the vista or interfering with the underground infrastructure.

An "urban living room" emerged under this metallic wing. Giving a sense of shelter rare in this big metropolis, it added a new dimension to the territory and framed the cityscape with modern determination. It offers a place to meet and relax, and its minimalist design respects the place and its history. The canopy also reveals the articulation between the upper and lower centers and acts as an elegant landmark that marks the stairs to the subterranean walkway-museum. It is a remarkable example of contemporary urban design.

Upgrading Squatter Settlements

Every notion we may have about planning and architecture evaporates here. What do you do about cities with over 10 million inhabitants? You cannot do them justice with "normal" planning or "normal" architecture, and that would suggest that the slower speeds of a traditional urban plan would work here. In Brazil, action is chronically overtaken by events. No time for consideration, no time for reflection. That's a European luxury, but here every city organization is powerless against urban growth and sprawl. All that can be done is to try to keep things under control. Urban planning becomes a matter of policing rather than of political or cultural discipline. (Bosch 1999: 111)

In industrializing countries, the dynamism and gigantism of cities are taking ever more complex forms. The urban population of Brazil jumped sharply from 26 percent

Figure 11.5. The renovated Praça do Patriarca and the minimalist design of its steel canopy marks the underground pedestrian passage to Projeto Vale do Anhangabaú and generates a new place downtown. (Photo by Nelson Kon, www.nelsonkon.com.br)

in the 1940s to 80 percent in 1990—an increase of eighty-five million urban inhabitants. Imagine such a growth rate in tandem with the government's incapacity to invest in public housing and improve urban standards of living. In São Paulo, the picture is cruel: 40 percent of the population—four million people—lives in favelas, slums, pirate subdivisions, and other types of substandard housing, where people survive illegally and marginally, without the minimum appropriate urban infrastructure and public facilities (França and Bayeux 2002).

Clandestine cities spring up in spaces that are normally not conducive to urbanization; many environmentally protected areas become occupied: hills, floodplains, the watersheds of reservoirs, forests, and rural land on the urban outskirts. When a metropolis is unprepared to receive so much growth and so many migrants, truly illegal—but very real—cities appear and occupy different layers of the metropolis. Problems are of such a scale that it is no longer possible to discuss ideals—only possibilities. Despite all the planning from government agencies, the city expands on its own, and it is not possible to manage it on such a large scale. Planning happens after the fact, in an attempt to regulate an already imposed reality, and the government is constantly improvising solutions.

In this dramatic situation, São Paulo, like other Brazilian cities, sought alternative responses to the immense social problem represented by the demand for low-income housing. Programs for the urbanization of irregular settlements and the upgrading of favelas are attempts to provide these settlements with a minimum of livability through infrastructure and public facilities, and legalizing their status and better integrating them into the existing city.

In the first decade of the millennium, the city of São Paulo implemented Bairro Legal (*legal* has a double meaning: "legal" and "cool") a large-scale program to regulate land tenure and provide legal property deeds to families that had been living in favelas for more than five years (through adverse property rights as set forth in the Brazilian National Constitution; see the introduction to this book). Between 2005 and 2006 a total of 52,000 lots on public and private lands were regularized through the program. In parallel, the Programa de Urbanizacao e Regularizacao de Assentamentos (Program to Urbanize and Upgrade Settlements) outfits irregular subdivisions with appropriate infrastructure, improved housing, upgraded public spaces, recreational and green areas, and better accessibility to public facilities such as schools and health clinics. Between 2005 and 2006, 7,250 lots and 10,000 families benefited from the program.[12]

Another extremely important effort was Programa de Saneamento e Recuperacão Ambiental da Bacia do Guarapiranga (Program for the Sanitation and Environmental Rehabilitation of the Guarapiranga Watershed), jointly run by the city and the state sanitation and water authority to protect and slow the environmental degradation of the main water reservoir serving São Paulo. Even though Guarapiranga's watershed was technically under environmental protection, over the years it had been progressively and illegally occupied, first by illegal development and then by favelas containing a population of ninety-five thousand at the beginning of the program. Between 1991 and 1996 the population in the area grew at an average rate of 4.6 percent per year, while in the city as a whole the yearly rate was 0.4. This statistic demonstrated the need to keep settlements around the dam at high densities in order better to control them and to minimize environmental impacts by keeping the rest of the area free of development.

Using funds from the International Bank for Reconstruction and Development (IBRD), a branch of the World Bank, the program most importantly addressed the regularization of land tenure and the upgrading of more than one hundred favelas and illegal subdivisions around the reservoir—its major sources of pollution. This project concentrated on urban improvements, such as installing public facilities and infrastructure, but included the relocation of families from dangerous or unhealthy sites, and the recovery and preservation of environmentally sensitive areas (fig. 11.6).

The city government hired several design firms to develop these projects, mostly through public competitions. The work of Paulo Bastos & Architects can be cited as an excellent example, and their projects for the Jardim Floresta and Imbuias I favelas received the grand prize for urbanism at the 1999 International Architecture Biennial in São Paulo (fig. 11.7). The first favela occupies the slopes of a hill, while the second is at the bottom of a valley and subject to flooding. The design process started in 1997 and involved resident participation from its inception, "allowing them to participate in the formulation of their own public and family spaces, first by identifying the nature of the problems to be solved, then by discussing alternative solutions" (P. Bastos 2003: 213–21). This process allowed the community to participate not only in the

Figure 11.6. The Jardim Souza favela is on a hill that slopes down to Guarapiranga Reservoir. (Photo by João Urban, from França 2000: 108)

Figure 11.7. Paved streets, new infrastructure, and a new park on top of a piped creek, in the award-winning project for Jardim Imbuias I favela, an environmental upgrading program for Guarapiranga Reservoir. (Courtesy of Consorcio JNS HagaPlan)

upgrading of their own settlement—from analysis to implementation—but also in its management.

As in several of the projects for Guarapiranga, some families had to be relocated to new housing in other parts of the same favela, either because they had settled on hazardous areas or allow for much-needed street widening, recreational areas, and public facilities. The standard city services were provided: garbage collection; piped potable water, storm-water, and sewage systems; and public lighting.

Urban Rearticulation in Mauá

The dynamics of the São Paulo metropolitan region are reflected quite dramatically in the transformations suffered by the structural nodes along the rail lines. In the case of the city of Mauá, located in the southeastern part of Greater São Paulo, its structure is strongly determined by the evolution of industry and the old Santos-Jundiaí Railway, a rail line now shared by the Companhia Paulista de Trens Metropolitanos (CPTM), which runs the passenger trains, and a private firm which operates the freight lines under federal license.

As Mauá evolved, the historic nucleus around Praça 22 de Novembro (November 22 Square) near the train station was engulfed by high-density industrial, residential, and commercial development beginning in the 1950s. Originally structured around a cathedral, a train station, and a main square (*praça*), the nucleus of Mauá became an extremely complex urban node. A new terminal replaced some of the historic open space, and residual spaces were occupied by street vendors and informal commerce. The lack of spatial organization encouraged unpredictable pedestrian flows across the railroad tracks, exposing them to constant risk.

On the other side of the railroad tracks a new locus of public activities emerged, generated by the 1975 Plano de Renovação Urbana (Urban Renewal Plan) by architect João Vilanova Artigas—one of the initiators of the Paulista modernism. In addition to carefully studying the traffic flows and proposing the relocation of the railway that cuts through the city's historic center, Artigas proposed a new, modern city hall surrounded by a renovated cityscape and a public park, the design of which would be completed by the internationally famous landscape architect Roberto Burle Marx. Unfortunately, the plan was only partially built, leaving out important elements such as the pedestrian bridges over the railroad tracks and the plan for the park. The remaining buildings and public spaces suffered in an area devoid of spatial articulation.[13]

Today, this heavily utilized area, the nexus of historic Mauá, is totally disjointed. Drawing from the existing studies and seeking to rescue some of the components of

Figure 11.8. The plan for Mauá, Greater São Paulo, includes landscaped areas and new public buildings on a platform over the railroad tracks, reconnecting the historic nuclei and integrating different modes of public transportation (Illustration by the author, adapted by Vicente del Rio)

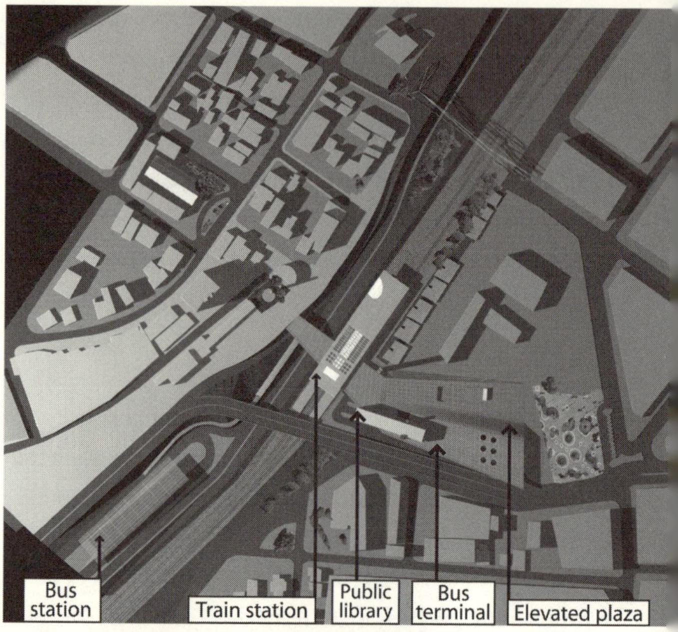

Figure 11.9. Digital model of the proposed platform and civic plaza in Mauá. (Illustration by the author, adapted by Vicente del Rio)

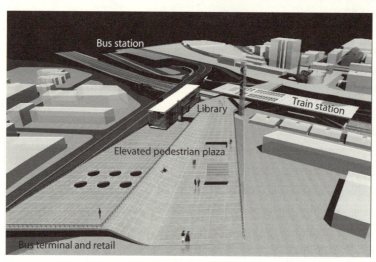

Artigas's 1975 plan, at the end of the 1990s the city government developed the first stage of another plan to renovate the area.[14] Then in 2002, architect Mario Biselli and I won a public competition and were hired to develop an urban design proposal to implement the plan's final phase.[15] We started by reviewing Artigas's original ideas, but realized implementing them would be a complicated process not only because of the project's scale, but also because of the need to negotiate with various public agencies, planners, environmentalists, local politicians, community representatives, and other stakeholders.

In May 2003, after developing four design alternatives, we presented a preliminary version of the final plan to the public in Praça 22 de Novembro. A giant projection screen showed the proposal, and renderings and models were exhibited to the public. The ensuing debate generated still more changes to the project, which evolved through a continuous process of public participation. The use of different presentation methods was of vital importance: although CAD programs can easily generate three-dimensional simulations and can be easily revised throughout the review process, the use of physical models was absolutely fundamental for discussing the project with the public.

The final urban design proposal will restore Mauá's historical nucleus and rearticulate its fragmented territory (figs. 11.8 and 11.9). Some of the project's goals are new and others date back to Artigas's original modernist ideas: (a) to generate an urban element that integrates fragmented spaces and connects the two urban nuclei on either side of the railroad tracks; (b) to integrate existing public transportation systems; (c) to preserve the existing open spaces; (d) to enhance public use of the center; (e) to generate a space with complementary uses; (f) to rehabilitate the public realm; and (g) to strengthen the city's historic centrality. The proposal will inject new life into the historical center with a series of complementary projects.[16]

The central urban nucleus will be reconnected through a pedestrian esplanade on a platform above the railroad tracks, linking the city's two main historic public spaces, Praça 22 de Novembro and Largo da Matriz (Cathedral Square). This new structural element will also integrate the three public transit stations for metropolitan trains, intercity buses, and city buses. On top of the platform, the esplanade features a new two-story-high city library with a café on the top story. Under the platform and directly connected to access streets and the station are shops and the headquarters of the Secretaria Municipal de Educação (City Education Secretariat).[17]

The plan also includes the completion of some components from Artigas's original plan: the Parque do Paço (a large city park next to the city hall) and an indoor sports complex. Our design for the park is based on a grid that structures the different uses and landscape typologies in a mosaic complemented by two long metallic canopies highlighting the main pedestrian walkways. The city started construction on this project in late 2004.

Conclusion

The projects discussed in this chapter reflect the immense contradictions in the enormous and complex metropolis that is São Paulo. On one hand, urban revitalization, architectural renovations, and urban structures of global magnitude act as metropolitan agents in the global network. The metropolis in transformation reflects this complexity. To provide new functionality to deteriorated spaces is the alternative now preferred over the modernist "blank-slate" approach. Community needs must direct urbanism, and its resulting projects and architecture must be based on the essential, not the superfluous. There is no room for experimentation or for postmodernization of historic façades, fake place-making, and irresponsible gentrification.

On the other hand, the city annexation of land invasions and the provision of facilities and urban services in favelas in environmentally sensitive areas are examples of the immense challenges that developing countries face in their overpopulated cities. Once the land invasion is irreversible or the favela is established, urban planning must operate within the limits of the possible: to create minimum conditions for urban life, to reconnect the territory at its edges and integrate its spaces to the surroundings, to transform the haphazard settlement into a neighborhood, and to help society integrate a marginalized population. A more equitable contemporary metropolis is possible through the provision of basic public facilities and services and the consequent improvement in the lives of *favelados*. They require integration into the legally constituted city territory and the granting of their universal right to full citizenship.

The fundamentals of appropriate urban interventions in São Paulo—and in Brazil—arise from a balanced understanding of a place's geography and its most pressing needs, even if they are global in nature, always in the context of promoting social justice. In this sense, projects for rehabilitation of consolidated historic areas (Luz and Patriarca), for integration of illicit settlements (Guarapiranga), and for territorial rearticulation (Ma"á) clearly illustrate these possibilities: fewer artificially derived uses and more functional essence in urban actions in post-Brasília Brazil.

Notes

1. I use the French expression *terrain vague* as conceptualized in a classic text by Ignasi de Solá-Morales (1995). On one hand, the word *terrain* means a piece of land larger than a simple tract, on the other *vague*, through its Latin origins, implies two complementary meanings. The first is a void, not occupied but available. The second meaning comes from *vagus*, or imprecise, without clear limits, uncertain, and vague. In the United States, the phenomenon of *terrain vagues* is more often described by the less precise terms *wastelands* or *brownfields* (Southworth 2001).

2. Agenda 21 is a United Nations program of environmental action that envisions the promotion, on a planetary scale, of new standards for development that reconcile environmental protection, social justice, and economic efficiency. Governments and institutions from 179 countries contributed to the plan over two years, culminating in the UN Conference on Environment and Development (UNCED, or Earth Summit) in Rio de Janeiro in 1992. In the

realm of built environments, the plan calls for sustainable urban planning (see "Agenda 21 Brasileira" at www.mma.gov.br/port/se/agen21/index.cfm; retrieved December 26, 2003).

3. *Palimpsest* is used by Benedito Lima de Toledo (1983) to characterize the urban evolution of São Paulo as a city that has been rebuilding itself one layer on top of another in the same space.

4. Project by Jorge Wilheim and Jamil Kfouri, with landscape architecture by Rosa Kliass.

5. The association's name plays on the many meanings of the word *viva* in Portuguese: to salute someone or something, to be alive, to experience a place, or to live in it.

6. The Monumenta program started by addressing four of Brazil's most important historical towns (Ouro Preto, Olinda, Salvador, and São Luiz) and areas in its three main ports of entry (Rio de Janeiro, Recife, and São Paulo). Today, twenty-six cities and their historical areas have been added to the program. See www.monumenta.gov.br/site (retrieved on March 6, 2008).

7. For this project, Paulo Mendes da Rocha, one of Brazil's most important architects, was awarded the Mies van der Rohe Prize in Latin American Architecture. He subsequently won the Pritzker Prize in 2006. On his work, see Andreoli and Forty (2004) and Spiro (2001).

8. Pólo Luz Cultural Project was designed by Regina Meyer and UNA Arquitetos (Meyer and Izzo 1999).

9. The Memorial de América Latina is a complex of cultural facilities, exhibition halls, and buildings for public events celebrating the integration of Latin America. It was designed by Oscar Niemeyer for São Paulo's state government in 1989.

10. Projects by Nelson Dupré (architecture and urban design) and Rosa Kliass (landscaping). Total project area: 58,134 square meters (627,847 square feet); restored area: 26,630 square meters (287,604 square feet); parking garage and public square: 31,504 square meters (340,243 square feet); total project cost: US$25.7 million.

11. Portuguese stones are small cubic cobblestones of white, dark, and red granite that are laid out in mosaic-like patterns. This popular method to pave sidewalks in Brazil is a tradition inherited from the Portuguese in colonial times and can also be found all over Portugal.

12. See http://portal.prefeitura.sp.gov.br/secretarias/habitacao (retrieved March 3, 2008).

13. The original Plano de Renovação Urbana is available on CD-ROM, published in 2001 by the library of the Faculdade de Arquitetura e Urbanismo, Universidade de São Paulo, and the Fundação Vilanova Artigas.

14. Developed by Mariluce Rossi and a team at the Municipal Public Works Department, City of Mauá.

15. Developed by GPA Arquitetura, São Paulo (architects Mario Biselli, Carlos Leite, Arthur Katchborian, Monica Brooke, and associates).

16. The complete project envisions a 68,137-square-foot sports complex, a million-square-foot municipal park (Parque do Paço), a 124,200-square-foot elevated pedestrian esplanade, and a 23,760-square-foot city library. Total estimated cost of the project is US$5 million.

17. The complete project is published in *Revista Arquitetura & Urbanismo* 124 (São Paulo: Pini, 2004).

CHAPTER 12

Upgrading Squatter Settlements into City Neighborhoods
The Favela-Bairro Program in Rio de Janeiro

Cristiane Rose Duarte
and Fernanda Magalhães

Favela-Bairro is a program for upgrading favelas (squatter settlements) and irregular subdivisions run by the city of Rio de Janeiro. It is considered innovative as a public policy for low-income populations, particularly for its recognition of the social, cultural, and political importance of favelas in the city. The irregular subdivisions included in the program were ones that had initially been approved by the municipality but could not be regularized due to the absence of the minimum required infrastructure. One of the principal characteristics of the program, launched in 1994 by the city government, is to consider these agglomerations as part of the urban structure and to seek their integration into the existing official city. Many experts on housing policies in Brazil have observed that the Favela-Bairro program and the projects developed under its umbrella have shown themselves to be relatively efficient in promoting community development and in the integration of those informal settlements into the formal city.

On one hand, Favela-Bairro has sought to improve the quality of urban space by means of infrastructure networks and public services like piped water, electricity and sewers, new streets, and community-use spaces such as playgrounds and recreation areas. On the other hand, the program promotes community development through educational and income-generating projects seeking the organization of local work cooperatives. Occasionally, the project includes construction of community buildings, such as day-care centers, and a limited number of residential buildings, in this case to relocate persons whose dwellings are in areas of risk such as on unstable hillsides or floodplains.

Special attention is given to architectural aspects and urban design, which is reflected in the multiple project solutions proposed by teams of architects and planners contracted by the city and chosen by competition to develop the projects for the different favelas targeted in the first phase of the program. In this article we shall discuss the Favela-Bairro program and its effects on its communities and the city as a whole, and we shall address the primary urban design aspects of some specific favela projects taken as examples.

Favelas and Previous Housing Policies

A favela, or land invasion, is an unauthorized group of self-built dwellings, often devoid of urban infrastructure and official streets, and basically occupied by low-income populations.[1] The *favelados*—residents of favelas—do not have legal property deeds to their homes. The name originated from Morro da Favela, a hill in downtown Rio de Janeiro where the first known land invasion was located.[2] The name spread throughout Brazil and is now used generically to designate any illegal occupation with an irregular urban pattern and a lack of public utilities.

Usually dwellings in favelas start as shacks and are improved by their residents over time, but most do not offer decent living conditions. Favelas are normally densely built up, and their population growth rates are higher than those of the formal city. They may be small, with only a handful of dwellings, but in large cities like Rio de Janeiro they may hold thousands of residents. According to census data, in 2000 the largest favelas in Rio were Maré (which is really a complex of six different favelas) with almost seventy thousand people, and Morro do Alemão with more than fifty-six thousand. However, city estimates are almost 20 percent higher than these census estimates. The favela is a complex urban phenomenon that for more than a century has "developed its own typologies of form and use, consolidating itself definitively in the framework of great Brazilian cities" (Duarte 2004: 303).

The majority of favela residents are among the lowest-income socioeconomic groups, and many live there simply because they do not have other options. Some choose life in a favela to be closer to work and to have urban comforts easily accessible. Others, even if they improve their income somewhat over time, prefer to remain in the favela for sentimental reasons and because of the social networks they have created there. On the other hand, there are those who reside in a favela because they profit from renting out a piece of their land; by building tenements and renting out rooms; or by leasing out illegal hookups to water and electricity networks or other illegal practices.

Favelas have been the object of various government plans since the first decades of the twentieth century, but these have always proposed unrealistic or inappropriate solutions for the reality of the *favelados*. Until recently, public policies generally repressed favelas and commonly promoted residents' eviction and relocation to new public housing projects at the city's edge.

In 1950 Rio de Janeiro had 2.5 million inhabitants, a high percentage of whom were migrants from either the interior of the state or other parts of Brazil. Census data for the decade of 1950–1960 show that while Rio's urban population grew by 38 percent, the highest rate of the century, the population in favelas doubled. A similar phenomenon was happening in other large cities such as São Paulo, Salvador, Belo Horizonte, and Recife.

But it was in the 1960s that government policies took a radical approach by viewing favelas as a malaise that should be removed from cities. Large programs and projects started eradicating favelas within the city and relocating the residents to large public housing complexes. Not uncommonly, such projects were designed for populations of more than five thousand people packed into small, low-quality apartments, which the families had to pay for through long-term mortgages. Most of this housing was on the urban periphery, more than twenty-five miles from the city center, and lacked efficient public transportation. Soon after the military took power in 1964, a national housing policy was established through a strong institutional and financial apparatus, the Banco Nacional da Habitação (National Housing Bank), and state and local regional housing agencies.[3]

During the 1970s and until the end of the military regime in 1985, favelas were regarded mostly as places of political resistance and their removal continued with the widespread collusion of the middle and upper classes. In the 1970s Rio's population passed the four million mark, of which almost 13 percent was living in 162 favelas (the total number of squatter settlements according to the city's official database). At the beginning of that decade, the city had spread the terror of forcible eviction among the poor, and 175,785 people had been forced out of their favelas and into new public projects on the city's periphery (IPLANRIO 1993). Many favelas were demolished, particularly those occupying attractive sites near the coastline and in middle-class neighborhoods, due to the potential value of that land on the property market.

Nevertheless, even at the peak of repression, a number of planners, architects, researchers, and intellectuals did not consider eviction as the best solution, defending instead the upgrading of favelas and a "respectful" urbanization. This movement consolidated in 1976 during the First International Habitat Conference in which Brazilian representatives participated.

In the 1980s, with the re-emergence of urban social movements combined with Brazil's return to democracy, the removal of favelas was no longer socially nor politically viable. The federal government began to implement alternatives programs such as site-and-services and core housing, all relying on mutual or self-help practices, following the World Bank's recommendations. In 1988 the new Brazilian National Constitution transferred many prerogatives for urban development and housing to municipal governments, including the development of housing policies. In this new context several cities recognized that *favelados* had a right to urban land and turned to programs to regularize property rights, legalize favelas, and provide more socially relevant public housing.[4]

Meanwhile, in 1982 in Rio de Janeiro a left-wing candidate won the first elections for state governor after the military era. The newly empowered government prioritized policies aimed at upgrading existing squatter settlements and illegal subdivisions in trying to integrate them into the formal city through programs that provided them with infrastructure and public services, such as garbage collection. In the 1980s, however, the city of Rio de Janeiro was suffering from the deepening national economic crisis and experienced a surge of street and drug-related crimes. Consequently, residents of the formal city continued to associate favelas with crime regarding them as "enclaves of criminality."

In Brazil and in Rio de Janeiro, politicians and institutions began to realize that the solution to illegal settlements could not be reduced simply to repression and the massive production of public housing. As Turner and Fichter (1972) and other committed professionals advocated, the housing problem was recognized as a social problem whose solution requires implementing more realistic policies that foster better housing conditions and access to public services and to the market. This philosophy was at the heart of the resolutions approved at the United Nations Second Conference on Human Settlements in Istanbul (Habitat II, 1996), and the United Nations together with the World Bank launched a global campaign titled "Cities without Slums." This new approach was incorporated into the policies and loan programs of the Inter-American Development Bank (IDB) and other international organizations (Brakarz, Greene, and Rojas 2002).

In the 1980s and 1990s, the poverty rate in Rio de Janeiro was higher than in 95 percent of Brazilian municipalities. According to census data, the total number of favelas in the city increased from 441 in 1980 to 661 in 1994, when the total number of squatters exceeded the one million mark. Part of this growth was due to the economic depression, but the 2000 census revealed that the situation continued to worsen even after economic recovery: almost half of Rio's population earned less than one minimum salary per month, and approximately 1.5 million people—25 percent of the total city population—lived in illegal settlements.[5]

In 1993 a new mayor was elected on a platform calling for "urban order"—a very attractive political platform to middle-class and upwardly mobile groups. Among other high-impact initiatives, the new mayor called for integrating favelas into the formal city so that their inhabitants could gain full citizenship and enjoy public services, and argued that opening up these settlements would eliminate the enclaves that facilitated drug trafficking.[6] City officials from different agencies that had accumulated years of experience in dealing with favela upgrading and services programs were gathered into the Secretaria Municipal de Habitação (SMH, Municipal Housing Secretariat), a new city secretariat especially created to deal with the housing issue.[7]

This new secretariat began to implement a series of policies, some set forth in the Plano Diretor Decenal da Cidade (Ten-Year City Master Plan) in 1990, prescribing new and flexible programs for the so-called areas of social interest, among which were favelas. In recognition of the long-term social and economic community investments that they represent to their residents, removal was no longer the goal, but rather their urbanization was. Among these programs, Favela-Bairro stands out. Its mission is to create the conditions for the favelas to become integrated with the official city and to overcome the stigma of physical, social, and cultural segregation that their inhabitants have been experiencing for years. According to the municipal decree that created Favela-Bairro, its objective was "to complement and construct the principal infrastructure and to offer environmental conditions for the perception of the favela as a neighborhood of the city" (Decree 14.332, November 7, 1995).

The technical and managerial competence of the staff in the new SMH contributed decisively to the successful implementation of the first phase of Favela-Bairro, which is a very complex program. The participation of international agencies such as the IDB was also fundamental. The IDB acted as a facilitating agent, sharing knowledge it had acquired from projects in other countries. The international partnerships enabled the project criteria and technical procedures to be established up front, thus avoiding political interference and philosophical differences during project implementation.

Planning and Urban Design

Fundamentally, Favela-Bairro's vision is that favela residents have "a right to the city" (S. Magalhães 2002: 67). The program aims to make squatter settlements part of the formal city and give them access to public services (water, sewer, garbage collection, electricity) and "an officially recognized address." On the other hand, these benefits would also place new obligations on the residents from the moment they receive their new property titles, such as payment of city property and utility taxes.

As part of their process toward official recognition as a city neighborhood, the favelas also would gain access to the services of professional architects and urban designers. According to the leaders of the program, those professionals would not only introduce "symbols of modernity," if these corresponded to the cultural aspirations of the inhabitants, but would also create conditions for the integration of these ghettos with officially consolidated neighborhoods around them.[8] For architect Demetre Anastassakis, then president of the Instituto dos Arquitetos do Brasil–RJ (IAB–RJ, Brazilian Institute of Architects–Rio de Janeiro) and of the national IAB for 2004–2006, urban design of favelas represented a tremendously exciting challenge to architects and urban planners because it represented an opportunity "to invent such designs, whether of architecture or of urban design, that integrate and that are beautiful, very beautiful, so that the favela might be accepted by everyone, and the *favelados* would be proud of it" but that "this new design will not be culturally exogenous modernism, socializing luxury, nor will it be a contextualized mimicry romanticizing poverty: it shall be a design that will emerge from day-to-day concerns and that represents modernity at the service of popular culture" (quoted in Duarte, Silva, and Brasileiro 1996: 14).

The first phase of the Favela-Bairro program had an unusual beginning in June 1994 with the launching of a competition for methodological proposals open to teams of architects and urban planners from Rio de Janeiro. Organized by the IAB–RJ, the competition attracted entries from thirty-four interdisciplinary teams involving some 150 professionals, which represented a very significant response rate given the still small number of offices dedicated to designing low-income housing in Rio de Janeiro. Fifteen teams were selected and contracted by the municipal government to implement their proposed methodology in one favela each, as an experimental pilot project. Favela-Bairro anticipated that the pilot methodologies would be improved in the next phase of the project (later designated Favela-Bairro II), when the program would be expanded to a greater number of favelas. The teams were required to demonstrate that their methodologies would be capable of satisfying the enormous diversity and sociocultural and spatial complexity of the different favelas targeted by the program.

The convocation of architectural firms to propose methodologies for favela interventions was in itself an innovation because it meant the incorporation of the "informal city" as a "real client" of the firms, not merely as an object of interventions by the state. Furthermore, this process went beyond the proposed specifications of the project areas, promoting "a deepening of reflection about the urban Carioca phenomenon" (Duarte, Silva, and Brasileiro 1996: 181).

While the upgrading of the physical infrastructure was Favela-Bairro's main goal, the program also responded to the community's basic social needs through projects such as health clinics, day-care centers, schools, and clinics for vulnerable groups (drug addicts and the like). Complementary social projects such as job creation, community awareness, programs for the elderly and youth, cultural projects, and hygiene and environmental education were also provided.

The pilot projects in phase one were developed by the winning teams under the coordination of the SMH, which was also responsible for reviewing the projects to ensure feasibility and compliance with the program's general criteria and objectives. The projects were to include new access roads, upgrading of pedestrian walkways, public infrastructure (sewage, water, storm drainage, electricity), garbage collection, public spaces and recreational facilities, environmental rehabilitation and landscaping, and income-generation programs.

On the other hand, in respecting the personal investments the residents had made in building their own homes, the projects avoided disturbing the existing houses, which were only removed when located on dangerous sites (subject to flooding, mudslides, or other hazards) or if absolutely necessary (for road construction, for instance). The program limited the percentage of the population that could be moved from their houses in any project to 5 percent of that community, and they were to be relocated to new homes within the same favela.

The social projects were developed in tandem with the urban improvements and were financed by the city government and implemented by the city social services agency under SMH coordination. In response to community demands, the second phase of the program included more widespread social actions—such as activities to develop young leaders, to increase school retention and provide tutoring, and to build small community libraries—and social welfare and family support were increased. As the first phase was considered experimental, procedures were adjusted as problems arose, and a more fixed methodology was employed in the second phase.

The city project managers (staff from the SMH in charge of supervising the project teams) were also charged with creating bridges among designers, the major city service providers, and the community. Often, however, groups representing favela communities would contact the design firms directly, and the managers became more like monitors assuring timely project execution. Various public meetings and direct contact with favela residents associations encouraged community participation, and the final projects had to be approved by the communities to ensure the legitimacy of the intervention.

According to the architects who worked on phase one, the relationship with the communities was very productive, and in the great majority of cases the proposed improvements were largely well accepted.[9] During project execution, however, there was not enough open communication between community members and project teams. In some favelas where there were gangs linked to drug trafficking, SMH staff attempted to communicate with them as well as the residents associations, to convince them that the urban interventions did not represent police actions but strictly physical improvements to the neighborhood. Sometimes the local criminal gangs would infiltrate their agents into community meetings when the projects were presented. In the great majority of cases, however, there were no major problems with implementation, primarily because the community members had demonstrated great acceptance of the urban improvements that were intended.

Some design teams reported conflicts between different municipal agencies that were not used to working together.[10] Frequently, the SMH ran into project components that required the cooperation or approval of other secretariats such as Social Development, Environment, Sports and Recreation, Urban Planning, Education, or Health. For example, the architectural plans for a new day-care center in a favela would have to be submitted simultaneously to the secretariats of Education and of Health, who did not always share the same views as the staff in the secretariats of Housing and Urban Planning. Nevertheless, the architects reported that none of these conflicts compared to the difficulty of coordinating between state and municipal agencies, principally because at the time their directors were affiliated with different political parties. Not unusually, the infrastructure and sanitation projects, for example, faced difficulties in getting approval from the responsible concessionary, the state water and sewage company (CEDAE).

Another important initiative in the Favela-Bairro program was POUSO—Portuguese for a place to land or crash in—which stood for Posto de Orientação Urbanística e Social (Station for Urban and Social Orientation). A POUSO in each favela ensured governmental presence on-site through an office staffed by architects, engineers, and social workers. This staff ensured that any new construction by residents was not placed in public or high-risk areas and that it aligned with the streets, while also preventing new invasions and expansion of the favelas during the projects. The POUSOs proved to be efficient in participating effectively in the urban improvements and curbing the proliferation of improvised new construction by residents energized by the upgrading of their communities.

By 2002, Favela-Bairro I and II had encompassed 45 percent of the city's population living in favelas, a total of around 500,000 inhabitants in 149 communities, of which 82 had average populations between 500 and 2,500 inhabitants (SMH 2003). By 2002, the first phases of Favela-Bairro totaled more than US$600 million in public investments (Brakarz, Greene, and Rojas 2002: 102).

In both phases the total budgets as well as the average and maximum expenditures per housing unit were fixed by the operating rules agreed upon between the city government and the IDB. In 1995 for Favela-Bairro I these rules stated that the cost of investments per domicile should not exceed (a) a US$4,000 maximum and an US$3,500 average per family for any favela; (b) in the case of illegal subdivisions, the maximum would be US$3,500 and the average US$2,000 per family. In 2000, during Favela-Bairro II, these values were adjusted to a maximum of US$4,500 and an average of US$3,800 per family in a favela, and a maximum of US$3,500 and an average of US$2,600 per family in a subdivision. In 2006, with Favela-Bairro II still under way, the city estimated the total cost of this second phase at US$300 million, which is financed by a new IDB loan of US$180 million and city matching funds of US$120 million (Brakarz, Greene, and Rojas 2002).

In light of the history of low-income housing and urbanization projects in Brazil, Favela-Bairro represents an incredible step in the right direction, particularly with regard to its methodologies and its recognition of residents' property rights. In this sense several aspects of the program were innovative, influencing other programs in Brazil and overseas and recently being considered a model for "neighborhood upgrading" by the IDB (Brakarz, Greene, and Rojas 2002: 98). Following Favela-Bairro's success, the city government independently initiated similar programs such as Bairrinho (Little Neighborhood), targeting twenty-nine small illegal settlements of one hundred to five hundred houses, and Grandes Favelas, targeting larger favelas.

From Favelas to Neighborhoods: Comments on Four Projects

In this section we briefly discuss four projects from Favela-Bairro I. It is important to note that each project was unique because of the very different and challenging sociocultural, economic, physical, and environmental situation of each community. Therefore, it is not possible to consider any one project as representative of the whole because each one demanded different processes and solutions. Our intention is solely to illustrate the complexity and the depth of the process and the appropriateness of the projects.

Following, we will discuss the projects for the favelas of Vidigal, Parque Royal, Ladeira dos Funcionários, and Mata Machado, all in different city districts. The projects were all developed in 1995, and construction started at the beginning of 1996 and was finished by 1997.

Favela Vidigal

Located in the Vidigal district, this favela enjoys an extremely beautiful site surrounded by forests and with breathtaking views of the Atlantic Ocean, São Conrado Beach, and Pedra da Gávea Mountain (fig. 12.1). The street that accesses the favela

Figure 12.1. Favela Vidigal, Rio de Janeiro, with São Conrado beach and Pedra da Gávea mountain in the background. Some of the Favela-Bairro upgrades are visible in the photo, such as the sports facilities. (Courtesy of Jorge Mário Jauregui)

starts off Avenida Niemeyer, a panoramic road that meanders between the mountains and the sea, linking the elegant districts of Leblon (to the east) and São Conrado (to the west). At the time of the project, Vidigal had 9,900 inhabitants (around 2,600 families) in an area of around fifty-eight acres.

According to project director and architect Jorge Mário Jauregui, the design concept was born from "reading the place's structure, that was the key, the point of departure for project development."[11] Given the site's rugged topography, there were not many alternatives for new roads, so the goal was rather to streamline the flow of pedestrians and vehicles through the existing thoroughfares. The favela's main street was renovated and received a lot of design attention to make it function as the "backbone of the community." Along this one-mile promenade accommodating the site's topography, a series of community facilities and parks were distributed to support community events and generate social encounters. Marking the beginning of this

Figure 12.2. The new gateway plaza at the corner of Avenida Niemeyer leading to Favela Vidigal, Rio de Janeiro. (Courtesy of Jorge Mário Jauregui)

promenade and the access to the favela from Avenida Niemeyer, a new gateway park was built on a corner site, with a striking portico in vivid colors enclosing a small amphitheater, as an invitation for passersby to visit the community (fig. 12.2).

Starting from the gateway park, the project provided along the promenade a building for the theater group Nós do Morro (We from the Favela), two community parks, two day-care centers, a community center with computer rooms, and a scenic overlook on the highest, most panoramic spot. The project also included a communal space for washing clothes, a symbolic representation of an almost extinct tradition of conviviality in favelas dating from the time when the women gathered at a river or spring to do their daily washing. At the end of the promenade, the topography permitted the construction of a sports complex named the Olympic Village: a soccer field, an indoor multi-sport court, and other facilities (fig. 12.3).

As deforestation caused by squatters clearing the hillsides was a major concern, the project proposed a retaining wall to establish a physical limit to the settlement. Community environmental awareness was enhanced by educational programs, by an ecological park, by designating areas for reforestation—such as steep slopes—and by hiring people from the favela to conduct the planting.

Since Favela Vidigal is close to large hotels and important tourist and beach attractions, and because of its spatial configuration and beautiful setting, the original project proposed incorporating tourist activities as a means to attract visitors, increasing income-generation activities and social integration with the city. A cable car to the overlook was proposed, which would also have increased accessibility for residents on the upper slopes. However, this was a controversial proposal much criticized by the outside public, who denounced its high costs and feared it would act as an incentive for more growth in the favela. When the new city mayor took office, the cable car proposal was shelved.

Due to the challenging topography and the high density of the Vidigal favela, the project displaced 220 families from their original homes—a large number in comparison to other projects in Favela-Bairro I.[12] New housing units were provided for these families, but most chose a cash payout and just moved out of the community.[13] Nevertheless, the installation of the much-needed infrastructure—sewage, piped water, and electricity—was well received by the community which was also supportive of the new parks, sports facilities, and day-care centers.

The total project cost—including design and construction—was around US$6 million at the time (1996), and residents report that their quality of life did in fact improve. On the other hand, although community members report intense use of the public spaces and that the new facilities have indeed improved their quality of life, the desired social integration with the surrounding official city has yet to happen. On the other hand, improvements also generated some degree of gentrification, as they added value to many of the buildings. Some of the older residents—primarily

Figure 12.3. The Olympic Village at the top of the hill at Favela Vidigal: before (*above*) and after (*left*) construction. (Courtesy of Jorge Mário Jauregui)

renters—eventually left the favela in search of cheaper housing elsewhere and were replaced by newcomers.

Ladeira dos Funcionários

Ladeira dos Funcionários (Steep Street of the Public Servants) is a favela located on 6.8 acres in the industrial district of Caju next to the port area and close to Guanabara Bay. In 2006 there were 3,274 residents in 927 housing units. Caju was originally settled in the eighteenth and nineteenth centuries as a vacation and spa area, but in the early twentieth century it underwent a total transformation through successive landfills to accommodate industrial and port activities, two major cemeteries, a military arsenal, and a public hospital. Residential use is practically restricted to the favela, which was started in the 1940s by hospital workers who squatted on the hillsides. The area is bounded by major freeways—Avenida Brasil, Linha Vermelha, and the loops to access the Rio-Niterói Bridge—which isolate it from the rest of the city grid.

Like in other Favela-Bairro projects, the design for Ladeira dos Funcionários sought to improve its fragile linkages to its surroundings and to the formal city. In an interview with the authors, architect Pablo Benetti—principal at Fábrica Arquitetura, the firm hired for this project—said that the design solution was based on a new ring road around the community that would act as the backbone of a network of new public spaces with parks, soccer fields, and other public facilities. Starting at Rua Carlos Seidl, the most important street leading into the Caju district, a new two-way loop road for limited vehicular traffic was built around the favela (fig. 12.4). The road was pushed to the property line of the neighboring military arsenal, making room for sixty-six new housing units for the families displaced by the project (fig. 12.5). The road also facilitated the construction of new infrastructure networks and allowed more efficient garbage collection by reducing the average collecting distance from 500 meters (1,650 feet) to 30 meters (99 feet).

Improving local accessibility and providing a network of public facilities around it, the ring road became a magnet for social interaction rather than just a thoroughfare. Not unlike in Favela Vidigal, this concept mirrors the culture of favelas, where public spaces are appropriated for collective and social activities as extensions of the home space, making them a binding element for community life and for integration with the surrounding city.

The project respected residents' social habits by rehabilitating spaces that were already being used by the community and redesigning them for public use. The new square Praça Clemente Ferreira, for example, was built where the populace used to gather under a group of existing trees and in front of a bar. The soccer field was re-

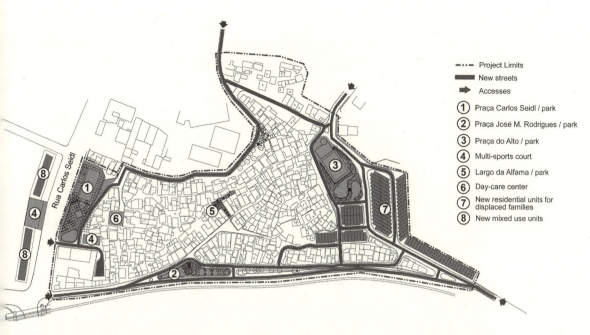

Figure 12.4. Site plan of the Favela-Bairro project for Ladeira dos Funcionários, Rio de Janeiro. (Courtesy of Pablo Cesar Benetti/Fábrica Arquitetura, adapted by Vicente del Rio)

Figure 12.5. Aerial view of housing units, sports ground, and park built as part of the Favela-Bairro project at Ladeira dos Funcionários, Rio de Janeiro. (Photo by Fábio Costa Silva)

built in its former location, and another square was located where many community members met to chat and play cards. At the southern end of Rua Carlos Seidl, the Praça Ladeira dos Funcionários serves as the gateway to the favela, with a 185-square-meter (2,000-square-foot) multipurpose sports field and a 370-square-meter (4,000-square-foot) community center in an old converted shed that used to belong to the nearby military arsenal.

Social and recreational facilities were geared to different age groups, and a distinctive architecture design was used to reinforce the neighborhood's new identity. Form, color, and landscaping were used to impart character to the new buildings and public spaces, although the architects chose to use inexpensive and easily maintained finishing materials so that the architectural imagery would not be too foreign to the community. Among the new public facilities, two day-care centers were built and presently serve two hundred children.

Several participatory workshops ensured that design decisions reflected community expectations, and the final project was well accepted. In 2006, almost ten years after completion, we can say that the project had positive effects and significantly improved the residents' quality of life. Also, the new facilities serve not only the favela residents but also the workers and the small population of the industrial district around it, thus promoting social integration.

Parque Royal

The Parque Royal (Royal Park) favela is on Ilha do Governador (Governor's Island), the largest island in Guanabara Bay where the international airport, an air force base, and a cluster of related facilities are located, along with several middle- and lower-middle-class residential neighborhoods. The favela occupies around 17.8 acres bordered on the north by the bay, on the east and west by two canals, and on the south by Avenue Canárias-Tubiacanga, an important thoroughfare to the north shore of Ilha do Governador. The grounds of the international airport are beyond the canal on the west side. Because the favela is in a floodplain, the first *favelados* built their shacks on stilts and over time infilled the space beneath their homes with dirt, rocks, and other materials. When the project started in 1995, the community had 4,146 residents.

The Favela-Bairro project for Parque Royal was awarded to Archi 5 Arquitetos Associados, who concentrated on improving the settlement's existing physical structure. Although this was a compact favela with well-defined edges, it had a discontinuous fabric and many of the existing roads did not interconnect. There was ample open space, including two generously sized soccer fields that were eventually incorporated into the final design (figs. 12.6 and 12.7).

Similarly to the previous projects, the design for Parque Royal aimed at establish-

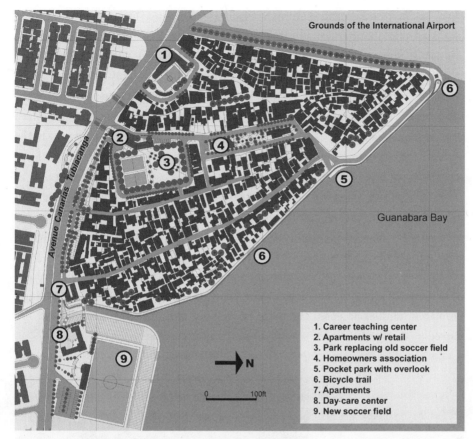

Grounds of the International Airport

Guanabara Bay

Avenue Canárias Tubiacanga

1. Career teaching center
2. Apartments w/ retail
3. Park replacing old soccer field
4. Homeowners association
5. Pocket park with overlook
6. Bicycle trail
7. Apartments
8. Day-care center
9. New soccer field

N

0   100ft

Figure 12.6. Site plan for the Favela-Bairro project in Parque Royal, Rio de Janeiro. (Courtesy of Pedro da Luz Moreira/Archi 5 Arquitetos, adapted by Vicente del Rio)

ing linkages between the settlement and the surrounding neighborhood via a new street along the shore starting at Avenida Canárias-Tubiacanga. This street would play an important role in the community by connecting with the entire internal roadway system, integrating the settlement to the waterfront, and creating a strong social and physical reference. Its design prioritized pedestrians and provided a bike path, tree plantings, landscaping with local species, a specially designed viewpoint, and a series of small public spaces with appropriate street furniture—such as benches and tables—where the community could socialize and enjoy the views to the bay and the distant mountains. Additionally, the street functions as a physical impediment to the construction of new squatter shacks on stilts and the further growth of the favela.

The connections between Parque Royal's road network and the surrounding urban fabric were improved by eliminating dead-end streets and widening some thoroughfares, which facilitated services such as garbage collection and access by delivery trucks, and contributed to a proper integration to the city context. Since its extension to the favela's southern edge, Avenida Canárias-Tubiacanga may now be used as an alternate route to other parts of Ilha do Governador, making the community more accessible, eliminating its "dead-end" image, and providing it with a new face.

The two largest existing open areas were turned into community parks with soccer fields and other sports and recreational facilities. A day-care center and one of the new soccer fields were located in a 56,000–square-foot site on the favela's western edge next to Avenida Canárias-Tubiacanga and along the canal perpendicular to the bayfront. They became part of a larger city plan for a bayfront park with recreational and sports facilities around the Ilha do Governador.

Social facilities were located along the edges of the community to encourage joint use with the surrounding population. This is the case, for instance, with buildings for a day-care center for one hundred children (4,400 square feet) and the Center for Continuing Education (4,500 square feet). Thirty-six new housing units were built for residents displaced by the project, including eight apartments above retail spaces on the edge of the favela for income generation and integration to the surroundings. Displaced families accepted the changes willingly, and only very few sold out and moved to another favela.

Figure 12.7. Aerial views of Parque Royal (*top*) before, and (*bottom*) after Favela-Bairro project. Existing community open spaces were respected and used to structure the design. (Courtesy of Pedro da Luz Moreira/Archi 5 Arquitetos)

Figure 12.8. View of Mata Machado favela, half-hidden in the mountains and forests of Rio de Janeiro. (Photo by Cristiane R. Duarte)

According to Archi 5 Arquitetos Associados, their design concept for Parque Royal sought to reduce the physical discontinuities between the community and the surrounding city in order to integrate the two. It was also important to create a clear distinction between the public and private realms, in order that the public space become regarded as the collective patrimony of the community. These were fundamental concepts for keeping public spaces free from further invasions and improper use. The quality of the design solutions together with the location of the new community, retail, and residential units along the edges of the favela represent an effort toward greater integration with the surrounding city. Now, years after implementation, the design concepts for Parque Royal proved to have met their objectives; they helped the community to acquire a new image and contributed to its economic and social development.

Mata Machado

The Mata Machado favela is located on twenty-five acres of mountainous terrain cut by rivers and springs in Floresta da Tijuca (fig. 12.8). Considered one of the world's largest urban forests, this park resulted from extensive government-sponsored reforestation of a big coffee plantation in the 1930s. Most of the favela's current 2,400 residents are descendents of the rural workers who migrated there for the reforestation project (Soares, Duarte, and Costa 1996).

The project for Mata Machado was designed in 1995 and construction began a year later.[14] Initial design research showed that although residents valued living close to the forest, they dumped waste directly into the rivers that cross the settlement (Duarte et al. 1995). Consequently, along with addressing fundamental concerns over the installation of basic infrastructure and waste collection services, the design strategy focused on strengthening the community's relationship with the embracing natural setting (forest and rivers), prioritizing environmental quality, open spaces for social interaction, and access to public amenities.

The designers believed that by implementing physical and visual connections to the rivers and forest—the major physical limitations on the design—the project would motivate residents towards conservation and provide them with a stronger sense of belonging to the land. Access to these natural elements became a design priority, and the widening of streets and alleys for vehicular access became an opportunity to generate new vistas for those passing through the favela. Pedestrian paths with pocket parks were proposed along the two riverbanks, which would help stabilize them and prevent further erosion, in addition to encouraging residents to invest in the quality of buildings along the banks.

The design for the small Magnolia Lake sought to reclaim its original function as a meeting place for residents, who in the past had used it as a swimming pool and for social gatherings, barbecues, and recreation. Over time these uses had been abandoned because of erosion, silt from land invasions upstream, and misuse by residents who used it as a waste dump. The favela's new piped water and sewage systems helped address the dumping problem, and the lake's environmental revitalization included cleaning up garbage and alluvial debris, replanting riparian vegetation, and starting a new community orchard upstream. The orchard displaced ten families from precarious houses with open sewers, unhygienic conditions, and free-range domestic animals, which were polluting the watershed and causing erosion and mudslides. These families were accommodated in new 450–square-foot housing units elsewhere in the favela.

A new community park in an existing and centrally located open space was proposed, and on the recommendation of the designers, the city purchased a site from an abandoned factory at the favela's edge for a new park to promote social integration between Mata Machado and the surrounding communities (fig. 12.9). The new park included landscaped areas, soccer and sports fields, kiosks for the sale of local crafts, and a community center.

Unfortunately, the US$1.8 million allocated by the city for this favela was insufficient, and the original proposal was never fully implemented—the river promenades, for instance, were left unfinished. There were unexpected cost increases when excavation for the sewage pipes revealed subterranean boulders that had to be removed by hand since the use of explosives was impossible, and a retaining wall had to be built along Estrada de Furnas, the major road that passes by the favela.

The poor coordination between state and municipal governments also hindered the proposed interventions, particularly in the case of the sewage system which, in

Figure 12.9. Park and community facilities proposed for Mata Machado. Located at a site next to the entrance to the favela from an important road, these facilities integrate the community with the surrounding neighborhood. (Rendering by Cristiane R. Duarte)

Rio de Janeiro, is operated by a state company. Even after the city installed the sewage pipes in Mata Machado, the raw sewage had to be dumped into the river downstream since there was no connection to the main system available at that point.[15]

Although the integration of the favela with adjacent neighborhoods is limited to social contacts among users of the new park at the former factory site, Brasileiro (2000) reported that the community, including the families relocated to the new units, readily accepted the changes introduced by the project. In spite of the increase in property values at Mata Machado, in 2006—ten years after completion of the public works—the majority of residents were still living in the favela and many had beautified their home exteriors, an indicator of their desire to remain. On the other hand, the project had collateral implications: new families started to squat in the surrounding forest—an area designated for environmental protection—in hopes of being included in similar projects and gaining access to urban improvements and property titles.

Conclusion

The success of Favela-Bairro can be assessed by first analyzing how much the quality of life really improved for the communities directly served by the projects, particularly with regard to infrastructure, accessibility, social facilities, housing conditions, and public services, and also in terms of new employment opportunities and revenue-generating activities. In his study of the Favela-Bairro program, Cardoso (2002) points out that whereas in 1991 only 59.9 percent of the residential units were supplied with potable water, in 2000 after project implementation this percentage had gone up to 90.2 percent. Sanitation also improved notably: adequacy of sanitary facilities in homes rose from 43.9 percent to 85.7 percent in the same period (Cardoso 2002). In Parque Royal, one of our case studies, 41.2 percent of homes did not have piped water in 1991, a rate that fell to 2.5 percent in 2000.

Brakarz, Greene, and Rojas (2002: 65) observed similar results in other favelas served by the program. In Morro da Formiga (Ant's Hill), the percentage of houses with piped water increased from 17 to 77 percent. In Três Pontes (Three Bridges) only 2 percent of homes were linked to the city sewage network and 3 percent had septic tanks in 1994; in contrast, 37 percent had been connected to the sewer system by 2000.

A city survey of resident satisfaction with Favela-Bairro reveals very positive results: 70 percent of respondents said that there was significant improvement in the water supply, sewer systems, recreation areas, garbage collection, road network, and public lighting (Brakarz, Greene, and Rojas 2002: 53). Sixty-four percent considered that the quality of community life had improved, and 47 percent believed that the relationship of their favela with the surrounding community had improved. The same survey indicated that the program had changed the population's attitude toward the city government, as 70 percent of respondents judged the government's actions as either average or good.

Brakarz, Greene, and Rojas (2002: 53) also report that the same survey revealed that residents in favelas served by the program generally perceived a general improvement in their quality of life; 36 percent of respondents considered that life was better than five years earlier, whereas only 28 percent responded that there had been no improvement whatsoever. Another survey by the Secretaria Municipal de Trabalho (Municipal Labor Secretariat) in eight favelas in the program counted four hundred small businesses that employed almost seven hundred persons, 45 percent of which were begun after the projects were completed (Brakarz, Greene, and Rojas 2000).

The surveys indicate that Favela-Bairro achieved one of its major goals: to correct the discontinuities in street grids, infrastructure, and public services by means of a qualitative improvement in the urban conditions of the favelas. The data also seem to indicate that the communities experienced significant improvements in sanitary conditions and in accessibility within the favela, to places of work outside, and to public facilities and urban services.

In settlements where the Favela-Bairro defined new Alignment Projects,[16] their rights-of-way were officially demarcated through a formal definition between public and private realms. This not only allowed homes to have official city addresses—an important step toward giving residents access to small loans and full citizenship—but was also important in forcing public agencies to assume their share of responsibility for maintaining the public spaces and providing the necessary services. Abramo (2002) reports on recent research showing that the majority of residents in communities affected by Favela-Bairro use their complete address when asked about their place of residence, whereas in other favelas, residents use only the name of their neighborhoods. A clear distinction between public and private realms also enabled the establishment of condominiums, the most feasible form of property ownership in favelas given the complicated and intertwined physical conditions of the dwelling units.

On the other hand, Favela-Bairro encountered several complications. First, the city still faces several legal constraints in order to resolve land conflicts and provide property titles to residents, in addition to the bureaucratic obstacles imposed by public notaries for property registration (*cartórios de registro de imóveis*), a long-established national and state system.[17] To date, the city government has not been able to confer property titles to the majority of residents in favelas affected by the program.

Second, although the increase in property values is an indicator that living conditions in the favelas have indeed improved the accompanying gentrification is not an entirely positive outcome. When evaluating Favela-Bairro, the IDB used increased market values as an indicator of added benefits, but these increases also favor a speculative property market that is particularly harmful for renters. In Parque Royal, one of our case studies, the market value of homes increased by more than 40 percent due to Favela-Bairro, according to an estimate by the president of the residents association (Pontes and Schmidt 2001). In Mata Machado, another case study, an average two-room house was priced around R$14,272 (US$4,921) before the project, and the market value rose to R$23,571 (nearly US$8,128) after the project (Abramo and Faria 1998). These researchers also reported that in favelas affected by the program the average market price for a house rose from R$12,280 (US$4,234) to R$20,045 (US$6,912), prices that are higher than those for houses of the same size in some of the lower-middle-class neighborhoods of the formal city.[18] Pontes and Schmidt (2001) also reported that rents for houses or apartments in favelas served by Favela-Bairro also increased significantly. At the time of their study the average rent in a favela not served by the program was around R$200 (US$69.00), whereas in Vidigal, one of our case studies, rents reached R$500 (US$173) per month (Pontes and Schmidt 2001).[19]

Not surprisingly, these studies show that gentrification is a perverse market mechanism inevitably caused by the improvements: the poorest residents are unable to afford the increase in rents and housing costs and move to a cheaper favela—one that lacks public facilities or is farther away from the better city neighborhoods and employment opportunities. The vacated properties are then occupied by somewhat better off families who migrate from less costly favelas or are pushed out of the formal city due to its rising costs. This is a cruel social logic that exists to a greater or lesser degree in all our case studies as well as in the majority of the communities served by Favela-Bairro.[20]

Critics of Favela-Bairro also point out that it was unable to control the growth of favelas. Indeed, since the program focused on correcting physical deficits without implementing any complementary citywide policies to meet the demand for new low-income housing projects or even to contain further land invasions, the projects tended to attract new residents to either the favored favelas or to land around them. Quite commonly, newcomers invaded environmentally sensitive or forested areas, as mentioned in the case of Mata Machado. The city should have promoted a set of parallel actions to impede the formation of new favelas and to regulate the growth of existing ones, as well as undertaking broader and longer-term policies to expand access to different low-income housing options. It is also worth emphasizing that by transferring all responsibility for house construction to the residents, the city abdicated its control over housing conditions and encouraged low construction standards and precarious living conditions, to which many low-income residents have to submit.

Clearly, a program such as Favela-Bairro alone will never fix the housing problem in a city such as Rio de Janeiro, far less in Brazil. Nevertheless, it was very successful in consolidating a new type of governmental policy toward the favela, one that considers it a legitimate housing and urban alternative. The program resulted in concrete social benefits that made it a national and international model for public policies in cities facing similar problems. Moreover, Favela-Bairro's methodology introduced into the Brazilian public arena several steps toward better low-income housing policies and actions.

First, Favela-Bairro established a new, effective process for low-income urban developments through having government officials manage the work done by private firms chosen through public competitions. On one hand, this enabled the city to undertake more projects simultaneously than its staff could have accomplished on their own, in addition to making the process more responsive and the results more flexible. On the other hand, the program introduced innovative design and implementation methods, creatively developed by different firms independent of the city bureaucracy. The designs deserve praise both for their effectiveness and for their creativity in endowing spaces considered to be of "low yield" with good-quality architectural and urban works, which previously had been reserved for the formal city.

Second, the government guidelines for Favela-Bairro embodied great social responsibility in their respect for community participation and for the existing environmental and cultural peculiarities of each site. Third, the program led the way toward a new culture of city management in which the actions of different public agencies and levels of government—federal, state, and municipal—are coordinated. The program overcame political changes in state and local administrations, removed blockages to inter-institutional relationships, and included different stakeholders—all of which were fundamental achievements for public policies and programs of this type.

Fourth, Favela-Bairro teaches us that in low-income communities in large cities, residents acquire a new perception of the value of the place where they live and of belonging to a community through participating in projects to improve their own favela. By participating in the reconstruction of their own built environment, they build social ties and strengthen local identity, important steps towards full citizenship (Soares, Duarte, and Costa 1996). Although Favela-Bairro did not entirely succeed in promoting the formal integration among the multiple physical and cultural spaces that make up the city, it did enhance the importance of these settlements (Soares, Duarte, and Costa 1996). We understand that the recognition of such a creative potential is fundamental to establishing action guidelines in informal neighborhoods.

Finally, by and large, the fundamental principles guiding Favela-Bairro were absolutely correct in recognizing the high social and economic investments that residents had already made in their favelas and their homes, as well as their right to participate in the official city. With Brazil's return to democracy and the expansion of citizenship and civil rights, the city could no longer turn its back on a process that became more of the rule than the exception in the construction of the city. Through Favela-Bairro, the residents of favelas achieved a new social status, moving a step away from the segregated city. These families now have access to infrastructure and public services, they have formal addresses, and they have to pay fees and taxes. By recognizing the favela's needs, the city feeds and strengthens notions of property, crystallizes a feeling of community power, and fosters citizenship.

Notes

1. For more on favelas, see the classic studies by Perlman (1976), Gay (1994), Pino (2007), and del Rio (2004). An incredible research resource is a recent study by Valladares and Medeiros (2003), who reviewed almost seven hundred publications on favelas, tracing their development as objects of policies, theory, and reflection.
2. Historians write that the majority of the first inhabitants of these shacks were probably veterans returning from the Canudos civil war (1896–1897) in Bahia, Northeast Brazil. The hill and resulting slum were named because the soldiers found there a beanlike plant (*fava*) very much like one found in the combat area (see Zylberberg 1992; Zaluar and Alvito 1998).

3. For a study of these policies and their consequences, see Perlman (1976).
4. See Kowarick (1994), Edesio Fernandes (2000), and Valladares and Medeiros (2003).
5. In the 1980s the minimum wage corresponded to US$100 per month. However, 12.3 percent of the city's inhabitants lived below the poverty line which corresponded to a monthly income of less than R$82 (approximately US$30). See *Relatório sobre o Desenvolvimento Humano no Brasil—1996*, a report by the Instituto de Pesquisas Economicas Aplicadas and the United Nations Program for Development, published in 1996.
6. Another of the high-impact initiatives of this government was the Rio Cidade program, discussed by Vicente del Rio in chapter 10.
7. The Secretaria Municipal de Habitação was made up mainly of technicians from the secretariats of Social Development, Urban Planning, Environment, Public Works, and Education, and from municipal sanitation, energy, and water utilities.
8. This aesthetic concern was much less important to the favela population than to the wealthy classes which, as opinion surveys demonstrate, are much more bothered by the "unfinished" appearance of favela buildings than by the housing conditions of favela dwellers per se.
9. Information provided by SMH staff in interviews with the authors.
10. Information provided in interviews conducted for this study.
11. Interview with Jorge Mário Jauregui by the authors. In recognition of his involvement with several Favela-Bairro projects, in 2000 Jauregui was awarded Harvard's Veronica Rudge Green Prize in Urban Design (see R. Machado 2003).
12. Data supplied to the authors during interviews with planners from the SMH.
13. The SMH was unable to give the current whereabouts of families who chose to be paid off.
14. Project by architects Duarte, Costa, Silva, and Soares.
15. These problems are discussed in more detail in Brasileiro (2000).
16. Projeto de Alinhamento (Alignment Project) is a legal instrument used in the city of Rio de Janeiro to define rights-of-way, road cross-sections, front setbacks, and sometimes even building heights along avenues and major streets.
17. For an analysis of the difficulties in legalizing favela properties see Edesio Fernandes (2000).
18. Abramo and Faria (1998) note that some residents chose to stay in the favelas even though the market value of their homes had risen to match that in the formal city because of the social networks that they had built over time and because in a favela they can expand their houses in order to accommodate a growing family or add a room for rent to provide an additional source of income.
19. The minimum wage at the time was R$260 (US$90) per month.
20. Based on interviews with city staff and technicians from the SMH. Because of the difficulty in obtaining property titles and the nonexistence of formal rental contracts, it is impossible to obtain precise data on the percentage of residential mobility in the favelas analyzed in this chapter.

Conclusion Lessons from Contemporary Brazilian Urbanism

William Siembieda

The time period for this book coincides with Brazil's evolving democratization process since the end of military government rule in 1985. It is also the period when globalization started to gain strength in terms of changes in transnational capital, adjustments in the use of labor, and the emergence of what have come to be called global cities. These forces create a very dynamic period for Brazil's cities that cannot be simply analyzed by any one theory or doctrine. To assist us in telling the story of contemporary urbanism in Brazil, we apply a spatial political economy approach. Such an approach recognizes that culture occurs in specific places and is constructed to reflect the dominant economic means of production, the impact of property capital, and the alignment of political power and influence at both the national and local levels (Cuthbert 2006). This approach allows us to inquire into the territorial logic(s) utilized in the different types of space being produced in the built environment.[1]

To understand the form of contemporary urbanism being practiced in Brazil, or for that matter in many other countries, we need to see it as a process embedded in an ever-changing set of spatial relations between property capital and civil society. We also need to understand the state's evolving role as an agent manipulating the social and economic equilibrium (be this maintaining or altering the status quo). In this instance we are trying to understand in what ways contemporary urbanism in Brazil reflects the broader analytical framework of postmodern urbanism per se.

Brazil is a modernizing country whose democracy is getting stronger every day, a process which is reflected in the way that contemporary urbanism shapes its cities. The 1988 Brazilian National Constitution accepts the continuous reformation of the city as the appropriate place to reflect and fulfill people's needs and desires. In addition, the municipal and national governments now recognize different kinds of city-building processes that allow for diversity and respond to different publics while accepting different cultural forms of expression. The Statute of the City (Federal Law 10.257), enacted in 2001, exemplifies one way the state has responded to these contemporary concerns. This statute, signed into law after ten years of national debate, is an attempt to legitimize a new, socially orientated urban-legal order at the level of the municipalities (Fernandes 2007).

Foremost among the many innovative aspects of this legislation is its conception of the social function of urban property. The statute alters the long-held 1916 Civil Code doctrine that recognized only the property rights of a single owner, instead recognizing the city as a higher order of collective social ownership. This means that the right to use urban property is ensured if it meets a social function as determined by local legislation. This leads us to ask, What is the territorial logic used in Brazil to create, plan, and regenerate cities? Does this territorial logic reflect the desired social contract between the state and society, or does it simply reflect property capital and globalization at work? What processes are at work in the urban realm to satisfy the needs of the individual and the market? These are among the questions explored by the contributors to this book. The purpose of this conclusion is to provide a more analytic view in terms of how Brazil's cities serve contemporary society and what lessons can be learned from this experience that can apply to other cities throughout the world.

The emerging territorial logic is best expressed by Lineu Castello who, in writing about the city of Porto Alegre, states that postmodern Brazilian city design seeks to promote places that "value the city memory, preserve its environment, and avoid uneconomical and unnecessary expansions to the urban fabric" (chapter 8). The territorial logic is to refocus growth within the existing urban fabric and to use "boosterism" to enhance the value of properties that have some historic value. This logic is also reflected in Carlos Leite's analysis of São Paulo (chapter 11). There are institutional mechanisms and democratic powers in motion that work to control the polarity between public and private uses of urban space, and this is one of the typical manifestations of postmodernism (Zukin 1988: 47).

In each of the book's sections ("Late Modernism," "Revitalization," and "Social Inclusion") the contributors relate various ways in which the public and private realms are being reformulated to address social and cultural requirements, and grant one of the fundamental rights of citizens: the right to the city and its modern comforts and opportunities. The public realm is being created through a process of power sharing and varied implementation actions among ever-changing sets of stakeholders, within an established national legal framework. In Smith's (2006: 384) terms, what is under way is a highly unpredictable and contested process of "place-making." There can be many different outcomes of the place-making process, a fact that in and of itself reflects the forces of postmodernism at work.

Spaces of Late Modernism

Modernism was the dominant doctrine used by urbanists, urban designers, and architects to address territorial expansion for more than a century (beginning with the design for the new city of Belo Horizonte in 1895). During the contemporary democratic period, however, it is the existing built environment (the in-place stock of buildings and spaces) that has received progressively more of the government's attention. The older urban centers were considered as in need of regeneration and also preservation, as urbanists and the national and state governments began to accept the city as a polycentric entity composed of diverse elements, each with different social requirements. Such a "decentered" city, to use the language of postmodern urbanism, could not be planned as a whole project, but only as pieces that reflect various aspects of the whole city, which is itself constantly changing.

Modernism's core appeal was its assertion that it could bring improvements to society through built form. This notion, while philosophically appealing, has not proved valid in practice. The shift away from modernist thinking is based on the empirical fact that Brazilian cities have grown faster than expected, and in some cities more than half of the houses are in places that are not contained within the master plans.[2] This is not surprising given the rise of non-plan-conforming (irregular) settlements throughout the world (Davis 2006). The sociocultural dynamics and territorial logics of urbanization were simply not well understood by urbanists or public policymakers, who tended to view the city as static rather than dynamic. But people occupy the "real city," not the "designed city." When the designed city cannot meet the people's needs, the real city emerges as a necessary condition of social order.

Modernism simply cannot cope with such a duality, and this explains much of the need to adopt other modes of territorial logic based on some type of polycentric system of spatial organization that has the capacity to address a social-spatial agenda that includes local as well as citywide needs. Modernism still has a role to play in the production of new spaces at the periphery of metropolitan areas or in new towns where rationalism can make a positive contribution to the design of transportation networks and infrastructure.

No longer do Brazilian urbanists view city building as a finite product based on a single rationale. In terms of urban design, they have moved from a "total urban design" approach to "all of a piece" or "plug in" approaches (Lang 2005). Mixed efforts based on market, cultural, social, and environmental dynamics are now the objects of government attention and private partnerships. Contemporary urbanism—and also high modernism (Dear 2000)—recognizes and embraces the existing built environment and uses this context as a link to the past and a portal to the future. Working with what is there and making improvements that draw new users to a street, square, railroad yard, dock area, or aging commercial street are elements of this emerging postmodern design protocol.

In the contemporary Brazilian experience, "projects" are used to regenerate space and to open more opportunities to create and re-create the urban realm (public or semipublic). This is most clearly demonstrated in the chapters on social inclusion, where a polycentric, unarticulated structure of the city is accepted, and each project generates the substance needed to enhance daily life within the local public realm. The territorial logic then pursues a spatially specific result that may or may not benefit other parts of the city. A project-based approach was also a key element in the Barcelona experience, where there also was a focus on reconstituting neighborhoods (Herzog 2006). Although projects are limited in scope, these interventions do represent partial efforts to respond to the broader role of the Brazilian city in promoting social justice. Nevertheless, the project-based approach does not mean the end of modernism as a philosophy. Modernism is not dead in Brazil; it continues to be utilized as part of a set of overreaching conceptual tools to produce a more just city and for the regeneration of the public realm.

The belief that government can use urbanism and the urban design process to respond to an existing territorial logic is the basis for the social inclusion projects discussed in São Paulo and Rio de Janeiro. In these cities, local government actions are required to link deteriorated public spaces in an effort to facilitate their reuse. The reconfiguration process, however, must take place in a contemporary context. In the case of São Paulo, the context is that of a global world city where the use of modernist design elements—such as the use of enormous canopies reconnecting the old downtowns in the capital and in the antiquated railroad suburb of Mauá—restores the public realm and brings new life to deteriorating areas. As tools for creating the contemporary urban realm, "projects" are preferred over more comprehensive approaches that require extensive intervention by the state.

The new towns of Brasília and Palmas demonstrate that modernism alone does not produce a better city; it simply yields a city with a distinct spatial structure based on formal principles. The original intent of building Brasília was to direct population growth toward the country's interior and promote economic development there. The rate of economic development and its spatial expression (sprawl and multi-nucleation at the city's edge), however, demonstrates that modernism lacks the flexibility needed to accommodate demand for urban space and the complexities of market-driven forces. Over time, the periphery drives urban form more than the center does. The strict concentrations of uses contemplated in the Pilot Plan have shown themselves to be too rigid to adapt to changing societal needs. Brasília would have benefited from having a regional plan as a complement to the Pilot Plan, in order to accommodate and channel growth. The La Defense zone in Paris and the Santa Fe zone in Mexico City are examples of areas designed to accommodate the global demands for new commercial property capital expansion outside of the historic core city.

If we ask why so many of São Paulo's residential buildings (and in fact those in any large city in the country) tend to take the same form—high tower blocks set back from the street and separated from it by gates and walls—an answer can be found in Silvio Macedo's chapter. It provides an example of how modernist regulation shapes the public realm and creates social segregation. Although their objective was to force residential developers to provide more open space in residential tower developments, the São Paulo zoning laws instead created islands of social segregation, resulting in fewer people using the streets, fewer public parks, less interaction in the public realm, and greater reliance on automobiles. Each tower building and condominium becomes its own self-contained world, with its own parks and amenities, separate from the rest of the city. The territorial logic that produces such self-contained spaces does not recognize the negative symbolism it creates: the symbolism that says, "Stay away, we do not want to share" and "We do not need the street or to be part of its public realm."

Another transitional trend in the postmodern process is the proliferation of the shopping center and its role in city development. The expansion of Brazilian shopping centers is a contemporary phenomenon, an imported concept that reorganizes space and replaces the traditional street shopping. These shopping centers emerge by taking pieces from European and American examples and making them Brazilian "projects." They impact the neighborhood, but at the same time are adaptive to changing social and consumer needs. In this sense the shopping centers are closer to meeting the public's need for local spaces, at least for those consumers who have time and money to spend on nonessential items.

The two shopping centers examined by Bruna and Vargas are magnets of social life in their zones and provide one means for regeneration of areas left behind by changing market forces. Bruna and Vargas explain that shopping centers can also serve to concentrate urban activities at the periphery and thus to create centralities in suburban areas. Hence, they have form-making properties and are not necessarily linked to any formal plan. They certainly restructure space for consumption. In built-up (mature) urban areas, the shopping center can be used to "requalify" those areas in need of economic improvement, at least in the limited sense of providing local people with access to goods. In both instances they serve as part of the public realm even though they are privatized spaces that can at times serve as transition spaces to the public street. Brazilian shopping centers are quite adaptive to local needs, changing and reforming themselves in terms of context and culture. Bruna and Vargas see them as potential instruments for organizing urban space and forming nodes of attraction because of the influence they exert on surrounding areas. Once places of consumption, Brazilian shopping centers are now consumed as places, fitting well within what Sklair (1991) calls the "culture-ideology of consumerism" of a global market. Given the abandonment of the street as depicted in Macedo's chapter on the vertical city, the shopping center gains currency as an urban policy tool and a significant influence on the territorial logic of a local area.

Places Revitalizing Cities

Regeneration of existing spaces is a theme of contemporary urbanism. This is exemplified in Rio de Janeiro's Cultural Corridor Project, where partnerships between the public and private sectors become the dominant tool of urban action. Here a coalition of building owners and community associations working with the project Technical Office join hands to craft appropriate solutions to complex urban issues of transit, deterioration, security, and public use of space. The territorial logic here is one of preservation, modernization, involvement, and evolution—solutions that are place-appropriate for local and nonlocal users. Context does count here. Globalization of space by transnational capital is not what stakeholders discuss as the key issue. This example of Brazil's contemporary urbanism supports the proposition that the city is in constant transformation and exists to serve a social purpose. Such a view is also post-Marxist, as both the social and economic functions of the city are recognized and validated. This experience, along with the chapters in the "Social Inclusion" section, demonstrates the movement toward participatory democracy as defined by Sklair (1991: 232) has some validity in Brazil.

Establishing a working territorial logic that promotes the creation and maintenance of the historic public realm is not a simple task. The city of Salvador in Bahia provides us with clear evidence of the contradictions in contemporary urban Brazil. Reversing the deterioration of this former colonial national capital city (founded in 1542) has been the subject of nearly forty years of federal, state, and municipal government efforts, beginning in the early 1970s with the establishment of the development-node and metropolitan-region policies supported by the military government. The most intense effects, spanning a period from 1992 through 2005, have been focused on the Pelourinho, an area in the old city.

The Salvador case demonstrates that there can be two or more different forms of territorial logic at work at the same time. In the 1970s the state government built new roads to urbanize the periphery and located new government headquarters in these outlying areas. Simply put, they subsidized and modernized the metropolitan area. This was an efficient modernist scheme that led to growth and economic development in the expanding suburban areas while encouraging private-sector disinvestment in the old city. The periphery became the focus of investment, and the colonial center continued to deteriorate due to lack of maintenance, becoming the place where the poorest and least desired people could find shelter and create their own sense of community. Such a process is not unique to Salvador; it is seen in many colonial Mexican cities and other urban areas of the world.

The Pelourinho renovation and regeneration is part of a series of economic development initiatives that link history and culture to entertainment and leisure as a tourist attraction strategy. As noted by Fernandes and Gomes, "place marketing" in Salvador is both an attempt to attract the people from the metropolitan area and sell the city to tourists as a means to nourish social cohesion in a city that is increasingly fragmented and segregated. The packaging of history (reflected in buildings and public spaces) and culture (Carnaval, music, street events, and local informality) are central to the Salvador strategy. This strategy, which at first sought to drive out the human element perceived as undesirable, yielded poor results until housing improvements were included to keep local people, who provided the area's cultural element, from taking their food, music, and folkways elsewhere. This revised strategy recognized that historic buildings alone are not enough to sustain urbanity and a sense of place, which relies on human dynamics and sociocultural factors to make important and continuous contributions. Had the government urbanists and urban designers read more of Lefebvre's (1971) theories on the production of social space they would have known not to take for granted that authentic culture could not be replaced by a designed and staged environment.

The Navegantes Commercial District outlet mall in Porto Alegre is a great example of postmodern urbanism. There, private developers believed in a vision which, supported by a legitimate industrial past, helped them to create a popular shopping destination. Urban design did not clone history but used the existing structures and their symbolic power to support economic development. The regeneration of the surroundings soon followed, with the city government taking a secondary role as a hands-off supporter, and then a partner in expansion of the area's public realm. The developers were, in the words of Harvey (1990), "reterritorialising" the space as a function of property capital investment.

In the northern coastal city of Belém, the re-creation of the public realm relied on the conversion of functioning historic buildings to match the cultural and social values of a contemporary population that accepts the use of semi-commoditized forms of space. The construction of a cultural landscape on the waterfront as opposed to a focus on a single monumental landmark has enabled the municipal government to meet social needs and create a postmodern type of semipublic realm. Both the Belém and Porto Alegre cases are in line with Hayden's (1995) notion of establishing a symbolic dialogue with the past as a condition for effective urban landscape design. Symbolism provides the cultural ties to a postmodern spatial solution.

The Social Role of Urban Space

The movement toward social inclusion means improving what exists and adding elements that support the productive uses of the public realm. A key aspect of contemporary urbanism in Brazil is the relationship between urban elements and favelas, or squatter settlements. After decades of first trying to remove and then just ignoring them, the Brazilian state has come a long way. By allowing favelas to become consolidated into the formal city the Brazilian government has recognized in practice the social right of occupation. Recognizing favelas as part of the formally built environment—not simply as illegal and haphazard settlements—creates the basis for a dialogue between residents and the city government that is "project specific" and socially and culturally appropriate. The *favelados* (favela residents), as Duarte and Magalhães state, have a "right to the city." And as we have mentioned elsewhere in this book, this is a superior form of human right (Lefebvre 1968).

The 1995 Favela-Bairro project is instructive in understanding the "social right of occupation" logic and also in recognizing the social and physical investments made by residents of these areas. The projects in Rio de Janeiro provide clear examples of postmodernism and spatial "reterritoriality" at work. Here the architects and planners worked directly with the residents and accepted the majority of the built space as a fixed context rather than trying to reconfigure it to modernist design rules. The object was to design into the existing spaces features of the formal city that directly benefit local users: street alignments that support transportation; access to potable water; better sanitation; and improved public spaces, public buildings, and community development programs. To accomplish this, the architects and the municipal agencies were challenged to adopt new methods of work, ways of "formalizing the city," and avenues for mutual learning among the participating parties. Not only are new public areas and services created that serve local needs, but also new channels are opened to expand the public realm in the favelados' daily life. In this way the city becomes more "democratic," by embracing participatory democracy in a particularly Brazilian form.

Such improvements also impact the land markets, however, and property and rental prices within the favelas do rise. As favelas replicate amenities of the "formal city," the cost of living there begins to find an overall submarket equilibrium. Some gentrification appears, as households with more income compete with those of lesser income for improved space in the favela. This competition for space reflects the value of the public improvements paid for by the government being expressed in market price adjustments. Since the government has no price control policy for favelas, such price increases are a natural result of local property market demand forces. In a social justice sense, projects such as Favela-Bairro tend to discriminate against the poorest sectors of the city, thus the need does exist to spread out such upgrading efforts as much as possible, in order to encompass a great number of favelas and dilute these market forces.

Curitiba is a city where urban plans have been in place for more than six decades (beginning in 1943). From this chapter we learn that it is not the plans alone, but rather how they are implemented, that counts the most. Originating in a master plan from the mid-1960s, the 1974 primary strategy was to build transportation axes to accommodate and guide the city's growth. Historic preservation and environmental protection strategies followed, all implemented by a publicly created single-purpose company, IPPUC. Since that time, acting as a design-build agency, IPPUC's dominant practice has been to devise a series of quickly implementable projects to support development and address social and environmental requirements. The recognition of the relationship between spatial and social issues and the ability to respond to them rapidly have greatly contributed to the success of Curitiba.

Irazábal (chapter 9) identifies three converging elements that explain Curitiba's success: the coalescing of dominant interests around a single project; the marketing of the city's image; and the providing of material advancement for the lower classes. To these we can add long-term stability of leadership and expansion of the public realm for use by the broader society. Irazábal's criticism of the planning system focuses on the types and degrees of citizen participation, the absence of metropolitan-level planning to match the local planning, and the issues of economic and environmental inequality between Curitiba and its surrounding municipalities. Balancing the economic and social benefits of urbanization between a center and its periphery is a dynamic process, not easily, if at all, controlled in a market-based or semi-directed economy. The reshaping of socioeconomic relations in geographic terms (Curitiba versus its periphery) is an expression of adjustments to capital requirements and the dominance of the IPPUC as an agent influencing regional spatial adjustment and economic equity.

Postmodernist urbanism is also represented in the Rio Cidade project in Rio de

Janeiro, which reflects the city government's recognition of the need to enhance the public realm as a strategic effort to rehabilitate Rio's international image. As in the famous Barcelona model, revitalizing the quality of the city's public spaces, strengthening community identity, and supporting the city's tourist industry were "boosterism" strategies recognized in Rio's strategic plan of the early 1990s. Despite the lack of good coordination with other important citywide and much-needed efforts, such as an integrated public transportation system and more effective law enforcement, the Rio Cidade program proved relatively successful in recuperating the public spatial realm in many city districts.

Final Comments

All territorial logics are influenced by economic dynamics, changing social relations between the individual and the state, and the overall forces inherent in the urbanization process (Cuthbert 2006). The social meaning contained in what we consider the built environment must be recognized before it can be addressed by an urbanistic action (plan, project, regulation, and so on). More than one territorial logic coexists in every city; thus, adjustments to issues of metropolitan balance and equity will require a balancing of logics based on the extent of inequality and public realm requirements. Implementing the Statute of the City process throughout the country will certainly support localized experiments in this direction. Such experiments have already been seen in Puerto Alegre, where needed efforts to construct low-cost subdivisions with public services have occurred.

The Brazilian contemporary urbanism model tells us that in order to balance the inherent inefficiencies in urban land markets, the remaking of the public realm and the "requalification" of urban places needs to be a continuous process. The logic of postmodernism as applied to existing space in the city requires more shared responsibility between the social sectors and the property capital sector. If citizens have a "right to the city," they also have a responsibility to the city.

Real property investments, mostly following global patterns, will promote projects of various scales that influence the organization of urban space to match its interests. Real property capital has created its own set of agents that promote the symbols of investment as well as a uniformity of finance, sales, and construction.

Countering these forces will require Brazilian urbanism to recognize that processes are more influential than projects. These processes and logics determine who gets what in material and symbolic terms. The challenge throughout the urban world is how to address peripheral growth together with the strengthening of the existing city in a nonintegrated way, and how to establish access to the material and symbolic values of the continually changing city and its environs. If there is an overreaching territorial logic for the Brazilian city, then this is it.

This book points to three major lessons of Brazilian contemporary urbanism, and they undoubtedly put Brazil at the forefront of contemporary urban thinking. First is the importance of regarding the city as a tool for social justice. In this regard, Brazilian contemporary urbanism is pursuing the city as a shared dream, a place that provides opportunities for personal, social, cultural, political, and economic development for all its citizens. Second, Brazil teaches us the importance of recognizing the value in having different territorial logics in the city, as long as they can strengthen the public realm and increase different forms of accessibility. In this case, the success of a place is not proportional solely to the quality of its design, but also to the pluralism of its urban solutions and its cultural and social responsiveness. Third, the expansion of participatory democracy, together with the recognition of different social and territorial logics, is leading Brazilian contemporary cities to more inclusionary planning and design processes. This path is directly related not only to the quality and accessibility of places, but also to the processes that produce, regulate, and maintain them. Most importantly, this path recognizes the city as *res publica*, or as the place for public life.

Notes

1. Territorial logic is a political economy framework that explains the allocation of urban space. It is influenced by what Michael Peter Smith (2006) calls the crisscross of political economic relations of power that link people to places and obliterate distinctions between the inside and outside and the global and local.

2. In 1916 only 10 percent of the population lived in urban areas, whereas in 2006 more than 86 percent are considered urban

Bibliography

Abbud, Benedito. 1986. *Vegetação e Projeto: Estudos de Caso em São Paulo com as Reflexões de um Arquiteto.* Master's thesis, Faculdade de Arquitetura e Urbanismo da Universidade de São Paulo.

Abers, Rebecca. 1998. Learning Democratic Practice: Distributing Government Resources through Popular Participation in Porto Alegre, Brazil. In *Cities for Citizens: Planning and the Rise of Civil Society in a Global Age,* edited by Mike Douglass and John Friedmann. New York: John Wiley and Sons.

———. 2000. *Inventing Local Democracy: Grassroots Politics in Brazil.* Boulder, Colo.: Lynne Rienner.

Abramo, Pedro, coord. 2002. *Estudo Detalhado em Doze Favelas do Município do Rio de Janeiro.* Relatório Técnico Final vol. 4. Rio de Janeiro: IPPUR/Universidade Federal do Rio de Janeiro, and IPP/Prefeitura da Cidade do Rio de Janeiro. Photocopy.

Abramo, Pedro, and T. C. Faria. 1998. Mobilidade Residencial na Cidade do Rio de Janeiro: Considerações sobre os Setores Formal e Informal do Mercado Imobiliário. In *Anais do XI Encontro Nacional de Estudos Populacionais da Associação Brasileira de Estudos Populacionais.* Rio de Janeiro: Associação Brasileira de Estudos Populacionais. Available online at www.abep.nepo.unicamp.br/docs/anais/pdf/1998/a139.pdf (retrieved on July 23, 2003).

Abreu, Maurício de. 1987. *Evolução Urbana do Rio de Janeiro.* Rio de Janeiro: IPLANRIO/Zahar.

Agier, Michel. 1991. Introduction to *Cadernos CRH. Cantos e Toques: Etnografias do Espaço Negro na Bahia.* Salvador: Centro de Recursos Humanos, Universidade Federal da Bahia.

Akamine, Rogério. 1998. Avenida Central Paulistana: Procedimentos de Desenho Urbano. Master's thesis, Faculdade de Arquitetura e Urbanismo da Universidade de São Paulo.

Almandoz, Arturo. 2002. Urbanization and Urbanism in Latin America: From Haussmann to CIAM. In *Planning Latin American Capital Cities, 1850–1950,* edited by A. Almandoz. London: Routledge.

Anastassakis, Demetre. 1996. Programa Favela-Bairro: Como Selecionar Profissionais e o que Fazer nas Favelas. In *Favela, Um Bairro,* edited by Cristiane Duarte, Osvaldo Silva, and Alice Brasileiro. Rio de Janeiro: Pro-Editores/Prefeitura da Cidade do Rio de Janeiro.

Andreoli, Elisabetta, and Adrian Forty, eds. 2004. *Brazil's Modern Architecture*. London: Phaidon.

Arantes, Otilia, Carlos Vainer, and Erminia Maricato. 2000. *A Cidade do Pensamento Unico—Desmanchando Consensos*. Rio de Janeiro: Editora Vozes.

Azevedo, Sergio. 1990. Housing Policy in Brazil: 1964–1986. Paper presented to the Housing Debates/Urban Challenges Conference. Paris.

Bacellar, Jeferson Afonso. 1979. *A Realidade e o Futuro do Pelourinho*. Salvador: Instituto de Patrimônio Artístico e Cultural, Governo do Estado da Bahia.

Bahia, Estado da. 1969. *Levantamento Sócio-Econômico do Pelourinho*. Salvador: Fundação Patrimônio Artístico e Cultural, Secretaria de Cultura.

———. 1970. *Plano Geral de Recuperação da Área do Pelourinho na Cidade do Salvador, Estado da Bahia, Brasil*. Salvador: Fundação Patrimônio Artístico e Cultural, Secretaria de Cultura.

Barnett, Jonathan. 1996. *The Fractured Metropolis: Improving the New City, Restoring the Old City, Reshaping the Region*. New York: HarperCollins.

Barthes, Roland. 1972. *Mythologies*. Selected and translated from the French by Annette Lavers. New York: Hill and Wang.

Bastos, Maria Alice Junqueira. 2003. *Pós-Brasília: Rumos da Arquitetura Brasileira*. São Paulo: Perspectiva.

Bastos, Paulo. 2003. Urbanização de Favelas. *Estudos Avançados* [Instituto de Estudos Avançados, Universidade de São Paulo] 47: 212–24.

Belém, Prefeitura Municipal de. 1993. Plano Diretor Urbano do Município de Belém—PDU. Lei Municipal nº 7.603. *Diário Oficial do Município de Belém*, January 13, 1993. Available online at www.belem.pa.gov.br/new/index.php?option=com_content&view=article&id=4115:plano-diretor-urbano-de-belem&catid=148:segep&Itemid=172 (retrieved on July 29, 2003).

———. 2000a. PRO-BELÉM: Plano de Reestruturação da Orla de Belém. Belém: Secretaria Municipal de Urbanismo. Photocopy.

———. 2000b. Projeto Ver o Rio. Belém: Secretaria Municipal de Urbanismo. Photocopy.

Berman, Marshall. 1988. *All That Is Solid Melts into Air: The Experience of Modernity*. New York: Penguin.

Bonduki, Nabil. 1998. *Origens da Habitação Social no Brasil*. São Paulo: Estação Liberdade.

Borges, Celina Lemos. 1995. The Modernization of Brazilian Urban Space as a Political Symbol of the Republic. *Journal of Decorative and Propaganda Arts* [Wolfsonian–Florida International University], Brazil Theme Issue, 21: 219–37.

Bosch, John, Juliette van der Meijden, Maurice Nio, Wim Nijenhuis, and Nathalie de Vries. 1999. *Eating Brazil*. Rotterdam: 010 Publishers.

Brakarz, Jose, with Margarita Greene and Eduardo Rojas. 2002. *Cities for All: Recent Experiences with Neighborhood Upgrading Programs*. Washington, D.C.: Inter-American Development Bank.

Brandão, Maria de Azevedo. 1981. O Último Dia da Criação: Mercado, Propriedade e Uso do Solo em Salvador. In *Habitação em Questão*, edited by L.P. Valladares. Rio de Janeiro: Zahar.

Brasileiro, Alice. 2000. Espaços de Uso Comunitátrio em Programas Habitacionais: Entre o

Discurso e a Prática. Master's thesis, Faculdade de Arquitetura e Urbanismo, Universidade Federal do Rio de Janeiro.

Bruand, Yves. 1981. *Arquitetura Contemporânea no Brasil*. São Paulo: Perspectiva.

Bruna, Gilda Collet. 1982. *Processos de Dimensionamento de Áreas Comerciais*. São Paulo: Pini.

Bruna, Gilda Collet, and Sheila Walbe Ornstein. 1990. Revitalização Comercial ou Renovação do Ambiente Construído? *Sinopses* [Faculdade de Arquitetura e Urbanismo, Universidade de São Paulo] 14: 34–42.

Bucci, Ângelo. 2004. Anhangabaú, o Chá e a Metrópole. Ph.D. diss., Faculdade de Arquitetura e Urbanismo, Universidade de São Paulo.

Buechler, Simone. 2006. São Paulo: Outsourcing and Downgrading of Labor in the Less-developed World. In *The Global Cities Reader*, edited by Neil Brenner and Roger Keil. New York: Routledge.

Caldeira, Teresa P. R. 2000. *City of Walls: Crime, Segregation, and Citizenship in São Paulo*. Berkeley: University of California Press.

Cañete, Voyner Ravena. 2003. Pesquisa de Oferta e Demanda Habitacional no Centro Histórico de Belém. Final research report. Belém: Prefeitura Municipal de Belém. CD-ROM.

Cardoso, Adauto L. 1997. Reforma Urbana e Planos Diretores: Avaliação da Experiencia Recente. *Cadernos do IPPUR* [Instituto de Pesquisa e Planejamento Urbano e Regional, Universidade Federal do Rio de Janeiro] 11 (1–2): 79–111.

———. 2002. O Programa Favela-Bairro: Uma Avaliação. In *Avaliação de Projetos IPT: Habitação e Meio Ambiente, Assentamentos Urbanos Precários* [seminar proceedings]. São Paulo: Páginas e Letras.

Carmona, Matthew, Timothy Heath, Taner Oc, and Steve Tiesdell. 2003. *Public Places, Urban Spaces: The Dimensions of Urban Design*. Oxford: Architectural Press.

Carr, Stephen, Mark Francis, Leanne G. Rivlin, and Andrew M. Stone. 1995. *Public Space*. 2nd ed. Cambridge, Mass.: Cambridge University Press.

Castello, Lineu. 2000a. Marketing, Consumption, and the Traditions of Place—Marketing Tradition: Post-Traditional Places and Meta-Urbanism. *Traditional Dwellings and Settlements—Working Paper Series* [University of California, Berkeley] 124: 1–21.

———. 2000b. Revitalização de Áreas Centrais e a Percepção dos Elementos da Memória. In *Hands across the Hemisphere*: *Proceedings of the 23rd International Congress of the Latin American Studies Association*. Miami, Fla.: Latin American Studies Association.

———. 2005. Place. In *Encyclopedia of the City*, edited by Roger W. Caves. London and New York: Routledge.

Cavalcanti, Lauro. 2003. *When Brazil Was Modern: Guide to Architecture, 1928–1960*. New York: Princeton Architectural Press.

CDP [Companhia das Docas do Pará]. 2004. Portos e Hidrovias Administrados pela CDP. Available online at www.cdp.com.br/portobelem.htm (retrieved on July 29, 2004).

Cervero, Robert. 1995. *Creating a Linear City with a Surface Metro: The Story of Curitiba, Brazil*. Berkeley: Institute of Urban and Regional Development, University of California Berkeley and National Transit Access Center.

Choay, Françoise. 1994. L'Empire de l'Urbain et la Mort de la Ville. In *La Ville* [exhibition catalog], edited by J. Dethier, T. Grillet and A. Guilleu. Paris: Centre Georges Pompidou.

CLAN/OTI. 1970. *Plano de Turismo do Recôncavo.* Salvador: Governo do Estado da Bahia.

Clemente, Isabel. 1997. Interior é Novo Paraíso dos Shoppings. *Jornal do Brasil* (Business and finance edition), January 23, p. 17.

CODEPLAN [Companhia de Desenvolvimento do Planalto Central]. 1991. *Pesquisa Domiciliar de Transporte.* Brasília: Companhia de Desenvolvimento do Planalto Central.

CDP (Companhia das Docas do Pará). 2004. Portos e Hidrovias administrados pela CDP. Available online at www.cdp.com.br/porto_belem.htm (retrieved on July 29, 2004).

Costa, Lucio. 1987. Brasília Revisitada. *Diário Oficial do Distrito Federal no. 194.* Brasília, DF.

———. 1995. *Lucio Costa: Registro de uma Vivência.* São Paulo: Empresa das Artes.

CTB [Companhia de Turismo de Belém]. 2003. Complexo do Ver-o-Peso. Available online at www.belem.pa.gov.br/belem/português/index.htm (retrieved on July 23, 2003).

Cuthbert, Alexander R. 2006. *The Form of Cities: Political Economy and Urban Design.* Malden, Mass.: Blackwell.

da Matta, Roberto. 1991. *Carnivals, Rogues and Heroes: An Interpretation of the Brazilian Dilemma.* Notre Dame: University of Notre Dame Press.

Davis, Mike. 2006. *Planet of Slums.* London: Verso.

Dear, Michael. 2000. *The Postmodern Urban Condition.* Oxford: Blackwell.

Deckker, Zilah. 2001. *Brazil Built: The Architecture of the Modern Movement in Brazil.* London: Spon Press.

del Rio, Vicente. 1990. *Introdução ao Desenho Urbano no Processo de Planejamento.* São Paulo: Pini.

———. 1992. Urban Design and City Images of Brazil: Rio de Janeiro and Curitiba. *Cities: The International Journal of Urban Policy and Planning* 9 (4): 270–79.

———. 1997. Restructuring Inner-City Areas in Rio de Janeiro: Urban Design for a Pluralistic Downtown. *Journal of Architectural and Planning Research* 14 (1): 20–34.

———. 2002. Making Livable Streets: Urban Design for a Commercial District in Rio de Janeiro—The Case of Projeto Rio Cidade Méier. Paper presented at the Making Livable Cities annual conference. Monterey, Calif.

———. 2004. Favela. In *The Encyclopedia of the City*, edited by R. Caves. London: Routledge.

del Rio, Vicente, Carlos Ferreira, José Kós and James Myamoto. 1987. Nascimento e Apogeu do Shopping Center. *Revista Módulo* 94: 34–47.

del Rio, Vicente, and Haroldo Gallo. 2000. The Legacy of Modern Urbanism in Brazil. *DOCOMOMO International Journal* 23: 23–27.

del Rio, Vicente, and Ana Cristina Santos. 1998. A Outra Urbanidade: A Construção da Cidade Pós-Moderna e o Caso da Barra da Tijuca. In *Arquitetura: Pesquisa & Projeto,* edited by Vicente del Rio. São Paulo: Pro-Editores.

Duarte, Cristiane Rose. 1997. Favelas. In *Encyclopedia of Vernacular Architecture of the World*, edited by Paul Oliver. Cambridge: Cambridge University Press.

———. 2004. *Favelas.* In *Enciclopédia de Guerras e Revoluções do Seculo XX*, edited by Fernando T. Silva et al. Rio de Janeiro: Elsevier.

Duarte, Cristiane Rose, Lucia Maria Costa, Francirose Soares, Osvaldo Silva and Luis Carlos Rolemberg. 1995. Diagnóstico de Mata Machado—Programa Favela-Bairro. Project report. Rio de Janeiro: IPLANRIO, Prefeitura da Cidade do Rio de Janeiro. Photocopy.

Duarte, Cristiane Rose, Osvaldo Silva, and Alice Brasileiro, eds. 1996. *Favela, um Bairro:*

Propostas Metodológicas para Intervenção Pública em Favelas do Rio de Janeiro. São Paulo: Pro-Editores and Grupo Habitat, Universidade Federal do Rio de Janeiro.

el-Dahdah, Farès. 2005. *Lucio Costa: Brasilia's Superquadra.* New York: Prestel; Cambridge, Mass.: Harvard Design School.

Ellin, Nan. 1999. *Postmodern Urbanism.* 2nd ed. New York: Princeton Architectural Press.

Espinoza, Rodolfo. Slum Dunk. Available online at www.brazzil.com/pages/cvrjun97.htm (retrieved on December 12, 2003).

Evenson, Norma. 1973. *Two Brazilian Capitals: Architecture and Urbanism in Rio de Janeiro and Brasilia.* New Haven: Yale University Press.

Faccenda, Marcelo Borges. 2003. Entre Davis e Golias. As ações (boas e más) dos museus na dinâmica urbana. *Arquitextos* 34 (3). Available online at www.vitruvius.com.br/arquitextos/arq034/ arq034_03.asp (retrieved on February 8, 2004).

Fava, Maria Luisa G. 2000. Espaços Comerciais: A Arquitetura em Dois Shopping Centers em Londrina. Master's thesis, Faculdade de Arquitetura e Urbanismo, Universidade de São Paulo.

Fernandes, Ana, and Marco Aurélio A. de Filgueiras Gomes. 1992. Centro Antigo de Salvador da Bahia—Invertendo o Tempo Perdido. *Boletim de la Real Sociedad Geográfica* [Madrid, Spain *127*: 217–36.

———. 1995a. O Passado tem Futuro? Os (Des)Caminhos da Requalificação do Pelourinho (Salvador/Ba). In *V Encontro Nacional da Associação Nacional de Pesquisa e Pós-Graduação em Planejamento Urbano e Regional.* Vol. 1. Belo Horizonte: ANPUR, Universidade Federal de Minas Gerais, and CEDEPLAR.

———. 1995b. Operação Pelourinho: O Que Há de Novo, Além das Cores? In *Estratégias de Intervenção em Áreas Históricas,* edited by Silvio Zanchetti, Geraldo Marinho, and Vera Millet. Recife: Universidade Federal de Pernambuco.

Fernandes, Edesio. 2000. The Legalization of *Favelas* in Brazil: Problems and Prospects. *Third World Planning Review* 22 (2): 167–87.

———. 2001. New Statute Aims to Make Brazilian Cities More Inclusive. In *Habitat Debate* [United Nations Centre for Human Settlements] 7 (4): 19.

———. 2007. Constructing the 'Right to the City' in Brazil. *Social Legal Studies* 16 (2): 201–19.

Fernandes, Edesio, and Marcio Valença, eds. 2001. Urban Brazil. *Geoforum* (special issue) 32 (4): 415–566.

Ferreira, Nadia Somekh. 1987. A (des)verticalização de São Paulo. Master's thesis, Faculdade de Arquitetura e Urbanismo da Universidade de São Paulo.

Firkowski, Olga. 1998. Curitiba e a Região Metropolitana. Paper presented to the Geography Department, Federal University of Paraná, Curitiba. Photocopy.

———. 1999. O Processo Recente de Localização Industrial na Area Metropolitana de Curitiba: Concentração ou Desconcentração. In *Dinâmica Econômica, Poder e Novas Territorialidades,* edited by Eliseu Sposito. Presidente Prudente, São Paulo: Universidade Estadual Paulista.

———. 2000. A Pertinência da Nova Lei Diante da Necessidade de um Plano Diretor Metropolitano. In *Cadernos de Gestão Pública* vol. 2. Curitiba: Fundação Pedroso Horta.

Frampton, Kenneth. 1992. *Modern Architecture: A Critical History.* 3rd ed. New York: Thames and Hudson.

França, Elizabeth, ed. 2000. *Guarapiranga: Recuperação Urbana e Ambiental no Municipio de São Paulo*. São Paulo: M. Carrilho Arquitetos.

França, Elizabeth, and Gloria Bayeux. 2002. Favelas Upgrading. A Cidade como Integração Dos Bairros e Espaço de Habitação. Arquitextos 27. Available online at www.vitruvius.com.br/arquitextos/arqo27/bases/ootex.asp (retrieved on June 27, 2003).

Fraser, Valerie. 2000. *Building the New World: Studies in the Modern Architecture of Latin America, 1930–1960*. London: Verso.

Friedmann, John, and Goetz Wolff. 2006. World City Formation: An Agenda for Research and Action. In *The Global Cities Reader*, edited by Neil Brenner and Roger Keil. New York: Routledge.

Gay, Robert. 1994. *Popular Organization and Democracy in Rio de Janeiro: A Tale of Two Favelas*. Philadelphia: Temple University Press.

GDF [Governo do Distrito Federal]. 1977. *Plano Estrutural de Ocupação Territorial do Distrito Federal—PEOT*. 2 vols. Brasília: Convênio Seplan/PR-GD.

———. 1982. *Plano de Ocupação Territorial do Distrito Federal—POT*. Brasília: Governo do Distrito Federal.

———. 1986. *Plano de Ocupação e Uso do Solo do Distrito Federal—POUSO*. Brasília: Convênio SVO/DAV/Terracap.

———. 1991. *Relatório do Plano Piloto de Brasília*. Brasília: ArPDF/CODEPLAN/DePHAGDF.

———. 1992. *Plano Diretor de Ordenamento Territorial—PDOT. Relatório Técnico Anexo e Lei 353/92*. Brasília: Secretaria de Obras e Serviços Públicos—SOSP.

Goldsmith, William, and Carlos Vainer. 2001. Participatory Budgeting and Power Politics in Porto Alegre. *Land Lines* [Lincoln Institute of Land Policy] 13 (1): 7–9.

Gomes, Marco Aurélio A. de Filgueiras. 1984. Le Patrimoine Historique au Brésil: mythe de l'identité et de la mémoire nationale et (re)production capitaliste de l'espace. Ph.D. diss., Université de Paris Rabelais.

Gorovitz, Matheus. 1995. Brasília—Sobre a Unidade de Vizinhança. In *IV Seminário sobre Desenho Urbano no Brasil*, edited by Frederico de Holanda and Maria E Kohlsdorf. Brasilia: Faculdade de Arquitetura e Urbanismo, Universidade de Brasília.

Gruen, Victor. 1962. Retailing and the Automobile: a Romance Based upon a Case of Mistaken Identity. In *Stores and Shopping Centers*, edited by James S. Hornbeck. New York: McGraw-Hill.

Hannigan, John. 1998. *Fantasy City: Pleasure and Profit in the Postmodern Metropolis*. London and New York: Routledge.

Harvey, David. 1990. *The Condition of Postmodernity*. Oxford and Baltimore: Blackwell.

———. 2000. *Spaces of Hope*. Berkeley: University of California Press.

Hawken, Paul, Amory Lovins, and L. Hunter Lovins. 1999. *Natural Capitalism: Creating the Next Industrial Revolution*. Boston: Little, Brown and Co.

Hayden, Dolores. 1995. *The Power of Place: Urban Landscapes as Public History*. Cambridge, Mass.: MIT Press.

Herzog, Lawrence A. 2006. *Return to the Center: Culture, Public Space and City Building in a Global Era*. Austin: University of Texas Press.

Holanda, Frederico de. 2000. Brasilia beyond Ideology. *DOCOMOMO International Journal* 23 (August): 28–35.

———. 2002. *O Espaço de Exceção*. Brasília: Editora Universidade de Brasília.

Holanda, Frederico de, Ana Maria Passos Mota, Antônio Alexandre Cavalcante Leite, Laura Regina Simões de Bello Soares, and Patrícia Melasso Garcia. 2002. Eccentric Brasilia. *Urban Design International* 7: 19–28.

Holston, James. 1989. *The Modernist City: An Anthropological Critique of Brasilia*. Chicago: University of Chicago Press.

Huxtable, Ada Louise. 1997. *The Unreal America. Architecture and Illusion*. New York: New Press.

IBGE [Instituto Brasileiro de Geografia e Estatística]. 2000. Censo Demográfico, 2000. Rio de Janeiro: IBGE.

IPHAN [Instituto do Patrimônio Histórico e Artístico Nacional]. 2003. Inventário Nacional de Bens Imóveis e Sítios Urbanos Tombados/Belém. Relatório Final de Análises e Conclusões. Belém: IPHAN. Photocopy.

IPLANRIO. 1993. Favelas Cariocas: Alguns dados estatísticos. Rio de Janeiro: Instituto de Planejamento e Estatística do Rio de Janeiro. Photocopy.

IPPUC [Instituto de Pesquisa e Planejamento Urbano de Curitiba]. 2003. Pensando a Cidade. Available online at www.ippuc.org.br/pensando_a_cidade/index_pensando_ingles.htm (retrieved July 2003).

Irazábal, Clara. 1999. Behind the Scenes in Wonderland: Re-Assessing Curitiba's Planning Model. *AULA: Architecture and Urbanism in Las Américas* 1 (spring): 92–103.

———. 2004. Architecture and the Production of Postcard Images: Invocations of Tradition vs. Critical Transnationalism in Curitiba. In *The End of Tradition*, edited by Nezar AlSayyad. London: Routledge.

———. 2005. *City Making and Urban Governance in the Americas: Curitiba and Portland*. Aldershot, UK: Ashgate.

Jacobs, Jane. 1961. Death and Life of Great American Cities. New York: Random House.

Jameson, Frederick. 1991. *Postmodernism, or the Cultural Logic of Late Capitalism*. Durham, N.C.: Duke University Press.

Jáuregui, Jorge. 2003. Urbanistic, Social and Economic Structuration of the *Favelas* in Rio de Janeiro. Available online at www.jauregui.arq.br/favelas2_ing.html (retrieved on July 25, 2003).

Jencks, Charles. 2000. *Architecture 2000 and Beyond: Success in the Art of Prediction*. Chichester, UK: Wiley-Academy.

Jones, Gareth A. 2004. The Geo-Politics of Democracy and Citizenship in Latin America. In *Spaces of Democracy: Geographical Perspectives on Citizenship, Participation, and Representation*, edited by Clive Barnett and Murray Low. Thousand Oaks, Calif.: Sage.

King, Anthony D. 2004. *Spaces of Global Cultures: Architecture, Urbanism, Identity*. New York: Routledge.

Kohlsdorf, Maria Elaine. 1985. As Imagens de Brasília. In *Brasília, Ideologia e Realidade: O Espaço Urbano em Questão*, edited by Aldo Paviani. São Paulo: Editora Projeto.

———. 1987. O Planejamento da Imagem da Cidade: Por Exemplo, Brasília. In *Percepção*

Ambiental: Contexto Teórico e Aplicações ao Tema Urbano. Special publication no. 5, 39–42. Belo Horizonte: Instituto de Geociências, Universidade Federal de Minas Gerais.

———. 1996a. Brasília em Três Escalas de Percepção. In *Percepção Ambiental: A Experiência Brasileira,* edited by Vicente del Rio and Lívia de Oliveira. São Paulo: Studio Nobel.

———. 1996b. Brasília, Mosaico Morfológico. In *IV Seminário História da Cidade e do Urbanismo,* vol. 2, edited by Denise P. Machado. Rio de Janeiro: PROURB/FAU and Universidade Federal do Rio de Janeiro.

———. 1997. Brasília Hoje: Cidade-Patrimônio, Cidade-Capital, Cidade-Real. In *Guia de Arquitetura, Urbanismo e Arte de Brasília,* edited by Andréa Braga and Fernando Falcão. Brasília: Fundação Atos Bulcão.

Kotler, Philip, David Gertner, Irwin Rein, and Donald Haider. 2006. *Marketing de Lugares: Como Conquistar Crescimento de Longo Prazo na America Latina e no Caribe.* São Paulo: Pearson/Prentice Hall.

Kowarick, Lucio, ed. 1994. *Social Struggles and the City.* New York: Monthly Review Press.

Lang, Jon. 2005. *Urban Design: A Typology of Procedures and Products.* Oxford: Elsevier/Architectural Press.

Lara, Fernando. 2006. Brazilian Popular Modernism: Analysing the Dissemination of Architectural Vocabulary. *Journal of Architecture and Planning Research* 23 (2): 91–112.

Leach, Neil. 1999. *The Anaesthetics of Architecture.* Cambridge, Mass.: MIT Press.

Lefebvre, Henri. 1968. *Le droit a la ville.* Paris: Editions Anthropos.

———. 1971. *The Production of Space.* Translated by Donald Nicholson Smith. Oxford: Blackwell.

Leitão, Francisco C. 2002. Brasília 1956–1964: Tirando a Poeira. Master's thesis, Faculdade de Arquitetura e Urbanismo, Universidade de Brasília.

Leitão, Geronimo. 1999. A Construcao do Eldorado Urbano: O Plano Piloto da Barra da Tijuca e Baixada de Jacarepagua 1970–80. Niteroi, RJ: Editora da Universidade Federal Fluminense.

Leme, Maria Cristina Dias, ed. 1999. *Urbanismo no Brasil, 1895– 1965.* São Paulo: Studio Nobel/FUPAM.

Lima, Evelyn F. W. 2004. Configurações Urbanas Cenográficas e o Fenômeno da Gentrificação. *Arquitextos* 46 (3); Available online at www.vitruvius.com.br/arquitextos/arq046/arq046_03.asp (retrieved on August 2, 2004).

Lins, Elizabeth de A. 1989. *A Preservação no Brasil: A Busca de uma Identidade.* Salvador: Faculdade de Arquitetura e Urbanismo, Universidade Federal da Bahia.

Loukaitou-Sideris, Anastasia, and Trijib Banerjee. 1998. *Urban Design Downtown: Poetics and Politics of Form.* Berkeley: University of California Press.

Lynch, Kevin. 1981. *Good City Form.* Cambridge, Mass.: MIT Press.

Macedo, Silvio Soares. 1987a. *Higienópolis e Arredores. Processo de Mutação de Paisagem Urbana.* São Paulo: Pini/Editora da Universidade de São Paulo.

———. 1987b. São Paulo, Paisagem e Habitação Verticalizada: os espaços livres como elementos de desenho urbano. Ph.D. diss., Faculdade de Arquitetura e Urbanismo, Universidade de São Paulo.

———. 1999. *Quadro do Paisagismo no Brasil.* São Paulo: Projeto Quapá/Laboratorio da Paisagem, Faculdade de Arquitetura e Urbanismo, Universidade de São Paulo.

Machado, Lia Zanotta, and Themis Quezado Magalhães. 1985. Imagens do Espaço: Imagens de Vida. In *Brasília, Ideologia e Realidade—Espaço Urbano em Questão*, edited by Aldo Paviani. São Paulo: Projeto Editora.

Machado, Rodolfo, ed. 2003. *The Favela Bairro Project: Jorge Mario Jauregui Architects.* Cambridge Mass.: Harvard University Graduate School of Design.

MacLachlan, Colin. 2003. *A History of Modern Brazil: The Past against the Future.* Wilmington, Del.: Scholarly Resources.

Magalhães, Fernanda, and Candido Malta Campos Neto. 2002. Favela-Bairro: Um Estudo de Caso no Rio de Janeiro. In *Proceedings of the 30th IAHS World Congress on Housing*, edited by Ural, Abrantes, and Tadeu. Coimbra: International Association of Housing Studies.

Magalhães, Sérgio. 1998. Rio de Janeiro: Una Perspectiva Actual de la Ciudad. In *La ciudad del siglo XXI. Experiencias exitosas en gestión del desarrollo urbano en América Latina*, edited by E. Rojas and R. Daughters. Washington, DC: Inter-American Development Bank.

———. 2002. *Sobre a Cidade: Habitação e Democracia no Rio de Janeiro.* São Paulo: Pro-Editores.

Magnavita, Pasqualino. 1995. Quando a História vira Espetáculo do Poder. In *Estratégias de Intervenção em Áreas Históricas*, edited by Silvio Zanchetti, Gilberto Marinho, and Vera Millet. Recife: Universidade Federal de Pernambuco.

Magnoli, Miranda M. E. M. 1983. Espaços Livres e Urbanização: Uma Introdução a Aspectos da Paisagem Metropolitana. Bachelor's thesis, Faculdade de Arquitetura e Urbanismo da Universidade de São Paulo.

Margolis, Mac. 1992. A City That Works. *World Monitor,* March.

Maricato, Erminia. 1997. Brasil 2000: qual planejamento urbano? In *Cadernos do IPPUR* [Instituto de Pesquisa e Planejamento Urbano e Regional, Universidade Federal do Rio de Janeiro] 11 (1–2): 113–30.

———. 2001. *Brasil, Cidades—Alternativas para a Crise Urbana.* Rio de Janeiro: Editora Vozes.

Marx, Murilo. 1980. *A Cidade Brasileira.* São Paulo: Melhoramentos/Editora da Universidade de São Paulo.

Masano, Tadeu Francisco. 1993. Shopping Centers e suas Relações Físico-Territoriais e Sócio-Negociais no Município de São Paulo. Ph.D. diss., Faculdade de Arquitetura e Urbanismo da Universidade de São Paulo.

Mattedi, Maria Raquel, Marusia Rebouças, and Sueli Barreto. 1989. Salvador: O Processo de Urbanização. In *Comissão de Planejamento Econômico Habitação e urbanismo em Salvador*, 337–64. Salvador: CPE.

Menneh, Márcia Halluli. 1997. Morfologia da Paisagem Urbana Verticalizada: Conflitos e Padrões Urbanísticos. Master's thesis, Faculdade de Arquitetura e Urbanismo, Universidade de São Paulo.

Meyer, Regina M. P. 2001. Atributos da Metrópole Moderna. *São Paulo em Perspectiva* [Fundação Seade, São Paulo]: 14: 3–9.

Meyer, Regina, Marta Grostein, and Ciro Biderman. 2004. *São Paulo Metrópole.* São Paulo: Editora da Universidade de São Paulo.

Meyer, Regina, and Alcino Izzo Jr. 1999. *Pólo Luz: Sala São Paulo, Cultura e Urbanismo.* São Paulo: Ed. Terceiro Nome.

Morales, Anna Maria. 1991. Blocos Negros em Salvador: Reelaboração Cultural e Símbolos de Baianidade. In *CADERNOS CRH. Cantos e Toques: Etnografias do Espaço Negro na Bahia*. Salvador: Centro de Recursos Humanos, Universidade Federal da Bahia.

Moreira, Antonio Cláudio. 1997. Administração Municipal Paulistana e a Questão dos Impactos Ambientais. *Sinopses* [Faculdade de Arquitetura e Urbanismo, Universidade de São Paulo] 28: 19–25.

Moreno, Manuel F. N. 2001. Qualidade Ambiental nos Espaços Livres em Áreas Verticalizadas da Cidade de São Paulo. Ph.D. diss., Faculdade de Arquitetura e Urbanismo, Universidade de São Paulo.

Moura, Rosa. 2000. Regulación de Uso del Suelo Urbano: Discusión Sobre el Caso de Curitiba. Paper presented at the Law and Urban Space workshop, International Research Group on Law and Urban Space (IRGLUS), Cairo.

Moura, Rosa, and Maria de Lourdes Kleinke. 1999. Caracterização das Regiões Metropolitanas Institucionalizadas, vol. 4. IPEA/DEPRU/CGEPUR and UNICAMP/NESUR. Draft version, photocopy.

MIT [Ministério do Trabalho e Emprego]. 1999. *Cadastro de Estabelecimentos Empregadores: Base Estatística e Cadastral* [CD-ROM]. Brasília: MTE, Governo Federal.

Nacif Xavier, Helia, and Fernanda Magalhães. 2002. Case study of Rio de Janeiro prepared for *Global Report on Human Settlements 2003–City Report of Rio de Janeiro*. Rio de Janeiro: UN-Habitat.

Nascimento, Oswaldo. 1997. *O Guia Mapograf*. São Paulo: Mapograf Editora.

Nesbitt, Kate, ed. 1996. *Theorizing a New Agenda for Architecture: An Anthology of Architectural Theory 1965–1995*. New York: Princeton Architectural Press.

Nobre, Eduardo Alberto Cuce. 2000. Reestruturação Econômica do Território: Expansão Recente do Terciário na Marginal do Rio Pinheiros. Ph.D. diss., Faculdade de Arquitetura e Urbanismo, Universidade de São Paulo.

Nunes, Brasilmar Ferreira. 2003. A Lógica Social do Espaço. In *Brasília: Controvérsias Ambientais*, edited by Aldo Paviani and Luiz Alberto de Gouvêa. Brasília: Editora Universidade de Brasília.

Oliveira, Augusto S. de Sá. 2002. Do Botequim à Boutique: A Redefinição do Imaginário Social na Reconstrução do Pelourinho. Master's thesis, Faculdade de Comunicação, Universidade Federal da Bahia.

Oliveira, Cloves Luiz Pereira. 1998. O Negro e o Poder: Os Negros Candidatos a Vereador em Salvador, em 1988. In *Cadernos CRH. Cantos e Toques: Etnografias do Espaço Negro na Bahia*. Salvador: Centro de Recursos Humanos, Universidade Federal da Bahia.

Oliveira, Dennison de. 1995. A Política do Planejamento Urbano: O Caso de Curitiba. Ph.D. diss., Universidade Estadual de Campinas.

Omholt, Tore. 1998. Strategic Rationality as a Basis for Town Centre Revitalization and Management. Paper presented at the Recent Advances in Retailing and Services Science conference, Baveno, Italy.

Outtes, Joel. 2002. Disciplining Society through the City: The Genesis of City Planning in Brazil and Argentina (1894–1945). *Bulletin of Latin American Research* 21 (1): 99–127.

Paviani, Aldo. 1985. A Metrópole Terciária. In *Brasília, Ideologia e Realidade: O Espaço Urbano em Questão*, edited by Aldo Paviani. São Paulo: Editora Projeto.

———. 1999. Gestão do Território com Exclusão Socioespacial. In *Brasília—Gestão Urbana: Conflitos e Cidadania*, edited by Aldo Paviani. Brasília: Editora Universidade de Brasília.

Paviani, Aldo, and Luiz Alberto de Gouvêa, eds. 2003. *Brasília: Controvérsias Ambientais*. Brasília: Editora Universidade de Brasília.

Peixoto, Nelson B. 1998. *Paisagens Urbanas*. São Paulo: Senac/Marca D'água.

Pereira, Margareth Dias. 2002. The Time of the Capitals: Rio de Janeiro and Sao Paulo: Words, Acts and Plans. In *Planning Latin American Capital Cities, 1850–1950*, edited by Arturo Almandoz. London: Routledge.

Peres, Francisco da R., ed. 1987. *Protesto contra a Demolição da Sé, 1928*. Salvador: Centro de Estudos Bahianos, Universidade Federal da Bahia.

Perlman, Janice. 1976. *The Myth of Marginality: Urban Poverty and Politics in Rio de Janeiro*. Berkeley: University of California Press.

Pinheiro, Augusto Ivan. 1986. Corredor Cultural, um Projeto de Preservação para o Rio de Janeiro. In *II SEDUR—Seminário sobre Desenho Urbano no Brasil*. São Paulo: Editora Pini.

———. 2002. Preservar, Conservar e Modernizar: um Novo Paradigma para a Reabilitação do Centro do Rio. Rio de Janeiro: Instituto Light. Available online at www.light.com.br/foster/web/aplicacoes/documentos/instituto/artigos/documentolist.asp (retrieved on May 19, 2002).

Pinheiro, Augusto I., and Vicente del Rio. 1993. Corredor Cultural: A Preservation District in Downtown Rio de Janeiro, Brazil. *Traditional Dwellings and Settlements Review* 4 (2): 51–64.

Pino, Julio Cesar. 2007. *Family and Favela: The Reproduction of Poverty in Rio de Janeiro*. Westport, Conn.: Greenwood Press.

Pontes, Fernanda, and Selma Schmidt. 2001. A Invasão Silenciosa das *Favelas*. O *Globo*, January 21, 2001, p. 18.

Porto Alegre, Prefeitura Municipal de. 2003. *Porto Alegre: Um Outro Mundo é Possível*. Porto Alegre: Prefeitura Municipal de Porto Alegre.

Rabinovitch, Jonas, and Josef Leitman. 1993. Environmental Innovation and Management in Curitiba, Brazil. In *Urban Management and the Environment*. Working Paper no. 1. UNDP/UNCHS (Habitat)/World Bank. Photocopy.

Rio de Janeiro, Prefeitura da Cidade do. 1996a. *Plano Estratégico da Cidade do Rio de Janeiro*. Relatório da Cidade 2. Rio de Janeiro.

———. 1996b. *Revista Rio Cidade*. Rio de Janeiro: IPLANRIO.

———. 1996c. *Rio Cidade: O Urbanismo de Volta às Ruas*. Rio de Janeiro: IPLANRIO/Editora Mauad.

Recamán, Luiz. 2004. High-Speed Urbanization. In *Brazil's Modern Architecture*, edited by Elisabetta Andreoli and Adrian Forty. London: Phaidon.

Rego, Maria Elizabeth Pereira. 1996. The Relocation of Itá. In *Traditional Dwellings and Settlements*. Working Paper Vol. 81. Berkeley: Center for Environmental Design Research/IASTE, University of California, Berkeley.

Reis, Nestor Goulart. 1996. O Processo de Urbanização—A Proposito do Programa de Cidades de Porte Médio. In *Urbanismo e Planejamento no Brasil, 1960/1983*, Cadernos do Laboratório de Arquitetura e Planejamento #11. São Paulo: Faculdade de Arquitetura e Urbanismo, Universidade de São Paulo. Photocopy.

Relph, Edward. 1987. *A Paisagem Urbana Moderna*. Lisbon: Edições 70.

Ribeiro, Ana Clara Torres, and Grazia de Grazia. 2003. *Experiêcias de Orçamento Participativo no Brasil*. Petropolis, RJ: Forum Nacional de Participação Popular/Editora Vozes.

Ribeiro, Luiz Cesar. 2001. Cidade, nação e mercado: genese e evolução da questão urbana no Brasil. In *Brasil—Um Século de Transformações*, edited by Ignacy Sachs, Jorge Wilheim, and Paulo Sergio Pinheiro. Rio de Janeiro: Companhia das Letras.

Ribeiro, Luiz Cesar, and Adauto Cardoso. 1994. Planejamento Urbano no Brasil: Paradigmas e Experiencias. *Espaço e Debates* 37: 77–89.

———. 1996. Da Cidade `a Nação: Genese e Evolução do Urbanismo no Brasil. In *Cidade: Povo e Nação—Genese do Urbanismo Moderno*, edited by Luiz Cesar Ribeiro and Robert Pechman. Rio de Janeiro: Civilização Brasileira.

———., eds. 2003. *Reforma Urbana e Gestão Democrática. Promessas e Desafios do Estatuto da Cidade*. Rio de Janeiro: Observatório IPPUR/UFRJ-FASE, Editora Revan.

Rioarte/Iplanrio. 1985. *Corredor Cultural: Como Recuperar, Reformar ou Construir seu Imóvel*. Rio de Janeiro: Prefeitura da Cidade do Rio de Janeiro.

Robinson, Jennifer. 2006. *Ordinary Cities: Between Modernity and Development*. New York: Routledge.

Rodrigues, David. 1999. O Uso Extra-Fiscal da Tributação do Ordenamento Urbano. Master's thesis, Programa de Pós-Graduação em Direito, Universidade Federal do Rio de Janeiro.

Rodrigues, Edmilson, and Márcio de Meira. 2004. Porque o Ver o Peso é Candidato a Patrimônio da Cidade. Belém: FUMBEL. Available online at www.fumbel.com.br/patrimonio1.htm (retrieved on July 27, 2004).

Rogers, Richard. 1998. *Cities for a Small Planet*. Boulder, Colo.: Westview Press.

Rolnik, Raquel. 2000. *São Paulo Leste/Sudeste—Reestruturação Urbana da Metrópole Paulistana: Análise de Territórios em Transição*. São Paulo: Puccamp/Fapesp/Polis.

———. 2001. Territorial Exclusion and Violence: The Case of the State of São Paulo. In *Urban Brazil. Geoforum* (special issue) 32 (4): 471–82.

Rykwert, Joseph. 2000. *The Seduction of Place: The City in the Twenty-First Century*. London: Weidenfeld and Nicolson.

Sachs, Ignacy. 2001. Quo-Vadis Brazil. In *Brasil—Um Século de Transformações*, edited by Ignacy Sachs, Jorge Wilheim, and Paulo Sergio Pinheiro. Rio de Janeiro: Companhia das Letras.

Sakata, Francine M. G. 1994. As Linhas Projetuais da Arquitetura Paisagística no Desenho dos Espaços Livres dos Edifícios de Apartamentos. Research report. São Paulo: Faculdade de Arquitetura e Urbanismo, Universidade de São Paulo. Photocopy.

Sánchez, Fernanda. 1996. O City Marketing de Curitiba: Cultura e Comunicacão na Construcão da Imagem Urbana. In *Percepcão Ambiental: A Experiencia Brasileira*, edited by Vicente del Rio and Livia de Oliveira. São Paulo: Studio Nobel and Universidade Federal de São Carlos.

———. 1997. *Cidade Espectáculo: Política, Planejamento e City Marketing*. Curitiba: Editora Palavra.

Sant'Anna, Márcia. 2003. A Cidade-Atração: A Norma de Preservação de Centros Urbanos no Brasil dos Anos 90. Master's thesis, Faculdade de Arquitetura e Urbanismo, Universidade Federal da Bahia.

Santos, Carlos Nelson dos. 1985a. Para Cada Forma de Dominação a Utopia que Merece.

Arquitetura Revista [Faculdade de Arquitetura e Urbanismo, Universidade Federal do Rio de Janeiro] 3: 86–90.

———. 1985b. *Quando a Rua Vira Casa*. São Paulo: Projeto Editora.

Santos, Milton. 1959. *O Centro da Cidade do Salvador*. Salvador: Universidade Federal da Bahia.

———. 1975. *The Shared Space: The Two Circtuis of the Economy in the Underdeveloped Countries and Their Spatial Repercussions*. London: Methuen.

———. 1987. *O Espaço do Cidadão*. São Paulo: Nobel.

Santos, Milton, Maria Adelia A. de Souza, and Maria Laura Silveira, eds. 2002. *Território: Globalização e Fragmentação*. São Paulo: Hucitec/ANPUR.

Santos Neto, Iaias de Carvalho. 1991. Centralidade Urbana: Espaço e Lugar. Ph.D. diss., Faculdade de Arquitetura e Urbanismo, Universidade de São Paulo.

São Paulo, Prefeitura Municipal de. 1985. *Plano Diretor do Município de São Paulo*. São Paulo: Secretaria Municipal de Planejamento.

———. 2002. *Plano Diretor Estratégico*. Lei #13,430 (September 13, 2002). São Paulo: Câmara Municipal de São Paulo.

———. n.d. *Coletânea das Leis e Decretos de Parcelamento, Uso e Ocupação do Solo*. São Paulo: Secretaria Municipal de Planejamento.

Sassen, Saskia. 1998. *As Cidades na Economia Mundial*. São Paulo: Studio Nobel.

Schmidt, Benicio Viero. 1983. *O Estado e a Politica Urbana no Brasil*. Porto Alegre: Editora da Universidade/L&PM.

Schwartz, Hugh. 2004. *Urban Renewal, Municipal Revitalization: The Case of Curitiba, Brazil*. Falls Church, Va.: Higher Education Publications.

SEADE [Fundação Sistema Estadual de Análise de Dados.] 2000. Secretaria de Estado dos Negócios, Economia e Planejamento, Estado de São Paulo. Available online at www.seade.sp.gov.br (retrieved on March 13, 2004).

Segawa, Hugo. 1998. *Arquiteturas no Brasil: 1900–1990*. Sao Paulo: EDUSP.

Sennett, Richard. 1974. *The Fall of Public Man*. Cambridge: Cambridge University Press.

Serra, Geraldo. 1991. *Urbanização e Centralismo Autoritário*. São Paulo: EDUSP/Nobel.

Sisson, Raquel. 1986. Marcos Históricos e Configurações Espaciais, Um Estudo de Caso: Os Centros do Rio de Janeiro. *Arquitetura em Revista* [Faculdade de Arquitetura e Urbanismo, Universidade Federal do Rio de Janeiro] 2: 57–81.

Sisson, Raquel, and Elizabeth Jackson. 1995. Rio de Janeiro 1875–1945: The Shaping of a New Urban Order. *Journal of Decorative and Propaganda Arts* 21: 139–54.

Skidmore, Thomas E. 1988. *The Politics of Military Rule in Brazil, 1964–85*. New York: Oxford University Press.

———. 1999. *Brazil: Five Centuries of Change*. Oxford: Oxford University Press.

Sklair, Leslie. 1991. *Sociology of the Global System*. Baltimore, Md.: Johns Hopkins University Press.

Smith, Michael P. 2006. The Global Cities Discourse: A Return to the Master Narrative. In *The Global Cities Reader*, edited by Neil Brenner and Roger Neil. London: Routledge.

SMH (Secretaria Municipal de Habitação do Rio de Janeiro). 2003. Programa Favela-Bairro. *Revista Cidades do Brasil*. Available online at www.cidadesdobrasil.com.br (retrieved on July 25, 2003).

Soares, Francirose, Cristiane Rose Duarte, and Lucia Costa. 1996. Uma Análise da Ocupação

Irregular de Florestas Urbanas do Rio de Janeiro. Paper presented at Forest 96: IV International Symposium on Forest Ecosystems. Belo Horizonte, Brazil.

Solá-Morales Rubió, Ignaci. 1995. Terrain Vague. In *Anyplace*, edited by Cynthia C. Davidson, 118–23. Cambridge, Mass.: MIT Press.

Somekh, Nadia. 1994. Cidade Vertical e o Urbanismo Modernizador: São Paulo 1920–1939. Ph.D. diss., Faculdade de Arquitetura e Urbanismo, Universidade de São Paulo.

Southworth, Michael. 2001. Wastelands in the Evolving Metropolis. Institute of Urban and Regional Development Working Paper Series, Paper WP-2001–01 (April 1, 2001) Berkeley: Institute of Urban and Regional Development, University of California, Berkeley. Available online at http://repositories.cdlib.org/iurd/wps/WP-2001–01 (retrieved January 15, 2008).

Souza, Marcelo Lopes de. 2003. *ABC do Desenvolvimento Urbano*. Rio de Janeiro: Bertrand Brasil.

Souza, Maria Adélia Aparecida de. 1994. *A Identidade da Metrópole: A Verticalização em São Paulo*. São Paulo: Editora Hucitec and Editora da Universidade de São Paulo.

———. 1999. O II PND e a Politica Urbana Brasileira: Uma contradição evidente. In *O Processo de Urbanização no Brasil*, edited by Csaba Deak and Sueli R. Schiffer. São Paulo: Editora da Universidade de São Paulo.

Spiro, Anne. 2001. *Paulo Mendes da Rocha: Works and Projects*. Zurich: Arthur Niggi Verlag.

Tângari, Vera Regina. 1999. Um Outro Lado do Rio. Ph.D. diss., Faculdade de Arquitetura e Urbanismo, Universidade de São Paulo.

Toledo, Benedito L. 1983. *São Paulo: Três Cidades em um Século*. São Paulo: Duas Cidades.

Trancik, Roger. 1986. *Finding Lost Space: Theories of Urban Design*. New York: Van Nostrand Reinhold.

Trindade, Saint-Clair Cordeiro Jr. 1997. *Produção do Espaço e Uso do Solo Urbano em Belém*. Belém: NAEA and Universidade Federal do Pará.

Tschumi, Bernard. 1994. *Event-Cities: Praxis*. Cambridge, Mass.: MIT Press.

Turner, John and Robert Fichter. 1972. *Freedom to Build: Dweller Control of the Housing Process*. New York: Macmillan.

Underwood, David. 1991. Alfred Agache, French Sociology, and Modern Urbanism in France and Brazil. *Journal of the Society of Art Historians* 50 (June): 130–66.

Valença, Márcio 1999. The Closure of the Brazilina Housing Bank and Beyond. *Urban Studies* 36 (10): 1747–68.

Valladares, Licia. 1988. Urban Sociology in Brazil: A Research Report. *International Journal of Urban and Regional Research* 12: 285–301.

Valladares, Licia, and Lidia Medeiros. 2003. *Pensando as Favelas do Rio de Janeiro, 1906–2000: Uma Bibliografia Analitica*. Rio de Janeiro: Relume Dumará.

Vargas, Heliana C. 1992. Comércio: Localização Estratégica ou Estratégia na Localização. Ph.D. diss., Faculdade de Arquitetura e Urbanismo da Universidade de São Paulo.

———. 2000. 'Shopping Caixote' Tem os Dias Contados em São Paulo. *Gazeta Mercantil* [São Paulo], June 19, pp. 1, 5.

———. 2001. *Espaço Terciário. O lugar, a Arquitetura e a Imagem do Comércio*. São Paulo: SENAC.

———. 2003. City Center Management: Learning from Shopping Malls. In *Proceedings of the XII International Conference on Research and Distributive Trades*. Paris: ESCP-EAP.

———. 2004. A Magnitude do Comércio: de Ambulantes à Shopping Centers. In *São Paulo, Metrópole em Trânsito: Percursos Urbanos e Culturais*, edited by Candido Malta, Lucia Gama, and Vladimir Sacchetta. São Paulo: SENAC.

Vasconcellos, Patricia. 2002. *Interiores—Corredor Cultural: Centro Histórico do Rio de Janeiro*. Rio de Janeiro: Editora Sextante.

Vaz, Lilian Fessler. 1994. Uma História da Habitação Coletiva na Cidade do Rio de Janeiro: Estudo da Modernidade Através da Moradia. Ph.D. diss., Faculdade de Arquitetura e Urbanismo, Universidade de São Paulo.

———. 2002. *Modernidade e Moradia: Habitação Coletiva no Rio de Janeiro, Séculos XIX e XX*. Rio de Janeiro: Sete Letras.

Villac, Maria I. 2003. Um Novo Discurso para a Megacidade. Projeto Praça do Patriarca. Available online at www.vitruvius.com.br/Minha_Cidade/Vitruvius_arquivos/tex.asp (retrieved on June 27, 2003).

Villaça, Flávio. 1998. *Espaço intra-urbano no Brasil*. São Paulo: Studio Nobel/Lincoln Institute.

Virilio, Paul. 2000. *A Landscape of Events*. Translated by Julie Rose. Cambridge, Mass.: MIT Press.

Watson, Sophie, and Kathrine Gibson, ed. 1995. *Postmodern Cities and Spaces*. Oxford: Blackwell.

Wilheim, Jorge. 2001. Metrópoles e Faroeste do Século XXI. In *Brasil—Um Século de Transformações*, edited by Ignacy Sachs, Jorge Wilheim, and Paulo Pinheiro. Rio de Janeiro: Companhia das Letras.

Zaluar, Alba, and Marcos Alvito, eds. 1998. *Um Século de Favela*. Rio de Janeiro: Editora da Fundação Getúlio Vargas.

Zukin, Sharon. 1988. The Debate over Postmodern Urban Form. *Theory, Culture and Society* 5 (2–3): 431–46.

Zylberberg, Sônia. 1992. *Morro da Providência: Memórias da Favela*. Rio de Janeiro: Secretaria Municipal de Cultura, Prefeitura do Rio de Janeiro.

Contributors

DENISE DE ALCANTARA is a practicing architect and lecturer, School of Architecture and Urbanism, Federal University of Rio de Janeiro.

LINEU CASTELLO is retired as full professor from the School of Architecture, Federal University of Rio Grande do Sul, Porto Alegre, Brazil, and is now a guest professor in the Graduate Program in Architecture.

GILDA COLLET BRUNA is retired as full professor from the School of Architecture and Urbanism, University of São Paulo. She coordinates the Graduate Program in Architecture and Urbanism at Mackenzie Presbyterian University, São Paulo.

CRISTIANE ROSE DUARTE is full professor, School of Architecture and Urbanism, Federal University of Rio de Janeiro.

ANA FERNANDES is associate professor, School of Architecture and Urbanism, Federal University of Bahia, Salvador.

MARCO A. A. DE FILGUEIRAS GOMES is full professor, School of Architecture and Urbanism, Federal University of Bahia, Salvador.

FREDERICO DE HOLANDA is associate professor, School of Architecture and Urbanism, University of Brasília.

CLARA IRAZÁBAL is assistant professor of international urban planning, Columbia University, New York.

GUNTER KOHLSDORF is retired from the School of Architecture and Urbanism, University of Brasília, and now coordinates the Center for Design at UNIEURO university in Brasília.

MARIA ELAINE KOHLSDORF, retired as full professor at the School of Architecture and Urbanism, University of Brasília, coordinates the Program in Architecture and Urbanism at UNIEURO, a university in Brasília.

CARLOS LEITE is associate professor and research coordinator, School of Architecture and Urbanism, Mackenzie Presbyterian University, São Paulo.

SILVIO SOARES MACEDO is full professor of landscape architecture, School of Architecture and Urbanism, University of São Paulo.

FERNANDA MAGALHÃES is associate professor, School of Architecture and Urbanism, Federal University of Rio de Janeiro. She is a planning specialist for the Inter-American Development Bank in Brazil.

ALICE DA SILVA RODRIGUES is a planner with the City of Belém and teaches in the School of Architecture, University of the Amazon, Belém.

SIMONE SILENE DIAS SEABRA is associate professor, School of Architecture, University of the Amazon, Belém.

DIRCEU TRINDADE is director of the Institute Attílio Corrêa Lima for Urban Planning and Research, Goiânia.

HELIANA COMIN VARGAS is full professor, School of Architecture and Urbanism, University of São Paulo.

Editors

VICENTE DEL RIO is full professor in the City and Regional Planning Department, College of Architecture and Environmental Design, California Polytechnic State University, San Luis Obispo. From 1978 to 2001 he taught at Faculdade de Arquitetura e Urbanismo, Federal University of Rio de Janeiro, where he was full professor. He has been a fellow at Johns Hopkins University and the University of Cincinnati. He is a visiting professor of urbanism at the Universidade Lusófona in Lisbon, Portugal. Specializing in urban design, he has worked, published, and lectured extensively internationally. Among his many publications are the books *Introdução ao Desenho Urbano no Processo de Planejamento* (1990), *Percepção Ambiental: A Experiência Brasileira* (1996), *Arquitetura: Pesquisa & Projeto* (1998), and *Projeto do Lugar* (2002).

WILLIAM SIEMBIEDA is full professor and head of the City and Regional Planning Department, College of Architecture and Environmental Design, California Polytechnic State University, San Luis Obispo. He is former director of the Center for Research, School of Architecture and Planning, University of New Mexico. He has lectured extensively in Mexico, Central America, and Brazil. He was a Fulbright Fellow at the University of Guadalajara, Mexico, and a CNPq Fellow at the University of São Paulo, Brazil. He is internationally known in the areas of urban land policy, master-planned community development, and disaster mitigation planning. He has served as a consultant and planner to new towns in the United States and Mexico.

Index

demand for, 258; Favela-Bairro program and, 288–89; in Rio de Janeiro, 12–13; state public housing agencies and, 86; for workers, 7

Maricato, Erminia, xxiii, 27–28
Marx, Roberto Burle, 4, 9, 261
Mata Machado favela (Rio de Janeiro), *283*, 283–85, *285*, 287, 288
Mauá, 261–63, *262*, 294
Méier (Rio de Janeiro), 228–35, *229*, *230*, *232*, *234*
Mercado de Ferro (Belém), 166–67, 169, *174*, *175*, *175*
Metropolitan planning: agencies for, 16–17, 23; in Curitiba, 216–18
Military regime: architecture and urban design during, 11–23; national housing policy of, 268
Ministério das Cidades (Ministry of Cities), 33
Ministry of Education and Health, 3, 4, 6
Modernism: in Brasília, 9, 42–44, *47*, 47–48, *49*, 50–52, 294–95; in Brazil, 40; core appeal of, 293; end of, 10–11; functional, 13–14; Late Modernism trend, xxvi, xxviii, 37, 293–96; military and technocratic, 11–23; Paulista, 254, 261; peak of, 6; peripheral, 52–55, *53*, *54*; positivist paradigm in, 37; in São Paulo, 294, 295; urbanism and, 1–2; Vargas and, 2–4
Modernization: in Brazil, xxiii–xxiv, 65; of Rio de Janeiro, 126–27
Monumenta program, 252, 253
Morphological types in Brasília: classic modernism, *47*, 47–48, *49*, 50–52; land invasions, 55–56; peripheral modernism, 52–55, *54*; postdating modernism, 57–61, *57*, *59*, *60*; vernacular, 45, *46*, 46–47
Movimento Nacional da Reforma Urbana, 24–25

National Agency of Urban Transportation (EBTU), 17
National Association for Education in Architecture and Urbanism (ABEA), 26
National Association for Research and Graduate Studies in Urban and Regional Planning (ANPUR), 26
National Commission of Metropolitan Urban Regions and Urban Policy (CNPU), 17
National Council of Urban Development (CNDU), 17
National Heritage Site for Preservation, 148–49, *149*, 150
National Housing Bank (BNH), 13, 14, 15–16, 23, 268
National Program for Faculty Training (CAPES), 26
National Research Council (CNPq), 26
National urban planning, 11–12, *12*, 13–14, 23
Navegantes Commercial District, 188–93, *190*, *191*, *192*, 297
Niemeyer, Oscar, xiv, 4, 6, 249, 265n9
Nova Olaria Commercial Center (Porto Alegre), 194, *194*
Núcleo Cultural Feliz Lusitânia (Belém), 169, 176–78, *177*, *178*, 179, *179*

Occupation, social right of, 298–99
Open spaces: acclaimed, xiii; landscaping of, 98–99; quantity and quality of, 94; verticalization and, 91–94, *92*
Operação Urbana Centro (São Paulo), 251
Ópera de Arame (Curitiba), 209, *209*, 222n11

Palmas: city center, *72*, 72–73; construction of, 77–79; design for, 38–40, 66, 67–69; evaluation of, 79–81; grid in, 69, *69*–76; orienting principles of, 68; problems in, 80–81; recreation and leisure in, 75–76; regional development and, 79; residential areas in, 73–75; site selection for, 66–67, *67*; traffic and transportation in, 70–72, *72*
Parks: pocket, in Rio de Janeiro, 231, 236

PT (Labor Party), 30, 219
Public housing, modernism and, 7–8

Quarteirão Cultural and Praça das Artes e
    da Memória (Salvador), *159*

Recife, 102
Rede Integrada de Transporte (RIT), 204–5,
    205, 207, 208, 216
Re-democratization of Brazil, xviii, 23,
    121, 268–69. *See also* Brazilian National
    Constitution (1988)
Reforms, institutional and judicial, xxii
Reidy, Affonso, *8,* 8–9
Reis, Nestor Goulart, 13
Residential areas: Cultural Corridor
    Project and, 139–40; in Curitiba, 207;
    high-density, 102; high-rise apartments,
    87, *87*; in Palmas, 73–75; Pelourinho
    revitalization and, 156, 157–58. *See also*
    low-income housing
Revitalization, xxviii, 15, 121, 296–98
Ribeiro, Luiz Cesar, 12, 13, 25, 27
Rio Cidade program: Avenida Rio Branco,
    139; background of, 225–26; budget issues,
    242; community participation in, 242–43;
    competitive bid process, 227, 240; inter-
    vention areas, 228; IPP and, 227; Leblon,
    235–38, *236, 237, 239, 240*; lessons from,
    238, 240–43; Méier, 228–35, *229, 230, 232,
    234*; multidisciplinarity of, 241; overview
    of, 200, 224; postmodern urbanism in,
    299–300; strategic plan and, 226–27; suc-
    cess of, 243–44; timelines for, 240, 242
Rio de Janeiro: Agache plan for, 4–6,
    5, 127; Barra da Tijuca and Baixada
    de Jacarepaguá, 18–20, *19*; Corredor
    Cultural, xiii, 24; downtown of, 126–28,
    128; Downtown shopping center, 110, *111*;
    favelas in, xix, 7, 267–70; friendliness of,
    xxi–xxii; Le Corbusier plan for, 6, *7*; low-
    income housing in, 12–13, 16; master plan
    for, 12, *13,* 25–26, 226–27, 270; Parque do
    Flamengo, 8–9, *9*; Pedregulho Residential

Complex, 7, 8; population of, xxi; prob-
    lems in, xix–xx, 225; verticalization in,
    85, 93. *See also* Cultural Corridor Project
    (Rio de Janeiro); Favela-Bairro
Rio Grande do Sul, 185–86. *See also* Porto
    Alegre
RIT (Rede Integrada de Transporte), 204–5,
    205, 207, 208, 216
Riverfront. *See* waterfront
Rocha, Paulo Mendes da, 253, 255
Rolnik, Raquel, 27
Rykwert, Joseph, 45

SAARA area (Rio de Janeiro), 134, 135, *136,*
    139
Sachs, Ignacy, xx, 30
Salvador, Bahia: Aeroclube center, 110,
    111; height limits of, 84; historic center
    of, 144–45, *145*; history of, 144; plan for,
    20–21; territorial logic and, 296–97. *See
    also* Pelourinho district (Salvador)
Santos, Maria Adelia dos, 17
Santos, Milton 1987, 68
São Paulo: Alphaville, 29–30; apartment
    buildings in, *87,* 88–89; Avenida Paulista,
    84, *85,* 115, 249; city center of, 249–57, *250*;
    as compartmentalized, 117; contradictions
    of, 246; EMPLASA, 17; horizontal areas
    of, *96,* 96–97; Iguatemi shopping center,
    110, *113,* 113–15, *114*; land-use regulations,
    84; as local metropolis in global world,
    247–49, 264; Luz district, 252–53, 254, *255,
    256*; master plan for, 32–33; modernism
    in, 294, 295; Pátio Higienopólis shop-
    ping center, 110, *113,* 115–17, *116*; Plano de
    Avenidas, 3; population of, xx–xxi; Praça
    do Patriarca, 254, 255, 257, *258*; renovation
    in, 200–201; shopping centers in, 104,
    105–9, *107, 108*; Shopping Light center,
    118, *118*; squatter settlements in, 257–61,
    260; territorial logic and, 292; verticaliza-
    tion of, 40–41, 82, *87,* 90–92, *101*
Sassen, Saskia, 247
Satellite towns of Brasília, 53–55, *54*

Secretaria Municipal de Habitação (SMH), 270, 272–73
Segawa, Hugo, 18, 23
SERFHAU (Federal Service for Housing and Urbanism), 14–17, 18, 33
Serviço de Patrimonio Historico e Artistico Nacional (SPHAN), 3
SFH (Sistema Federal de Habitação), 14
Shopping centers: attractions at, 112; in Brazil, 104–5; central city compared to, 41; construction of, 112–13, *113*; definition of, 105; design of, 109–11, *110, 111*; form of, 104; functions of, 111–12, 117–18; Iguatemi, 113–15, *114*; Navegantes Commercial District, 188–93, *190, 191, 192*; Nova Olaria Commercial Center, 194, *194*; Pátio Higienopólis, 115–17, *116*; postmodern urbanism and, 295–96; in São Paulo, 105–6, *107*; Shopping Total, 194–95, *195*; types of, 106–9, *108*
Silva, Luiz (Lula) da, xxii, 196
Sistema Federal de Habitação (SFH), 14
Skidmore, Thomas, xx, xxii
Sklair, Leslie, 296
SMH (Secretaria Municipal de Habitação), 270, 272–73
Smith, Michael Peter, 292, 301n1
Social function of urban property, 292, 295–96, 298–300
Social Inclusion, xxviii–xxix, 199, 294
Social justice, city as tool for, 301
Spatial segregation, and cities, 27–30, *29*
SPHAN (Serviço de Patrimonio Historico e Artistico Nacional), 3
Squatter settlements. *See* favelas
Statute of the City, xviii, 31–32, 199, 292, 300
SUDAM, 11
SUDENE, 11–12
SUDESUL, 11
Superquadras (superblocks): in Brasília, 48, 60, 83, *84*; in Palmas, 68
Sustainability, 182–84, 202

Taguatinga, *54,* 54, 55
Taniguchi, Cassio, 214, 217
Terrain vagues, 201, 246
Territorial logic, 292–97, 300–301
Tocantins, 65. *See also* Palmas
Tourism: Bahia and, 144; Belém riverfront redesign and, 168; Cultural Corridor Project and, 136–37; in Palmas, 75–76; Pelourinho district and, 158–60
Tower-in-the-green model, 28–29, 40, 295. *See also* apartment buildings; verticalization
Trancik, Roger, 46
Transamazonia, 12
Transportation: in Belém, 171; in Brasília, 62; in Curitiba, 204–5, *205, 207, 208,* 216; in Palmas, 70–72, *72;* parking issues, 154
Turner, John, 269

UNESCO World Heritage Sites, 122. *See also* Brasília
United Nations: Agenda 21, 31, 248; Conference on Environment and Development (Earth Summit), 31, 182, 225–26
Urban design: in Brazil, xv–xvi; evolution of, xv; market economics, legal rights, and, xv; sustainable, 182–84
Urbanism: academia, professional organizations, and, 26–27; Anglo-Saxon, 183; birth of, 2–11; in Brazil, xvii, xxiii–xxv, 33–35, 291–93, 300–301; concept of place and, 184–85; criticisms of, 10–11; definition of, xvii; dualities of, xix–xx; education in, 26; equity and, xvii–xviii; functional modernism and, 13–14; goal of, xxvi; inequality and, xx–xxii; modernism and, 1–2; National Constitution and, 25; optimistic tone about, xxv; postmodern, 34–35; re-democratization and, 23–24; in São Paulo, 246, *247;* segregation, fragmentation, and, 27–30, *29;* as tool, 199

Vainer, Carlos, 27–28
Vale do Anhangabaú (São Paulo), 250–57, *251*
Valença, Márcio, 23
Vargas, Getúlio, 2–4, 6, 7, 65
Ver-o-Peso (Belém), 166, 173–76, *174*, 179
Ver o Rio (Belém), 169, *170*, 171, 179
Verticalization: apartment buildings, 87,
    87, 88, 88–90; areas subject to, 97–98;
    articulation between buildings and open
    spaces, 92–94; in Brasília, 83; in Brazil,
    84–87, 94–95; in Copacabana, 83–84; defi-
    nition of, 83; effects of, 102; landscaping
    and, 98–99; land-use regulations and, 90;
    lifestyle and, 102; models of, 98; norms,
    codes, and spaces, 94–96, *96*; overview of,
    82; principal expansion fronts of, 86–87;

in São Paulo, 84, *85*, 90–92; skylines and,
    99; of urban territory, 101–2
Vidigal favela (Rio de Janeiro), 274–78, *275*,
    276, 277, 287
Vila Paranoá (Brasília), 52, 55–56, *56*
Vila Planalto (Brasília), 52, 53, *53*
Villaça, Flávio, 14, 27

Walled cities, 60–61, 62. *See also* "city of
    walls"; gated communities
Waterfront: of Belém, description of, 164–
    67; of Belém, redesign of, 122–23, 167–78,
    297–98; of Copacabana, *20*, 21, 225; of
    Curitiba, 207; of Porto Alegre, 186
Wolff, Goetz, 28
World Social Forum, 187